We Alone Will Rule

Living in Latin America

Robert Levine
General Editor

We Alone Will Rule

*Native Andean Politics
in the Age of Insurgency*

Sinclair Thomson

THE UNIVERSITY OF WISCONSIN PRESS

The University of Wisconsin Press
1930 Monroe Street
Madison, Wisconsin 53711

www.wisc.edu/wisconsinpress/

3 Henrietta Street
London WC2E 8LU, England

5   4   3   2   1

Printed in the United States of America

Library of Congress Cataloging-in-Publication Data
Thomson, Sinclair.
We alone will rule: native Andean politics in the age of insurgency / Sinclair Thomson.
pp.   cm. — (Living in Latin America)
Includes bibliographical references and index.
ISBN 0-299-17790-4 (cloth: alk. paper)
ISBN 0-299-17794-7 (pbk: alk. paper)
1. Quechua Indians—History—18th century.   2. Aymara Indians—History—18th century.
3. Quechua Indians—Wars.   4. Aymara Indians—Wars.   5. Quechua Indians—Politics and
government.   6. Aymara Indians—Politics and government.   7. Peasant uprisings—Andes
Region—History—18th century.   8. Tupac-Amaru, José Gabriel, d. 1781.   9. Peru—History—
Insurrection of Tupac Amaru, 1780–1781.   10. Peru—Politics and government—18th century.
I.Title.   II. Series.
F2230.2.K4 T54 2002
980´.013—dc21   2002004975

Contents

Illustrations

Figures

Maps

Preface and Acknowledgments

A powerful realization that emerged for me out of the research and reflection for this book was the significance of long-term historical connections and cycles in the highland Andes. Fundamental aspects of Andean community politics today—both structural and cultural—have their origins in the eighteenth century. Late-colonial processes—such as the constitution and breakdown of mediatory political relations between Andean communities and the dominant institutions of the state—have been followed by comparable ones in the late-nineteenth and twentieth centuries.

After finishing the writing of the book, this awareness was reinforced by the dramatic popular uprisings, involving mobilizations across the Bolivian altiplano as well as in the highland valleys and lowlands, that took place in April and September 2000. During the road blockades in the highlands, Indian peasant communities drew upon many of the same collective resources and strategies that they had employed in the uprisings of the colonial period. During the three-week siege of La Paz, the memory of 1781 was on the minds of urban residents cut off within the basin of the capital city, and it was equally alive for the movement's leaders, as their statements at the time made clear. The town of Guarina, featured in this book, proved to be a flashpoint in the confrontations between mobilized popular sectors and state military forces. On September 28, three men— peasant farmers Cirilo Choque Huanca and Toribio Chui, and rural schoolteacher Joaquín Morales—died of bullet wounds when, according to witnesses, an air force plane opened fire on assembled protesters. Their lives came to an end not far from the site where Túpaj Katari's execution had taken place two hundred years before, and while they were not protagonists whose names are likely to be recorded in future annals, their lives and deaths are part of one ongoing history.

A symbol of warfare in Aymara peasant culture is the sling *(k'orawa)*, which transforms itself from a pastoral implement into a dangerous weapon during moments of conflict. When used for purposes of combat, the sling manifests the supernatural potency of the snake *(katari)* that is contained within it. The serpentine weave and coloring of the sling bears the marks of this powerful, unpredictable, and fearsome creature associated with subterranean forces. In her inspired design for the cover, Bolivian artist Martha Cajías has taken the image of the sling as animated serpent to represent aesthetically the historical process recounted in the book. The figure of the katari at the head of each chapter is also her handiwork. I am delighted that she has been able to add her creative spirit to the book, and would also like to thank Omar Tapia for his assistance with the computer graphics for the cover.

Many other friends, colleagues, and institutions have contributed to the making of this book, and my gratitude to all of them runs deep. Social Science Research Council and Fulbright-Hayes fellowships funded the original dissertation research. A grant from the Ibero-American Studies Center at the University of Wisconsin–Madison made possible a preliminary visit to the archives, and a University of Wisconsin Fellowship allowed me to organize substantial archival data and begin writing up the results. To complete the book project, support for follow-up research and writing was provided by a Goddard Fellowship from New York University and grants from NYU's Center for Latin American and Caribbean Studies, the Wenner-Gren Foundation for Anthropological Research, and the National Endowment for the Humanities.

My historical training is due in the first place to my professors and fellow graduate students in Latin American history at the University of Wisconsin. At the start of my graduate studies, Tom Skidmore acted as a kind and wise elder; and in the dissertation phase, Francisco Scarano offered welcome help, criticism, and encouragement. Frank Salomon was a challenging, influential teacher and his scholarship on the Andes a source of inspiration. Florencia Mallon's work originally drew me into history, and her intellectual creativity has continued to freshen and enliven it for me. Steve Stern's exceptional commitment as a teacher and scholar have been an example of great value to me. His sustained interest in this project and his lucid observations on successive drafts of the manuscript have been of enormous benefit.

In Madison, the intellectual and social interaction with friends and fellow graduate students was a constant source of stimulation, and the basis for ongoing important ties. I owe particular thanks to Karl Zimmerer, Medora Ebersole, and their family for the generosity with which they received me during the final phase of the dissertation work. At the University of Wisconsin Cartography Lab, my thanks go to Onno Brouwer,

Qingling Wang, and Erik Rundell for production of the maps. I am also grateful to the staff at the University of Wisconsin Press for publishing the book, and especially to Rosalie Robertson with whom I worked originally, Mary Magrey for her excellent copyediting, and Erin Holman for seeing the final version into print.

In New York, I found a congenial environment in which to bring the research and writing of the book to a conclusion. Among the colleagues and students at New York University who have provided support and thoughtful comments on the project are Ada Ferrer, William Roseberry, Tom Abercrombie, Molly Nolan, Greg Grandin, Forrest Hylton, Mark Healey, and the participants in the New York City Latin American History Workshop.

The most important stage of the project took place in Bolivia. Archival staff at various repositories kindly facilitated the research. In particular, I would like to acknowledge the late Gunnar Mendoza of the Archivo Nacional de Bolivia and his fine assistants; Alberto Crespo Rodas, René Arze Aguirre, and Eliana Asboun, successive directors of the Archivo de la Biblioteca Central of the Universidad Mayor de San Andrés; and Elizabeth Cipoleta of the Archivo General de la Nación in Buenos Aires. I am also grateful to Monseñor Alberto Aramayo and Monseñor Gonzalo del Castillo of the Archbishopric of La Paz for their consideration while I was working in the ecclesiastical archives.

At the Archivo de La Paz, a number of friends and colleagues created a lively atmosphere for historical and archival work. In particular, I appreciated the collegiality and cooperation of Florencia Ballivián, Roberto Choque, Laura Escobari, Ximena Medinaceli, Mary Money, and María Luisa Soux who have all served as formal directors or informal authorities.

A host of other historians and intellectuals contributed to the project through encouragement, support, and exchange at different stages. I cannot adequately acknowledge all of them nor their full importance here, but I would like to signal my appreciation to Xavier Albó, Silvia Arze, Cristina Bubba, Martha Cajías, Ramiro Condarco Morales, Marisol de la Cadena, Mercedes del Río, James Dunkerley, Marcelo Fernández, Laura Gotkowitz, Orlando Guanca, Olivia Harris, Herb Klein, Jim Krippner–Martínez, Erick Langer, Ana María Lema, Clara López, Jaime Mejía, Ramiro Molina Rivero, Scarlett O'Phelan Godoy, Johnny Orihuela, Tristan Platt, Silvia Rivera Cusicanqui, Gustavo Rodríguez, Sergio Serulnikov, Enrique Tandeter, Ruth Volgger, and Ann Zulawski. Through ongoing collective discussion and collaboration, the comrades of *autodeterminación*— Jean Paul Guevara, Seemin Qayum, Gonzalo Rojas, Luis Tapia, and Fabian Yaksic—have shaped my thinking about politics since I began to work in Bolivia. Over the years, it has also been a pleasure to work closely with Rossana Barragán in the endlessly fascinating field of Bolivian history. I have admired Brooke Larson as a scholar and colleague since I first entered the field, and this book has benefited greatly from her insightful comments. I also thank the other readers of the manuscript when it was under review for publication. Mark Thurner, Dwight Heath, and another anonymous reader offered perceptive, helpful suggestions for revisions.

I am especially grateful for the moral and spiritual support of my family and a wide community of excellent friends. Seemin Qayum has backed this work with unfailing generosity since its inception. She has participated in its elaboration through constant discussion of the findings and arguments, and it is my good fortune to have her personal and intellectual companionship.

We Alone Will Rule

1

Contours for a History of Power and Political Transformation in the Aymara Highlands

To some, civilization itself seemed to hang in the balance in 1781. To others, it seemed the dawning of a new day, when men and women could live freely and with dignity. In that year, the most powerful anticolonial movement in the history of Spanish rule in the Americas was sweeping across the southern Andes. For Spaniards and the colonial elite as well as for Indian insurgents, it was a decisive time matched only by the sixteenth-century conquest of the continent. Indian leaders imagined now a counterconquest, a "new conquest" of their own; colonial officials likewise saw their campaigns of repression as a "new conquest" or "reconquest" of the realm.[1] One of the two primary theaters of the violent Andean civil war in the early 1780s was La Paz (in present-day Bolivia), a region situated around the southern rim of the Lake Titicaca basin in the heartland of the Aymara-speaking indigenous population. As an exploration of Indian community and peasant politics, this study sets out to recover and illuminate the history of the Aymara people of La Paz in the age that produced the momentous pan-Andean insurrection.

Since the 1720s and 1730s, the Andean region had been the scene of growing turmoil. Local conflicts flared up with increasing frequency throughout the countryside. The exploitative commercial practices of provincial Spanish governors not only wrought hardship among communities but also stirred trenchant opposition. Indian protests poured into the courts. Anticolonial sentiment found expression in prophecies, conspiracies, and occasional revolts. In the 1770s, after Bourbon state officials imposed a set of universally unpopular measures (including higher taxation and stricter control of trade), Andean society reached an explosive conjuncture.

In 1780, a chain of riots expressing Indian, mestizo, and creole discontent with the Bourbon reforms broke out in highland, valley, and coastal cities.[2] In the countryside near Potosí, the fabled source of Spain's wealth in silver, local community struggles turned into an armed regional insurgency led by an Aymara-speaking peasant, Tomás Katari. In Cuzco, the preconquest capital of Inka territory, José Gabriel Condorcanqui Túpac Amaru, an Indian *cacique* (community governor) and nobleman stepped forth as the direct descendant of the last native sovereign who had been executed by Viceroy Toledo in the sixteenth century. Túpac Amaru called for the expulsion of all Europeans from Peruvian soil and a profound social reordering. The powerful movement that looked to him as its symbolic leader succeeded in liberating a vast expanse of the southern Andean highlands, an area that today encompasses southern Peru and Bolivia. Its repercussions were felt even more broadly, up and down the cordillera ranges from what is today Colombia in the north down to present-day Argentina in the south and from the deserts of the Pacific coast to the tropical lowlands of the Amazonian interior. When the key struggles shifted to La Paz, where the Quechua-speaking commanders from Cuzco teamed up with the Aymara peasant commander Túpaj Katari, the civil war entered its most acute and most violent phase.[3]

From their camps in El Alto, on the rim of the Andean altiplano, or upland plateau, tens of thousands of Aymara peasant warriors looked out over an impressive scene. Below them opened up a wide basin created by the drainage, over tens of thousands of years, of an ancient sea whose waters had flowed down from the highland elevation of thirteen thousand feet (four thousand meters) through highland valleys and lowland foothills out onto the continental floor of the Amazon. Eerily beautiful limestone badlands, in ashen gray, ochre, and reddish earth tones, formed steep walls around the basin. Across the basin and above it, thrusting up into the brilliant Andean skies, the insurgents gazed upon the massive glacial peaks of Mount Illimani (twenty-one thousand feet high, or sixty-four hundred meters), which they worshiped as an awesome ancestral divinity. Beneath its towering tutelary presence, successive waves of settlers over thousands of years had occupied this basin, farming its hillsides, mining its soils for gold, and pasturing native camelids. When the members of the first Spanish expedition arrived in the sixteenth century, they were unaware of the landscape's numinous powers and the layers of human history it had sustained. A Spanish township named La Paz was founded in 1548, in the location that diverse native ethnic groups speaking Aymara, Quechua, and Pukina languages called Choqueyapu.

La Paz served thereafter as the most important commercial nexus between Cuzco and Potosí. It was also the main point of Spanish settlement and colonial political control in a highland expanse overwhelmingly occupied by people the Spaniards called "Indians." Yet now, after two and one-half centuries of colonial rule, the city was under full siege and Spanish power was on the verge of destruction.

The Aymara camp was the scene of constant hustle and bustle. Spies brought reports on developments within the city, and messengers conveyed news and letters from northern and southern provinces. The combatants, coming and going from communities around the altiplano, were organized in twenty-four political assemblies *(cabildos)*. At their head, exercising political, military, and spiritual authority, was the fearsome Túpaj Katari, whose name signified "resplendent serpent" in Aymara. Under a vast canopy, Katari presided over the meetings of his military tribunal and celebrated daily mass conducted by captive Spanish clergy. The corpses of enemies and traitors hung from gallows over the city as a terrifying sign of justice.

Streams of Indians wound up and down the ascending walls of the basin, some with mules or llamas bearing weapons and supplies. From the heights of El Alto, the Spanish city far below was a puny cluster of adobe rooftops, rectangular streets, and barricaded walls within which the Spaniards had taken refuge. Outside the walls, all Spanish haciendas had been abandoned. The surrounding Indian parishes had become burnt-out battlefields in which the opposing armies skirmished.

Within the walls of the city, a dwindling population of Europeans, creoles, mestizos, and their Indian dependents held out against attack, hunger, disease, and demoralization. At night Indians stirred up a steady din to keep their enemy on edge. Families were reduced to eating horses, mules, dogs, cats, even animal skins and praying to the Virgin for succor. Church bells tolled in steady mourning.

The siege of La Paz, in its two phases, lasted a total of 184 days. Only in late 1781, and with difficulty, did royalist counterinsurgency troops sent from Buenos Aires finally manage to lift the siege and subdue the main insurgent forces. Katari was captured and quartered in a brutal ceremony, held in the name of God and the king, before a massive assembly of stunned Indians from around the lake district. Subsequent campaigns of pacification swept the La Paz countryside in 1782, wherever pockets of resistance held out. Colonial forces also continued to crack down on new signs of rebel activity elsewhere in the Peruvian realm. In the aftermath of the war, there were ongoing local demands, threats, and mobilizations and a test of strength as communities, local elites, and the Bourbon state sought to redefine colonial power relations.

Approaching Indian and Peasant Politics

The late eighteenth century was a time of deep political upheaval in distant territories of the Atlantic world. In Europe and the Americas, established political regimes and structures of colonial rule were under attack, and revolutionaries espoused and fought for alternative visions of social order. Andean communities rose up almost coincidentally with insurgents in North America and shortly before the *sans culottes* in France and "black Jacobins" in Saint Domingue (Haiti). Three decades later, creole Spaniards launched the wars that finally achieved independence from Iberian political authority. Given the simultaneity of these movements, it is interesting to note that the pan-Andean insurrection has received scarce mention in the conventional Western historiography of the Age of Revolution.[4] Is this accidental, a case of historiographic oversight? Is it a more significant exclusion? Was insurgency in the Andes, while coincidental in its timing, categorically different from other revolutionary movements of the day?

One possible explanation for the scarce attention is that Iberia and Iberian America are often seen as peripheral to the northern Atlantic axis of power emergent in this period. The empires of Spain and Portugal were indeed straining to reorganize themselves in the late eighteenth century and to compete against their more dynamic imperial neighbors and rivals. It is also the case that France, North America, and England, rather than Spain and Portugal, were the originary sites for the liberal political culture and capitalist political economy that are normally taken as paradigmatic in the revolutionary Atlantic world.

One of the classic assumptions about revolution in this era is that the ideals and examples of liberation swept like a tide from France and North America throughout the rest of the Atlantic world. And yet there is next to no evidence that the pan-Andean insurrection was inspired by French *philosophes* or prompted by the successes of North American creoles. Nor was it provoked by British secret agents hostile to the Spanish Crown. Unlike the Haitian revolution, which developed in close connection with multilateral political dynamics in the Americas and Europe, the Andean case here again falls outside the conventional paradigm for the revolutionary Atlantic.

Another possible explanation is simply that "enormous condescension of posterity," (E. P. Thompson's memorable phrase) that history shows toward those whose struggles were not victorious and whose aspirations were not in line with what subsequent thinking deems "modern." It is true that the successful revolutionary war waged by slaves in Haiti—which led to the first independent nation in Latin America and the Caribbean and the first to abolish slavery anywhere in the Americas—has met with similar condescension. Yet if the significance of the Haitian revolution has long been displaced from Western historical narratives, the same problems of "silencing" and trivialization have affected, even more acutely, treatments of the pan-Andean insurrection.[5]

Where it has been addressed, the character of the Andean movement is often measured, and found wanting, by dominant liberal and national norms for what constitutes viable, legitimate modern political projects. Túpac Amaru and his followers did not spurn monarchical sovereignty for republican ideals. The ethnic leaders and institutions controlling power staked their political claims on ancestral hereditary, communal, and territorial rights rather than on abstract and ostensibly timeless notions of human rights and individual citizenship. Democracy was present neither as a novel political philosophy nor a system in which a detached stratum of special intermediaries administered public affairs, but as lived forms of communal, decentralized, and participatory political practice. Some writers have miscast the movement as backward looking, seeking to restore a preconquest social order or an early colonial pact with the Spanish Crown. Others have treated it as a typical millenarian, messianic, or utopian nativist revolt—an irrational or doomed expression of the desperation of the downtrodden rather than a political phenomenon worthy of study on its own terms.

Exploration of anticolonial insurgency in the eighteenth-century Andes offers one way to reconsider revolutionary political culture and political organization in a wider light. It allows for a shift away from the standard Western models of the birth of democracy, nation-state formation, and capitalist "modernity," which privilege the northern Atlantic region and bourgeois or creole political agents. It reveals a broader array of revolutionary subjects and emancipatory projects in circulation at the time and the way in which these were produced locally, rather than as a reflection of northern Atlantic experience and consciousness.

The revolutionary Atlantic was less a single oceanic tide than multiple currents flowing simultaneously, with some converging and others following a more separate course. The Andean highlands did not lie outside of a discretely delimited revolutionary world in the eighteenth century, nor is it a site that begs for inclusion within a Western geography of modernity. Like other revolutionary struggles of the time, the Andean insurrection of 1780–1781 was a liberation movement that sought to, and temporarily did, overturn the preexisting regime of domination and place formerly subaltern subjects at the head of the political order. Unlike the others, it was a movement against colonial rule and for self-determination in which *native American* political subjects made up the fighting corps, held positions of leadership, and defined the terms of struggle. The specific ways in which they envisioned liberty and self-rule and the specific local and regional dynamics out of which their political visions and practices emerged are the primary themes of this book.

In the Andean region itself, the distinctiveness of the great insurrection and its importance are not in question. It has received abundant attention, in proportion to its enormous impact. The events of 1780–1781 affected not only colonial society and imperial reform in the late-eighteenth-century Andes but also the nature of the independence process and subsequent nation-state formation in the nineteenth century. Two centuries later, the insurrection has acquired potent symbolic significance in national political culture and popular movements. In Peru, for example, both the reformist military regime of Velasco Alvarado (1968–1975) and the conservative regime of Morales Bermúdez (1975–1978) invoked the insurgent leader from Cuzco while instituting new agrarian and social policy. In Bolivia, the figures of Túpaj Katari, his consort Bartolina Sisa, and his sister Gregoria Apaza have become sources of inspiration for Aymara intellectuals and political and trade-union organizations in the contemporary phase of ethnic mobilization since the 1970s.

In historical scholarship—only one dimension of the broader public memory in the Andes—the insurrection has inspired magisterial and impassioned work, keen controversy, and ongoing cycles of specialized research. This study has been shaped by the rich scholarship even as it attempts to bring to light certain realms of history that have remained in the shadows. The historiography will be treated more carefully in the following chapters; however, there are questions of approach that I do wish to address here at the start.

To begin with, my underlying purpose is to convey a sense of the vitality and intensity of Indian peasant politics, and this appreciation entails inquiry into the "internal" political dimension of Indian society and community. The eighteenth century was a time of particular political effervescence in the Andes. The Viceroyalty of Peru witnessed the kinds of

collective political actions—such as spontaneous or short-lived village revolts over land, subsistence conditions, and local exactions or protests
over Bourbon state reforms—that were relatively widespread in colonial
Latin American history. Yet the Andes also became the site of bold and
original anticolonial mobilizations that were rare in other Latin American
regions prior to independence.[6] The late-colonial Andean case thus lends
itself particularly well to the study of peasant political engagement and
culture as well as the anticolonial and insurgent politics of native American peoples.[7] What I wish to explore, however, are not only the direct
confrontations with external adversaries but also the inner workings of
Indian society and the ways in which they shaped such confrontations.
These interior political spaces and intimate political histories matter in
and of themselves—after all they absorbed the greater part of Aymara political energies. At the same time, the internal dynamics relate back to the
negotiations and conflicts with outside forces and to the general set of
causal processes that shaped the colonial Andean world.[8]

This is a study of an age rather than an episode. I am concerned with
the long-term historical context within which the insurrection occurred
and within which it must be understood. The events of the civil war are by
now well established, even for the less prominent regions within the insurrectionary territory, and my approach is therefore closer to other long-term
analyses of Indian peasant resistance and rebellion than to conjunctural
narrative accounts of insurgency.

These long-term works, however, have tended in two directions: toward a panoramic view of Andean territory as a whole and toward a
structural-economic materialist analysis of the causal factors leading to the
insurrectionary rupture of 1780–1781. My aim, which I see as complementary to these contributions, is to explore a less familiar history at the regional and local levels, and in the internal political and cultural spheres of
Indian society.[9]

This inquiry centers on two issues. First is what I take to be a major
transformation occurring within communities over the course of the eighteenth century in the southern Andes. In this period, the traditional system
of authority and the form of community government by a native lord—
known as *cacicazgo*—entered into irreparable crisis and gave way to a new
and very distinctive arrangement of community political power. The struggles over cacicazgo afford exceptional insight into the complex dynamics
within Indian towns and communities in this period. They also show the
implications of changing internal conditions for external relations and rural
society at large. As I will argue, broad regional and structural forces set these

changes in motion at the local level, yet intracommunity transformation also determined the way that colonialism in the Andes unfolded and unraveled. In this respect, the local and internal approach will reveal how broader regional and structural processes of crisis and change were shaped from the bottom up.

The Aymara "community" can be conceived of as a specific political formation, that is, a structural whole in which a set of power relations are specifically articulated.[10] As I will show, for instance in discussions of the cacicazgo and the hierarchy of communal authority posts *(cargos),* the emphasis on relations of power gives this concept greater depth and dynamism than would a functionalist, institutionalist approach to community politics. The internal political focus will concentrate on dynamics of power; on axes of hierarchy, differentiation, and solidarity; and on community mediation, representation, and legitimacy. This focus works against stereotypes of the community as a unified, discrete agent that simply resists, re-creates itself, or breaks down in the face of hostile external forces.

At the same time, the structural conception of the "community" is perfectly compatible with a specifically historical understanding. The notion employed here of a political formation does not reinforce the view of the *ayllu*—the traditional Andean communal unit—as possessing an ahistorical, self-reproducing essence, nor as a primordial relic. My view is that a fundamental transformation in community political structure took place in this period. I will argue that as complex struggles proliferated in the second half of the eighteenth century, the locus of community power shifted to the base of the political formation. This historical process was one of democratization along communal, not Western liberal, lines. It involved definitive change and political self-(re)creation, and it laid the political foundations for Aymara communities until the present.[11]

The other central issue is the meaning of insurgency and the nature of political consciousness for Andean peasants and their leaders who participated in anticolonial mobilizations in this period. According to Bartolina Sisa, the Aymara commander Túpaj Katari roused his peasant army with the prospect that "they would be left as the ultimate owners of this place, and of its wealth." Indian combatants in 1781, she observed, spoke with anticipation of the moment when "they alone would rule."[12] Such visions of emancipation and self-determination were not unprecedented in La Paz, though earlier historiography has failed to record them. As local conflicts increased in frequency and intensity in the eighteenth century, they occasionally sparked movements that directly challenged the twin foundations of colonial political order: Spanish sovereignty and Indian subordination. These visions also coincided to varying degrees with the projects of anticolonial insurgents in other southern Andean regions in 1780–1781—the Chayanta movement headed by Tomás Katari, the Cuzco uprising under Inka leadership, and the Oruro mobilizations which brought into brief alliance Indian communities and urban creoles. By surveying the range of anticolonial projects pursued in eighteenth-century La Paz and in the southern Andes in 1780–1781, we can identify the common and varying contours of the political imagination of Indian insurgents, and the specific peasant visions of Andean utopia.

Túpaj Katari, the peasant commoner who emerged to coordinate the siege of La Paz and Aymara forces throughout the region in 1781, has been remembered in polar images, either as an audacious, charismatic hero or a shadowy and vicious brute. I wish to reconsider Katari's identity and leadership in order to appreciate his actual complexity and political creativity. At the same time, reflection on his strategies of leadership, his use of spiritual power and symbolic performance, and his masculinity can serve as an initial key to the political culture of the Aymara insurgency which he led. Just as Katari's fierce warrior conduct is often seen in contrast to the noble figure of the Inka Túpac Amaru, the phase of war in La Paz is commonly distinguished from the earlier Cuzco phase for its radicalism, racial antagonism, and violence, as well as for the powerful expression of base-level community forces within it. I will be concerned with the ways in which Katari's movement was politically connected to and shaped by other regional insurgencies, the ways in which it differed from them, as well as how its dynamics can clarify more general patterns throughout the southern Andes.

By connecting the question of community transformation to the analysis of insurgent politics, we can obtain valuable insight into the crisis of colonial order in the eighteenth-century Andes and the nature of the insurrectionary experience in 1780–1781. From midcentury on, as local struggles over community government grew so frequent and widespread as to undermine the cacicazgo, they had the simultaneous effect of destabilizing the colonial political order. The cacicazgo was a long-established and crucial form of political mediation between the Indian communities and the state, regional authorities, and other local elites. Its demise meant the breakdown of the classic mechanisms of indirect colonial rule through local ethnic lords. While both communities and the state would strive to renegotiate forms of political mediation and representation in their own interest, this test of forces would endure until the end of the colonial period and prove inconclusive. A viable regime of colonial domination in the countryside was never successfully restored.

Just as the community transformation contributed to the general crisis of colonial Andean society, it set political preconditions for the Aymara insurgency in 1781 and shaped the specific nature of anticolonial mobilization in this period. My findings indicate that, virtually without exception, native lords or caciques did not participate in such mobilizations in La Paz. The insurgencies were marked by powerful base-level forces pursuing communal aims, and their leadership was either decentralized or highly sensitive to communal demands. The autonomy and strength of these communal forces reflected the transformation going on at the time within communities, with the collapse of the cacicazgo and the devolution of power to the base of the political formation.

Ultimately, in my view, the crucial connection between Aymara community transformation and insurgency in the eighteenth-century Andes was the issue of self-rule. The local struggle for self-rule was at the root of community conflicts with their caciques throughout the late-colonial period. The same political aim was also at the heart of anticolonial projects among Andean people in the eighteenth century. While in the end the great insurrection of 1780–1781 did not culminate in lasting triumph for Indian peasants, the aspiration for autonomy was kept alive afterwards at the local level. It has manifested itself subsequently in republican history, in the form of cyclical struggles to reassert control over the spheres of political representation and mediation with the state, and it continues to be present in Aymara political culture today.

Aymara Identity and Politics

In Andean ethnography and ethnohistory, Aymara ethnic identity is attributed to a predominantly rural and peasant population that speaks the Aymara language and is geographically concentrated on the highland plateau and adjacent valleys of the southern Andes.[13] Historically, the distribution of *"Jaqi aru,"* the language described since colonial times as Aymara, was far more extensive than it is today. Aymara-speakers were organized within regional kingdoms or ethnic federations that came under Inka rule by the early fifteenth century. Within the Tawantinsuyu realm controlled by the Inka, there was an approximate correspondence between the region of Qollasuyu and what is now recognizable as Aymara territory. Aymara federations extended nearly as far north as Cuzco and further south than Potosí. Within the area of our study, the Qolla federation controlled the area to the north and northeast of Lake Titicaca; the Lupaqa occupied the western shore of the lake; and the Pacaxes were based to the south.[14]

With Spanish conquest, ethnic and local distinctions among Andean peoples—who of course shared common cultural parameters despite their differences—were blurred in the vision of a colonial state which generically typed its native subjects as "Indians." Over the course of colonial and modern history, Aymara territory continued to shrink with the advance of the Quechua linguistic frontier. Today, Aymara and Quechua linguistic borders still shift and overlap, and a sizeable Aymara population has taken up urban residence, primarily in the greater metropolitan area of La Paz and El Alto. A reduced Aymara population is found in northern Chile, while another larger concentration exists in southern Peru around Lake Titicaca. The majority of the population resides in Bolivia, and the Aymara core is located in the lake district and the region of La Paz.[15]

The ethnohistorical attribution of Aymara identity—to people speaking a common language and sharing a given set of cultural conditions and a general territory—should not be taken to imply that there existed historically a sharp, self-conscious ethnic contrast between Aymara- and Quechua-speakers in different parts of the southern Andes. In eighteenth-century La Paz, after the older ethnic federations had disappeared and indigenous social organization had been reorganized and reduced to the level of colonial town jurisdictions, there was no explicit or self-referential ("-emic") category of "Aymara" ethnic identity. Nevertheless, with this caveat in mind, we can make such an attribution and conceive of indigenous people in La Paz who spoke Jaqi aru or Aymara as the "Aymara" ancestors of those who call themselves Aymara today. In recent decades, Aymara identity has been increasingly adopted self-consciously as part of a general galvanization of peasant political organization and a rise in ethnic consciousness in Bolivia.[16]

The older ethnographic literature painted a picture of the Aymara as generally sullen, suspicious, and long-suffering, but with a pronounced streak of cruelty and belligerence. The North American anthropologist Adolph Bandelier wrote, "Cupidity, low cunning, and savage cruelty are the unfortunate traits of these Indians' character." Citing Spanish chroniclers, he continued, "These traits are not, as sentimentalism would have it, a result of ill-treatment by the Spaniards, but *peculiar to the stock,* and were yet more pronounced in the beginning of the Colonial period than at the present time" (the emphasis is Bandelier's). Drawing from his field-work impressions, he added: "The stranger, who remains but a short time among the Aymarás, is easily misled by their submissive manners, their cringing ways, and especially by their humble mode of greeting the whites. Upon closer acquaintance, however, the innate ferocity of character cannot remain concealed."[17]

Such a view was not peculiar to visiting foreign anthropologists. Bautista Saavedra—Bolivian criminologist, author of a treatise on the ayllu, and later president of the republic—voiced a similar impression, even if it was "sentimentalist" by Bandelier's standards: "It may be said that, by means of selection, there has been a sharpening of these weapons of defense [the instincts of mistrust and cunning] against the brutal depredations of the Spaniards and the abuses and exploitations of the priest, soldier, and corregidor [canton authority]. . . . Hence, when the Indian is in contact with whites, he feigns abject submission, because he knows his impotence. But when he finds himself in a position of evident superiority, he is haughty, stubborn, bold. . . . If his hatred and rancor burst out, he transforms himself into a fearsome beast with distorted visage and bulging eyes."[18]

The comments of Bandelier and Saavedra have a typical ring for turn-of-the-twentieth-century Latin America, especially insofar as they echoed the recent scientific discourse on race. Yet both ethnographers' notions about the sinister side of Aymara character derived in large part from the elite's historical experience of uprisings in La Paz. Both were writing in the wake of the Mohoza massacre in 1899, when Indians killed a contingent of creole soldiers during the 1899 civil war. Both were also aware of the insurrection that had taken place a century earlier. The eighteenth-century political violence left its mark in the minds of elites and ethnographers, and the colonial discourse about Aymara savagery that arose in 1781 has persisted, with modern racist accretions, into the late twentieth century. A critique of these clichés about Aymara character that surface in the colonial sources and endure in some of the historiography of the insurrection will help to clarify how and why Aymara peasants did engage in political uprisings and violence in the eighteenth century. The study of late-colonial Aymara politics will also allow insight into the political profile of the community today and one of its key features—its distinctive democratic content—to which recent ethnography has called attention. At the same time, I wish to show that the Aymara political vitality so striking in contemporary ethnic organization and mobilization has a history reaching back over two centuries.[19]

The Age of Insurgency

In a major overview of the revolts and rebellions in the Viceroyalty of Peru during the eighteenth century, Scarlett O'Phelan carefully charted the convulsions of the late-colonial Andean world. She found three critical conjunctures each marked by a cluster of uprisings. The first was the period of 1724–1736, when conflict broke out over fiscal and administrative reform. The second was the period of 1751–1758, when the *repartimiento de mercancías* (the coercive distribution of commodities by provincial governors) was legalized. The third was the decade of the 1770s, when Bourbon reforms further disturbed colonial society and set up the general insurrection. In another broad vision of late-colonial rebellion in Peru, Steve Stern offered a methodologically sensitive periodization of an insurrectionary age between 1742, when Juan Santos Atahualpa led his neo-Inka movement against Spanish domination, and 1782 when the movement headed by Túpac Amaru family of Cuzco was finally suppressed.[20]

How does the periodization of late-colonial social conflict appear from the local and regional vantage point of La Paz? My findings, based on archival research for the period from the opening decades of the eighteenth century through the first decade of the nineteenth, show a proliferation of conflict from the 1740s on.[21] This initial cycle of conflict reached a peak in the early 1770s, a moment of great instability in much of the highland countryside and one which prompted serious concern in the highest spheres of the colonial state. No insurrectionary leadership emerged, however, to channel the political ferment among Aymara communities in the southern Andes. After the siege of La Paz in 1781, which was directed by Túpaj Katari, local conflict, community mobilization, and real or imagined uprisings kept the region in a state of agitation. A second siege of the city would take place in 1811, but this time Aymara communities would be under mestizo leadership, and headed into a very different kind of independence process.[22]

Stern's lofty view of an "age of insurrection" implicitly related the Andean historical experience to the "age of revolution" which was discussed above. Taking a ground-level perspective from La Paz, it is possible to add another dimension to the characterization of the period. In the Aymara region at least, the eighteenth century was a time of a ground swell or surge of forces from the base of Indian society. More so now than ever before, power could flow from the bottom up because it was located below with peasant community members belonging to local ayllu units. In this deep sense, the movement in power relations at the community level—and not

15

only the violent eruptions in times of open mobilization—allows us to think about this era as an "age of insurgency."

The Highland Regional Landscape

By the mid-eighteenth century, the territory of Upper Peru—corresponding to the administrative district of the colonial court *(Audiencia)* of Charcas based in La Plata—was emerging from a secular demographic and economic decline. While growth in most regions was limited, La Paz showed relatively more dynamism as a key point on the southern Andean commercial circuit, and as the leading region, outstripping Cuzco, for production of coca leaf. A royal treasury report in 1774 waxed enthusiastic over regional fortunes: "In truth, coca is such a valuable good, enjoying such favorable circumstances in the flow of trade, that there may be nothing like it in all the world. . . . The residents of La Paz who devote themselves to cultivation of the leaf have in it the great source of commerce that creates the grand opulence of this city."[23] In this period, La Paz nearly equaled Potosí as the most important regional source of revenue within Upper Peru, and surpassed it as the city with the largest population in the district. By the end of the century, La Paz also ranked with Cuzco and Lima as the most important sources of tribute for the Crown, and it had the highest indigenous population anywhere in the Andes.[24]

At the northern end of the Audiencia of Charcas, La Paz fell within the jurisdiction of the Viceroyalty of Peru up until 1776, when Charcas was reassigned to the newly created Viceroyalty of Buenos Aires. (For this exposition of the study region, refer to maps.) In the ecclesiastical sphere, La Paz constituted a bishopric that was subject to the higher authority of the archbishopric of La Plata, and that bordered to the north on the bishopric of Cuzco. In the early 1780s, Bourbon authorities introduced a new territorial and administrative system. The region of La Paz, which formerly had no secular administrative status of its own, became an intendancy; the provinces of the region, formerly called *corregimientos,* were now dubbed *partidos;* and the provincial governor or magistrate, who exercised supreme military, political, and judicial authority within the provincial jurisdiction, changed from the *corregidor* to the *subdelegado* or subdelegate.

Beyond formal administrative divisions and jurisdictions, which began to mutate at an accelerating pace from the late 1770s on, the social, economic, and political unity of colonial La Paz was reflected in the geography

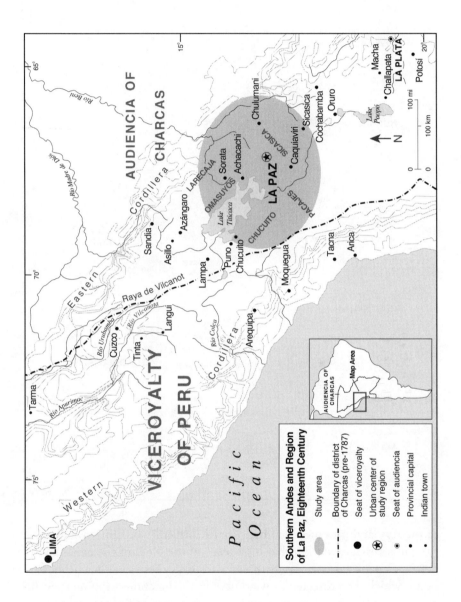

Southern Andes and Region
of La Paz, Eighteenth Century

Study area
— · · —	Boundary of district of Charcas (pre-1787)
●	Seat of viceroyalty
⊛	Urban center of study region
◉	Seat of audiencia
•	Provincial capital
·	Indian town

AUDIENCIA OF CHARCAS

VICEROYALTY OF PERU

Pacific Ocean

LIMA

Tarma

Cuzco

Tinta

Langui

Río Apurímac

Río Vilcanota

Río Urubamba

Raya de Vilcanot

Río Colca

Arequipa

Moquegua

Tacna

Arica

Sandia

Asillo

Azángaro

Lampa

Puno

Chucuito

LARECAJA

OMASUYOS

Sorata

Achacachi

CHUCUITO

Lake Titicaca

LA PAZ

Caquiaviri

SICASICA

PACAJES

Chulumani

Sicasica

Cochabamba

Oruro

Lake Poopó

Macha

Challapata

LA PLATA

Potosí

Cordillera

Eastern

Western

Cordillera

Río Beni

Río Madre de Díos

AUDIENCIA OF CHARCAS

Map Area

N

0   100 km
0   100 mi

15°

20°

65°

70°

75°

Pacajes Province and Chucuito Province, Eighteenth Century

— — — Boundary of province

⊛ Urban center of study region

◉ Provincial capital

• Indian town

of the Aymara movement led by Túpaj Katari in 1781. On November 14, 1781, in a ritual execution that took place in the plaza of the Sanctuary of Peñas, Túpaj Katari's limbs were tied with heavy ropes to the tails of four horses which then careered forward in separate directions, ripping apart his body. As a terrifying demonstration of Spanish justice and to reassert symbolically Spanish power throughout the region, Katari's head and limbs were then distributed for prominent display in the areas where his influence had been greatest.[25] His head went to the regional capital, and was placed

upon the gallows in the central plaza of the city and above the gate leading to the hill of Quilliquilli, where Katari had set up his own gallows and hung captive enemies.

Katari's right arm was fixed on display at the center of the town plaza in Ayoayo, his home and original political base, and then transferred to

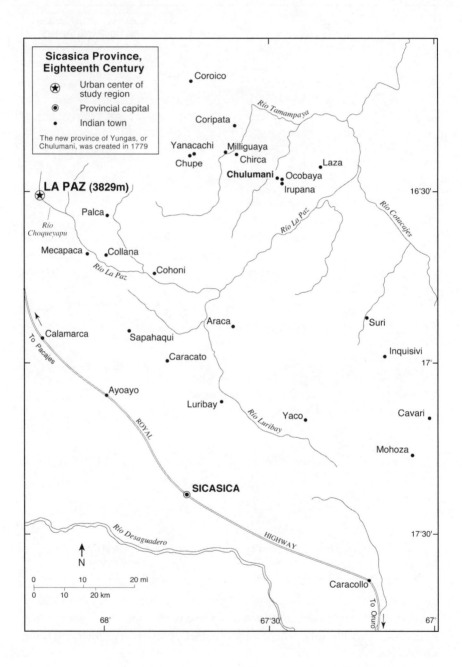

Sicasica Province, Eighteenth Century

⊛   Urban center of study region

◉   Provincial capital

•   Indian town

The new province of Yungas, or Chulumani, was created in 1779

Coroico

Río Tamampaya

Coripata

Yanacachi   Milliguaya

Chupe   Chirca

Chulumani   Ocobaya   Laza

Irupana

16°30'

⊛ **LA PAZ** (3829m)

Río Choqueyapu

Palca

Río La Paz

Río Cotacajes

Mecapaca   Collana

Cohoni

Río La Paz

Araca   Suri

Calamarca   Sapahaqui

To Pacajes

Caracato   Inquisivi

17°

Ayoayo

Luribay   Yaco   Cavari

Río Luribay

ROYAL

Mohoza

◉ **SICASICA**

17°30'

Río Desaguadero

HIGHWAY

↑ N

| 0 | 10 | 20 mi |
| 0 | 10 | 20 km |

Caracollo

To Oruro

68°   67°30'   67°

neighboring Sicasica, his birthplace and the capital of the colonial province of Sicasica. Lying to the south and east of the city of La Paz, Sicasica was one of the largest and wealthiest provinces in the colonial Andes. It spanned from the altiplano, on the highly trafficked royal highway between Cuzco and Potosí, down into agriculturally rich subtropical valleys which included the coca-growing Yungas. The size of the province and the difficulties of governing it—not only logistic but political, since peasant communities in Sicasica proved notoriously insubordinate— caused colonial officials to divide it into two after the disturbances of the 1770s.

Katari's right leg was sent to the town of Chulumani, which had become the capital of the new province of Yungas or Chulumani in 1779. The Yungas drew in seasonal Indian labor for the coca harvest as well as permanent migrants looking to gain small landholdings as tenants in the expanding hacienda sector. The free communities in Yungas engaged in vigorous commerce and barter involving coca with petty Indian traders from around the altiplano and especially from the Sicasica highlands.[26]

Katari's left arm was sent to nearby Achacachi, the capital of the highland province of Omasuyos. Bordering the eastern rim of Lake Titicaca, the province was situated along the eastern cordillera of the Andes, whose peaks look down upon the plaza of Peñas. Omasuyos had exceptionally fertile lands and some larger agricultural and livestock estates owned by provincial and regional elites. It formed one of the two corridors connecting La Paz along the lake to the northern provinces of Chucuito, Paucarcolla, Azángaro, Lampa, and Carabaya, which were also included within the district of Charcas until their separation in 1796.

Katari's left leg was sent to Caquiaviri, the capital of Pacajes. This province combined with Sicasica to form the southern altiplano range of La Paz, bordering to the south on the Aymara region of Oruro. With infertile soils and extreme climatic conditions, Pacajes was primarily suited to livestock raising. It had little hacienda penetration, and its communities were known, like those of Sicasica, for their indomitability and propensity to revolt.[27]

The other integral province of La Paz that makes up our study area was Larecaja, with its capital Sorata. Economically and politically more peripheral than the other provinces, the Larecaja valleys were articulated primarily with upland Omasuyos, and from preconquest times they were the site of important colonization by altiplano Aymara federations and Inka *mitmaq* settlers. The province was suited for agricultural production, especially of corn, and extraction, primarily of minerals, in the lowlands.[28]

These then were the provinces of La Paz whose Aymara communities rose up and came together under Túpaj Katari to besiege the Spanish capital city. With the capture and death of their maximum leader, the powerful political movement cohering on a regional scale was dismembered and its forces dispersed into the countryside whence it had arisen.

To a lesser but still significant extent, the compass of this study also includes the province of Chucuito, which bordered Pacajes on the western side of the lake. As noted above, Chucuito fell within the district of Charcas until the end of the century, and it displayed many similar political dynamics to the La Paz provinces. Chucuito province derived from the preconquest Aymara-speaking Lupaqa kingdom, and its late-colonial indigenous nobility was integrated through marriage and commercial enterprise with the noble families of Pacajes. Located along the royal highway, it was a center of profitable livestock production and transport. The study will also occasionally refer to archival material for the provinces of Paucarcolla and Azángaro, which lay to the north of the lake.

Each province consisted of a set of Indian towns (the *reducción* or *pueblo* in Spanish was known as a *marka* in Aymara), with a parish-style religious organization *(doctrina),* whose jurisdiction covered the surrounding countryside. Most were founded in the sixteenth century, although, especially in the last decades of the eighteenth century, a number of new sites appeared as offshoots of original colonial towns. In the *reducción* scheme devised by Viceroy Francisco de Toledo, following the pattern from the Spanish peninsula, these towns were designed to act as a medium of civilization and a point of political and spiritual control over the rural population.[29]

According to the Laws of the Indies, no "Spaniards"—meaning non-Indians—could reside in the towns, although this prescription was only loosely observed in the colonial period. As the eighteenth century wore on, mestizos and creoles who were looking for parcels of land, access to Indian labor, and local power increasingly infiltrated and took up residence in the town centers. Nevertheless, the Spanish Crown originally did intend to guarantee the land-base of communities and to protect Indians from the abuse of other colonial subjects, in order to ensure its own vitally important appropriation of tribute.

Given the evangelical purpose of the towns, priests were the only "Spaniards" legally permitted in them. While they often complained of the poor Indian attendance at Sunday ceremonies of mass, they did oversee an annual calendar of Christian festival celebrations in which Indian communities participated fully. Priests played important political and economic, as much as spiritual, roles in local life. They sought to take full personal advantage of community resources and labor, and often became embroiled in local disputes involving other local notables such as the cacique, the corregidor or his agents, or other town-residents.[30]

The state extracted two principal forms of tribute from communities. First was a payment in cash by landholding Indian families. For the purposes of tribute collection, state officials kept registers *(padrones)* which defined community members according to a set of tributary categories: *originarios,* who were natives to the community and held inherited land within it; *agregados,* who held lands but were attached to the community in a less integral way; and *forasteros,* or recently arrived outsiders. After ongoing, complex, and contested reform of the tributary system since the late seventeenth century, Indians in all of these categories paid tribute on a prorated basis by the end of the eighteenth century.[31]

The second form of state extraction was the *mita,* a corvée system of rotating drafted labor for work in the distant silver mines of Potosí. Community members normally fulfilled their mita obligations by making the long trek to the mines and performing their annual service turn at three different times in their lives. Mita service was so grueling and loathsome that many Indians chose to abandon their communities rather than be enrolled as *mitayo* laborers. In general, however, though tribute meant a significant economic burden for them and the mita was especially onerous, Indians made their contributions to the Spanish sovereign in the understanding that the Crown in turn guaranteed them protection of their lands and the conditions for community reproduction. Tristan Platt has conceptualized this as a colonial pact of reciprocity bearing important continuity with arrangements between communities and the state in the period of Inka rule.[32]

Due to the sixteenth-century restructuring under Toledo, indigenous communities in La Paz entirely lacked the higher levels of segmentary organization that characterized the preconquest ethnic kingdoms. At the local level, they retained the dualism and nested layering that were traditional in Andean social organization. The highest existing level of organization coincided with the Indian town *(marka)* and its jurisdiction. This unit was in turn divided into two halves or moieties *(parcialidades)* usually termed *Anansaya* and *Urinsaya,* each of which had its own Indian governor or *cacique* (a Taino appellation applied by the Spaniards to the Andean lords known as *kuraka* in Quechua and *mallku* in Aymara). Each moiety was comprised of a cluster of local units called *ayllus,* represented by their own *hilacata* authorities. The local ayllu consisted of a set of hamlets *(estancias)* made up of closely kin-related peasant households.[33]

In this study, the use of the term "community" follows the practice of Indians themselves in the colonial documentation. Indians spoke of their "community" *(comunidad* or *común* in Spanish) in a way that retained the multivalent resonance of the segmentary social organization. They applied the term to the local ayllu, to the moiety, or to the town-level units that they belonged to, depending on the referential context. In Andean ethnography and ethnohistory, allowing for variations in period and place, it is common to refer to the general structure and principles of this system as ayllu organization. Some evidence indicates that, outside of the more formal colonial settings that usually generated the documentation available today, Indians in eighteenth-century La Paz did retain the term "ayllu" as a general referent for collective social organization at varying scales. The term "community" in this study is therefore approximately equivalent to the term "ayllu" in its general connotation. Nevertheless, to avoid confusion I will usually reserve the term "ayllu" for the local subunits that together composed the moiety or town level of organization. Also, as we will see, by the late-colonial era Indians had absorbed the Spanish term for "community," making it their own in a culturally consistent, politically conscious fashion, and employing it freely outside of formal or institutional discursive contexts.[34]

Contours of a History

After this general survey of the regional setting, we may turn to the distinguishing political features of late-colonial Aymara communities in La Paz. Chapter 2 will look at the structure of community political authority and hierarchy as it had evolved over the course of colonial history. This chapter will set up an understanding of the political transformation of community that took place in the eighteenth century. Chapters 3 and 4 examine the proliferating, acute conflict in the La Paz countryside in order to explain the breakdown of community government. This internal process was bound up with a clash of political forces at the local and regional levels. Thus the challenge, which emerged from the base of the Aymara community, to constituted political relations and regimes reflected a definitive crisis in the colonial Andean political order. This community challenge and colonial crisis would reach fullest expression in the great insurrection of 1780–1781.

From the general process of community struggle in the preinsurrectionary phase, chapters 5 and 6 take up the more exceptional anticolonial projects and the political vision of Indian insurgents. In order to situate the movement led by Túpaj Katari, chapter 5 examines more closely the cases of clear anticolonial mobilization in La Paz prior to 1781, and the other regional movements within the overall Andean insurrection. Chapter 6 is devoted to the figure of Katari and the key issues associated with the war in La Paz: radicalism, racial antagonism, and violence, as well as the power of peasant community forces. Chapter 7 considers the postwar period in terms of community relations with the Bourbon state and local elites. It also returns to the question of intracommunity political structure and its transformation that was raised in chapter 2. Here my aim is to demonstrate the devolution of power and democratization of the political formation that was under way in this period. The conclusion reflects on the importance of these political processes for our understanding of late-colonial crisis as well as subsequent nineteenth- and twentieth-century relations between communities and the Bolivian state. It establishes the eighteenth century as a constitutive moment for Aymara communities on the Bolivian altiplano today, and one that helps to understand subsequent cycles of political mediation, legitimacy, and crisis.

A final compositional note: My interest is as much to evoke local political life in Indian towns and communities as it is to trace the patterns and processes of regional history within the wider Andean context. The region of La Paz was one of grand scope: each of its provinces encompassed a multitude of rural Indian towns, approximately eight to twelve original municipal districts along with other towns of more recent formation. For the most part, my approach will be to skip freely from locality to locality, and across the provinces, in order to illustrate general points. In order to portray local life more fully, however, not only do I resort to occasional "thick" description, but recurrently return to one town in particular. A practical reason for focussing on Guarina, in the province of Omasuyos, is that a respectable body of documentation about it remains extant in Bolivian, Argentine, and Spanish archives.[35]

In one respect, then, my purpose for returning to Guarina throughout the book is to allow a more fine-grained, intimate sense for individual figures, families, and local affairs, and to follow through longer-term processes at the local level. Guarina's local history was of course rich and distinctive, as is the local history of every one of the dozens of towns throughout the region. In other ways, however, Guarina is of interest precisely because it did not stand out as an especially unusual site. In this respect, my second aim is to discern the ways in which the dynamics in one "ordinary" location reflected the common processes unfolding in towns throughout the region.[36]

In the eighteenth century, the district of Guarina was home to a sizeable and growing population of Indian community members (including an ethnic minority of native Urus) and hacienda peons. Their number at century's end was close to 10,000, while the number of non-Indian town residents was minimal. According to the local priest, there were no more than six or seven "Spaniards," "by which I mean mestizo Spaniards because none of them are of pure blood."[37]

The town itself was nestled below a small hillside along the eastern shore of Lake Titicaca. According to Andean creation mythology, the lake was a cosmic navel and birthplace of humanity. From the time of the ancient Tiwanaku civilization, through Inka occupation of Qollasuyu, as well as in colonial and modern times, the lake has continued to be perceived as a source of great spiritual potency. It attracted streams of pilgrims to its sanctuaries, as well as Andean ritual specialists who renewed their powers in seasonal ceremonies. Like a huge mirror, its waters reflected the changing phenomena of the heavens: the intense azure of clear skies, the piercing rays of a brilliant sun, the vivid whiteness of fleecy cloud formations, the dark tones of overcast, roiling atmosphere.

Streams and marshlands around the lake not only favored agriculture but afforded fertile pasture for large herds of livestock. The Urus, descended from an early Pukina-speaking population living along the fringes of the lake, specialized in fishing and gathering of other lacustrine resources. In the eighteenth century, more so than ever before, small-scale trade coursed through Guarina, connecting the town with the urban entrepôt of La Paz, the provinces of Lower Peru to the north, and the valley lands spilling down over the eastern flank of the Andean cordillera range. It was not only in demographic and economic terms, however, that late-colonial society was stirring. In others ways as well, the pulse of local life beat with a quickening rhythm.

2   The Inherited Structure of Authority

Since the sixteenth century, the noble Calaumana and Yanaique dynasties had ruled continuously over the two moieties of Guarina in the province of Omasuyos. Sometime around 1730, Anansaya and Urinsaya were brought together under the command of Simón Calaumana, evidently due to intermarriage and the absence of any male Yanaique heir. In 1742, his son Matías Calaumana Yanaique was formally recognized as cacique of Guarina by the viceroy in Lima, over the rival pretensions of Francisco Calaumana. Matías could trace his ancestry from his father all the way back to don Diego Calaumana, "the ancient first cacique, the trunk of our lineage." According to Matías, Francisco could not claim the same "excellence and superior prerogative" since he descended from Diego's progeny by a second marriage.[1]

Less than ten years later, Matías was forced to return to the courts of La Plata and Lima to fend off another challenge from Francisco. After obtaining the viceroy's confirmation once again, Matías insisted that the corregidor hold a public ceremony in the plaza of Guarina to demonstrate once and for all to the community that he was the rightful heir. In December 1751 the corregidor complied, since "the Indians were unsure who their own cacique was" and since it was his role to set their minds at rest. He had the viceroy's proclamation read in Aymara to an assembly of Indians, including community authorities and elders, in the presence of the town priest and his auxiliary. Finally he took Matías Calaumana by the hand and seated him in the throne of honor, in the absence of objections by anyone present.

During the following decades, Calaumana continued to enjoy the confidence of the Omasuyos corregidores. In compliance with the demands of the colonial state, he oversaw the collection of tribute payments and the allocation of mita laborers. He ensured local social order, bearing in mind the state's injunctions that Indians occupy themselves in productive labors, avoid idolatry and dissension, and live according to the norms of "civilized," Catholic subjects.

Calaumana was renowned among community members as a "true descendant of the primordial native lords and monarchs of these American dominions."[2] He also fulfilled the typical responsibilities expected of caciques by their communities. In the courts he waged battles to defend community lands, drawing on his own personal wealth and documents in his possession, which dated back to the early seventeenth century. He held off the encroachments of landlords *(hacendados)* and sought to regain control over the community's fertile valley lands, possessed since the time of the Inka, in the neighboring province of Larecaja. He also demonstrated cacique "reciprocity" and patronage when he supplied foodstuffs to mitayo families on their way to Potosí, not out of legal obligation but as a "voluntary act based solely on fairness and kindness."[3] Many of his community subjects, however, also knew him as "very vengeful and of rancorous temperament." Indians from nearby Viacha (Pacajes), after facing off against him in a land boundary dispute, called him "a violent and greedy tyrant" who had wrought havoc in the fields, horribly murdered one woman, and jailed any who opposed his will.[4]

Despite initial difficulties with his succession to the position of cacique governor (cacicazgo) and other occasional minor conflicts, Matías Calaumana maintained a firm grasp on power. Because of his unusually long reign of forty years, his unusually concentrated authority (given the political fusing of both moieties), his alliance with colonial officials, his traditional ethnic prestige and paternal custody of the community, and his fearsome personality, he serves as one of the most notable examples of eighteenth-century dynastic patriarchs in La Paz. Over this fairly stable if by no means idyllic period, there was little to foreshadow what would come— the shattering of the Guarina cacicazgo with the 1780s insurrection.

During the cacique's heyday, subordinate community authorities present an understandably low profile in the documents. Yet what about other members of his clan and the indigenous elite? Appealing for state recognition of his noble stock, Francisco Calaumana, the vanquished pretender to the cacicazgo, was awarded an honorary and obsolete title of authority *(alcalde mayor de naturales)* for the entire province. The post apparently brought with it no material benefits, and the Indians of neighboring Carabuco announced they had no use for such an authority. Joseph Calaumana acted as a companion authority *(segunda persona)* for his brother Matías until community members, unwilling to tolerate his despotism, forced him from office; Indians in Laja also rejected his improbable bid for the cacicazgo in their district. Other Calaumanas similarly took on rotating authority posts in town or married into the families of mestizo townspeople with modest landholdings and occasional employment in the provincial bureaucratic apparatus. The noble Yanaique line, which had controlled the Urinsaya cacicazgo into the eighteenth century, faded back into the toiling peasantry.[5]

In Guarina, as more widely in the Aymara highlands, long-term developments had led both to the consolidation of cacique power and to the waning fortunes of the indigenous nobility as a distinctive stratum of colonial society. Other Indian commoners normally lived their lives and met their obligations to community, religious forces, and the state under the aegis of their cacique. The hierarchical exercise of power within the community could often be blunt or abrasive, yet it was invested with a seemingly natural legitimacy and durability. It was also perfectly in keeping with the familiar tensions of Andean colonial order in which Spanish domination of the native population operated through the mediation of ethnic community representatives.

This chapter will explore the community polity that had been formed out of the earlier phases of colonial history. It traces the structure of authority and the symbolic as well as functional importance of hereditary and rotating political posts. It will also focus on a set of issues that are relatively sketchy in the colonial documentation and historiography. One is the ambivalent identity of Indian nobles and their historical decline. Another is the shadowy figure of *principales* (ranking community members, especially elders, with informal authority) and the multiple connotations of *principal* status. A third issue is the loose institution that was the community *cargo* system (an integrated arrangement of subordinate authority posts). Overall the established community formation was marked by centralized, hierarchical, and patriarchal power relations flowing from Andean as well as Spanish sources. As we will see later, these power relations would undergo major transformation over the increasingly turbulent course of the eighteenth century.

The Apex of Authority: Classic Cacique Patriarchs

The fact of Spanish conquest in the sixteenth century set the underlying contours of power and political relations until the last of the royalist military forces surrendered in the nineteenth century. The caste segregation of the "republic of Indians" from the "republic of Spaniards," as well as the obsession with honor and rank in colonial Spanish mentality, fixed the space and significance of political mediation between the republics and between the local Aymara community and the wider colonial order. From the Spanish vantage point, the crucial intermediary—the cacique, or Indian community governor—was by law identified with the (effectively subordinate) Indian republic, yet was also certified as a native lord with the honors and privileges that befitted a nobleman. Community members recognized his backing by the colonial state and, at the same time, expected the cacique to uphold certain traditional norms of Aymara lords (mallkus). Given the ambivalence of his position and the keenly felt contradictions of status in this dual social order, what was the real nature of cacique power? How did the cacique manage the Spanish and Andean sources from which his authority flowed? And where did the cacique actually stand in the colonial political world?

The colonial historiography has shown that caciques played a dual economic role. On one hand, they engaged actively in colonial commerce and accumulated sometimes substantial private fortunes. On the other, in exchange for their privileged access to community lands and labor, traditional norms of economic reciprocity obliged the cacique to show his largess with material favors, support for the needy, and subsidies in time of want or bad harvest. While these activities could be complementary, with private accumulation serving community economic reproduction, they could also enter into contradiction if caciques abused their privileges or failed to meet their obligations to the community.

Caciques were legally understood to be "Indians," as the descendants of noble Indian ancestors, and colonial law ostensibly allowed no one but Indians into community government. Yet generations of intermarriage with mestizo and creole families meant that they were at the same time effectively "mestizos" or "cholos" of mixed "blood," or mixed birth. This racial factor overlapped with other features of apparent cultural ambivalence. Not only did caciques often marry into "Spanish" (meaning non-Indian, whether European, creole American, or mestizo) families, but they were "Indians" who dressed, bore themselves, and professed their faith in much the same way as did the members of the ethnically and legally distinguished "Spanish republic."[6]

A similar tension emerged regarding the cacique's political power and identity.[7] However, caciques should not be portrayed as eternally ambiguous, intrinsically amorphous, forever betwixt and between the essentialized poles of "Spanish" and "Andean" identity. The following section shows, through a set of short commentaries, that the double sources of cacique authority in fact converged politically and symbolically to shape classic cacique patriarchy. This will be followed by a brief consideration of a neglected political element in discussions of cacique legitimacy, namely the role of the patriarch as community protector. The following chapters will indicate how the long-standing tensions surrounding cacique power were ultimately worked out, leading to the demise of the native patriarch.

Andean Sources of Authority

Early colonial legislation in the Andes reflected a tension over whether Indian communities were to be ruled by state appointees or the hereditary successors of native lords. In Central Mexico, over the course of the sixteenth century, a significant split developed between community governors and caciques *(tlatoque)*. Local caciques maintained the honors and privileges attached to their noble title, yet the post of governor often passed into the hands of others such as those who enjoyed the political confidence of state officials.[8] In the Andes, by contrast, no such separation of powers took place. Maximal, state-sanctioned political authority in Indian towns remained under the firm control of local noble lineages. Men like Matías Calaumana could thus declare themselves cacique governors under formal circumstances, though it was normally enough to invoke the title of cacique in order to signal governorship.[9]

Since caciques relied upon ascriptive hereditary authority, they were highly preoccupied by genealogy and ancestral stock, not unlike lords and aristocrats in other cultural and historical settings. Leaving aside speculation about matrilineal descent in precolonial times, by the eighteenth century the obsession with lineage in cacique families primarily meant a fixation on the fore*fathers*. The myriad succession conflicts over cacicazgos in this century demonstrate the keen knowledge that pretenders possessed not only of their own genealogy but of that of their kin and rivals. It was not uncommon for a cacicazgo pretender to stake his claim on a subtle point of kinship in the sixteenth century. Lucas de Meneses Cutimbo in the town of Chucuito (Chucuito province), for example, argued in 1722 that his local rival descended from a Spanish interloper who arrived from southern Charcas at the time of Gonzalo Pizarro's rebellion in the mid-sixteenth century.[10]

An especially damning argument against a rival was that it was not known who had sired him. In 1763 in the town of Curaguara de Pacajes (Pacajes), the cacique in office was challenged on the grounds that "he is a low Indian whose father is not even known." In Chulumani (Chulumani), the cacique Martín Mamani dismissed his rival in the same terms, as a "low-grade Indian whose ancestors are unknown, since he is from outside the community and of obscure origin."[11] To be without genealogy meant to be without noble rank and without claim to authority. Knowledge of the forefathers *(los antepasados y abuelos),* which could be attested to by community elders or by colonial state titles and *probanzas,* was a requisite of power.

The intimate association between nobility and (historical) origin explains the recurrent references by caciques to their "authors" since the days of the gentiles *(la gentilidad)* or pre-Christian era. In Ancoraimes (Omasuyos), Bernardo Callacagua declared himself the rightful noble heir to the cacicazgo possessed by his fathers and grandfathers since the time of the gentiles.[12] Many cacique families in the La Paz region could legitimately claim to have been recognized as nobles under Inka rule or to have descended directly from Inka lineages. The cacique of Juli (Chucuito), Manuel Francisco Chiqui Inga Charaja, held that his gentile ancestor had been confirmed as nobleman by the Inka king of Peru Guayna Cápac "from the beginning" *(ab initio).*[13] The eminent Cusicanqui family of Calacoto and Caquingora (Pacajes) traced its line back to sixteenth-century nobles Felipe Tupa Yupanqui and Gonzalo Pucho Guallpa, who were themselves descendants of the "great" lord Tupa Inga Yupanqui. One family member affirmed in 1783 that the very name Cusicanqui evoked the family's purity of stock and its right to govern.[14]

These references from La Paz reflect a widespread cultural-political consciousness of Andean origins and identity, which developed in the late seventeenth and eighteenth centuries into a "neo-Inka nationalist movement" (Rowe) among educated Indian nobles and caciques.[15] Inka descendants in Cuzco, for example, frequently commissioned paintings of their genealogical line. In some cases caciques even invented fictitious claims that the Inka had recognized their ancestors in the preconquest period.[16] The extent of this neo-Inka culture among caciques in La Paz was relatively limited compared to Cuzco, Lima, and other parts of the Lima audiencia. Aymara caciques from La Paz had few political or kinship ties to Cuzco families, few had studied in the elite schools for Indian nobles, and there were no urban festivals, as in Cuzco and Lima, in which noble families would parade their ancestral prestige. Nevertheless, earlier Inka occupation of the region did leave a set of legitimate descendants, and caciques did manipulate Inka motifs to enhance their authority.

The outstanding example of neo-Inka culture among Aymara caciques in La Paz comes from the powerful Guarachi dynasty of Jesús de Machaca (Pacajes). The two caciques evidently most influenced by the new trends were Pedro Fernández Guarachi, who governed through the 1660s and 1670s, and his son José Fernández Guarachi, who succeeded him in 1682 and ruled until his death apparently in the late 1730s. Their exposure to the late-seventeenth- and eighteenth-century cultural currents was probably due to their Cuzco education, and we know that José visited Lima on at least one occasion.[17] It seems that Pedro caught the portrait fever of his cacique contemporaries and had his likeness captured on canvas. Such portraits were commonly included in cacicazgo petitions and claims to nobility made to the colonial administration in the eighteenth century. His son also commissioned paintings and had in his possession, for example, a portrait of Inka Yupanqui and his consort. Into the nineteenth century, Guarachi descendants continued to commission works that depicted the Inka dynastic successors and included annotations on their noble lineage.[18]

In their genealogical accounts, the Guarachis traced their ancestry back to the Aymara lord Apu Guarachi who ruled prior to Inka expansion over a vast altiplano domain, from Desaguadero to Quillacas with valley outliers in Potosí and Chuquisaca. According to family legend, Apu Guarachi sent his two sons to witness Manco Cápac's manifestation in Pacarictambo, and one son aided the Inka in subduing the Qolla people around Lake Titicaca, for which service he was rewarded with a splendid vestment (*unku*).[19] The Guarachis also declared themselves blood descendants of Viracocha Inka, Cápac Yupanqui, Sinchi Roca, and Maita Cápac, having married into the Tito Atauchi family, an Inka clan from Copacabana, in the latter seventeenth century. It was, in fact, none other than Pedro Fernández Guarachi—most likely motivated by the new Inka prestige he would have been exposed to during his Cuzco student days—who secured this Inka ancestry by marrying Juana Quispe Sisa, daughter of the cacique of Copacabana.[20]

In the 1730s, José Fernández Guarachi listed among his belongings the ancient tunic, or *unku*, supposedly awarded by the Inka to his forefathers for their loyalty and military collaboration, as well as a litter upon which Andean lords were traditionally transported.[21] While the Guarachi patriarchs and other caciques commonly dressed in Spanish fashion, presumably they also found public ceremonial occasions to don Inka raiments, which would inspire awe and respect on the part of their local subjects. In the eighteenth century, the Guarachis also brandished the staff of authority of *alcalde mayor de los cuatro suyus de este reino*. In 1555 Carlos V had originally granted this peculiar title, with its echoes of imperial Inka domain (Tawantinsuyu), to Alonso Tito Atauchi (an Inka ancestor of José Fernández Guarachi's mother) for his services in capturing Francisco

Hernández Girón. The title was reconfirmed at José Fernández Guarachi's request in 1720, though he felt obliged to ask that authorities clarify the exact grade and jurisdiction of the post.[22]

Inka identification, and native nobility generally, served as a potent source of authority vis-à-vis ordinary community members. But it was an authority subject to abuse. One unpopular cacique of Mocomoco (Larecaja) sought credibility by declaring himself, truthfully or not, to be of "the royal blood of the Inka kings."[23] In Carabuco (Omasuyos), community members charged that: "They tell us that we are obliged to serve them, as native lords [*señores naturales*], offering our selves, our belongings, and our pack animals, . . . [and that] they have the right to seize anything we own, down to the very floor of our homes. . . . Sometimes they take away our children, grandchildren, nieces, nephews, and relatives. They call this tyrannical thievery of boys and girls the *chaco* and believe that children born to unwed or widowed mothers belong to the caciques by natural dominion."[24]

The Colonial Realignment of Andean Inheritance

In some cases, colonial Spanish codes and customs introduced distortions that subtly undermined traditional Andean practices. One example concerns ascriptive hereditary authority. While the Spanish Crown officially recognized existing hereditary ethnic authority, it did so largely according to its own principles and on its own terms. Native nobility was conceived of within the framework of feudal status hierarchy on the Old World peninsula, with Andean caciques being simply a curious, novel variant of familiar Spanish hidalgos. Cacicazgo authority was deemed a piece of titled family property, the rights to which were set out in the Castilian legal code for entails *(mayorazgos)*.

This code will be examined more closely below (see chapter 3), yet suffice it to mention one aspect here. In eighteenth-century cacicazgo succession conflicts, much genealogical contention revolved around the privilege of first-born male children to accede to the cacique post. This privilege was extended, if not introduced, by Spanish mayorazgo rules, signifying an important shift in older Andean succession principles, which were more flexible and, because they included competence as a criterion for eligibility, could permit more effective ethnic leadership. Traditionally, leadership could pass from a deceased lord to his brother, primogeniture was not similarly privileged, and women were eligible to exercise authority.[25] Female inheritance rights were one of the few traditions that the Crown was willing to recognize formally in the Andean setting, if certain unusual circumstances obtained. Yet the Spanish juridical definition of a woman's natural "incompetence" caused her husband to assume the roles of official administrator of her property and functioning governor.[26] Therefore, colonial state regulations significantly recast notions of Andean nobility and contributed to cacique family obsessions with male forebears, lineage "purity," and "blood" origin. Also, as we will see in more detail in the next chapter, the introduction of stricter Spanish patriarchal principles of succession contributed to the long-term structural decline of colonial Andean rulership.

The Colonial Politics of Andean Noble Cultural Expression

Returning to the question of cacique historical memory and the new-found prestige attached to native nobility in the eighteenth century, what did the revalorization of traditional Andean sources of authority mean for cacique relations with the colonial political order and Spanish Crown? Though the problem is complex, two contrasting interpretations, drawing on the existing cultural historiography, may be noted here. According to one view, the proliferation of cacique portraits, urban processions in Inka regalia, and noble appeals to the Crown for privileges and recognition, to cite only a few features of the "Inka nationalist movement," remained largely within the formal coordinates of colonial Spanish culture. In its reformist political variants, it served to legitimate the Spanish Crown as successor to the Inka monarchy of the past. The political proof of this hypothesis, one might go on to argue, lies in the fact that throughout the age of insurgency most caciques shunned rebellion and tended instead to back the reactionary forces of colonial order.[27]

By another account, the mixture of Andean and Spanish cultural forms and motifs in the neo-Inka movement followed a set of symbolic strategies by caciques to use colonial elements in such a way as to subtly subvert colonial hierarchies at the discursive level. Cacique appeals to the past glory of Tawantinsuyu and to the ruling Spanish sovereign contained a critique of their subordination within the Peruvian viceroyalty and an ideological gravitation towards Andean autonomy. In fact, this argument concludes, the distinction between loyalist "moderate" caciques and rebel leaders was narrow indeed—as in the case of Túpac Amaru, the radicals were commonly frustrated reformists—and the conceived continuity between Inka and Spanish monarchy could logically extend to a utopian restoration of Inka kingship.[28]

Clearly, further research and broader vision are necessary to resolve this problem. The meaning of cacique "loyalism" is in itself a complex issue, and the artifacts of neo-Inka cultural renaissance cannot be understood only at a formal level through textual readings, however sophisticated. Moreover, while the political potential of the neo-Inka movement was indeed double-edged, we must ultimately pin down the practical applications of the ideology and the political conduct of its bearers under shifting historical conditions.[29]

The historical dynamics in La Paz, to be discussed in the following chapters, do not support the idea of a covert anticolonial project cultivated by caciques. The critical, counter-hegemonic strain of neo-Inka ideology associated with an "Andean utopia" was indeed historically significant in given regions at given moments.[30] Yet neo-Inka revival and Andean utopia did not always go hand in hand. Their respective historical courses were in fact complex and, however historically entwined, distinct. In the end, to understand the sharp differences within the cacique sector and the fact of cacique collaborationism, we must take seriously both a revolutionary project (Andean utopia, in its ideological dimension and political expression) and a conservative, at best cautious and at worst self-serving, loyalism that could also partake of neo-Inka inspiration. As a revolutionary ideology, Andean utopia might have circulated widely while gaining only limited acceptance, and it probably produced an ideological and political counter-reaction among much of the noble Indian sector. Insofar as the neo-Inka movement remained a sectoral campaign—to augment noble prestige and accede to education as well as ecclesiastical, bureaucratic, and legal positions within the viceroyalty—it lacked a true proto–national consciousness, whether conceived of in cross-class (i.e., noble/peasant or "Indian" nationalist) or interethnic (i.e., noble/creole or "Peruvian" nationalist) terms. In this sense, a categorical association between "neo-Inka" and "national" elements would be overstated.[31] In some cases it is surely valid, as with Túpac Amaru, while in others, as with the Guarachi patriarchs, it is manifestly not.

The conservative portrait of caciques that emerges from the study of La Paz draws not only on caciques' own declarations—which after all must be taken with a certain reserve, as discourse set within an official colonial context—but on their actual political conduct. The political identity of caciques within the Andean colonial order must be assessed not only in terms of cacique self-representation before the Crown and in relation to colonial authorities and elites, as with much of the neo-Inka cultural and political expression, but also in relation to their own communities. As will be shown in subsequent chapters, in La Paz the actual political conduct of caciques in relation to their communities rarely contributed to the subversive projects of "Andean utopia," and it ultimately proved decisive in undermining cacique power.

Local evidence from La Paz reveals how caciques, including those most influenced by the neo-Inka movement, drew authority from identification with the reigning Spanish sovereign. Alongside the portrait of the Inka and his consort, José Fernández Guarachi displayed another painting in his Jesús de Machaca residence. Described in his will of 1734 as a gold-framed depiction of the Inka and Spanish kings, it almost surely was a copy of the image of the royal dynastic successors made famous by the 1725 engraving attributed to Alonso de la Cueva, a Lima priest and intellectual.[32] Recent art history criticism has convincingly sought to tone down the loyalist interpretation of this work—seen in the past as a colonial appropriation of native symbols in order to legitimate Spanish rule—by exploring its peculiar significance for caciques, and their creole sympathizers such as de la Cueva, within the neo-Inka movement that we now know helped to produce it. Whether or not one accepts this reading of destabilizing discursive strategies within the engraving, there is no dispute that the image of dynastic succession suggests that Inka and Spanish sovereignty could be collapsed into a single, historically continuous source of authority for caciques. It is difficult to gauge the diffusion of such a notion in the countryside, among less urbane caciques outside the core areas of neo-Inka renaissance. Nevertheless we can note the case of the cacique of Laza, Asencio Campos Alacca, whose lineage, it was asserted, had been "confirmed by the king since the time of the gentiles."[33]

Recent criticism has also studied loyalist expressions in other paintings commissioned by La Paz cacique art patrons. *The Triumph of María* (1706) shows José Fernández Guarachi in the same entourage as the Spanish monarchs Carlos II and Felipe V, who uphold the Immaculate Virgin. In a mural in the Carabuco church, dated around 1768, cacique Agustín Siñani and his wife are shown in the train of Roman emperor Enrique IV, who penitentially pays obeisance to the pope. According to the critical analysis, there is a sometimes subtle subtext to these and other works that predicates cacique loyalty to Spanish kings on the subordination of secular to divine authority.[34]

The caciques' assimilation of feudal European symbolic codes and identification with metropolitan royalty is further evidenced by the adoption of heraldic emblems, especially in the family coat of arms. In 1720, the Crown conceded official permission for José Fernández Guarachi to employ the royal coat of arms. The Guarachi family shield contained an extraordinary assemblage of elements, from Bourbon royal arms to those granted by Carlos V to the Inka Paullu in the sixteenth century. The Cusicanqui family, who traced their ancestry back to Túpa Inga Yupanqui, drew their coat of arms from the shield conceded to Felipe Túpa Yupanqui and Gonzalo Pucho Guallpa by Carlos V in 1545.[35]

Just as caciques could take improper advantage of their prestige as Andean nobles, they could abuse the authority vested in them by the Crown. The cacique of Yunguyo (Chucuito) in 1755 arbitrarily seized the property of deceased peasants, saying that he was only acting on behalf of the king. In 1756 in Guaycho (Omasuyos), the cacique denied charges that he called himself "king" during local disputes; he had only asserted that the king had installed him in power to carry out the royal will.[36] Such reliance on Crown backing would increase as caciques came under fire from their own communities in the eighteenth century.

The Merits and Honor of Cacique Nobles

Cacique authority derived directly from the sovereign's recognition of hereditary nobility and governorship, yet it was also reinforced by the merits and services performed on behalf of the ruler. While caciques could cite services to both the Inka and the Spanish Crown, once again it seems clear that colonial Spanish codes informed cacique family claims. This is especially evident from the fact that caciques very frequently cited their family's military services. Since the reconquest of the Spanish peninsula—the seizure of Moorish territory for the Catholic kings—military exploits on behalf of the Crown had been recognized as a legitimate claim to nobility. This same logic was transferred to the New World and the importance of its adoption by Andean caciques must not be underestimated.

When cacique families enumerated their military merits in order to strengthen their claims of authority, they explicitly affirmed their loyalty to the king and implicitly assumed, to one degree or another, a Hispanic vision of history. Insofar as the peninsular reconquest and New World colonialism both involved territorial and political dominion over heathen peoples, be they Moors, Jews, or Indians, the caciques adopted a Spanish ideology of civilization and historical supremacy. Generally for caciques in the Andean context, the legitimacy of the conquest was reconfirmed historically in ongoing episodes, over the centuries of colonial rule, in which they and their families loyally participated and at times perished. The most dramatic of these episodes was—ironically enough—the "pacification" of neo-Inka insurrection in 1781.[37]

Evidence for this comes again from José Fernández Guarachi's collection of paintings. One work in his possession, entitled *The Battle of the Urus,* celebrated Pedro Guarachi's suppression of the revolt by the "infidel" Uru people on the Desaguadero River in 1676. For this service to the Crown, the Guarachi clan was awarded the formerly Uru lands of Iruitu. Pedro Guarachi's services also included marching on La Paz to help subdue disturbances in the 1660s and leading expeditions to dislodge highway bandits in the Moquegua valley along the Pacific coast and in the Llangabamba valley of Sicasica province. When enemy English vessels were spied off the coast, he was also named Captain General of the Pacajes Indians enlisted for the defense of the port of Arica.[38]

When Martín Mamani set out to defend his right to the cacicazgo of Chulumani in 1799, he declared that his forefathers had been the first caciques "from the time of the conquest." He noted his own exploits on the lowland frontier as chief commander of the company of Indians who participated in the conquest (also described as the "mission," "new discovery," and "new reducción") of the "barbarians" in the Mosetenes territory. His merits included working indefatigably to open roads and building the church for the Indians of Bope (mistaken for Chiriguanos). He also laid forth the loyal military services of his family during the 1781 insurgency and pacification. When insurgent leaders—allegedly Túpac Amaru himself—sought to recruit his father for the movement, Dionicio Mamani promptly tipped off the corregidor. Dionicio and his sons subsequently served in different campaigns against the insurgents, one of which cost him his life.[39] In much of the late-colonial documentation, cacique families recited their heroism and sacrifices during the civil war and new conquest of 1781. They also boasted of their official Spanish military titles and produced certifications of their deeds by prominent colonial officials.

While military prowess and services to native lords may well have been important in Andean society in pre-Hispanic times, there is a patently Spanish and colonial quality to cacique proclamations of merit in the eighteenth century. Such services and merit were significant for cacique claims to nobility under colonial rule and to the prerogatives of rank, what one cacicazgo pretender termed "employment, honors, and privileges."[40]

Cacique honor, as a code of individual virtue and social rank, flowed from the Andean sources of hereditary nobility as well as the Spanish political sources that invested cacique governors with hierarchical status. It is hardly surprising to find that just as Spanish colonial power refounded cacique authority, it also influenced the practices and discourse of cacique honor in the eighteenth century. When Guaqui cacique Pedro Limachi came under attack from his community in 1771, he felt compelled not only to repudiate the plot against him but, in proper Spanish fashion, "above all to vindicate my honor, credit, and worthy conduct, which I publicly profess."[41]

It is especially important to note how cacique nobility, firmly established within Andean traditions, could dovetail with the Spanish colonial code that defined honor through superiority over vanquished Indians.[42] In such cases, honor for cacique nobles meant "distinction" from Indian "commoners." To justify their own rectitude and conduct, caciques did not hesitate to employ the Spanish colonial discourse about Indians as pathetic, rude, irrational, deceitful, and generally uncivilized beings. In the same dispute in Guaqui in 1771, the cacique Limachi denounced the "infidel and libertine customs" of the Indians, while his backers contrasted the cacique's "urbanity" with the "falseness" of the "cowering brutes" who opposed him. Faustino Pabon, cacique of Irupana (Chulumani), assailed his own "lazy and swindling" subjects as "the children of fickleness, falsehood, and evil." "Their primary aim is not truth," he held, "but rather influence and sedition."[43]

A pair of examples further illustrates how caciques manipulated royal sanction for their authority, and shows particularly how cacique honor as distinction from Indian subjects was acted out at times in feudal rituals of political subordination. Community members from Jesús de Machaca described how their cacique, Pedro de la Parra, routinely charged arbitrary fees in the name of the king and ordered Indians to do his bidding like a "lord of vassals." His subjects were expected to show him "reverence" by baring their heads and removing their plug of coca in his presence. When the community took Parra to court for his abuses of authority, they reported that "since we had no one to stand up for us, we could only seal our lips and render the customary genuflections of humility, which the cacique ordered we perform endlessly."[44]

But a second example may be given as well, since it could be argued that Parra was really a mestizo interloper in the cacicazgo and therefore not representative of illustrious noble families. When the house of the patriarch Diego Choqueguanca of Azángaro (Azángaro) was challenged, the cacique's son, José, staked his family's defense on the Crown, claiming that only the king had the authority to remove his father from the cacicazgo. After receiving the title of Commander General for four provinces during the military repression of the 1781 insurgency, José Choqueguanca forbade any Indians from wearing their native headgear in his presence.[45]

Colonial Andean Signs of Authority

While there is limited evidence regarding the traditional prestige and ritual practices surrounding caciques' privileged rights to land and labor services within the community, we do know that they antedate the conquest. These rights were subsequently reconfirmed and regulated by the Crown in keeping with the feudal Hispanic code of nobility. If caciques were seen as a New World variant of the peninsular hidalgos, then they also stood to enjoy their natural perquisites as did the Spanish gentry. For eighteenth-century native lords, their privileged control over designated community lands and laborers stemmed from both local Andean hereditary tradition and from colonial royal sanction.

Besides the caciques' coats of arms, which combined Andean and Hispanic insignia within a European heraldic form,[46] another political emblem wielded by cacique governors was the staff of authority *(vara* or *bastón de mando)*. Archaeological evidence exists to suggest there was a pre-Columbian antecedent of the colonial staff of authority in the Andean region, yet the Spaniards introduced the colonial staff for ethnic rulers throughout their American dominion.[47] As a compressed sign of local ethnic authority and of colonial state sovereignty, the staff was invested with a peculiar and sometimes unstable symbolic complexity. During the turbulent eighteenth century as state legitimacy faced growing threats, the staff of authority could switch from a source of prestige to an object of anticolonial antipathy.[48]

Cacique governors formally gained possession of cacicazgo authority at the ceremony in which they ritually "received the staff." For such occasions, the corregidor summoned all community members, whether authorities, elders, or commoners, to the town plaza where they were joined by local Spanish residents and authorities such as the parish priest and the provincial protector of Indians. With the corregidor as presiding official, the ceremony was held at the entrance to the church cemetery on Sunday at the hour of high mass. The town crier read the corregidor's decree, which granted authority to the incoming cacique, instructed him in his governing duties, and admonished community members to obey him. The corregidor then gave the cacique "actual corporal possession." He grasped him by the hand and seated him in the traditional throne of Andean lords known as the *tiana,* presumably also extending to him at this point the staff of authority. The cacique took a vow as owner of the caci-cazgo *(jure domini vel quasi)* before God and the corregidor to govern his subjects with love and justice. After the corregidor once more enjoined the Indians to take him as their cacique, great gaiety broke out as they rushed up and competed to embrace their new ruler and to demonstrate their satisfaction with his appointment. Afterwards the cacique hosted a grand banquet to please his subjects and display his own good will toward them.[49]

There are several points to make about this typical political ritual. Among the different "traditional" Andean features of the ceremony—which would include the community's rejoicing and embracing of the ca-cique as well as his reciprocal feast—the most striking is the tiana, a vestige of pre-Hispanic political ceremony that evoked the memory of all the past cacique forefathers who had sat in it. In the "magnificent" celebration held for the cacique of Chulumani, Dionicio Mamani sat in a gold tiana built by the community and reserved for hereditary successors to the post.[50]

Naturally, however, the significance of a single cultural form shifts ac-cording to the specific historical context, and the eighteenth century was a far cry from the preconquest setting. In this case, while the tiana could conceivably acquire a counterhegemonic potential for the community, as a reminder of its once autonomous political tradition, the corregidor orches-trated the seating of the cacique as a symbolic exercise subsuming ethnic authority to colonial state power.

Last of all, it is important to note the passive role of the community in the performance and the paternalism of the ritual script. The community participated only at the end of the ceremony when cued to offer its approval of the cacique who was already "seated" by the corregidor. The ritual sug-gests the absence of formal mechanisms for community control over its governor and major limits to cacique accountability.[51] There did exist in practice an informal negotiation of cacique legitimacy, involving a set of traditionally defined expectations for conduct, which was indeed in effect until the late colonial era. Yet as cacique legitimacy eroded more deeply in the eighteenth century, the formal limits to greater democratic participation in community politics proved increasingly problematic. Discontented com-munity members turned toward state courts to resolve internal disputes, generating voluminous litigation in our period, and when legal recourse proved inadequate, collective violence became the final response to the con-straints upon the community. The ritual of cacicazgo possession, a symbolic compound of Andean and Spanish cultural elements, provides a glimpse of these same colonial and patriarchal constraints.

The Patriarchal Protector

The colonial historiography has observed how the some-times tenuous negotiation of cacique legitimacy depended upon the ambivalent economic and cultural roles of the cacique in colonial society. It is also important to consider, however, a more directly political factor, infrequently noted in the literature, that contributed to that legitimacy. The common image of the cacique as intermediary between the community and other colonial forces, such as the state or the market, accurately describes the cacique's structural position in society at large. Yet ordinary community members perceived the cacique as more than an intermediary or an inhabitant of middle ground. In this sense, what concerned Aymara peasants was not only the cacique's function in collective material reproduction or as maximal community representative (that is to say, as officially sanctioned interlocutor or legal delegate before the state) but also his role as community *guardian* in local political conflicts.[52]

The colonial cacique served partly as state agent and partly as administrator of local resources. For the community, he also exercised a crucial political authority when, for instance, he engaged in court litigation on its behalf, stood up for its territorial boundaries, and handled the vital information in its archive of documents concerning lands, tribute, and the ancestors and lords of the past. While the cacique's role as community protector could overlap with state definitions of his function as legal guardian or tutor of peasant minors, in fact his role meant much more to local peasants. While this meaning is not readily accessible to us, since the documents left by the colonial bureaucracy focus on the state's own interest in cacique functions, it is possible to gain a sense of it.

As we will see in the following chapter, peasants counted on caciques to "defend," "protect," and "shelter" them. During the great insurrection of 1781, they expressed this sentiment while professing their loyalty to Túpac Amaru: "Our Gabriel Inca lives. We swear to him, then, as king because he comes legally and we receive him. All Indians perceive [that] he defends their rights."[53] Under more ordinary circumstances in the 1750s, community members in Palca (Sicasica) insisted on the cacique's "obligation" to support them as their patron *(patrocinar)*.[54]

This patronage was also understood in explicitly paternalist ways. Cayetano Berrasueta was said to have boasted that, during his twenty-six years as cacique of Chucuito (Chucuito), "he never harmed any Indian, which is why he is renowned as 'father' to all in his moiety." One elder from Irupana spoke of "the obligation that governors used to have and still have, since their place is that of a father and ours that of his children, to care for us and watch over us."[55] We might rightly wonder whether this patriarchal discourse of protection was not a form of colonial rhetoric adapted by Indians for strategic purposes in the courts and before the state. Yet the evidence shows that this discourse was not restricted to the sort of formal bureaucratic settings that left a documentary record. As witnesses sometimes later reported, it also surfaced spontaneously within the community and especially during moments of tension.

Furthermore, there is evidence that the notion of the patriarchal protector belongs to an Aymara tradition antedating the conquest. In Ludovico Bertonio's Aymara dictionary from 1612, the term "father, [one] who succors another person as if he were a father" is semantically associated with "shelter," "defender," "refuge," exalted terms signifying "one in whom they find full shelter." These glosses are derived metaphorically from the Aymara words for "fortress" and for the rock walls built as boundaries for plots of land and to keep away animals who preyed upon the fields.[56]

Beneath the Cacique Apex: The Tasks, Appointment, and Obedience of Subordinate Authorities

The structure of traditional authority in the Andes— below the level of cacique governance—has remained obscure to us given the tremendous variety of forms at the local level and the scarcity of ethnographic and historiographic studies. Over the decades, anthropological community studies have yielded a wealth of data about local authorities, but the peculiarity and diversity of situations, along with the modest interest in community politics generally, have limited more general and comparative analyses. Historical transformations involving the structure of community authority, which are of primary interest here, have also received little scrutiny.[57]

This same local diversity was found throughout the La Paz region, for example in the case of Indian officers in town government: *alcaldes, regidores,* and *alguaciles.* From Viceroy Toledo's original sixteenth-century mandate, to the prescriptions of the Laws of the Indies compiled in the early seventeenth century to Viceroy La Palata's ordinances based upon Toledo in the late seventeenth century, official legislation was itself not perfectly uniform. It is unsurprising, therefore, that in eighteenth-century towns there was no set scheme for alcaldes, and the presence of regidores and alguaciles could be fairly random.[58]

This section will review the functions and designation of local political authorities and will end with a comment on their relationship to caciques prior to the collapse of the cacicazgos. I have not framed this discussion exclusively in terms of cabildo, or town government, as might a historian of colonial Mexico. The cabildo was not nearly so consolidated an institution in the southern Andes as it was in New Spain, and such a crucial figure as the hilacata was a local ayllu authority without town jurisdiction. Nor have I chosen to focus on the civil-religious cargo system, the evidence for which will be examined in the following section. As we will see, the historical presence of Spanish cabildo, *cofradía* (religious lay brotherhood), as well as cargo-ladder institutional forms in the La Paz countryside cannot be understood apart from lasting ayllu organization and the deeper dynamics of local power relations.

The second-ranking authority who served at the side of the cacique was the *segunda persona de cacique.* The segunda post was a holdover from preconquest times, with a subordinate but complementary status that should be understood within the dualist logic of traditional Andean social organization. In the eighteenth century, the segunda's functions were primarily tributary, though there is evidence that he could also step in as surrogate when the cacique was absent. As his status corresponded formally to that of the cacique, his sphere of power was also the moiety and his base, the town. Acting under the aegis of the cacique and outside the colonial legal dispositions regulating town government, the segunda could serve longer terms in office than other authorities.[59]

In principle, given his high position within the scheme of community segmentation, one would expect the segunda to have been a more powerful figure than the alcalde or hilacata. In fact this does not seem to have been the case, apparently due to a long-term degradation of his authority. While informally recognized by regional colonial authorities, the segunda did not receive official state sanction as did alcaldes, nor was he treated as a strategic intermediary for colonial rule. In earlier periods, his activities presumably would have been far more extensive. By the eighteenth century, as they diminished to the functions of tribute exaction, his role was less central than that of the hilacata who roved from hamlet to hamlet collecting directly from peasant families.[60] Another sign of the institutional weakness of the post was the irregular appearance of the segunda in community legal depositions and collective mobilization.

In the occasional documentary register that lists the set of community authorities, it is true that the segunda is mentioned first, followed by alcaldes, regidores, alguaciles, and finally hilacatas. Yet given his narrowing functions and conspicuous absence in the crucial affairs of the community, we can infer a discrepancy between rank and power. Also, in some communities the segunda seems to have been simply nonexistent, finally rendered redundant over the course of colonial history.

The Indian authorities who served official town government—alcaldes, regidores, and alguaciles—were initially conceived by Viceroy Toledo according to the model of the peninsular cabildo institution. Their local representation and administration—defined under La Palata as official *gobierno económico*—did not originally include tributary responsibilities, and in the case of alcaldes and alguaciles, it principally involved judicial and police functions.[61] To take one ordinary example from Tiahuanaco in 1766, the alcalde was formally empowered to arrest any wrongdoers within the town's jurisdiction, to hear any cases involving lesser crimes, and to dispense punishment accordingly. Crimes considered "grave," such as homicide or mule-rustling, were to be turned over to the corregidor. In these cases the alcalde could embargo the property of the accused. He was to protect families, livestock, and lands from non-Indian assailants or rebels. He was also to censure marital infidelity, drunkenness, and idolatry and to ensure the punctual payment of tribute, regular church attendance, and public order generally.[62] Despite the faculty legally accorded them, the documentary record provides little evidence that Indian alcaldes actually heard suits and administered justice as magistrates in the first instance. They appear rather as enforcers of the law, acting at the behest of caciques, the corregidor and his agents, priests, or other visiting colonial functionaries.

This suggests that in practice there was significant divergence between the original Spanish blueprint for cabildo authorities and local political practice in the Andean countryside. The evidence also shows that alcaldes carried out any number of other activities, once again not following formal state guidelines so much as the contingent needs of the community and the command of superior authorities. These activities could range from witnessing legal writs, such as wills in case of emergency, summoning the principales to a community assembly held by the cacique, or guarding confiscated property along with an alguacil.[63] During the intendancy period beginning in 1782, efforts were made to enhance the jurisdiction of Indian town government authorities. In the decades of the 1780s and 1790s, subdelegates in rural areas acted to formalize the election of alcaldes, alguaciles, and regidores.[64] Also, the alcaldes no longer served solely as ministers of justice, but could assume a new responsibility in the tributary regime. Article 10 of the Ordinance of Intendants permitted alcaldes to collect tribute in towns where colonial authorities had not named proper collec-tors.[65] This shift occurred as part of a larger reshuffling of late-colonial po-litical relations between state and community.

Two other authorities introduced by Toledo were the alguacil and the regidor. The alguacil is sometimes described as a constable, essentially a low-ranking auxiliary to the alcalde. He acted at times as judicial emissary for the alcalde or other authorities, as guard or bailiff, or as member of a "posse" to round up criminal suspects within the jurisdiction.[66] In prac-tice, the number of alguaciles and regidores could vary from town to town.

According to Spanish cabildo design, the regidor was a town-council member, of higher rank than the alguacil, who participated in elections and sundry administrative tasks. His low profile, even obscurity, in the La Paz documentation suggests precisely the vagueness of this institution in the countryside. He is mentioned as a prisoner escort, indicating police duties, and also as a voter in the election of alcaldes, although references to this role are few indeed and even dubious, perhaps deliberately misleading attempts to impress the authorities with the image of a "properly" func-tioning town government.[67] In the absence of a more clearly defined polit-ical function, we can assume the regidor was an officer of low status—equivalent to that of the alguacil—who performed varying activities at the call of other authorities.

Aside from their different internal functions, all authorities acted to-gether as political representatives of the community vis-à-vis outside pow-ers. Their collective presence was symbolically important in ritualized po-litical events such as the delivery of tribute, the reception of a visiting dignitary, or the demarcation of community land boundaries. Like ca-ciques, these authorities bore staffs of authority entrusted to them during the annual possession ceremonies. The alcaldes, upon their election, were also granted certified state titles attesting to their status as officials of the republic. The alcalde, regidor, and alguacil all served one-year terms, as did the other important local authority, the hilacata.

The hilacata was ostensibly the lowest-ranking authority since he lacked the town jurisdiction of other figures. Representing his own local ayllu alone, he held no influence over members of other ayllus within the same moiety. This formal subordination is evident in the ranked lists of author-ities present during public gatherings—hilacatas are always mentioned last, after regidores and alguaciles. Their crucial role in the tributary re-gime, however, and the primacy of the local ayllu as vital cell for commu-nity organization as a whole are what account for the hilacata's special im-portance in our period. As we will see, the transformations of local power relations in the latter eighteenth century bestowed new and greater responsibilities on hilacatas, the enduring, irreplaceable representatives of the community's base.

Though not officially certified as part of the local town government, like the cacique and the other authorities introduced by Toledo, the hilacata's role as tribute collector at the ground level was clearly recognized and it made him indispensable to the colonial state. As with his tributary function, the hilacata generally served as the link between the local ayllu, on the one hand, and the cacique, town center, and community at large, on the other.

Let us take another concrete example of this, essentially a variation on the same tributary role. According to local custom, hilacatas were responsible for collecting from their ayllus all the food and gifts for hosting the corregidor and his entourage during visits to the town of Calacoto (Pacajes).[68] Whether attending to the corregidor or running errands for caciques, we have many examples of hilacatas performing services for authorities in town. But the documentation also shows that what was undoubtedly customary service gave way over time to increasingly arbitrary abuse and unjust manipulation of hilacatas, as well as other community authorities. This naturally provoked resentment and intensified the political significance of these authorities.

The hilacata also provided symbolic representation of the ayllu on ritual occasions and practical political leadership under more spontaneous circumstances, especially when pressured to do so by superior authorities or by the majority of ayllu members. Such leadership could involve spurring peasants into battle to defend land boundaries, or heading a legal suit to protest abuses against the community. This political role, rather limited in the first half of the century, grew to new dimensions in an age of social turmoil, peasant mobilization, and community transformation.

One other point may be made here in this discussion of authority functions: there is no evidence that hilacatas controlled the principal administrative affairs of the local ayllu. Instead, as we noted in the previous chapters, it seems that caciques were in charge of coordinating land distribution to peasant families and agricultural production on community plots, designation of mita service turns in town, festival sponsorship, and so on. Here again there were significant shifts by the end of the century, with the hilacata's function broadening well beyond the tributary sphere.[69]

Since the election of alcaldes and other town government officials was a formal concern of the colonial state, there is some documentation from which to reconstruct the appointment of these authorities. The selection of segundas and hilacatas, on the other hand, fell outside the purview of the state and hence there is little evidence to draw upon. Nevertheless, we may take one example from Laja (Omasuyos) in 1802. On the Sunday before the religious festival to honor Santiago in late July, the cacique Luis Eustaquio Balboa Fernández Chui called an assembly *(junta)* of the leading community members *(los de primer viso del gremio de indios)* in order to "name and elect" the segunda persona and hilacatas as well as the captain of the mita and that year's Potosí laborers *(cédulas)*. The packed assembly was held after mass in the cacique's own house and yard. Many seats were arrayed for the occasion and the cacique's staff of authority was prominently set upon the ceremonial table. Despite the objections of colonial officials who opposed him, the cacique insisted that these appointments were within his jurisdiction. A week or so later he held a similar assembly in Pucarani.[70]

This case allows for a few initial and general observations. First, segundas and hilacatas were designated along with other community servants outside the formal political structure. In contrast, the alcaldes and town government officials were elected in a separate political ceremony at a different time of year. Second, there was no outside intervention by the colonial state, as in the town government elections. In contrast to the election of alcaldes, the cacique presided over the ceremonies. Finally, the general assembly indicates the communal dimension to the designation of authorities. We saw in the previous section how the cacicazgo possession ceremony was attended by the community as a whole, but that community participation was reduced to a formality. Beneath the cacicazgo level, in the determination of community authorities, there was a great deal of base-level influence and a clear parameter for cacique power in traditional ayllu dynamics.

Where the cacique seems to have enjoyed the greatest autonomy was in naming his segunda persona. Over a decade earlier, Luis Eustaquio Balboa's own father, also cacique in Laja and Pucarani, affirmed "the ancient custom according to which I and my forefathers have collected tribute and named segundas to our satisfaction."[71] The basis for the selection of hilacatas is obscure in the documentation, yet the evidence regarding the functioning of the civil cargo system (see below) shows no significant divergences from present-day arrangements. We can therefore speculate that, like today, candidates were proposed by each local ayllu depending upon a set of economic and generational conditions at the household level. A male community member—accompanied by his female partner—would have taken up the post when it was his "turn" to serve and he was ready to move up a rung in the ladder of cargos. The cacique, as the maximum political authority and overall coordinator of ayllu rotation, may have reserved the right to veto or overrule ayllu proposals, but in most cases would have approved them.

Turning to the designation of town government officials—alcaldes, regidores, and alguaciles—the issue becomes somewhat more complex, and also controversial insofar as it touches even more directly upon the debate over Spanish and Andean institutional forms and the nature of community "democracy." If, as Roger Rasnake has indicated, autonomous cabildo officers elected by the populace were initially conceived of by Toledo as a counterweight to the traditional authority of caciques, it might be assumed that municipal authorities and caciques were at odds with one another politically.[72] Confusion also stems from the assumption that local elections of Spanish origin are the most obvious sign of democracy in community political participation and representation. What does the eighteenth-century evidence suggest?

First of all, the electoral system was a far cry from any peninsular Spanish model. Even in official correspondence or pronouncements, when subdelegates referred to the election of alcaldes, they virtually never mentioned the term "cabildo." The voting assemblies were called juntas (gatherings) and there is no evidence of a permanent cabildo site (such as a *casa de cabildo*) existing in Indian towns in La Paz.[73] The lack of a cabildo standard is also evident from the local variety in electoral practices. In his ordinance of 1783, attempting to reinstate and regulate local political practices in the wake of the insurrection, the Pacajes subdelegate spoke of the election of "alcaldes *and other customary officers*" (emphasis mine), revealing the lack of any legal norm for regidores, alguaciles, and other town representatives. The significance of local custom and the limits of colonial regulation in electoral procedure can also be inferred from, among other examples, the Paria subdelegate's notice that *vocales* (town council voters) had to explain to him about "ancient custom."[74]

The voting was held in town and following mass on the first day of January each year. The assemblies seem to have taken place commonly in the priest's residence or the plaza, and prominent community members were seated according to their rank. The officials elected were probably chosen in advance—we have no evidence of disputes or violence around voting time and one formulaic phrase that appears in the official transcripts proclaims the "unanimity and consent" of the elections.[75]

One of the colonial state's concerns in these elections was their supervision by a Spanish agent or delegate of the state. Naturally the corregidor or subdelegate could not be present for elections held around the province on one and the same day. Nor were there "Spaniards" in all the towns who could be commissioned with this task. Functionaries within the regional colonial bureaucracy discussed this problem explicitly at the time the intendancy system was put in place. Previously, we may assume, vigilance was not too strict, and priests or caciques were on hand to provide the names of the new authorities and informal accounts of the proceedings for the corregidor's record keepers.

In short, colonial state intervention or monitoring was always present in the designation of town government authorities, as in the case of cacique appointments. The Pacajes subdelegate was adamant that elected officials "shall not take possession of their post nor wield their emblem [the staff] until my tribunal is informed and I confirm them in His Majesty's name, issuing the order and commission to take their vow of loyalty and hand over to them the staff of justice. By any other procedure, the elections are null and void."[76] The corregidor's confirmation, the vow of loyalty, and the formal presentation of written certification and the staff of authority all linked the alcalde symbolically and from the start to the high power of the colonial state.

The question of who actually voted remains a bit blurry. This is not only because references to elections are scant, but because they do not always distinguish between those who voted and those who might have been merely present during the assembly or perhaps officiating. The occasional mention of "town council members" (vocales or *capitulares*) as voters is too vague to clarify matters. Allowing for local variation, it seems most likely that alcaldes, regidores, and principales (see below) were standard voters. If principales are understood to be former town officials, their participation fits with colonial law specifying past authorities as eligible voters. This legal clause would at the same time be contradicted, however, if outgoing authorities also voted, as the evidence suggests they did.[77] The documentation also points to the participation of priests and caciques in the assemblies. We should assume that priests had a symbolic and supervisory rather than direct electoral role. The role of caciques, however, is somewhat more ambiguous and, given its importance for our purposes, we will return to it for closer scrutiny.

It is important to note another communal dimension to the electoral process, one which has passed largely unnoticed in the historiography. I have already remarked on the key intervention of the colonial state and Iberian institutions, but this does not imply that such intervention was ultimately incompatible with or displaced traditional ayllu dynamics. The existing evidence shows that town government officials were designated on a rotating basis, consistent with the local-level cargo system and coordinated along ayllu lines. In this respect, alcaldes were much closer to hilacatas, as community authorities performing service turns, than we might suspect if we were to hold to a strictly dualistic institutional view of Andean and Spanish political power.[78]

The evidence of alcalde designation according to service turns is incontrovertible. In Ulloma (Pacajes), for example, community members objected to the pretensions of one Indian who sought to obtain the post of alcalde mayor for life: "It would be against the interests of other Indians who, for their merits, are rightful creditors to the position and should be named according to their turn."[79] It is safe to assume as well that alcaldes were chosen according to their ayllus or moieties of origin. As in the case of Guaqui (Pacajes), where the *alcalde de primer voto* was from Anansaya and the *alcalde de segundo voto* was from Urinsaya, it is not suprising to find both moieties represented by town alcaldes or one alcalde referred to as the "alcalde of Aransaya."[80] However dimly documented in its details, this logic of rotation and representation fits with our understanding of ayllu dynamics more generally, most notably with traditional mita principles for service turns, and is backed up by contemporary ethnography.[81]

The assumption that elections of subordinate authorities were settled in advance rests on our awareness of this internal arrangement combining individual and household conditions along with the dynamics of community organization, merging the unfolding sequences of the cargo system within the enduring patterns of ayllu structure. Yet one more element must be added to our analysis, in order to answer the question of how this collective arrangement was managed in practice. And here it is necessary to return once again to the role of the cacique.

As noted, the evidence points to cacique participation in town government elections, although it is difficult to determine whether the cacique actually voted, officiated, or simply sat in as distinguished observer. Colonial functionaries recorded his presence and sometimes even summoned him explicitly when calling an electoral assembly. The curiosity here is that legal statutes from the time of Toledo prohibited cacique participation in elections. One community leader from Laja (Omasuyos) in 1753 felt compelled to request that "caciques not attend the elections, as the ordinances stipulate, and that town regidores have full liberty to elect the alcaldes of their choice. . . . May the said cacique be excluded and without active or passive vote in the elections, in conformity with the law and justice." The audiencia's attorney for Indians *(fiscal protector general)* responded to this "lack of liberty suffered by voters [capitulares]" by recommending a ban on the cacique's intervention or attendance during elections.[82]

I can conceive of two possible explanations for the discrepancy between legal prohibition and cacique intervention in practice. The first and simplest is that local practice in the eighteenth century rarely matched legal regulations that had been devised much earlier and never fully enforced, and that pragmatic colonial officials acted in keeping with local reality. The other possibility is that there were points of contradiction within colonial legislation and administration. If Toledo's ordinances for the Peruvian viceroyalty did indeed ban cacique meddling in cabildo affairs, no such restrictions existed for town "governors" whose position could overlap with that of a cacique and who in fact headed cabildo proceedings in New Spain. It may have been that colonial authorities in Charcas, bowing to local custom and the caciques' unquestionable control, permitted their participation with the justification that caciques were formally recognized as governors.[83]

Whatever the explanation, it is clear enough that cacique presence was customary in town government elections and that cacique influence was important in the broader process of designating authorities. This influence surely also led to occasional abuse, as the Laja community member claimed. In another case from 1733 in Calacoto (Pacajes), the cacique saw that two alcaldes and two alguaciles to his liking were appointed from each moiety. He picked young men who would be "bosses" over others and "servants" to him. The cacique also played a role in coordinating the rotation of representatives—alcaldes, regidores, and alguaciles as much as hilacatas—from the different ayllus. The priest in Caquingora (Pacajes) reported, "The alcaldes are named not as the ordinances decree, but by the cacique who gives the staff to any Indian whose turn it is to serve, be he a simpleton or a drunkard, a troublemaker or a rebel."[84]

To conclude this overview of the designation of authorities prior to the political transformations of the late eighteenth century, we should note that the cacique was a key figure not only in the naming of segundas and hilacatas, but even in the case of town government officials who were legally supposed to be elected by the community without cacique interference. In reality, a three-way negotiation of authority appointments took place between the state, the cacique, and the community. It is important to consider what this arrangement tells us about local-level "democracy." In fact, formal electoral procedures introduced by Toledo following the Iberian cabildo model counted for far less than might be assumed at first glance. The elections were relatively predictable colonial political rituals, marked by an absence of conflict. Long-standing community political principles provided the basis for negotiating consensus and foreordained the elections of alcaldes, regidores, and alguaciles, as they did the appointment of hilacatas. Hence, for the real democratic content in the exercise of community authority, we must look elsewhere—to begin with, to those traditional principles of ayllu representation and participation by the ordinary community member, "be he a simpleton or a drunkard, a troublemaker or a rebel."

In the period prior to the onset of sharper political clashes within the communities, caciques exercised quite effective control over lower-ranking authorities. They could intervene, sometimes arbitrarily, in the appointment of town officials such as alcaldes. By the same token, a cacique, perhaps acting from a personal grudge or taking sides in a feud among families, might on occasion use his weight to control the designation of an hilacata who would not normally have been proposed by the local ayllu.

Besides such appointments, cacique control would have been evident in the service functions of authorities. Like mita laborers in town or in Potosí, town and ayllu authorities took their posts by turns and according to the logic of ayllu representation. The primary difference between mitayos and authorities was the prestige enjoyed by the political officers and bearers of the staff of authority. But they too served, and most immediately they were subordinate to and served their cacique. Because of their prestige, cacique control would not have been heavy-handed for the most part; after all, caciques had regular household and field servants already supplied for them by the ayllus. But caciques commanded obedience—whether formally, as in the hilacata's tributary subordination, or informally, as is evident from the alcalde's availability for errands. The formal judicial and political superior for alcaldes, regidores, and alguaciles was the corregidor who lived far off in the provincial capital. In his absence, and given the local supremacy of the cacique, the latter's presence loomed large from day to day in the towns.

Evidence of such informal control by caciques over authorities becomes especially clear after midcentury as conflicts between caciques and communities multiplied. When this occurred, such service was no longer taken for granted and cacique abuse of authorities—expected to be "bosses and servants"—became a frequent item on the list of peasant grievances. As local life became increasingly politicized, the significance of authorities within the community political formation—both their own power and control over them—was redefined.[85]

Unfixed Sites of Authority: Nobles, Principales, and the Cargo System

To round out this discussion of community political hierarchy and power relations, a few final issues that are especially peculiar or unfamiliar to us in the historiography need to be addressed. These are the paradoxes of provincial Indian nobility, the ever-present yet shadowy figure of the principales, and the open question of a civil-religious cargo system in the colonial period. These considerations will set up and anticipate an understanding of the community political transformation that took place in the eighteenth century.

Provincial Nobles in Decline

The schooled, urbane Indian elite who led the Inka cultural and political revival were concentrated in the Viceroyalty of Lima, including the traditional Inka district of Cuzco. In Charcas, there were far fewer numbers of nobles who, like José Fernández Guarachi of Jesús de Machaca, could claim some line of Inka descent and gain access to the upper echelons of Peruvian indigenous nobility. Most Indian nobles in eighteenth-century La Paz, and certainly those who no longer controlled cacicazgos, were less wealthy, less cultured (in colonial terms), and many justified their names not with highly prestigious Inka genealogies but as the descendants of any ancient cacique lineage.

In the towns, the noncacique nobles who concern us here comprised a decadent aristocracy, not in the usual moral sense but in terms of sheer numbers, wealth, and pretensions. The town with the highest population of nobles was Copacabana, the preconquest ceremonial site where numerous Inka families had resettled. But their demographic decline over two centuries of colonial rule was evident in the 1757 census, which registered only nine Inka males exempt from tribute because of their nobility. Their numbers were so few because many had already faded back into the peasantry, like the Yanaiques of Guarina, or married into the local town-resident *(vecino)* population as mestizos, like some of the Calaumanas.[86]

Some nobles solicited a formal certification from the state that due to their notorious poverty (as *pobres de solemnidad*) they should be freed from their financial obligations. Their pathetic condition is evoked by the case of Juan Esteban Catacora, who was the illegitimate son of Juan Basilio Catacora, the wealthy, distinguished, Cuzco-schooled cacique patriarch of Acora (Chucuito). In the 1760s, after the cacique's death, Juan Esteban and his brother Agustín sought to seize their inheritance, including Agustín's succession in the cacicazgo, from the clutches of their stepmother, the formidable *cacica* (female cacique) Polonia Fernández Hidalgo. In his legal statements, Juan Esteban presented a profile of a middle-aged man who was bankrupt, persecuted by his stepmother, and suffering from indisposition and swollen feet.[87]

There were evidently few economic alternatives for nobles who had lost the perquisites of land and labor that came with cacicazgo possession yet who scorned work in the fields. The most likely refuge was a town post, though not many of these were available. Some nobles could ply their trade as artisans in the provincial capital or occupy long-term, salaried positions in the local church.[88] Through informal apprenticeships, these posts could even be passed on from father to son and thereby perpetuate modest family rank. In a few places where their stock was not exhausted and their families retained prominence, nobles held onto vestigial control of authority posts in town, usually thanks to the favor of or kinship with the ruling cacique.[89] As we saw at the start of this chapter, this was the case of other members of the Calaumana cacique family in Guarina, while Francisco, the unsuccessful rival of Matías Calaumana, retained the largely symbolic honorary title of alcalde mayor for the province of Omasuyos.

The Tarqui lineage of Jesús de Machaca (Pacajes) provides an example of the slow downfall of a once prominent noble family, its slipping grasp of local political authority and near disenfranchisement by the late days of the colonial era. With documents dating back to 1604, Toribio and Jacinto Roque Tarqui could trace their ancestry back to the earliest generations of nobles in Machaca. Their forefathers had served successively in the post of segunda persona for the ayllus of Yawriri, Titicana, and Challaya. Francisco Alejo Tarqui, perhaps due to his rank as segunda, was even asked to assume the cacicazgo for an interim term in 1723. Through the mid-eighteenth century, the Tarquis also held the post of town scribe, a lifelong position for nobles who were fluent in Spanish and skilled in reading and writing. But Toribio and Jacinto could point to nothing notable about their father and grandfather, and by the first decade of the nineteenth century, as they sought in court to establish their lineage, they themselves apparently no longer occupied actual authority or scribe posts. Their main aim was to gain recognition from authorities and community members for the honors and exemptions that were conceded to noble ancestors since the early administrative survey *(visita)* of Viceroy Toledo.[90]

Given their modest circumstances, the status consciousness of local nobles like the Tarquis was especially keen. Above all, they were concerned with defending their legal privileges. Colonial law stipulated that caciques and their first-born sons as well as other subjects who could demonstrate genealogical descent from native lords, such as the Inka dynasty, enjoyed special exemptions. In practice this meant that nobles were released from labor services and sometimes from tribute.[91] Nobles like the Tarquis therefore had a strong material incentive to cultivate the sensitive historical consciousness and attention to colonial records that characterized caciques.

Nobles were also extremely concerned to uphold their distinction from other "commoners," meaning ordinary peasants without the status conferred by birth and bloodline. This concern is most evident in numerous confrontations between proud nobles and caciques who sought to impose their authority in the towns. Such battles over honor and power typically revolved around labor services, a mode of obedience and tribute seen by nobles as humiliating. José Araja complained in Laja (Omasuyos) that his cacique had subjected him to "low and mechanical" services—such as *pongo* (household servant) and mule herder—that were unfit for a person of his status. Felipe Inka Cari of Guancané (Paucarcolla) objected to being assigned the "low and humble services that plebeians must perform."[92] In the words of one sardonic lawyer at the Real Audiencia in La Plata, in these and other disputes it was the penchant of proud but impoverished provincial nobles "to blazon in quixotic tone" their family status, honor, and merits.[93]

The Enigma of the Principales

The eighteenth-century documentation of life in the rural provinces contains a common formulaic list of local political authorities: "the caciques, segundas, alcaldes, hilacatas, authorities *(mandones)*, principales, and the rest of the community of Indians." From similar passing allusions to the principales, we can quickly deduce that they comprised a leading stratum in the communities, yet their identity has remained vague to us. The vagueness is attributable, I believe, to overlapping categories of authority and status, which were undergoing important change until the end of the colonial period and which are not easily disentangled.

The colonial state recognized those nobles of cacique lineages whom we have just considered as privileged principales, whether or not they held a political office. Yet non-noble principales, usually acting authorities, were also recognized by the state and exempted from "ordinary and demeaning" labor services as were the nobles. Occasional showdowns pitted caciques against non-noble principales who complained, as the nobles did, of caciques failing to respect their honor and privileges. How can we sort out the confusion over the blurry meaning of principal status and exemptions—a confusion that evidently affected eighteenth-century contemporaries as it has twentieth-century historians?

A pair of references will suggest the range of interpretations of this problem. In 1756, witnesses sought to impugn the principal pretensions of Sebastian Nina from Guaycho (Omasuyos) by arguing that, though his wife was an *originaria* (a woman who belonged to the tributary category of originario) and his mother an originaria and principala, his father was a mere *yanacona* (hacienda peon), petty trader, and forastero from Paucarcolla. Nina could not, therefore, be a principal himself, or was at best "half-principal."[94] This hereditary explanation for principal status—one's own condition derives from that of one's parents—is consistent with definitions of noble status, though *principalazgo* and nobility are not assumed to be identical.

A half century later, in 1803, we get another look at the vexed question of principales from a frustrated cacique in Jesús de Machaca, Diego Fernández Guarachi. The district was becoming ungovernable, complained the cacique, because far too many Indians were claiming to be principales in order to avoid his authority and dodge community labor obligations. In the midst of the great drought and famine of those years, many subjects had fled rather than be enlisted in the Potosí mita, and the would-be principales refused to serve.

Guarachi presented the case of young Tomás Carita from Titicana ayllu as a typical example. Carita had obtained written certification from the subdelegate that he was a principal and therefore could not be obliged to travel for the mita. Before he became a cacique and learned their real motives, Guarachi explained that he himself had helped other Indians certify their noble ancestry—and here he was thinking of men like the Tarqui brothers from the same ayllu. He had done so "not so that they would be exempt from the mita of Potosí, but rather so that the magistrate, seeing the many services of their forefathers, would release them from low services such as *pongueaje* and others in town." But, he continued, these privileges were originally intended only for first-born sons, as the ancient noble titles granted by the viceroys showed, while now entire families were claiming them.

Guarachi also explained the more conventional notion of principal in Jesús de Machaca: "Among Indians in this area, the term or title is used for men who have completed their three labor turns [*tandas*] in Potosí and have been hilacatas, alcaldes . . . [deteriorated] . . . captains of the mita, and festival standard-bearer *[alférez de voto]*." Since Tomás Carita was not yet twenty-four years old and had not completed the tandas—"that are like steps for rising to the privilege of principal"—how could he possibly govern over others and enjoy the honors of principales?

Guarachi urged the subdelegate to clarify on what basis certification of principal status was to be conceded, and suggested that if granted it should only go to first-born sons of the family. Furthermore, he concluded, even if some Indians were exempted from town services, they should still comply with the Potosí mita; in this way they would be more likely to earn the status they sought.[95]

I propose a hypothesis to account for the varying criteria and definitions of the principalazgo. In early colonial Spanish America, chroniclers and bureaucrats employed the term "principal" rather broadly to refer to the noble kin or heirs of native lords and to lower-ranking leaders of indigenous polities.[96] While further research on the sixteenth and seventeenth centuries would be required to confirm this, the initial correspondence between nobility and authority, which was implicit in the notion of principal, gradually eroded with the decline of the provincial nobility. As commoners began to fill colonial political posts, they inherited the prestige and some of the perquisites of formerly noble office. The process was well advanced by the latter half of the eighteenth century, though by no means at an end. The significance of the term "principal" underwent corresponding change and now contained a new semantic range: principales who were recognized as hereditary nobles but were not necessarily authorities; principales who currently exercised political authority;[97] and principales who had attained elevated rank and seniority in the community after a lifetime of meritorious services and office-holding.

This process gave rise to variously ironic, contradictory, confusing, or frustrating situations for someone like Diego Fernández Guarachi. Younger men claiming nobility and commoners during the limited time of their office could approximate the status and enjoy the privileges of nobles and elders. Exemptions could become blurred: some nobles paid tribute while others did not; authorities paid no tribute and performed no services for the limited time of their tenure;[98] principales who had completed all their turns *(tandas)* were no longer subject to the mita and town services but continued to pay tribute. While the state was aware of principal elders who had fulfilled community obligations, it did nothing to certify formally or regulate their status (as it did with nobles and some acting political authorities).

The previously noted case of Sebastian Nina in Guaycho—whose full status was denied because his father was not an originario and principal—

raises another question: to what extent did principal and originario status coincide? The Omasuyos subdelegate in 1792 reported that, in relation to forasteros, yanaconas, and Urus, originarios considered themselves of "superior condition." Among other things, they were preferred over forasteros for public office and "the honorable post of captain of the mita." Forasteros, he added, lacked the "nobility" of originarios. The historical evidence supports the impression that originarios enjoyed notable status advantage over forasteros, and that originarios were normally the ones expected to fill authority posts, meet other community obligations, and eventually attain the rank of principal.[99]

There was, then, an unresolved tension over principal status defined in terms of heredity (with its state-sanctioned privileges) or community cargo service. Nevertheless, with the ongoing struggles of communities in the eighteenth century, principal elders—those who had attained principal status after fulfilling their community obligations—occupied an increasingly important place in the community political formation. Internally, they provided a stable complement to those rotating authorities whose experience or capacity may have been limited. As a collective body of elders, they would join authorities in directing community assemblies and decision making[100] and could afford political vision and leadership in times of community crisis. Their "shadowy" character—not regulated by the state, not permanently fixed by the strictures of town government, and not so directly subject to caciques as were official Indian authorities—gave the community a political advantage in conflicts with colonial authorities and local elites.[101]

A Colonial Cargo System?

When Diego Fernández Guarachi spoke of the various services and posts of the Potosí mitayo, hilacata, alcalde, mita captain, and alférez as "steps" *(escalas)* on the way to the prestigious rank of principal, he would seem to be describing a civil-religious cargo system such as we are familiar with in Mexico. Such a finding would be suprising since we have already pointed to the relatively limited formal development of cofradía and cabildo institutions in La Paz, while in Mexico, where they were more consolidated, a unified civil-religious hierarchy appears not to have emerged until the nineteenth century. With a virtual void in the Andean historiography, what does the La Paz evidence point to about a peasant cargo system?[102]

A handful of documents do confirm that community members rose up a ladder consisting of service turns (tandas) and honorific posts until they reached the elevated status of principales. At the "low" end of the hierarchy were labor services in town, say for the cacique or priest. Originarios were also expected—and obliged by the state—to perform three turns as mita laborer in Potosí. Town government posts such as alguacil and regidor would have ranked a bit higher but still were seen as somewhat marginal. They were rarely cited when community members recounted their cargo careers in the documents. Hilacata, alcalde, and segunda posts were definitely considered honorific, as was that of the mita captain, though he did not serve in a political capacity. Pascual Quispe of Achacachi (Omasuyos) declared that "I have fulfilled the Potosí mita services and the other obligations of Indian principales, such as segunda, alcalde, hilacata and town services."[103]

We can assume there was some variation in the patterns from one location to another, but one of the features that stands out is the apparent flexibility of the ladder. While some principales skipped certain posts, they might have served more than once as hilacata or alcalde, or for a longer period as segunda. Rasnake encounters the same flexibility in present-day Yura and insists on its contrast to the more fixed, systematic patterns in Mesoamerica.[104]

The limited information available to us for La Paz does not allow us to assume in general that religious cargos were integrated with civil ones, or that they contributed to determining principal status. We noted that Diego Fernández Guarachi did include a religious cargo, the alférez de voto, in his account of the cargo ladder in Jesús de Machaca, and he included this post at the top of his list of the steps leading to principal status. But no other evidence suggests such integration. Pascual Quispe of Achacachi, for example, did not mention it in his list of the obligations incumbent upon principales. Neither did Diego Guaycho of Santiago de Guata (Omasuyos): "I have fulfilled all the tandas, such as being alcalde pedáneo, segunda two times, captain of the Potosí mita once, and storekeeper *(pulpero)* for five years."[105]

We do know that festivals were sponsored individually, rather than by permanent cofradía resources or collective donations from the community, and that sponsorship—which could cost up to the exorbitant amount of two hundred pesos—brought great prestige.[106] In his will, Andrés Pacheco Chuquitancara, a principal of Callapa (Pacajes), proudly recorded that not only had he served as Potosí mitayo and hilacata once and mita captain three times, but he had sponsored Corpus Christi twice, the festival of Our Lady twice, and had offered other large contributions to the church of Callapa. Yet we lack the evidence to say that his principal standing derived from his religious patronage.[107]

Another example indicates that prestigious religious cargos did not guarantee the status of principal. Francisco Mamani, seventy-year-old originario of Zepita (Chucuito), affirmed that he had met all his personal service obligations in town, made all his tribute payments, labored in Potosí three times, acted as alférez once in the festival of Saint Peter and again in the festival of Our Lady of the Purification (spending one hundred pesos in each, plus miscellaneous expenses), and been elected four times as mayordomo of a festival dance troupe (spending fifty pesos). Nevertheless, when Mamani maintained that he had met all his obligations, he was speaking only as an originario. In his suit, he did not claim to be and was not recognized as a principal, presumably since he had not served in higher, honorific political posts.[108]

In the absence of earlier colonial and subsequent studies, we can only speculate as to the overall historical development of the cargo system. The civil hierarchy would have been established sometime after Toledo's introduction of cabildo institutional forms, though it remained to some extent in the hands of nobles. As suggested above, the slow decline of the nobility would have increasingly opened up the hierarchy of political posts to commoners and this in turn would have led, at least by the earlier eighteenth century, to the new cargo-based definition of principalazgo.[109] As permanently functioning cofradías with independent resources did not exist, in contrast to Lower Peru, individual sponsorship would have been the norm for festival organization and this condition should have facilitated the unification of civil and religious cargos. This integration could have been underway by the late-colonial period, as the cacique's testimony from Jesús de Machaca suggests; however, our limited evidence suggests a more unified system may not have coalesced in the region as a whole until the Republican era.[110]

Eighteenth-century La Paz therefore presents a contrast to existing images of Mexico, where an elaborate, integrated, and formal civil-religious system eventually developed, or of colonial Lower Peru, where the cofradía institution apparently assumed greater importance in restructuring Andean communities.[111] In La Paz, the cargo arrangement was flexible, locally varied, and probably only partially integrated. Both civil posts leading to principal status and religious festival organization were also structured in terms of enduring local ayllu dynamics.

The long-term evolution of the colonial cargo system reflected important processes at work within the Andean community. This chapter has suggested that it developed in conjunction with the slow decline of Indian nobility and that this process involved a new definition of principal identity. We have also seen that the community authorities who occupied cargo posts were subject to the maximal authority of their cacique. In combination, ayllu structuring of the cargo system, its loose and transitional nature, and the fact of cacique control indicate that this was not a discretely defined or autonomous institution and that it did not pose an intrinsic challenge to cacique authority as the apical site of power within the community political formation.

Classic cacique authority and noble rank in Aymara communities derived from convergent Andean and Spanish sources and they were defined in ascribed hereditary and patriarchal terms. While the apex of the political formation remained deeply marked by ascriptive authority well into the eighteenth century, a partial erosion of ascribed rank followed along with the slow decline of Indian nobility. This process meant a gradual shift towards broader community participation in the exercise of authority. In the following chapters, we will consider the further unfolding of this process with a decisive new development that took place in the eighteenth century.

The real motive behind Diego Fernández Guarachi's report in 1803 was his own loss of political control in Machaca. Young community members who obtained principal titles succeeded in evading community and Potosí mita services in a moment of agrarian crisis. But more importantly for Fernández Guarachi, they gained greater autonomy from the cacique and set an example of disobedience that he found profoundly disturbing: "These are haughty people who disobey their caciques' orders and are seducers responsible for the disasters and disorder that occur so frequently. . . . They lack the proper subordination of Indians and make a mockery of my command. They also set a bad example that causes others not to fulfill their duties when it is their turn to do so. Witnessing their public arrogance and rebelliousness towards me, others act just the same . . . and give signs of rising up with unfortunate consequences. . . . Because of them, this town is entirely insolent."[112]

While cacique-community relations had never been exempt from conflict and mutual testing of forces, the eighteenth century saw an unprecedented proliferation of conflict throughout the region. The major transformation of the community polity that occurred in our period was bound up with this "insolent" challenge from below and the ultimate crisis of cacique power.

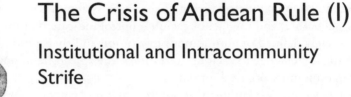

3 The Crisis of Andean Rule (I)

Institutional and Intracommunity Strife

In 1750, a handful of men led by Isidro Quispe came forth in the name of all the mitayos from Guarina to object to a variety of abuses perpetrated by their cacique, Matías Calaumana. The foremost complaint of the Indian witnesses who subsequently testified against him was that Calaumana did not supply sufficient provisions for the mita caravan that annually traveled to Potosí. Instead of giving two or three *cargas*[1] of foodstuffs to each traveler, he gave only one carga of *chuño* (dehydrated potato) and loaned one llama for transport. While there were two rich haciendas in the valleys of Larecaja to supply mitayos from Guarina, the cacique had usurped them and sold their maize harvests for private gain. He also forced the mitayos to pay tribute to the parish priest in Potosí, though that priest's stipend was supposed to be drawn from the aggregate tribute money of their town of origin. Some mitayos even preferred to remain in Potosí rather than return to their community and face the severity of the cacique and his burdensome exactions. He had taken over the lands of peasants within the community and obliged them to do onerous and uncompensated services. Those who worked for the cacique in his town store were required to perform added tasks. Mateo Choqueguanca, for instance, had to refinish the walls of the cacique's house and his wife had to serve as a weaver. The cacique was called an "intruder" in his post and the plaintiffs added that they were denied justice because of Calaumana's close ties to corregidores and the scribes whom they needed to draft their legal statements.

Matías Calaumana, in turn, declared the charges against him to be false. The valley estates had been under litigation for many years with local figures in Larecaja, and Guarina's control over the lands, despite the best efforts and expenses of the cacique, was slipping away. Furthermore, these properties had never been set aside for mitayo provisions, and there were no other communal lands for the purpose. By law, the transport costs of the mita were the obligation of mine owners in Potosí. If the cacique had provided community members with sustenance for their journey, it was a gratuitous display of his affection for them. The mitayos who were away from their home district were still required to pay their tribute in Potosí. He went on to clarify that the lands held by the cacique in the community were *yanapas,* legally assigned to him as to caciques in other towns, because of his governing status. These lands were not abundant and, given the regular frosts, drought, and bad harvests, they failed to meet his family's needs. If peasants did occasionally work in his fields, as was expected of them, they received food, coca, and *chicha* (a beer drink usually made from corn) in return. As for the town store, he had not rented it from the corregidor for the past five years because the earnings were low and it only incited the jealousy of his rivals. In the past, however, he paid two pesos, four reales to the woman chosen by the community to serve as vendor.

The cacique went on to allege that the suit against him was in fact a machination of his enemy, Francisco Calaumana, who had stirred up the town and schemed to take over the cacicazgo. The corregidor initially stepped in to obtain a retraction from Isidro Quispe and to offer a compromise whereby the cacique would henceforth provide two cargas of foodstuffs to mitayos. Shortly thereafter, irritated with the "facility with which Indians, whether willingly or induced, put forth such sinister complaints," the magistrate announced that the charges against the cacique had not been proven.

When the case appeared before the Real Audiencia in La Plata, the protector of Indians was not so willing to reject the testimony of community members, for this was the typical tactic used to conceal the misdeeds of caciques. The court's attorney general also acknowledged the frequent grievances against caciques—due to injuries and the usurpation of Indian lands and goods—and the regular complicity between caciques and corregidores "whose interests are mutually united in profit." The case was indeed a common one for the time, not only because of the nature of the grievances and the rebuttal but because of the dense intrigue clouding the explicit legal issues.[2]

After this short-lived dispute, Matías Calaumana met no other significant challenges to his authority, whether from cacicazgo pretenders, the community base, or meddling colonial officials. This was remarkable since conflicts flared throughout the region and cacique power was put to an extreme test in succeeding decades. One of the critical relationships for caciques was with the provincial corregidor, and Calaumana for the most part settled into a respectful, accommodating relationship with the successive governors of Omasuyos. One local Spanish landlord embroiled in a land conflict with the cacique and community of Guarina even remarked that the corregidor favored his adversaries because their satisfaction guaranteed the success of the corregidor's commercial *(reparto)* ventures.[3]

In the end, however, Matías Calaumana's individual fate curiously matched that of the institution he so eminently represented. Though he was a royalist who survived the civil war of 1781, the political authority of the old, ailing, and resented patriarch was bestowed by colonial officials upon a commoner during the ensuing reconstruction. With his powers ebbing away, and the future holding little promise, the cacique expired only one year after the devastating insurrection against colonial domination.

A Political Approach to the Colonial Cacicazgo

In recent decades, scholars of the colonial Andes have accumulated a rich store of empirical material about caciques and cacicazgos and this topic has become one of the key points in the historiography of the region. However, if we consider the conceptual notions, efforts at generalization, and debate about the cacicazgo, it seems the historiography has still not taken full advantage of this richness. The prevailing image in the literature is that of the cacique as "mediator" between community and colonial state, Andean culture and Western culture, ethnic economy and the market. It is an image conceived of with familiar tropes and a language of "ambivalence." Referring to his "bifrontal role," Sánchez Albornoz comments, "The position occupied by the cacique, or kuraka, within the colonial system was most delicate and thankless."[4] Glave characterizes it as a "core, ambiguous, and at times tragic position as the hinge between two worlds."[5] Other Janus-like conceptions speak of a "double language," a "double game," and a "double edge."[6]

The frequent preoccupation with the "structural ambiguity of the mediatory function"[7] reveals an implicit conceptual tendency that we could loosely term structural functionalist. Obviously, this focus on the function, the integration and reproduction, and the legitimacy of power does not assume a colonial social consensus, nor does it serve as historiographic apology for the colonial regime. On the contrary, the historiography reveals much sensitivity toward social tensions of every sort, and it takes as its conceptual point of departure a profound and constitutive social contradiction. Moreover, this historiographic tendency can claim a special justification due to the pressing need to understand how it was possible to erect an enduring social order out of such apparently contradictory social forces.[8]

Nonetheless, this image does reflect certain analytical limitations in the literature. The language of "ambivalence" and "doubling" sometimes serves as a rhetorical substitute for a more dynamic historical analysis. Fundamental questions remain open for us regarding, for example, the process of deterioration and collapse of the cacicazgo, or the patterns of cacique participation in the indigenous mobilizations at the end of colonial period. Thus, though the prevailing historiographic tendency can be justified— given the question of the colonial order's coherence, above all for the early colonial period—we still lack a full comprehension of change and historical process at a more specific level of analysis. This is no less true for the late colonial period when the mediations of power entered into irremediable crisis and the colonial order followed its accelerating decline.[9]

The historiographic difficulties consist of, first of all, *tracing* the colonial trajectory of the cacicazgo (the problem of periodization and historical specificity)[10] and, secondly, *explaining* the process of change and particularly the "crisis" of the cacicazgo. Let us take a few examples. Early colonial historians already indicate in this period serious threats to the legitimacy of caciques and processes of economic and cultural differentiation that distanced ethnic lords from local indigenous populations.[11] For the late seventeenth century, Glave observes of Bartolomé Tupa Hallicalla, cacique of Asillo (Azángaro), that "his system was collapsing, coming to an end like his life in abandonment."[12] Rasnake has recourse to the same criteria of private economic accumulation and cultural assimilation to explain the secular conflicts and the breakdown of the cacique system in Yura with the 1781 insurrection.[13] Hunefeldt also describes a process of "collapse" in cacique power in the early nineteenth century, with the delegitimation of indigenous elites occurring amidst polarized class relations within the community and a "whitening" of the indigenous elites.[14]

To sum up, the underlying problem is that, for the distinct historical periods, the historiography has often perceived a single phenomenon and sought to explain it in the same terms. The challenge, by contrast, is to elaborate a vision of the long-term evolution of the cacicazgo, of its successive phases throughout the colonial process.[15] How can we distinguish, for example, between the economic and cultural differentiation of caciques in the early seventeenth century and the late eighteenth century? How was this differentiation interpreted by the diverse sectors of rural society during these different moments?

To explain this evolution, the historiography has often associated the crisis of the cacicazgo with a "legitimacy crisis" within the community.[16] Our criteria for analysis of this legitimacy crisis, however, are still lacking in an important sense. Three criteria have often been employed to understand it. First is the lineage criterion: the cacicazgo entered into crisis with the extinction of "ethnic" caciques whose hereditary lineage earned them "rights by bloodline" *(derecho de sangre)*. With the proliferation of "intruder" caciques (whether by designation of the state and its agents or by other means), many of whom were mestizos and not natives of the community, it is assumed that "ethnic" legitimacy eroded.[17] The second criterion, which is even more familiar, also touches on ethnic-cultural identity: caciques lost legitimacy with their progressive cultural assimilation into the colonial elite, manifest for example in their dress, Christian faith, and matrimony with the daughters of Spaniards.[18] The third criterion is class position: taking advantage of the opportunities for accumulation of wealth within the colonial economy, and often exploiting the land and labor of their own community members, caciques were differentiated in class terms, integrating themselves within the regional economic elite and distancing themselves from the community with its traditional ties of reciprocity.[19]

All of these criteria contribute in fundamental ways to our understanding of the legitimacy of colonial Andean caciques. Yet we can emphasize here another neglected criterion that must be considered of utmost importance: namely, political identification. Filling out the political dimension of caciques offers a response to the historiographic limitations mentioned above and a key for a more dynamic and historically specific analysis. Adopting this political frame of reference, this study attempts to clarify two of the open questions for the historiography. It will provide a fuller vision of the definitive crisis and breakdown of the colonial cacicazgo and account for the lack of cacique participation in the anticolonial insurrection of 1781 in La Paz.

In this attempt to *trace* the history of the cacicazgo and to follow its decline, the archives afford an initial and very striking picture of overwhelming conflict in eighteenth-century La Paz. They contain dozens of cases from each province in the region, involving all manner of rivalry and conspiracy, power plays and violence. In certain towns, the cacicazgo battles lasted decades, like stubborn fires that flamed up time and time again to consume the once-great houses and estates of native lords. Such conflict engulfed most of the towns in every province at some point during the 1740s to 1770s, and a wave of attacks on caciques occurred with the conflagration of 1781. Subsequent struggle into the early nineteenth century left the cacicazgos like brittle shells of what they had been a century before, or simply reduced to rubble.

Colonial historians have certainly been aware of this abundance of documented conflict between caciques and communities in the eighteenth century. In fact, Nathan Wachtel points to the end of the seventeenth century as the time when community complaints first began to multiply.[20] While this conjuncture merits closer scrutiny, the evidence for La Paz indicates a major proliferation and intensification of conflict beginning in the 1740s and allows us to speak of fully fledged crisis only in the mid-eighteenth century.

There was also a geographically specific pattern to the process of decline.[21] To take the subregional differences within La Paz, the great patriarchal lineages were most prominent in Pacajes, Omasuyos, and Chucuito, the provinces that dominated the highlands and encircled the waters of Lake Titicaca. In the highland districts of Sicasica province, the "purity" of the dynastic lineages was somewhat more diluted by the mid-eighteenth century, while in the prosperous coca valleys of Yungas, indigenous families with noble pedigrees did maintain their cacicazgo pretensions. The cacicazgos were undoubtedly weakest in the southeastern valleys of Sicasica province and in the Larecaja valleys, for a variety of reasons. First, since the pre-Hispanic period, political organization was relatively more tenuous and vulnerable in these valleys and it derived from highland centers. Second, as outlier agricultural colonies for the highlands, Andean nobility had minimal presence in them. Third, after pre-Hispanic political ties between highlands and valleys were severed and valley production was rearticulated within the regional market, these peripheral areas (in contrast to the coca-growing Yungas closer to La Paz) were economically marginalized. Consequently, valley cacicazgos were not quite so attractive, compared to highland ones, as a base for accumulation.

In these valley areas, the eighteenth-century evidence presents us with fewer, less violent conflicts and a greater number of corregidor appointees and non-Indian caciques than in the core areas of the pre-Hispanic highland polities. While the highland core areas tended to have more powerful, stable cacicazgos, which entered into crisis more abruptly, the impression we get from the periphery is one of more gradual decline that was underway earlier.[22]

Judging from the evidence for La Paz, the cacicazgo crisis may be conceived of in terms of different forms of conflict, which for analytical purposes will be treated in three parts. First, I will consider the conflicts that did not immediately engage or revolve around the base of the community.

These included succession disputes and feuds among noble families as well as the conflictive "intrusion" of mestizos, outsiders who married into the hereditary family (*yernos* or sons-in-law), and caciques backed by self-interested colonial authorities. Second, of the increasing number of conflicts between caciques and communities, I will look at those cases not evidently bound up with the struggles against corregidores and the repartimiento de mercancías (reparto), or coerced consumption of commodities.[23] The cases of this sort frequently involved excessive exactions by caciques, misappropriation of community tribute and resources, political malfeasance, neglect, and violence. This chapter focuses on these two "interior" aspects of cacicazgo crisis.

The following chapter takes up the third set of conflicts, namely the reparto struggles and their critical significance for caciques throughout the region. With the reparto, we find mounting pressures upon communities and increasingly direct political intervention by colonial authorities in local government. Without losing sight of the full complexity of the historical process, in my view the decisive element in *explaining* the cacicazgo crisis is the shift in colonial power relations that accompanied the increasing economic extraction achieved by the reparto institution.

Throughout both chapters, the key to the analysis will be political. A broad political context will inform the discussions of particular community histories, and a political subtext—the negotiation of power—will emerge from consideration of local concerns and cultural practices. This will enhance our sense for individual elements in the conflicts—for instance, the succession of female heirs to the cacicazgo, corregidor appointment of cacique "intruders," or cacique abuse of peasant labor services. This analysis will also enable us to fit such phenomena, which were not necessarily new, into the historically specific process of cacicazgo crisis in the eighteenth century. These chapters will show, then, how the story of local cacicazgo conflict was entwined with wider regional political dynamics. As the second of the two chapters draws to a close, our gaze will increasingly extend beyond the crisis of the cacicazgos toward the unraveling of colonial order more broadly and society's overall movement toward the pan-Andean insurgency and civil war of 1780–1781.

Cacicazgo Succession and Intrusion Troubles

Battles over cacicazgo succession were by no means original to the eighteenth century, but they did acquire peculiar features and new significance within the broader political processes of the era. The Anansaya cacicazgo of Chucuito (Chucuito) provides one initial case of long-standing conflict among pretender families and an example of the intricacies and vicissitudes that could mark these dramas. Such succession disputes—in conjunction with different types of cacicazgo intrusion by mestizos, by outsiders who gained access to the cacique post through marriage, and by the clients of colonial state authorities—constitute the first aspect of my explanation for cacicazgo crisis.

The opening chapter in the Chucuito saga went back to 1710, when Simón de Sosa y Centeno appeared at the viceregal court in Lima to request state approval as the heir to the cacicazgo after Domingo Fernández Cutimbo died leaving no children.[24] He was granted interim title and the subsequent official investigation and testimony found that Simón was indeed the grandson of Diego Centeno and Isabel Taximolle and that Diego was the brother of Pedro Cutimbo, who was the son of Carlos Cari Apaza, the cacique governor of the city of Chucuito and the entire province. Don Carlos was himself the son of Apu Cari, captain general of the Inka king Guayna Cápac "in the time of the gentiles." Having established this genealogical record, Simón de Sosa was declared the rightful cacique successor.

Francisco Xavier Puma Inka Charaja, the cacique of Urinsaya who had also been serving on an interim basis in Anansaya, next appeared in the court asserting that Sosa was a mestizo, by law excluded from office, and that he was the true heir. Their dispute was finally resolved in 1720 with Sosa's rights to the cacicazgo being vindicated.

Two years later, it was the turn of Lucas de Meneses Cutimbo to challenge Simón de Sosa. The new pretender declared himself the illegitimate son of Aldonza Cutimbo, grandson of Margarita Cutimbo Vilamolle, and great-grandson of Chucuito cacique Pedro Cutimbo. Lucas agreed that his great-grandfather Pedro was the son of Carlos Cari Apaza, but diverged from Sosa's account when he held that Pedro was married to María Vilamolle and that she—"a very distinguished Indian woman"—was the child of Apu Cari.[25]

Lucas de Meneses Cutimbo broke the news that Sosa had deceived the court and seized the cacicazgo by fraud. The deceased cacique had indeed left a bastard heir, Juan Cutimbo, though he was demented. Since Juan was unfit to serve, the cacicazgo automatically should have passed to the deceased cacique's sister, Aldonza Cutimbo. And since she was a woman, and by law also "incompetent," the rightful heir was none other than her son Lucas, the deceased cacique Domingo's nephew.

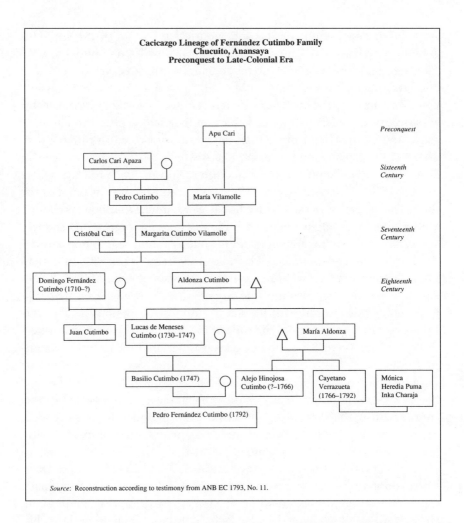

Cacicazgo Lineage of Fernández Cutimbo Family
Chucuito, Anansaya
Preconquest to Late-Colonial Era

Preconquest

Apu Cari

Carlos Cari Apaza ○

Sixteenth Century

Pedro Cutimbo — María Vilamolle

Cristóbal Cari — Margarita Cutimbo Vilamolle

Seventeenth Century

Domingo Fernández Cutimbo (1710–?) ○

Aldonza Cutimbo △

Eighteenth Century

Juan Cutimbo

Lucas de Meneses Cutimbo (1730–1747) ○

△ María Aldonza

Basilio Cutimbo (1747) ○

Alejo Hinojosa Cutimbo (?–1766)

Cayetano Verrazueta (1766–1792)

Mónica Heredia Puma Inka Charaja

Pedro Fernández Cutimbo (1792)

Source: Reconstruction according to testimony from ANB EC 1793, No. 11.

As the court finally acknowledged after receiving witnesses' testimony, Sosa had lied when he held that Diego Centeno was the brother of Pedro Cutimbo, and Sosa had induced other witnesses to fabricate the genealogical record. In fact, Diego Centeno was the Spanish conquistador who had come to the area from southern Charcas (where he had led the challenge to Gonzalo Pizarro's authority), and who was routed by Francisco de Carvajal in the Battle of Guarina in 1547. Furthermore, Centeno was never married to doña Isabel Taximolle, as Sosa maintained, but to the mestiza Luciana Medina.

The witnesses filled out the picture of events. In the seventeenth century after Cristóbal Cari, who had arrived from Canas province near

Cusco, had passed away, Domingo took over in lieu of his mother. Due to his failure to meet tribute payments, the corregidor deposed Domingo and placed in his stead Raphael Inka Charaja, who governed the other moiety of Chucuito. Domingo then died out of office and Simón de Sosa, serving as lieutenant for the provincial alguacil mayor, went to his estate to embargo his property. Sifting through his papers, Sosa came upon the cacicazgo titles and convinced the widow that he should hold them for safekeeping until Domingo's son was of age to replace his father. A few months thereafter, Indians were surprised to find Sosa governing their community with the corregidor's backing.[26]

The intricate dispute between Sosa and Meneses lasted for years. In 1728, the corregidor jailed Sosa for falling far behind in tributary payments and appointed Meneses to take charge of tribute collection and the mita draft. By 1730, the struggle was finally resolved in favor of Lucas de Meneses who was formally declared proprietary cacique by the Real Audiencia.

Don Lucas governed apparently uneventfully until his death in 1747, when he was succeeded by his first-born son, Basilio Cutimbo. Basilio, however, renounced his control over the cacicazgo (he was independently employed as bookkeeper by the provincial treasury in Carangas), transferring it by way of his aunt María Aldonza to her son Alejo Hinojosa Cutimbo. Basilio's sole condition was that he and his family continue to enjoy one-half of the lands, services, and perquisites legally attached to cacicazgo property. The new cacique ruled as governor through 1766 when his debts and arrears in tributary payments forced him to step down, transferring the cacicazgo to his brother, Cayetano Berrazueta, who had served the previous ten years as don Alejo's segunda persona.[27] In the conventional ceremony of possession, the corregidor of Chucuito duly led don Cayetano to the same throne (tiana) upon which his ancestors had sat. And he presided from it over the Anansaya community of Chucuito until the great insurrection ripped through the western lake district in 1781.

Berrazueta spurned the entreaties of Túpac Amaru, the movement's Inka leader, and organized his own Indian force to defend the Chucuito region under Commander Joaquín Antonio de Orellana. He saved the lives of prominent Spanish authorities, sallied into skirmishes against the superior numbers of enemy troops, and was among the last to evacuate when Crown forces finally gave way before the "rebel" tide. While he prided himself on having beheaded the rebel "Viceroy" Gregorio de Limachi, his own wife, Mónica Heredia Puma Inka Charaja, and his children were slaughtered during the war. Forced north due to military circumstances, Berrazueta wound up isolated and penniless in Cuzco where he labored as woodcutter and collier.[28]

Following the war, Berrazueta resumed his role as interim cacique, for he lacked the formal proprietary rights granted by the viceroy. Yet shortly after his return, he began to run into opposition. The three children of Basilio Cutimbo, who had relinquished power at midcentury, began to assert parallel hereditary claims to the cacicazgo. First they complained that Berrazueta failed to provide the cacicazgo benefits their father had secured for them. Then they challenged Berrazueta's right to serve at all as cacique, and Pedro Fernández Cutimbo came forth as the legitimate heir.

Don Cayetano deemed it improper to fight his own nephews, and in 1785 he offered to step down before being overwhelmed by litigation and exasperation. But the disputation and maneuvering was drawn out after his brother, the former cacique Alejo Hinojosa, intervened to block the retirement. Hinojosa insisted that he had obtained formal state approval as legitimate successor and that, therefore, the challenge to Berrazueta was unfounded. Nevertheless, Pedro Fernández Cutimbo subsequently procured a decree from the Real Audiencia in La Plata naming him rightful cacique.

Exhausted and resigned, Cayetano Berrazueta could only muster a pathetic objection that he had been treated unfairly. He did not insist on having hereditary legitimacy, but pointed instead to his twenty-six years of service and sacrifice to the Crown, his impeccable record in meeting tribute payments, and his benevolence toward his Indians "who gave him the epithet of 'Father.'"[29] The new cacique, he maintained, even had the gall to harvest the fields he had laboriously farmed and to remove his house attendant. This showed none of the respect due him for his merits and personal tribulations, his old age, and the ties of kinship between him and the younger Fernández Cutimbo. Describing his condition as one of "the most imponderable misery," Berrazueta requested that two ayllus continue to supply him and his descendants with laborers for their house and fields; he would commit himself to delivering over to the cacique the regular tribute and mita drafts from the ayllus.

The court assigned Berrazueta an attorney for indigent Indians and the case went through one last round in 1792.[30] The attorney reasserted his client's claims to the cacicazgo, citing his services during the insurrection and the royal decree of 1787 that called for all loyal caciques to be maintained in office as reward for their fidelity. But the legal dispute hinged on the rules of Spanish property inheritance (mayorazgo), and particularly the original transfer of the cacicazgo from Basilio Cutimbo to Alejo Hinojosa in the late 1740s. The opposing party argued that Basilio had intended only to substitute an auxiliary cacique in his absence and that he lacked the legal authority to alienate family property in any event. Mayorazgo property could only pass to a collateral line, like that of the Hinojosas, when there were no direct heirs.

Berrazueta's lawyer held that in fact there were no living heirs at the time of the transfer. Don Basilio obviously did not intend the property to go to his children since he had none. And once a mayorazgo passed from one line to another, it did not legally revert to the original line at any future stage.

The court ultimately ruled in favor of Pedro Fernández Cutimbo's hereditary cacicazgo rights and put off any decision on Berrazueta's requested reward for services to the Crown. We can imagine him living out his days in the impoverished circumstances of other provincial figures with noble pretensions, though lonelier and more embittered than most.

The story we have just reviewed in some detail presents many features common to succession conflicts in the eighteenth century. It involved contention over historical lines of descent, legal parameters set by the Spanish mayorazgo code, the ambiguity of interim cacique status, and noble competition over the material benefits of office. The story also gives us a foretaste of the significance that the civil war of 1781 had for cacicazgos—battering many lineages, establishing political loyalty to the Crown as a key criterion of legitimacy, provoking even more direct state intervention in the appointment of caciques. Also evident in the case is the overall erosion of a once eminent noble lineage, its patriarchal power slipping away as the cacicazgo became a piece of property that was increasingly available and, in effect, alienable.

This last point—the property condition of the colonial cacicazgo—is a neglected but especially interesting problem. It is brought forth quite clearly in the previous case because the succession conflict and its resolution in the Anansaya moiety of Chucuito did not involve overriding political intervention from above on the part of corregidores nor from below by community members. Cayetano Berrazueta introduced a variety of criteria to justify his claim to the post—his tributary record, his military services and loyalty to the Crown, and the community's filial love for and loyalty to him—yet, in the end, the determining element was hereditary property right as defined by the Spanish mayorazgo code.

As a specific form of property, the cacicazgo was ordinarily not commoditized, though at the very end of the eighteenth century there were occasional cases of corregidores illegally selling the post for handsome sums.[31]

Rather, it was an entail privately held and inherited within individual families. And herein lay a key political tension. The mayorazgo code existed to regulate the possession and transmission of cacicazgos, and the legal code was internally quite coherent and capable of clarifying the typical points of contention among pretenders, as in the Chucuito case.[32] The real problem, however, involved the significance of such property status for a political institution that, in principle and however tentatively, stood for and acted on behalf of both state and community.

Privatized property, ensuring the legal priority of hereditary right to the post, guaranteed a relative measure of institutional autonomy for caciques since they were not appointed directly by the state nor elected directly by the community. Yet as the political interests of state and community diverged more and more, cacicazgo autonomy came under increasing pressure from above and below. This assault curtailed the space for maneuver enjoyed by caciques as brokers, mediators, and representatives. At the community level, the very conditions that normally promoted autonomy could wind up, in an urgent political conjuncture, working against caciques. If caciques, relying on their legal status and property rights, ignored pressures from below, their integrity as community representatives could erode. Thus the influences of corregidores as well as rising community demands upon caciques brought on increasing degrees of cacicazgo "intrusion" and conflict surrounding the legitimacy of successors. Such conflicts, increasingly common in the polarized period of the eighteenth century, reveal institutional brittleness and inadequacy deriving, in an important way if by no means entirely, from the institutional tension between relations of property and relations of political legitimacy and power.

This tension was itself rooted in the transformations of Andean society wrought by colonialism. If caciques disposed of a margin of relative autonomy, the limits to autonomy were redefined by the colonial state when it introduced the new property form. As could be expected, cacique autonomy relative to the state was more limited than it was relative to the community. The property form juridically subsumed cacicazgos under state auspices and modified precolonial political relations by eliminating forms of indigenous social control over the succession of governors. As noted before, the mayorazgo code restricted the flexibility and competence of indigenous governance by privileging primogeniture as a principle of succession. We should also take note that a council of elders within the precolonial political formation was apparently responsible for determining who, within the leading dynastic families, should be the ruling successor.[33] With the entailment of indigenous rule and its regulation according to the mayo-razgo code, the political formation lost a certain capacity for this tradi-tional negotiation of leadership. As it became less subject to collective eth-nic determinations and more subject to those of the state, it also lost a degree of internal accountability and representativity.

One particularly interesting problem shows how cacicazgo succession practices in the colonial period could fly in the face of Andean principles and how the flouting of community norms and control could lead to a re-sentment of caciques. The eighteenth-century documentation provides ex-amples of a problem of intrusion we can identify as that of the "encroach-ing son-in-law." Colonial mayorazgo law gave sanction to the Andean custom allowing women to accede to the cacicazgo, though this was not initially contemplated by Viceroy Toledo. The provision could only apply if there were no eligible male offspring, and cacicazgo property for women did not carry with it effective governing power. Since women were deemed sexually unfit to hold office and exercise authority *(por sus débiles manos),* only a married woman could inherit the cacicazgo and actual control of it automatically fell to her husband.[34] Here again we can discern the lack of correspondence between property and political legitimacy, this time in a gendered dimension.

The "sons-in-law" in question, then, were those men who married into cacique families and thereby received the patriarch's benefits of resources, power, and prestige. Clearly such situations were symbolically charged within a metaphoric language provided by sexuality, kinship, and descent. These situations lend themselves to wide interpretive speculation, offering deeper insight into local cultural perspectives on cacique legitimation and community identity.

But let us begin by looking at concrete evidence that communities ex-plicitly conceived of such men as sons-in-law. At the same time during the 1750s that the Cachicatari clan in Yunguyo (Chucuito) was embroiled in an internal family squabble over succession, one of their own, Atanasio Cachicatari, had taken over the Anansaya moiety of Guaqui (Pacajes). Guaqui itself was caught up in serious turmoil that would eventually lead to the fission of Urinsaya and the founding of the new town of Taraco. Ca-chicatari justified his rights to the cacicazgo as the husband of Margarita Choqueguaman, the daughter of cacique Baltazar Choqueguaman who had died leaving no male heirs. Yet the community ultimately turned on him and demanded his removal. They declared him an "intruder" respon-sible for their mistreatment, agitation, and their failure to obtain justice. A writ on behalf of the fifty-four tributaries explained: "A cacique named don Francisco Xavier governed us as a son-in-law *(yerno)* many years ago and he ruined the entire town. He lost all our documents, which is why we have none today. The same thing could happen with don Atanasio. Subjecting us to his severe ways and failing to provide for us, it is as if there were no cacique. And most of the time he is off in his own town."[35]

The underlying problem in all cases of intrusion was the lack of community control over successors who took office and felt no obligation to answer to community social and political expectations. Yet the issue of abusive sons-in-law was especially keenly felt.[36] Peasant men who married into a given family as "wife-takers" commonly assumed the condition of outsiders of diminished status.[37] In the cacicazgo encroachment situation, there is also a metaphoric overlapping of family and community, with the encroaching son-in-law comparable to a forastero who attaches himself to the community having been unable to establish a patrimony of his own in his community of origin. As an outsider of lesser status, the forastero takes on a resemblance to the yerno.[38] The encroaching sons-in-law were legitimate hereditary successors according to state law, yet their sexual possession of the cacique's daughter and their arrogation of power and overnight accumulation of wealth combined to violate everyday codes of Andean morality and hierarchy.[39]

Another neuralgic point in succession and intrusion conflicts was cacicazgo control by mestizos or Spaniards. Spanish law explicitly banned mestizos from serving as caciques. Not only would their presence violate the formal separation between Indian and Spanish republics, but they were renowned for wreaking havoc in Indian towns.[40] Nevertheless, since many Indian noble families had intermarried with Spanish families since the sixteenth century, racial mixture did not rule out legal property rights over the cacicazgo. Hereditary descent from a ruling, proprietary lineage guaranteed indigenous noble status and overrode the fact of *mestizaje* in a family.[41]

Nevertheless, the racial factor was repeatedly raised by communities in legal petitions to end the abuse suffered at the hands of intruders who were mestizos or Spaniards. Most commonly these were interim appointees of the corregidor or subdelegate. Atanasio Villacorta was one such unpopular mestizo cacique appointed in Laja and Pucarani. His opponents described him as "a poor vagabond whose origin is unknown." His iniquities were attributed to "the unfortunate character of this interloper and his very nature since mestizos despise Indians. . . . This is surely why the laws of the kingdom strictly prohibit this bastard caste of people from becoming caciques in the towns of Indians."[42]

The mestizo intruders could also be sons-in-law married to a legitimate female heir to the property and hence legally recognized by the Real Audiencia. In the early 1750s in Italaque (Larecaja), Indians of the Pacauris moiety challenged their cacique Julián Ramírez for all manner of abuses. They also sought to disqualify him as racially unfit for governing them. They preferred Indian caciques "and not mestizos who abhor us." The testimony of witnesses confirmed that Ramírez was a mestizo or Spaniard— the term *viracocha* appears in one of the transcripts—and hence of "a different nature."[43]

The cacique's first argument of defense was that he had legitimately acceded to the post as the husband of Isabel Cutipa, the daughter of the previous cacique, now deceased. Following the death of the cacique Pablo Cutipa, the corregidor had first appointed him tribute collector, recognizing his marital status and wealth, and the Real Audiencia had confirmed his title in 1744, although apparently on an interim and not proprietary basis. Despite opposition and competing bids for the post, Ramírez held onto power for twelve years and was unseated only after authorities took the somewhat uncommon step of jailing him for his abuses.[44]

Disgruntled communities were also quick to point out cases of intruders who had entered office impoverished and quickly accumulated wealth as caciques. This could occur with dependent clients appointed by the corregidor or subdelegate or with others, often in league with the retiring cacique, who took office through local intrigues. In one dispute in Zepita (Chucuito), Indians protested against Francisco Sensano: "Before becoming cacique, this mestizo lived in utter indigence. Everyone knows how he used to dress in nothing but a cut of rough yellow cloth and supported himself by busting wild mules. Today, at our expense, he sports silks and brocades, fine cloth from Castille and frill. He spends his money on perpetual drinking and bribes for corregidores."[45]

Criticism of *arriviste* caciques could sound like a defense of traditional caste and patriarchal hierarchy. For example, one principal and son of a former cacique from Curaguara (Pacajes) assailed the new cacique as being a "low Indian whose father is not even known."[46] Yet it is quite clear that communities were concerned about newcomers with outside political backing and few ties binding them morally to the community or with little interest in negotiating moral economy pacts with their subjects.

In this sense, the primary target of community protest was the parasitical extraction visited upon them. And here again an example may show how the kinship idiom regarding sons-in-law is pertinent. During one flare-up in a long-simmering land boundary dispute in Anansaya moiety of Sicasica (Sicasica), hostile peasants from Collana ayllu challenged Asencio Sarsuri of Llanga ayllu. Sarsuri was said to own five hundred llamas and one thousand sheep and to control a large property "like any Spaniard." Because of his wealth, he managed to have his way, encroaching upon the lands of others. One witness said of Sarsuri that "as a son-in-law [yerno] he was called a presumptuous bum *[ysia alzado]* because of all his livestock."[47] The Aymara term *isilla* means lazy or idle, and its use here suggests that the economic accumulation of a yerno like Sarsuri was resented as parasitic. If this reading is correct, Sarsuri's situation helps illuminate the problem involving intrusive caciques.

This treatment of conflicts over cacicazgo succession and intrusion has retained a focus on encroaching sons-in-law not because they were quantitatively so abundant but because the problem was especially sensitive and revealing. Not only does the problem expose the typical elements of intrusion and their articulation but it also does so at the same time that it exposes the tension between cacicazgo legitimacy and property that was introduced by the colonial state. This tension took on particular importance in the eighteenth century as communities entered into conflict with caciques and came up against the legal and institutional limits to cacique political accountability.

A final example will bring together the critical elements that have emerged—kinship and sexuality, race, and class—and show how the illegitimacy of intruders could simultaneously derive from multiple criteria. The Indians of Moho (Paucarcolla) challenged their cacique, Gregorio Santalla, for a host of abuses including alcohol repartos, tithes, and clientelistic control over town officials. Santalla, they recounted, was a "white man" from Larecaja who arrived in the area with no fortune of his own. He befriended the cacique, found his way into the cacique's home, and finally married the man's daughter. He did this "without regard for the fact that she was an Indian woman and with the sole aim of obtaining a living. It is simply unthinkable that a white man would marry an Indian for any other motive."[48]

As political polarization deepened over the course of the century, there was increasing intervention from above and from below in cacicazgo succession. We have already seen the state's overriding legal authority to determine cacicazgo possession, whether on a "proprietary" or "interim" basis. It appears that fewer and fewer governors actually enjoyed full proprietary title to their posts even if the corregidor had accepted them as natural successors and their rights were well established. By law, it was the superior government of the viceroy, acting in representation of the king, that formally recognized a cacique and issued a proprietary title. This confirmation occurred after the Real Audiencia and its commissioner, who was usually the provincial corregidor, had heard the testimony of witnesses and verified the claims and suitability of the proposed successor (following the regulations of the *real provisión ordinaria de diligencias de sucesiones de hijos de caciques*). The entire procedure, however, especially if cacicazgo possession was contested, often took years to complete.[49] In cases where there was no heir apparent to a cacicazgo, the standard procedure for designating a cacique began with a public proclamation calling forth all interested candidates. If natural succession rights were remote or vague, other criteria—such as financial solvency, proven service and loyalty to the Crown, personal probity, and fluency in the Spanish language— were weighed to assess aptitude for government. The corregidor nominated three men to the audiencia, which would then, following the corregidor's recommendations, officially name the interim successor. Interim caciques were also called upon to fill in, for example, when the legitimate blood heir was not of age, when an unmarried or widowed cacica held possession, or while the cacicazgo post was vacant for other circumstantial reasons.[50]

The corregidor's role in these legal procedures was patently important, as it was in the more informal maneuvers and intrigue that characterized cacicazgo succession conflicts. Besides the common cases in which corregidores dispensed with legal procedure altogether and named interim caciques without authorization,[51] their intervention was also especially direct in the appointment of interim tribute collectors (*cobradores* or *recaudadores*). In these cases, the corregidor enjoyed his greatest liberty, since he could name whichever subject he saw fit, needing only to notify the audiencia of his selection. Officially, these interim tribute collectors were to serve alongside or in lieu of proprietary caciques, with no independent governing or tutelary status for the community. In practice, however, they often did exercise political authority, oversee community affairs such as the dispatch of the mita, and enjoy the perquisites of caciques—receiving the lands, services, and obedience due to rightful lords. Since these appointees were not officially caciques, corregidores could select not only subservient Indians, but mestizos or creoles who would favor their interests, especially in the reparto. Colonial administrators were well aware of these routine arrangements, yet given the practical advantages of filling the void in a cacicazgo, they rarely acted to prevent the jurisdictional confusion and overreaching operations of cacique–tribute collectors (*caciques cobradores*) until the final decade of the century.

Taken together, the steady proliferation of interim caciques and cacique–tribute collectors indicates a slow, subtle institutional erosion of the caci-cazgo. It is not necessary to view this as an objective demographic phe-nomenon of lineage exhaustion among the stratum of cacique families. It would be difficult to make such an argument since the category of indige-nous nobility was quite elastic, and more or less distant kin could eventu-ally be found to stake a valid claim within the Spanish mayorazgo code (i.e., possession of the cacicazgo could always move transversally to a par-allel line of descent). In the previous chapter, the decline of Indian nobles was seen to be less a demographic dynamic of absolute numbers than one of class and status within Indian society. We can be certain, however, of the institutional nature of the problem. Interim caciques, even those boasting the best noble pedigree, lacked the security and greater autonomy of full proprietary possession, and they or their families were more vulnerable to rival pretensions. The authority of cacique–tribute collectors was even less stable. Finally, the key role of the corregidor allowed for increasingly arbi-trary and illegitimate control over the post.

With ongoing political polarization in the eighteenth century, the ques-tion of hereditary rights and succession frequently became part of a broader, quite complex struggle over cacique authority and legitimacy. It was a struggle that involved multiple layers of legal, political, and cultural criteria each of which was subject to competing definition. In response to the pressures from above, intervention from below by the community also became common in eighteenth-century succession conflicts. By the 1790s, communities often came to play a striking role in these conflicts, at times even initiating pretender suits and propelling their candidates (whom we might want to consider clients more than patrons) directly into office. If there were indeed built-in limits to accountability in the cacicazgo as a property form (even when its possession was conceded only on an interim basis), the slow erosion of the institution also provided new openings for community intervention and pressure. At the same time, the very limits to accountability, as the need for cacique responsiveness grew more urgent, moved communities toward creative and audacious efforts to control their maximal authority from the base.

The Rising Community Challenge to Caciques

The midcentury suit brought against Matías Calaumana, noted in the prelude to this chapter, serves an example of the late-colonial proliferation of conflict between communities and caciques in La Paz. The Guarina episode was, in fact, rather mild and short lived compared to others. Calaumana survived it, reconsolidated power, and went on to govern without concerted opposition for another three decades. This section examines other instances of such conflict in order to apprehend the breakdown of political order within communities, the language of cacique delegitimation, and the emboldened strategies of base-level community forces. The section thus lays out the second major aspect of the cacicazgo crisis.

Conflicts between caciques and communities in this period centered around a number of different issues such as labor services and cash exactions, tribute, and the management of community resources. Each of them merits careful and deep treatment, yet these conflicts also involved less explicit and less immediately perceptible aspects than what usually dominate the court's attention and the arguments of the parties to the suits. The aim in the following reconstruction and commentary upon the successive episodes of conflict in Calacoto, a town set out upon the altiplano of Pacajes, is to bring out both levels—the explicit issues as well as the political dimension that underlay the ostensible legal dispute or subtly shaped each party's representation before the courts.

Calacoto was not the single most violent site in the eighteenth century, yet it is particularly interesting for our purposes since full-scale conflict broke out there very early and the community renewed its struggle against cacique abuse decade after decade. In Calacoto, the descendants of the Cusicanqui dynasty appear to have governed securely from the sixteenth until the early eighteenth century. In 1721 Juan Eusebio Canqui assumed power, and antagonism to him was present from the start. Community members declared that ever since his youth, Canqui had been arrogant, ill willed, and violent. They added that he had obtained his post through dubious maneuvering and by bribing the corregidor Pedro Ambrocio Bilbao la Vieja, his constant ally during the 1720s.[52] Canqui took firm action from the start, assembling an armed squad of mestizos from the town to rough up any who stood in his way or opposed him in the courts.

Ten years later, the antagonism against Juan Eusebio Canqui and his brother Francisco, who served as alcalde mayor, culminated in a formidable lawsuit filed in the audiencia. A full account of the grievances against the Canquis is not possible here, but the remarkable array of accusations, numbering in the dozens and touching upon even the most ordinary facets of daily life, illustrates the thorough resolve of the community in its campaign. The following is a general, if only partial, register of the alleged abuses of the Canquis:[53]

1. <u>Exactions in labor services and other contributions</u>: According to the testimony of peasants, the cacique had introduced unlawful and uncompensated labor services by Indian men and women. They served as house servant (pongo), firewood supplier, mail carrier *(chasquero),* mule keeper, general purveyor (the three *irasiris* were responsible for tallow and other kitchen provisions),[54] and caretakers of fields and harvested crops. Women house servants *(mitanis)* were obliged to spin and weave rough cloth for the cacique. Anyone who failed to serve was charged a monthly fee of seven pesos, four reales. Canqui rented bread-making and kitchen implements to his servants and gave nothing in return for Indian labor in his fields or for service in his retinue when traveling to the provincial capital or Topoco, the site of the annual mita dispatch.

    The cacique also took advantage of the twenty-two mitayos destined for Potosí, calling upon them for personal services before their trip to the mine. Four wealthier peasants named as *marajaques* would pay the cacique fifty-two pesos in order to be liberated from annual service, and their place was taken in the Potosí mita by others who should have been exempt or ineligible for it. Furthermore, he failed to provide the supplies that mitayos required and burdened them with his own private commercial interests. The designated vendor in his town store *(pulpería)* was saddled with a rental fee and provided insufficient merchandise to sell (also any unsold merchandise could not be returned to the cacique for discount). As a consequence, the Indian was unable to meet the overhead costs and routinely left the service turn indebted to the cacique. Servants were also obliged to sell bread and to repay the cacique in cash, whether or not all the bread had been sold.

2. <u>Appropriation of lands, animals, and community rents</u>: The cacique and his brother took over the finest community lands, leaving Indians with infertile plots into which the Canquis' livestock was allowed to wander in search of forage. Francisco Canqui claimed one livestock estate and prohibited Indians from pasturing animals on the land or even in the vicinity. When Indians took their mules to town, they were seized for the Canquis' purposes and later resold. The cacique also embezzled the rental income from a community loan *(censo de comunidad),*[55] which was meant to alleviate the needs of poor Indians.

3. <u>Political misconduct</u>: The cacique named two alcaldes and two alguaciles from both moieties, intentionally selecting younger men whom he could control *(mozos para mandones y serviciales).*[56] He dealt with them domineeringly and would put them to work making bricks for his house. He failed to defend Indians when residents of other towns encroached upon their pastures or pilfered from them. If the corregidor gave orders for him to administer justice, he displayed only indifference. He held the hilacatas responsible for the expenses of the corregidor during his visit to Topoco, the candles

burned during the Topoco trip, and the costs of other items such as balsa crafts for ferrying the river (while in fact pocketing much of the money for himself).

4. Physical abuse: The Canquis were pitiless in their treatment of Indians, and their violence caused some to flee, thereby jeopardizing tribute payments. One Indian who sought to escape Francisco Canqui's fury took refuge on the church cemetery grounds. The alcalde mayor felt no compunction, however, in battering the man on the spot before a large gathering of people. He likewise delivered fifty lashes to Andrés Pari, leaving him with permanent injury. Francisco Canqui boasted that he could kill as many Indians as he pleased and would have to pay no more than a fifty-peso fine.[57]

As the audiencia's investigation into the case proceeded in Calacoto, the cacique and his brother set forth on their way to La Plata with the aim of countering the campaign against them. Upon arrival they were imprisoned, and under interrogation Juan Eusebio Canqui provided a very different version of affairs:[58]

1. Exactions: According to Canqui, the pongo, firewood supplier, mail carrier, and mule keeper were customary attendants in town and at the royal post house or *tambo*. The cacique acknowledged calling upon them only occasionally when they were otherwise unoccupied, always duly paying them for their services. He maintained that their labor was necessary to tambo operations and that smaller towns, such as Jesús de Machaca, had even more tambo mitayos. The irasiri was responsible for organizing the service turns and provisioning in the tambo. Traditionally the irasiri supplied chilis, lard, candles, and other items, but the cacique had ended this practice years earlier; if on occasion the irasiri still did provide tallow, he was paid the fair price.

There were likewise six women who customarily served: a pantry keeper; one who sold goods to passers-by down at the shore of the river ("She is not harmed by this, rather it is to her advantage since she can sell her own items"); and four mitanis, allowed for in Viceroy Duque de la Palata's *retasa* decree of 1688, who spun and wove wool.[59] According to Canqui, the tambo mitayos as well as the women all were paid the equivalent of one peso, in cash or kind as they saw fit.

As for the marajaques, Canqui again asserted that it was customary for four peasants to serve as shepherds for the cacique's flocks. If a chosen peasant did not wish to serve, he could hire a substitute or commute his service by paying the cacique a given sum (fifty-two pesos in some cases, thirty or twenty pesos in others). As Canqui pointed out, the Duque de la Palata's retasa law granted the cacique four Indians who were reserved from tribute and two boys younger than eighteen (hence not of tribute age). He did not acknowledge that the marajaque practice was connected to the Potosí mita, that he availed himself of mitayos prior to their journey, or that he named ineligible substitutes to serve in Potosí. If mitayos had not received supplies for their turn, it was because no community resources existed to set aside for this purpose.

As for other charges, he insisted that the community work parties *(faenas)* in the fields set aside for the cacique were customary around the province and that he did indeed provide food, drink, and coca for laborers. During his two-week trips to Caquiaviri and Topoco to deliver tribute and mita parties, it was again customary for the community to provide him with four or five young men whom he properly fed; in the past, the retinue had been larger, as it remained in other Pacajes towns. He also declared that the priest, and not he, ran the town store.

2. Appropriation of other resources: He had taken over only those lands specifically designated by the community for him as cacique. On only four occasions had he requisitioned mules from peasants, always under orders from the corregidor or the priest and never for private benefit. He offered to give a full accounting for the community censo rents and to pay for any unjustified expenses.

3. Political conduct: He protested that he had always sought to protect the Indians from harm and had gone to great lengths to obtain titles to community lands, though so far his efforts had proven unsuccessful. He denied having obliged the alcaldes to serve him personally. The contributions of the hilacatas on behalf of the community, he held, were traditional in towns around the province.

4. Violence: The Canquis denied the malevolence attributed to them. As alcalde mayor, Francisco Canqui was justified in administering corporal punishment to Indians. The beating on church grounds took place when one Indian mocked his authority as he was assembling the community for Sunday mass.

In the end, then, the Canquis responded to the battery of charges by explaining their conduct and defending it as in keeping with local custom or by outright denial of the accusations as unfounded fabrications. They, and the witnesses who testified on their behalf, attributed Indian hostility to the Canquis' zeal in securing allegiance to "both Majesties, God and the king." The cacique alleged: "The Indians of the community have grown to hate him only because he has entreated them to live as Christians, attending the holy sacrifice of Mass and Christian sermon. In this he has taken special care, as he has also done in increasing the royal treasury [by raising the number of tributaries and exposing Indian efforts to dodge tribute]."[60]

In their defense, the Canquis and their witnesses declared that the audiencia's commissioner, Ignacio de Rejas, was guilty of encouraging the community members in their suit. In a sure sign of complicity, he had in fact been seen in their hamlets and huts, "eating and drinking with them to the point of inebriation."[61] Nevertheless, they never questioned that the community as a whole, in the end Anansaya as well as Urinsaya, was united against them. In many other such eighteenth-century conflicts, one faction or another in the community would favor the cacique or could be enlisted on his side. Nor did the Canquis suggest that the suit had been invented or pressed by rival members of the local elite. We saw an example of such a scenario in Guarina during the battle between Matías and Francisco Calaumana. The final evidence of the full split between cacique and community lies in the testimony of witnesses. While community members testified in droves against the Canquis, predominantly Spanish townspeople supported the cacique.

How should we interpret the Calacoto conflict? Unfortunately we lack evidence from the 1720s that might better indicate the initial fissures and how they widened with time into the deep split of the early 1730s. There seems little to sustain the Canquis' argument that the real problem was cacique enforcement of Catholic and tributary obligations.[62] Yet it is also important to look more closely at what was said (and left unsaid) by the community and at the strategic political dimension of its suit. It is probably safe to assume that the Canqui brothers were guilty of violent, reprehensible actions to enrich themselves and that their exercise of power went against collective values and interests. Also, they and their witnesses certainly did attempt to deceive the court with their testimony.[63] Nonetheless, there is more to this conflict than meets the eye, for in its legal interventions, the community did not tell the full story either, as we shall see. Ultimately then, we need to treat this case, and others like it, as less than absolutely transparent and susceptible to surface scrutiny. In many of these instances of colliding forces at the community level, we can discern instead points of such opaqueness and density that they do not yield to easy inspection. Beyond the limitations of historical documentation, it is important to recognize that these points derive from political strategy and maneuvering by each adversary and in relation to other significant forces, most notably the colonial state and its judicial apparatus.

A full apprehension of these conflicts requires that we identify, even if we cannot always disentangle, a set of elements: established local practices (which may be seen as "traditional" and "legitimate" and which may also be undergoing gradual historical change); the caciques' creative twisting of "tradition" to private benefit and redefinition of their own local functions; and the community plaintiffs' strategic maneuvers in the legal arena to attain political advantage (this could mean manipulating formal legal regulations that might otherwise be utterly ignored by peasants and caciques locally).

The complex and fascinating issue of services, contributions, and commutations is one that recurs in the successive Calacoto conflicts and merits sustained attention, keeping in mind this added political dimension. The cacique argued that all the services in question were customary when he took office and that in fact he had ended some of them as being illicit, even over Indian objections. The town and tambo laborers were not personal servants, according to him, though he clearly exercised control over them and did avail himself of their labor. He also cited La Palata's decree granting the cacique four women, four men, and two boys under tributary age as legal personal servants. Though Canqui was distorting the situation and presenting it to the court with a fictitious formal and legal coherence, so far his argument appears to have had juridically valid points involving local custom and state sanction in its favor.

The specific question of mita commutation and marajaques, however, reveals the cacique's deception of the court. Canqui simply argued that the marajaques were customary shepherds, the four servants allowed him by law, and he denied any link between them and the Potosí mita. He noted that if one of them wished not to serve, the Indian would hire another in his place or, if the cacique had contracted him, he would pay the cacique fifty-two pesos (or sometimes less). He denied ever having received illegal bribes (that is, cash commutation) from wealthier Indians to avoid the Potosí mita.

But a careful reading of all the testimony as well as earlier and later evidence available to us suggests a far more intricate problem and ultimately contradicts Canqui's account. If the shepherds were both customary and lawful servants, why did the cacique say he sometimes contracted them? Furthermore, the term "marajaque" means "person with an annual turn" (*"mara"* signifying "year" in Aymara), whereas La Palata's decree provided for servants with six-month terms. In fact, the cacique perjured himself when he asserted that these were his personal attendants ordained in the retasa. The reason he did so was to avoid admission of wrongdoing. While state officials were aware of local practices removing Indians from mita draft rolls and did little to prevent them, strictly speaking these practices were illegal.

If not the cacique's personal servants, then who were the marajaques? Evidence from the mid-seventeenth century sheds light on the original significance of marajaque practice in Pacajes. At the time of the province-wide assembly and mita dispatch in Topoco, the caciques would bargain and arrange labor contracts with Spanish owners of local livestock estates and mines. The contractor would advance the one-year salary of the laborer—known as a marajaque—and it would then be forwarded as a commutation *(rezago)* to a mining entrepreneur in Potosí. While this system was susceptible to cacique abuse, and in fact did give rise to crushing debt peonage on Spanish estates, it existed in the first place as an alternative, however onerous, to the dreaded labor in Potosí.[64] The account of the cacique's brother, Francisco Canqui, fits with the earlier evidence and affords proof of the connections between annual herders and mitayos. Since he was not cacique, he had no right to personal servants, yet he acknowledged that Indians hired themselves out to him in order to free themselves from service in Potosí: "Like anyone else who can afford to pay the Indians in exchange for pasturing his mules and livestock and guarding his fields, he normally pays fifty-two pesos a year to those Indians selected and drafted for the Potosí mita. . . . In order to avoid going to the mita, they accept his offer and pay money to their mita captains."[65] He tells us, first of all, that cash commutation of mita service did occur in Calacoto and that the labor of designated mitayos was effectively appropriated for the benefit of the cacique's family.

There are initial resemblances yet, also, a final distinction between seventeenth-century marajaques and Francisco Canqui's shepherds, on the one hand, and the marajaques under cacique Juan Eusebio Canqui, on the other. They appear similar insofar as both were associated with an annual labor term, usually herding livestock. Later evidence also confirms the community's claims (and thus belies the cacique's testimony) that eighteenth-century marajaques were peasants withdrawn from the mita draft. Hence a second similarity is that both types of marajaques were involved in alternatives to service in Potosí.

The significant difference is that the latter-day marajaques were selected to serve the cacique, rather than hired out to other estate owners and that they could cancel their obligation outright with a cash payment. The eighteenth-century references to marajaques include an apparent range of situations: the shepherds tending the cacique's flock (a usage similar to that of Juan Eusebio Canqui's and containing no mention of the mita); principales said to be "withdrawn," evidently from the mita, who paid the cacique a given sum (similar to *colquejaques,* who will be considered below, and with no mention of herding service); and shepherds taken from the mita ranks, who were considered responsible for a contribution worth fifty-two pesos and four reales.[66] In fact, these were not different situations but rather different facets of the same phenomenon.

Juan Eusebio Canqui twisted the truth when he held that marajaques were like other customary servants and allowed for by law. In fact, marajaque practice had an independent origin linked to the mita and had evolved since the seventeenth century into a mandatory corvée levy. It was the cacique's power and pivotal role in community administration that created the margin for arbitrary and self-interested operation. Francisco Canqui also slanted the truth when he attempted to present the labor contracts of shepherds as part of a free, fair, and transparent labor market into which Indians voluntarily entered. There were innumerable local distortions in the "market" for labor. For instance, in a specie-scarce rural economy, we can imagine that money often did not actually pass hands in these types of wage contracts. What the Canquis had special interest in disguising was the cacique's manipulation of the linkages of debt and obligation that constrained community peasants and his methods for turning the intricate mita apparatus to personal and family benefit.

Ultimately, of course, it was colonial extraeconomic coercion that set in motion an entire system of relations and gave rise to multifarious efforts, among them marajaque practice, to limit the impact of state-enforced labor drafts. If in the seventeenth century caciques coordinated marajaque service as a local buffer for Indians, now the Canquis stood accused of abusing it (in both its older and newer types) as well as other forms of rotating draftlabor in town, such as the cacique's personal services, tambo service, and town-store service. If commutation paid to Potosí mine or mill owners was originally a relief for peasants, commutations were now increasingly destined for Calacoto caciques themselves as part of their own personal mita network. The overall complex of labor obligation and labor's cash convertibility that irradiated out from Potosí—that critical site for the peculiar and vicious ensemble of colonial coercion and an emerging market in labor power—was replicated at the local level in the countryside and for the benefit of the Calacoto community's own constituted leader.[67]

Turning to the community argument, we should begin by noting that, throughout La Paz, Indian services in town and for the cacique followed familiar, traditional patterns of rotation and prestation and were not only the result of external imposition. To take one example, a Spanish townsman from Jesús de Machaca stated: "It is the custom in Pacajes province to *give* the cacique female servants, five in some towns, six in others, or more depending upon the number of ayllus."[68] The cacique even reported that the Indians interpreted it as a rebuff *(desaire)* on his part when he ended the irasiri's contributions years earlier. Such service was evidently seen as part of a morally imbued reciprocity arrangement. Despite the burden, the community provided the cacique with labor and other contributions under the assumption that he would suitably respond by fulfilling his own obligations to them and by favoring and protecting them. Furthermore, as noted above, the practices of marajaques and the commutation of Potosí mita labor were not of recent imposition; we also have earlier evidence of commutation for mita service in town.[69] Many community members had an interest in this form of commutation since it allowed a reduction in burdensome service obligations, as we have just seen, and since it actually could operate in accord with collective, redistributive norms in the community, as will be seen more clearly in the discussion below.

The question that follows, then, is why the community was taking issue with the Canquis for practices that were in place, understood, and relatively beneficial to many. I have already suggested that the denial and distortion in the Canquis' testimony was designed to cloak wrong-doing. It is also quite possible that over the previous decade, and indeed following shortly upon the great mortality of the 1719 famine, the Canquis had taken such extreme and unfair advantage of these practices as to be materially damaging to the community and morally outrageous. Continuing with this hypothesis, given the cacique's violation of existing quid pro quos and his manifest refusal to provide proper patronage, the community could have determined that "moral economy" and reciprocity claims upon the cacique were no longer effective. The only viable alternative strategy was to challenge the cacique directly and use the courts to unseat him. What is noteworthy in the suit is that the community did not simply argue that the cacique had taken advantage of legitimate traditional practices, as he most likely did. Rather, the plaintiffs intentionally neglected to mention established and legal practices, asserting instead that the exactions were new and intrinsically abusive. All of this adds up, therefore, to a pattern of things said and unsaid that cast the Canquis in the worst possible light before the court.

The problem of community "custom" is central to the general discussion here and leads to the core of the political dynamics in these conflicts. On point after point, the cacique refuted accusations of abuse by noting that he had only acted in keeping with the traditional practices he found in place when he took office and that were equally found throughout Pacajes. In this respect, interestingly enough, the problem cannot be reduced to one of community resentment over cacique disregard for traditional norms and custom.[70] It would seem, on the contrary, that communities were the ones willfully ignoring the existence of customary practices when they accused Canqui of certain inventions and violations, such as those involving labor prestations, the commutation of services, or the control of choice plots of land. The reason for this should now be clear. When communities deliberately failed to mention certain traditional prestations and accused the cacique, for example, of exacting excessive labor services, they were playing upon a delicate legal matter before a colonial state long sensitive to community instability and mita labor shortage. By portraying caciques as contravening local order and state legal injunctions, communities pinned them in a tight corner.

Compensation for labor services was another part of the dispute that brought the question of custom to the fore. In response to repeated charges that he failed to pay or provision laborers properly, Juan Eusebio Canqui upheld his own conduct on both legal and traditional grounds. He acknowledged availing himself of town/tambo laborers but insisted on having paid them as the law required. Likewise, he held that he did feed the young men who accompanied him on his tours to Caquiaviri and Topoco and that he served food, drink, and coca (the traditional Andean fare on such occasions) to work parties during the faena. Because compensation for services was legally required by the state, and had been since Toledo, communities insisted that its neglect was not only a moral violation of traditional reciprocity but also a punishable legal infraction. In the debate over custom, therefore, we can perceive both internal community and external overtones. Both sides in the struggle consciously engaged both criteria, traditional norms and expectations as well as colonial legal status, in order to press or defend their case.[71]

While the Canquis were being held under arrest in La Plata, the community moved to assert control over the cacicazgo. In May 1734, community members requested that they be named a new cacique to ensure fulfillment of their tribute and mita obligations. Juan Eusebio Canqui was unacceptable to them, and the other potential hereditary successors also lacked their confidence. They proposed instead three candidates who were trustworthy, and the principales personally offered financial guarantee for tribute payments under the new appointee.[72]

In early 1735 after lengthy investigations, the Real Audiencia finally ruled on the Calacoto dispute. It decided to absolve the Canquis and release to them their seized property. At the same time, the cacique was allowed to step down from his post while maintaining the rights and privileges due him. He was also required to restore to the community two hundred pesos in censo rents. On the problem of introduced services for caciques in Calacoto and throughout Pacajes, the audiencia enjoined the corregidor, under threat of heavy fine, to end all that were not provided for in La Palata's retasa. Those Indians who were legally assigned to provide labor should not be obliged to contribute anything else (presumably goods or cash) nor to serve in any capacity other than the one formally stipulated. Finally, the audiencia called upon the corregidor to admonish the Indians for "facile" engagement in litigation against their cacique. "If they persist in such disturbances and refuse to live with the proper conformity," it warned, "the principales will be severely chastised as an example for the rest of them."[73]

The early date of this extensive case as well as the provincial implications of the dispute over labor service give it special importance. Despite the injunction to end services for caciques, however, we do not have evidence that local custom in Pacajes changed significantly. On the other hand, the relative success of the community—despite the audiencia's admonition, they were able to unseat, if not convict, their cacique—served as an example of tactics and strategy that could be adopted by other communities. In effect, as the century wore on, we find similar cacique-community conflicts, with similar dynamics, recurring in Calacoto and throughout the region.[74]

Juan Machaca assumed the office of interim cacique in Urinsaya moiety of Calacoto shortly after the removal of Juan Eusebio Canqui, and within ten years he, too, came under fire from the community for a multitude of abuses. Personal services, reminiscent of those received by the previous cacique, were once again cited, as was the practice of cash commutation for services. The cacique demanded of each hilacata one Indian from among those named to the Potosí mita as well as one alguacil mayor (both of whose service could be redeemed for fifty-two pesos), one irasiri (forty pesos), one alcalde (seven pesos, four reales per month), one vendor in the town-store (nine pesos, four reales), and one mitani (either male or female, for seven pesos, four reales). He forced Indians to labor in his fields with no recompense and unjustly subjected them to corporal punishment. He charged each hilacata twenty-five pesos for the supposed costs of the corregidor's visit, and he pocketed some two hundred pesos in censo rents instead of distributing them to poor Indians.[75]

But the principal dispute in the late 1740s was over alleged tribute abuses by the cacique in league with the provincial scribe, Joseph Herrera. The cacique forcibly registered many Indians who should have been reserved or exempt from tribute: elderly men and youngsters, as well as beggars, the lame, and the disabled. Since they usually could not pay, the fiscal responsibility fell to ayllu tribute collectors. Once the cacique seized the livestock of hilacatas Bernardo Cruz and Pedro Calderón when they did not deliver tribute money for three underaged boys. Community witnesses attributed the improper enrollment to Machaca's malice toward them and his calculation that the burden of debt would keep the Indians subordinate. The scribe Herrera also was accused of charging a fee of two reales for all married and one real for all unmarried Indians at the time of their inscription in tribute rolls and the same amount for all mitayos in Topoco. This abuse was suffered by all Indians in Pacajes, not only those of Calacoto, and the scribe persisted with his exactions even after the audiencia had issued a decree calling for an end to the practice.

Juan Machaca responded to the charges from prison in La Plata, as had Juan Eusebio Canqui before him.[76] To begin with, he acknowledged that he had followed local custom in accepting fifty pesos from each Indian selected out of the mita contingent. This money was supposedly given in turn as a salary to another Indian who would be in charge of the livestock belonging to all the mitayos during their absence from the community. Machaca was evidently describing the marajaque practice acknowledged by Juan Eusebio Canqui—peasants were designated to bear the burden of herding livestock and could pay the cacique to be freed from service. But Machaca was now admitting the mita connection that the community had insisted on in the first dispute and that Canqui had denied. At the same time, in order to protect himself, he did not recognize, as Canqui had done, that the shepherds served him and watched over his own flock. In other words, Machaca presented himself as a neutral administrator of marajaque labor and commutation within the community framework for mobilizing Potosí mita drafts. Canqui, by contrast, based his defense on the established services provided for caciques. Neither wished to incriminate himself by acknowledging the overlap between mita labor and commutation for Potosí's Cerro Rico (rich mountain), on the one hand, and for the cacique himself, on the other.

Machaca's testimony also introduces a new wrinkle, namely the communal function of marajaque herders. This role may or may not have been performed by marajaques in reality. We lack other evidence to corroborate the assertion. If true, it would only enhance the comparison between the marajaque and the colquejaque, a slightly more familiar figure in the historiography. Despite certain similarities, they were not one and the same, and both of them could be found simultaneously in a single community.[77] The colquejaque (known as *colqueruna* in Quechua) was one of a number of wealthier peasants named by the cacique in addition to the regular mita party. He contributed a cash sum outright, often fifty-two pesos but at times as much as one hundred pesos, which excused him from service. The destination of these funds may well have been flexible, but generally the cacique would apply them as a subsidy for the costs of mobilizing the community labor force. In particular, colquejaque contributions were often used for sponsoring the copious feasts held for mitayos prior to their departure and for provisioning their caravan. Though considered exploitative and declared illegal by the colonial state, the logic of this practice for many community members is clear enough—the cash contributor was relieved of onerous duty, and the subsidy amounted to a sort of community economic redistribution insofar as wealthier peasants were underwriting collective costs.[78] In the case of marajaque practice, according to Machaca's version of it, the mitayos obtained the benefit of a herder for their livestock whom they would otherwise have had to contract individually and in exchange for other goods or services.

The foregoing discussion allows further speculation about the ways in which caciques took private advantage of these commutation practices. The most common abuse by caciques of colquejaques was to name an excessive number or demand an excessive amount and to appropriate their contributions rather than redirect them to meet communal needs.[79] When the cacique kept most or all of the colquejaque or marajaque money for himself, the commutation essentially became a *faltriquera* ("pocket") payment, like those received by the Potosí miners who simply elected not to hire a substitute laborer. With marajaques, if the cacique did find a substitute shepherd, he may well have offered some sort of nonmonetary compensation for his labor. Perhaps the substitute, like the seventeenth-century marajaque, would be relieved of obligatory mita service himself or relieved of other outstanding debts. It was noted above that the shepherds who served on Francisco Canqui's estate were formally similar to the seventeenth-century marajaques hired out to Spaniards for the price of mita commutation. Doubt was also raised about whether labor contracts were actually settled in cash. Though Francisco Canqui maintained that his shepherds worked for wages and commuted their mita service with money, this was evidently not necessary for the system to function, given his tight association with the cacique who oversaw the mita draft and commutation. In the end, we are left with the impression of extensive chains of debt and obligation controlled by Calacoto caciques, bringing cash to their coffers and ultimately—beyond certain redistributive potential in the case of colquejaques and marajaques—reinforcing the economic inequalities in the community. Prosperous peasants had a better chance for obtaining release from labor prestations, while at the end of the chain more vulnerable and disadvantaged peasants were the ones who eventually bore the burden.[80]

The cacique Juan Machaca also acknowledged the customary service of two Indian men and one woman who served him, and a second female laborer provided on a rotating basis by the ayllus who served monthly turns in the town store. He denied having received the services of an irasiri or of the alguacil mayor and alcalde and denied having received cash payments from any Indians in lieu of personal service. It was true that the hilacatas had contributed six pesos each and another Indian drawn from the Potosí mita had contributed fifty pesos for the feasting of the corregidor during his visits, but this was not an exaction introduced by the cacique. It existed since the time of his ancestors.[81]

In his defense against accusations of improper tribute administration, Machaca protested that he had not charged anyone unjustly. If any Indians had been included accidentally in the rolls, the cacique promptly notified the corregidor when advised of the error. If a few men had been reserved temporarily from tribute because of infirmities, they were obliged to satisfy payments upon regaining their health. Fraud, he argued, was impossible since the enrollment lists were drawn up during the corregidor's annual visit in the presence of the Indian principales and the priest, and he had never used separate account books for collection.[82]

Echoing his predecessor Juan Eusebio Canqui, Juan Machaca concluded that the Indians opposed him because he had fulfilled the duties of his office—"to extract them from their vices, depraved customs, and drunkenness and to attract them toward the holy cult, observance of divine law, and the other obligations that they ought strictly to follow."[83]

To make sense of this case, once again it is not sufficient to limit the inquiry to the manifest accusations and legal maneuvers. Tributary administration was the foremost issue explicitly under dispute, as it was in many other confrontations with caciques in La Paz, yet the core of the conflict lay elsewhere. In late November of 1744 in Topoco, the traditional setting for the delivery of the community's tribute and mita contingent, Bernardo Cruz and the rest of the hilacatas presented their collected money to Corregidor Francisco Xavier de Sosa and requested a notice of receipt. The corregidor, however, asked them to deliver the money later in Caquiaviri at which time he would give them the receipt. A rumor soon spread among the Indians: the corregidor had commented that he intended not to receive the money as tribute but as payment for his reparto debts, as he had attempted to do on a previous occasion; his term would soon be ending and he would no longer be able to collect what was owed him for the mules and rough cloth he had distributed.

The Indians also feared that once again they would be charged an additional sum by the provincial scribe Herrera. They had previously obtained a writ from the audiencia for the scribe not to charge his registration fees. The corregidor had publicly read the decree in Topoco before the entire assembly of Indians from the province, and he had turned it over to cacique Juan Machaca. Yet instead of using the document in defense of his community and of the others in the province who stood to benefit from it, Machaca hid it away and the scribe continued in his exactions. In the words of one Indian, "He hid it so the corregidor and scribe would maintain him in office as interim cacique. That is why he does not defend the Indians of his moiety; instead he has rebelled against them."[84]

The hilacatas boldly determined to take the tribute themselves directly to the Caja Real (royal treasury) in La Paz. For purposes of verification, the administrators of the Caja Real sent orders for the Pacajes corregidor to submit a copy of his account books. The corregidor was outraged. He vented his fury upon the Cañari Indian who bore him the message and twice refused to obey the request. He and the cacique put out a headhunting warrant for Bernardo Cruz and the other principales. They were forced to abandon their families and community and seek refuge in La Paz where they performed menial labor and fell deeper into debt. In revenge, the cacique, as always in complicity with the corregidor and scribe, then began his arbitrary registration of community members in tribute rolls.[85]

The Real Audiencia finally reached a decision in the case in 1750. It declared Joseph Herrera innocent of wrongdoing while ordering scribes throughout La Paz to refrain from charging fees for tribute and mita registration. The audiencia acknowledged the practice was widespread in the provinces but prohibited it thereafter regardless of local custom. Taking into consideration that the cacique had already languished in prison for three years, the audiencia acquitted Juan Machaca on most of the charges, including all those related to tribute administration. The court convicted him only for collecting money to sponsor the corregidor's visit and sentenced him to repay the amount to the community. It ruled that this and other services and contributions were improper, regardless of custom. The only services to caciques permitted by law were those regulated by the Ordinances of La Palata and for which the Indians were paid a salary. The conviction involved only minor delinquency on the part of the cacique, but it was sufficient to remove him from interim office. Following standard procedure, the audiencia ordered the corregidor to summon all hereditary pretenders to the cacicazgo or, in their absence, to nominate three suitable candidates to substitute for Machaca.[86]

As in the earlier case involving Juan Eusebio Canqui, there was more to this conflict than the explicit legal issues, this time involving tribute and personal services. Ultimately, it was the negotiation of local political power that was at stake. For the plaintiffs, the conflict concerned Machaca's political loyalties, and once again community members achieved their aim of unseating a cacique who had "rebelled against them." At the same time, the case shows how a conflict apparently internal to the community in fact related back to the colonial state apparatus (in the person of the corregidor) and colonial economic exploitation (in the form of the reparto) at the regional level.

The story of don Francisco Mauricio Marca provides us a rare glimpse of one of the many, usually faceless, authorities and elders who sustained the Calacoto community struggle during successive decades.[87] In December 1759, at the age of eighty, Francisco Marca made the long trek to the audiencia in La Plata in order to obtain a restraining order against the governing caciques who persecuted him and his family with special vengeance. It was not the first time that Marca had challenged hostile caciques nor appeared before the distant court. He had in fact been one of the original plaintiffs against the Canqui brothers in the early 1730s. In 1754, he was sentenced to ten years' labor in a textile workshop by the Pacajes corregidor, evidently for his political activities, but he managed to secure his freedom after presenting his case before the audiencia. In 1759, he dared to represent the community once again, in opposition to two new caciques who were introducing more personal service obligations and attempting to justify them as customary.

The first of these caciques was Gregorio Machaca, described by moiety members as "a pleb and drunkard with no right to the cacicazgo, an intruder and enemy of all the Indians of the community." He was denounced in one suit for favoring and protecting his son-in-law Salvador Mamani, a well-known thief, and appointing him hilacata against the wishes of the ayllu.[88] The second cacique was none other than Francisco Canqui himself, the brother of Juan Eusebio Canqui and notorious former alcalde mayor, who now had reclaimed the family's right to the post of governor.

Old Francisco Marca journeyed south that winter to La Plata and returned to Pacajes with a copy of the court sentence from the 1735 suit against the Canqui brothers, which decreed that the only legitimate services to caciques were those stipulated by La Palata in the previous century. The corregidor had no choice but to notify the caciques of the content of the ruling and publicly order that they observe the law. Of course Marca anticipated that Francisco Canqui and his fellow caciques—for the law applied throughout the province[89]—would not delay in punishing him for his insolence. By December, four months later, he was back in La Plata seeking the restraining order. The caciques of Calacoto and others from around Pacajes were "resentful and inflamed" against him and his four sons. He knew they would do as they had five years earlier, inventing lies about him and mounting a false trial. "United in hatred and rancor," they would influence the priests and the corregidor and brand him rebel, adulterer, assassin, or any other sort of criminal that they fancied. He requested legal protection for himself and his sons, who had already suffered extortions, humiliation, and whippings; he also requested that they be allowed to pay their tribute directly to the Caja Real in La Paz.[90]

With his successful maneuvering in the audiencia, don Francisco struck repeated blows against the community's aggressive local adversaries. Though we do not know how he ended his days, he was clearly one of many astute and courageous Aymara peasant leaders during the eighteenth century whose lives remain largely obscure to us today. Their anonymity is not only that of most ordinary peasants in history, a consequence of the fragmentary nature of the documentary record. Francisco Marca and others like him usually preferred obscurity and often chose to move in clandestinity. The few traces he did leave are enough to reveal that his accumulated experience and tactical and strategic intelligence were enduring political resources and that his example undoubtedly served in the formation of successive generations of leaders in Calacoto.

By this time in Calacoto, the cacicazgo conflict was intimately bound up with struggle over the corregidor's system of repartos. The community had first brought suit against Corregidor Salvador de Asurza's forced distribution of goods in 1758. Though its legal appeals were rejected by the Junta de Corregidores in Lima, the protracted battle would have major repercussions for colonial state administration. Based on this case, the audiencia in La Plata challenged Lima's hegemony, and in 1764 the Crown reduced the Junta's power to oversee all aspects of the legalized reparto system and restored the audiencia's judicial authority to rule on reparto conflicts within its own jurisdiction.[91]

In the midst of this struggle, at the time of old Francisco Marca's return to La Plata, two of his companions from Calacoto reinforced the case against cacique Francisco Canqui, alleging that he was coercing them to pay off their reparto debts to the provincial governor. It is also interesting to note that during the dispute an unnamed cacique from Calacoto complained that the corregidor was wrongly holding him in default for tribute arrears.[92] It is uncertain whether the cacique was Francisco Canqui himself or, rather, a new interim appointee; nor do we know if the cacique, under fire within the community, was forced by his own subjects into challenging the corregidor.[93] Important, in any case, are the extreme and contradictory pressures brought to bear upon the cacicazgo in this key moment. At the same time that the corregidor was attempting to collect his debts and the community base was mobilized against him, there were accusations levelled against the cacique for collaborating with Asurza and accusations by the cacique against the corregidor for unjust financial demands made upon him.

Open and violent antagonism between the caciques and community members in Calacoto in no way diminished in 1761 under the cacicazgo successors Miguel Cusicanqui in Anansaya and his son Pedro in Urinsaya. Many of the accusations were familiar: the caciques demanded excessive personal services and cash contributions, for all variety of purposes, from increasing numbers of Indians.[94] In Urinsaya, for example, Pedro Cusicanqui selected two mitayos from each of the five ayllus and charged each of them fifty-two pesos for the corregidor's visit. The custom prior to his entrance into office was for the hilacatas to pay five to ten pesos depending upon their capacities. Three more mitayos were each charged fifty-two pesos for tributary registration by the scribe, and a fourth was obliged to contribute the same amount as irasiri. Yet another three mitayos each paid fifty-two pesos for litigation expenses in land disputes involving the communities of San Andrés and Santiago de Machaca, Caquingora, and Callapa. The cacique separately collected money under the same pretext from other community peasants, accumulating over five hundred pesos in all. Yet he returned from the court in La Plata with only one decree that would have cost him no more than fifty pesos. The plaintiffs declared that Cusicanqui must have "eaten the rest of it" and that, in the end, he did nothing to benefit them.[95] The situation clearly exposes the extensive practice in the mid-eighteenth century of cash contributions and commutations of services that were handled by the cacique.

How are we to account for the persistence of these issues despite the audiencia's repeated injunctions? In his opinion on the Cusicanqui case, Indian Protector Antonio Porlier speculated that the caciques might have been simply unaware of the law when they entered office. This was clearly not the case, however. Witnesses recounted that when Indians showed Miguel Cusicanqui the decree forbidding contributions, the cacique became indignant and falsely declared before a large gathering that it had been repealed and that the king had issued him a new order for the exactions.[96]

Rather, it seems personal services and contributions to the cacique were charged with political significance involving the recognition of authority. As local conflict sharpened and polarization grew, especially in a period of ongoing battles over repartos, caciques would have demanded such recognition, in the form of contributions, as a matter of honor and principle. Community members, on the other hand, responding to the breakdown of cacique patronage, would have withdrawn their contributions and refused recognition of legitimacy.

This problem of authority was evident in the confrontations pitting caciques against ayllu authorities and principales, another issue that frequently surfaced in the eighteenth-century documentation of cacique-community conflict. Two days after Indians presented Miguel Cusicanqui with the audiencia's decree, he flogged the hilacatas Nicolás Tarqui and Agustín Mamani for having obtained a new copy of the 1735 ruling, and Mamani was detained in an unlit chamber in the cacique's house.

The public punishment of authorities was a brutal yet not uncommon political ritual in this period. Set within Spanish colonial political culture generally, these rituals of exemplary violence *(escarmiento)* demonstrated cacique power and implacability and sought to instill fear and subordination. As one witness told it, Pedro Cusicanqui humiliated and ravaged the body of former segunda persona Andrés Machaca: "He shut him up in one room after another, dragging him by the hair from place to place as if he were an ordinary scoundrel or delinquent. Ignominiously, he had him held down by four men and gave him a hundred lashes. He took an hour and a half to do it, so as to terrify us with his cruelty." The peasant's sin was to have defended his young nephew when the boy was charged tribute by the cacique. Cusicanqui allegedly menaced, "This rebellious Indian will die at my stern hand, and any judge will consider the deed well done." Community members particularly objected to this violence since these authorities and principales merited special honor and respect.[97]

Community members themselves explicitly commented on the local crisis of legitimacy, in the political sense and patriarchal idiom noted in the previous chapter. Not only did the Cusicanquis "tyrannize" them, but they failed to "defend" the community and its lands from outside encroachment. Rather than fulfill their obligations, the caciques had left the community neglected and helpless. Urinsaya Indians stated that Pedro Cusicanqui "has acted not like a father and protector, but like a bloodthirsty wolf or beast."[98]

The Calacoto conflict this time took on an added hue of political destabilization. Sebastián García, a principal from neighboring Caquingora, spoke out against the abuses, especially the punishments, suffered by those of his community. The Cusicanquis, he declared, had ruined the peace between the towns and provoked widespread resentment—"because of them there is risk of a tumult from one town to another."[99]

Protector Porlier in La Plata did not fear uprising, but the Calacoto case did lead him to express his concern about the community challenge to caciques throughout the northern district of Charcas. He began by questioning the veracity of community accusations. There were many examples of caciques who suffered long jail terms resulting from the charges levelled against them (in the summary testimony) yet who were later found innocent when they were able to testify and present witnesses on their behalf (in the plenary trial). (He considered Spanish witnesses, who commonly testified on behalf of caciques, to be more objective observers of cacique-community disputes.) Echoing the court's 1735 admonition to the Indians of Calacoto, Porlier remarked in his brief on the causes of the dubious suits against caciques: "This problem arises from the facile nature of Indians, their ignorance, and the influences to which they are subject because of the scheming of others who are not Indians and who use them to execute their desires. . . . [Also the Indians] can never bear the operations of their governors, who begin by compelling them to pay tribute, serve in the mita, attend mass, amend their vices, and fulfill their other obligations. This would be sufficient cause to treat Indians as enemies of their governors and, hence, to reject their testimony."

In the early 1760s, Porlier was responding to an already generalized problem and one that was shattering local social order. To illustrate his exposition, he cited other challenges to prominent caciques—Faustino Herrera in Caquiaviri (Pacajes), Diego Choqueguanca in Azángaro (Azángaro), Melchor Chuquicallata in Saman (Azángaro), and Felipe Alvarez in Ayoayo (Sicasica)—that were going on at the same time as the latest Calacoto conflict. The office of Indian protector threatened to become "an admirable workshop for disturbing the quietude and tranquillity of the Indians of this jurisdiction and for upsetting the government of the towns. . . . Protection of Indians must not distract from communal harmony nor afford easy credence to their particular declarations."[100] The protector's remarks ultimately reveal the state's awareness that the conflicts were of broad consequence and posed a real threat to colonial political stability.

In the early 1770s, the Calacoto community kept up its open denunciation of caciques, yet the issues of personal services and contributions, appropriation of resources, and violence no longer stood in the foreground. The conflict now narrowed down to a single outstanding issue, that of cacique collaboration with corregidores in the ruinous reparto de mercancías.[101] This was not a new problem—we saw it arise earlier in the dispute with Calacoto cacique Juan Machaca and again with cacique Francisco Canqui in 1760. But since it was, in a certain sense, a less localized problem, it is important to shift our gaze to the provincial and regional levels. The full explanation for the eighteenth-century crisis of the cacicazgo and Andean rule requires that we add to this account, in the following chapter, the fierce struggles against corregidores and their repartos.

The foregoing narration of cacique-community conflicts in Calacoto has allowed a glimpse at many of the issues that were commonly disputed in the courts. The sustained focus on one site has, no doubt, come at the cost of a wide perspective and a deeper discussion of the full set of issues that surfaced in La Paz over the course of the century. The one issue that did receive greater attention in this account is that of labor services and other contributions. The previous section of this chapter also explored the question of cacique intruders—whose succession rights and, often, ethnicity were challenged by their communities—while the cacique's role in the reparto system and ties to the corregidor will be examined in the next chapter. Bracketing off these questions of intrusion and reparto collaboration, a brief synthesis of the other typical issues found throughout the region is still in order and will help to show that the range of issues present in Calacoto was generally, if not perfectly, representative.

The accusations against caciques often took the form of lengthy lists of abuses, and their recurrence in the documents can begin to seem like standard formula for obtaining the indictment of community governors. Even if only one or two of the charges were founded, in the eyes of the court, the overall intent was to expose the cacique as an unsavory character unfit to rule. Two of the most common issues raised involved tribute and community lands. Communities charged that caciques demanded tribute of Indians who should have been exempt (such as young boys, widows, and the elderly as well as agregados and yanaconas) and that caciques kept parallel tribute rolls. Their in-house register included extra Indians who did not appear on the official rolls presented to the corregidor. In this way, the cacique raised more money than he actually submitted to the royal treasury, and he pocketed the difference.[102]

There were several common complaints over lands. The cacique often usurped individually held or common lands for private benefit, and he rented out uncultivated community lands to townspeople or landlords without consulting the community. Indians resented it when he accumulated large tracts within the community, like any Spanish estate owner, or when he failed to defend community lands under threat from outside forces.[103]

The Calacoto case has provided a fair description of the set of problems surrounding labor services, their cash conversion, and other community contributions and exactions. Local mita services were rendered in town and in the cacique's house, store, and fields. The cacique's wife usually supervised the labor of women weavers. The cacique also misappropriated the labor or commutation fees of Potosí mitayos. Contributions in cash or kind were ordinarily provided to the cacique for communal works and ceremonies.[104]

One issue that did not arise in Calacoto was cacique engagement in commercial abuses. Sometimes these involved the recruitment of community labor and requisitioning of livestock for marketing. In town, caciques often enjoyed a monopoly over sales to Indians and purchased peasants' products at unfair rates in order to resell them. Commercial risks were passed on to wealthier peasants enlisted as marketers who had to absorb any financial losses.[105]

Physical violence and cruel punishment were other regular complaints,[106] as were intimidation and control over community authorities.[107] Naturally there was also a plethora of other less common or less conspicuous abuses in each local setting.[108] It is important to note, in addition, that all of the above issues were subject to the kind of intricate contestation and deep ambivalence, conditioned by discursive and political strategy, that surrounded services and contributions in Calacoto and that make it so difficult to see at first glance the full dynamics of local conflict in the eighteenth century.

The Calacoto case is indeed illustrative of the diverse issues in these disputes, yet the real advantage of a long-term look at one town is the local political dimension that often emerges at the margins of the judicial proceedings and documentation. What our approach reveals is not merely that labor services for the cacique, to take one example, were an ongoing problem in Calacoto, but that they and other common issues are properly understood within a dense web of power relations and as part of often obscure political struggles. In this sense, the full meaning of cacicazgo conflict in our period cannot be reduced to the individual issues that recur in the court records.

At the heart of these political struggles was the question of cacique political loyalty to the community. As one peasant put it, when challenging interim cacique Juan Machaca in Calacoto, "He does not defend the Indians of his moiety; instead he has rebelled against them."[109] Litigation against one's own maximal authority—often involving an entire battery of accusations and protracted efforts and sacrifice on the part of numerous community members, principales, and authorities—was the ultimate tactic in campaigns to ensure the accountability of a cacique or to remove him altogether. The struggles aimed to renegotiate community power relations by exerting stronger base-level control over the post of the foremost community political representative and leader.

This chapter has taken up two key internal aspects of the eighteenth-century cacicazgo crisis. It began with an examination of the institutional conflicts bound up with cacicazgo succession and intrusion. Intricate succession disputes between rival pretenders hinged especially on family genealogical claims, the property rights established by the Spanish mayorazgo code, and the backing of colonial authorities and tribunals. Intrusion by illegitimate outsiders—who were usually in-laws of the rightful cacique family, mestizos, "social climbers" (Spalding), and/or the clients of regional state agents—combined with the proliferation of interim caciques and cacique-tribute collectors to erode the institutional stability of the cacicazgo as it had been consolidated over the previous centuries of colonial rule.

We have now also considered the acute intracommunity conflicts between caciques and their subjects. While these confrontations ostensibly involved a range of issues linked to community reciprocity and reproduction, administration and government, they have also brought to light an underlying contest over power relations that was sustained throughout this period. The Calacoto case shows that no simple moral economy equation or exclusively localist view can adequately account for the dynamics of this conflict. As was argued at the outset, a third conjunctural element of conflict—the repartimiento de mercancías and the powerful movements against it—is fundamental for understanding the full-scale crisis of the cacicazgo and the local bases of Andean rule.

4 The Crisis of Andean Rule (II)

The Reparto Connection and Breakdown of Mediation

The leading studies of eighteenth-century peasant movements in the Andes coincide in considering the repartimiento de mercancías, or forced distribution of commodities, to be a key economic factor in the cycles of social conflict that led up to the insurrectionary conjuncture of 1780–1781.[1] The repartimiento system was a peculiar and abhorred colonial institution that fused commercial capital with colonial political coercion. In a chain of debt relations that ultimately ended with local Indian "consumers," merchants advanced goods to provincial governors who then forcibly imposed them upon the Indian population at prices well above the market rate. The products distributed—including mules from Tucumán, cloth from Quito or imported from Spain, Yungas coca, and coastal brandy—were often useless or in poor condition. The reparto was a lucrative speculative enterprise for corregidores, many of whom bought their posts back in Spain at high cost and indebted themselves to merchants in the hope of fabulous returns. The system significantly benefited merchants faced with otherwise stagnant markets, and the Crown, whose income flowed from the sale of corregimiento offices even when the reparto was illicit. In the 1750s, the practice was legalized as the state sought to fill its coffers through taxation of reparto commerce.[2]

The aim of this chapter is to examine in greater depth the *political* significance of the reparto and its impacts. It is especially important to delve into the coercive nature of the distribution of commodities and to explore the erection of, and the shifts and tensions within, the political structure that constituted the regime of extraction. To ensure more effective extraction and to counter inevitable discontent or outright opposition to their exploitation, the corregidores moved to shore up their regional and local political apparatus in the eighteenth century. This could be achieved by introducing more state agents, especially deputies *(tenientes de corregidor)* and other private debt collectors (cobradores), and by consolidating their relations with caciques. But it was by no means a smooth or simple affair, and in the long run, it had drastic consequences for the colonial order.[3]

The relentless pressures from above brought on the full crisis of the caci- cazgos as community governors were forced into increasingly untenable positions as political intermediaries and representatives. While the corregi- dor effectively employed various methods to secure cacique compliance, Indian peasants sustained traditional political expectations of their ca- ciques and demanded that they fulfill their role as protectors ready to stand up for their own communities. As community struggles wore on and even gained in tenacity throughout the region and, indeed, the entire viceroy- alty, they threatened to converge with the radical political and cultural pro- jects of anticolonial rebels. Building upon the arguments laid out in the previous chapter, we now take up the third part of the explanation for the crisis of Andean rule. Widening our view from the local to the provincial and regional levels, we will now see more clearly how caciques fit within the field of colonial power relations and the overall dynamic of historical struggle in the eighteenth century as well as how the cacicazgo crisis ulti- mately involved the unraveling of colonial rule broadly defined.

The province of Sicasica (before its division in 1779) provides an especially vivid illustration of the rural rhythms of struggle. A reconstruction of these processes will show how a full cycle of politicization and polarization between communities and colonial agents worked to undermine cacique legitimacy and state order.[4] (See map on p. 20 for the following local and provincial historical account.) It is worthwhile to recall from the start the great importance of Sicasica at this time. According to the 1754 tariff that set the type, volume, and prices of legal reparto goods in each province, Si- casica had the second largest Indian population in the entire Peruvian vice- royalty as well as the reparto worth the highest value (226,750 pesos).[5] While the province was highly attractive for ambitious corregidores be- cause of the vast fortunes that could be accumulated there, it was also an early site of antireparto activities and became a zone renowned for the power of its community mobilizations. Sicasica played a leading part in the concatenation of revolts that would shake Peruvian colonial government in 1771. In 1776, the attorney general *(fiscal)* from the Real Audiencia of Charcas asserted: "No province has proven itself so inclined toward upris- ing as Sicasica."[6]

The conflicts between Aymara communities and the corregidor in the Yungas valleys dated back to the early 1740s. The complaints by the Indians

in the region against excessive and violent repartos from 1743 to 1747 provoked significant repercussions and were enough to disturb the king himself
back in Spain. Along with the reparto charges, the corregidor Juan Helguero, his deputy Juan del Cerro, and his reparto collectors stood accused of
a host of other abuses. Helguero had demanded a multitude of services and
cash contributions and had flogged two Indians to death. According to
their accusers, the collectors had also punished Indians cruelly, sold off
some as captive laborers in the textile workshops (obrajes), and taken the
lives of others. Furthermore, they had seized peasants' harvests and coca
fields and had set up a monopoly trade in coca. Using false weights, they
would buy cheap (from Chulumani and Chupe producers in particular)
and later sell dear to those Indians who traveled down from the altiplano.

The corregidor also unleashed an implacable campaign to break the opposition that was organized, especially in Chulumani and Chupe, against
his abuses. In 1742, the Indians who returned from La Plata with a decree
to investigate the excesses of the corregidor and his subordinates were arrested and submitted to corporal punishment in the textile workshop of
Diego Alarcón; then the corregidor used threats and blandishments to persuade them to drop the charges. He successfully maneuvered the removal
of the first judge named in the investigation, and the second judge, in
league with Helguero, acted only to silence the protest. When the corregidor later came under routine scrutiny after the end of his term, many of
the Indians who had instigated the 1742 suit were dead, others had fled,
and the remainder were left powerless to defend themselves and justify
their case. The corregidor left his post with his fortune secured and the first
battle won, but the resistance had grown and the political cost of Helguero's individual gains would be paid by his successors.[7]

During the 1750s, the level of conflict rose and resistance spread to the
other towns of Yungas. Community members in Laza, for example, protested against Corregidor Josef Serrano for his repartos and other abuses,
and they objected to the excesses of his collectors *(mozos cajeros)*. They appealed to be freed of such agents, including both lieutenants-general and
particular local deputies. They added that the collectors had introduced
new personal services, such as the *marcacama* for keeping mules, and that
they had abused Indian authorities in town, for example forcing the alguacil to labor during their harvests.[8]

Conflict in this period was focused, however, in the area of Palca and
Río Abajo. In 1753, the hilacatas and principales of Cohoni, Mecapaca,
and Palca protested against the corregidor's deputy in these towns because
of his "absolute power" and a series of abuses including the appropriation

of lands and repartos. The deputy defended himself with the argument that he had duly rented the lands from the cacique. He also questioned the validity of the suit since it was not presented by the cacique, as ordained by law. We should note here, first of all, that the cacique seems to have been compromised on the side of the deputy—he appears in the rental contract but not leading the defense of the community—and that the communities faced great difficulties in mounting a legal defense. They had to suffer repression at the hands of local authorities challenged in the suit. Also, they did not know how their case would be received by the court if it lacked the representation of the cacique, who in fact could be allied with the local colonial authority. Such circumstances could easily lead local conflict into increasingly polarized positions and result in the rupture of political relations.[9]

Only a few years later, the communities of Palca and Ocobaya were newly engaged in a confrontation with Corregidor Eusebio Yepes Castellanos because of his repartos and the conduct of his deputy (his legal substitute during the corregidor's absence). At first the cacique, Casimiro Andrade, and the principales held out together and obtained a decree for their protection. In spite of attempts to intimidate and separate him from the community defense, Andrade recognized that distributing the corregidor's goods would mean his own ruin within the community and he refused to do so. For this lack of cooperation, Yepes Castellano appointed his deputy Francisco Xavier Avendaño to harass the cacique until Andrade abandoned his office and left the community leaderless.

One witness testified that no deputy had ever operated in Ocobaya, a diminutive jurisdiction of only one league. Such an official was quite unnecessary since the corregidor and his deputy resided nearby in Chulumani and another deputy operated in the neighboring town of Palca. The corregidor's "golden pretext" for gaining legal confirmation of the new deputy in Ocobaya was that the jurisdiction was so vast. Yet Indians declared that a number of the places mentioned by the corregidor as part of the jurisdiction were "overgrown areas *(monte)* inhabited only by wild animals and not people." In truth, he had introduced the deputy to assure the reparto collection, which in Ocobaya alone was worth the extraordinary value of forty thousand pesos.

Once settled in, Avendaño's abuses were numerous. Aside from gratuitous cruelty, we can point to two principal aspects of the deputy's activities. First, he exercised supreme authority at the local level, along with his wife and two subordinate collectors. He controlled Indian alcaldes and alguaciles, forced many Indians into personal service, and assumed the function of the cacique in distributing communal lands (favoring certain clients within the community).

Second, the deputy's aim was maximum economic accumulation. As local intermediary, he established a commercial monopoly similar to the one imposed in Chulumani and Chupe. He set up a local outlet for tobacco and practiced his own reparto of this product. He restricted the custom by which the cacique's wife sold goods in town in order to meet tribute shortfalls and other community expenses. He also hurt local commerce by seizing the pack animals of Indian traders as they passed through town, prompting them to avoid it altogether. He also speculated on the collection of first fruits from the harvest *(primicias)* and arbitrarily grabbed peasant lands.

How was this conflict resolved by the high court? Protector of Indians *(Fiscal Protector General)* Ignacio Negreiros presented the community suit before the audiencia. He held that the corregidor was operating "so as to keep the Indians oppressed and drown their clamors no matter how great his hostility," and he cited the growing number of deputy posts (tenientes) as the cause of the trouble. There had never before been such an abundance of deputies in the province—there now were twelve, with six in the ten leagues of Yungas Chapes alone—and their only real function was to collect reparto payments. He argued that Indians would be better off without them and better able to meet their tribute obligations. Citing the Laws of the Indies and a viceregal order from 1661, he recommended that Avendaño and other unnecessary deputies be suspended. He warned, "The repetition of complaints may become numerous and intolerable in the future, if a remedy is not applied at the start." But Attorney General Joseph López Lisperguer rejected the argument and insisted that the 1661 order, allowing only one lieutenant general per province, had been revoked.[10]

The intensity of the local political maneuvers can be seen in the investigation carried out by an audiencia commission. The witnesses Tomás Cavachura and Miguel Millares, Indians who had previously obtained a royal decree in favor of the community, now denied the accusations against the corregidor and deputy. They indicated that they were obliged to request the decree by the cacique and his mestizo allies without knowing the content of the complaint. The cacique had informed them that it would be easy to obtain the order since Protector Negreiros despised the corregidor. As a result, the commission concluded that the suit had been presented for private purposes, and the new protector recommended that it be dismissed.

Later, community members came forth with another suit repudiating the commission and denouncing Cavachura and Millares who, in complicity with the corregidor, had hidden a decree emitted on behalf of seven towns. For siding with the corregidor, Cavachura had been named cacique in Palca. The community repeated its charges against the deputy for his reparto excesses and fraud.[11]

The community of Chulumani rejoined the struggle in the mid-1750s, protesting the mounting abuses of the corregidor Yepes Castellanos and all his deputies, ministers, and dependents.[12] Yepes had sold the post of lieutenant general to Juan León de la Barra for ninety thousand pesos, and he in turn practiced his illicit repartos so as to ensure the success of his speculation. In the words of the plaintiffs, "Since the price was so high, he had to try to exceed it and profit at our expense and subject us to greater misery." The politicization of the process is evident from the fact that any community member who did not wish to accept the reparto commodities was branded a "rebel." The suit also revealed that the magistrates *(oidores)* and the president of the Real Audiencia had united to remove Protector Negreiros because he favored Indians and opposed the appointment of deputies. They persecuted him until achieving their aim of having him step down and depart from La Plata. The new protector, Joseph López Lisperguer, they insisted, did not defend Indians and on the contrary always favored the corregidores and others of their adversaries.[13]

The complex conflict, with the fluid dynamic of alliances and rivalries within the local elite as well as critical divisions within the communities, persisted during the 1760s.[14] In 1766, the president of the Real Audiencia, commenting upon the most recent protest in the town of Sicasica and seeking to place the blame for the general discontent upon the Junta de Corregidores in Lima, issued a warning: "If His Majesty's royal clemency . . . does not prohibit, under severe punishment, the continuation of the repartimientos, these provinces will be destroyed."[15] Yet this was not to be the last time a voice of alarm went unheeded. The conflict sharpened even more at the end of the decade, spreading across the altiplano and valleys throughout the province until culminating in the uprising in the town of Sicasica in 1769.

In 1768 and 1769, Corregidor Marqués de Villahermosa and his deputies were challenged, even by Spanish townspeople and landlords, in repeated legal suits.[16] Community resistance reached a new level when Indians accepted the proposal of Tadeo Viveros, described by his adversaries as "a mestizo . . . who works as a scribe and is known for his depraved, troublemaking character," who offered to "defend" them and draft their petitions. In 1768, with the aid of Viveros, the communities of Sicasica, Ayoayo, Calamarca, Sapahaqui, Palca, and Ocobaya organized as a united front to appear before the audiencia.[17] A broad opposition, on a provincial scale and articulated between altiplano and valleys, was now coordinated.

The towns of Palca and Ocobaya were once again central in the conflict and sites of complex political intrigue. When the judicial commission sent by the audiencia arrived in 1769 to investigate the accusations, caciques and principales declared that they were content with the conduct of the deputies and the corregidor. They complained of the meddling of the "mestizo agitators" Tadeo Viveros and Diego Catacora, who in nocturnal gatherings had suggested to a few community members that they bring suit against colonial authorities. The pair had led them to believe that the king had already issued a royal pronouncement on the communities' behalf and that Corregidor Villahermosa had a tarnished reputation in the audiencia. The "agitators" had seduced them with the illusion that they could obtain decrees freeing the Indians from the reparto. In the end, the caciques of Yungas Chapes requested that the case against the corregidor be dismissed as false. They asked that the reparto be reinstituted and that the fine goods from Castille that they had previously returned as useless be delivered back to them, saying that their wives would take advantage of them.[18]

But later that year, the Palca and Ocobaya communities once again challenged the deputies, insisting that the testimony to desist from the case had been given without their knowledge. They stated that the caciques had supported the deputies out of fear and had been induced by promises of reward. They requested that the caciques not be permitted to intervene: "Since they distribute the reparto goods and profit from it, they are against the community."[19]

As the fiscal protector general observed, the problem was that deputies were by law excluded from involvement in reparto distribution or collection functions, but they could, as local agents of justice, oblige Indians to pay their debts, including for the reparto. If deputies did indeed practice repartos themselves, it was doubtless because they had purchased their post from the corregidor with that mutually understood intention. The law allowed the corregidor a 50 percent profit over the market price for Castilian goods, but this case was one of "intolerable robbery" with a margin over 250 percent.[20]

In 1768, six principales from Sicasica spoke out against the corregidor, his treasurer in town, and the cacique of Anansaya. The cacique was a mestizo "intruder" by the name of Tomás Celada who had received Castilian wares, worth over ten thousand pesos, for their forced distribution. When Corregidor Villahermosa had tried to summon all Indians to town to deliver them the goods, the cacique advised him it would be dangerous since there was already much resistance. He suggested instead that only the hilacatas convene at the corregidor's house. To avoid rioting, the cacique would distribute the goods himself to the hilacatas and they in turn would take them to the ayllus.[21] Responding to the legal complaints, and over the objections of the "intruder" Celada, the audiencia issued orders for the recall of all unwanted items, the adjustment of prices, and the return of useless goods to the corregidor. It also named another interim cacique, Fermín Paticallisaya, as a substitute for Celada.[22]

In neighboring Ayoayo, Indian authorities and principales stood up against both their caciques. They protested the corregidor's reparto and denounced the Anansaya cacique, Diego Olarte, because he collaborated with Villahermosa. For example, Olarte kept accounts of Indians for greater efficiency in the reparto and attempted to prevent the community from appearing before the magistrate in the audiencia's commission. They asserted, "[Olarte] is the cause of the disturbance, and he is responsible for all the confusion and chimeras."[23] The other cacique, Felipe Alvarez, whose cacicazgo property had been confirmed by the viceroy in 1749 and who descended from the Chipana cacique lineage, had already been convicted in 1763 for serving as a deputy under Corregidor Yepes Castellanos and committing various excesses in the reparto. Finally in 1769, after a local conflict in which the parish priest was killed, he retired from the post, "lacking the strength to contain and repress the arrogance of these people who are so insolent because of the impunity they have enjoyed in their misdeeds."[24]

The intensity of the conflict grew in mid-1769 with an open confrontation in Mohoza. According to witnesses, Deputy Josef Pardo de Figueroa arrested the Indian Miguel Colque for having complained (along with other community members) in April of that year against Figueroa for the repartos to Indians, mestizos, Spaniards, the elderly, and poor widows. Employing threats and corporal punishment, the deputy sought to discover who was behind the complaint. Figueroa was unable to break Colque's resistance before other Indians interrupted the torture and rescued him. Raising the alarm of an uprising, Figueroa took refuge in the church, which was held under siege for several days by community members. Indians finally withdrew from the town only after the corregidor arrived and acknowledged that the deputy's tyranny had provoked the disturbance. After collecting the goods distributed, he marched on to Yungas with the same purpose of pacifying the populace.[25]

In his defense, the deputy blamed the cacique Marcos Santos Quinaquina for upsetting the town and trying to take his life. But the new commissioner, Dr. Juan Antonio de Castro, named by the audiencia in August of 1769 to investigate the case, determined that Figueroa had committed "incredible excesses" in the town, serving himself of people and property as if he were their owner. His general opinion of deputies was severe: "They had no intention of administering justice, but only of showing off their sovereignty and oppressing Indians while advancing their own interests."[26]

Commissioner Castro pursued his investigation of the many accusations against deputies involved in repartos. The case of Deputy Josef Antonio Talavera drew his attention for several reasons.[27] First of all, there were suits against him in Cavari and Suri. It is worth noting, as well, that in the new town of Inquisivi, still attached to the ecclesiastical jurisdiction of Cavari, the cacique Diego Alcala Sacari lamented to the corregidor that the Indians "persecute me, insisting that I consented to the reparto that was forced upon them by Deputy don Joseph Talavera. . . . I, sir, am not to blame, so that they should refuse to pay me their tributes because of this reparto." Other Spanish witnesses confirmed that they denied him tribute and were at the point of revolt precisely because the cacique "does not defend them from the reparto."[28]

Second, Corregidor Villahermosa already had recognized diverse charges against Talavera in his edict of June 1769.[29] Because of the protests, he was aware of "the oppression suffered [by his subjects] due to the tyranny with which his deputies had distributed goods in his name." In order to "avoid in the future any threat of uprising like the one in Mohoza," he named in Cavari and Suri an alcalde supposedly to administer justice but evidently, above all, to maintain public order. He also installed a new collector to secure his reparto interests. Admitting the abuses of Talavera, he ordered that the distributed goods be recalled and assured the populace that with this measure there would be no more complaints.[30] On this last point, the corregidor was correct in a certain sense despite his bad faith: for all intents and purposes, the communities had virtually exhausted the benefits of legal recourse. However the new aggressions of Villahermosa and his agents, including Talavera himself, would sweep the process, soon thereafter, toward an outbreak even more violent than the one in Mohoza.

Despite prohibitions against it, the corregidor circulated throughout the agitated province from the month of August on. He collected reparto payments violently, seized property, and shut down the stores and houses of those who failed to cancel their debts, especially in the capital of Sicasica. At the same time, the new commissioner Castro inspected the towns and inquired into the conduct of royal authorities. Alejandro Chuquiguaman, an Indian with cape and staff who was accompanied by a troop of peasants, engaged the commissioner in Yaco in order to observe his procedures. Chuquiguaman told him to travel to the town of Sicasica, where he was cacique, in order to recall the goods distributed there. When Castro replied that he could not receive clothing and iron products since they were allowed by law, Chuquiguaman, whose influence extended to the jurisdictions of Ayoayo, Calamarca, Palca, and Sapahaqui, remained in Yaco inciting the Indians to return their goods until Castro commanded him to withdraw. Sensitive to the "signs of uprising," the Real Audiencia feared that the suspect cacique could prompt a riot if the items were not collected.[31]

In November, Chuquiguaman and the eleven hilacatas of Anansaya from the town of Sicasica objected to the abuses of Manuel Solascasas, Villahermosa's commissioned magistrate and reparto collector.[32] He was accused, among other things, of manipulating the three alcaldes of the town and arbitrarily depriving them of their staffs. He had battered alcalde Pascual Copa with his own staff until it shattered into pieces. With the population now thoroughly riled up, warnings of uprising began to be heard.[33]

In anticipation of the tribute payment due at year's end, Chuquiguaman and seven hilacatas traveled directly to the royal treasury in La Paz in order to deliver their tax. They suspected that if they delivered it to the corregidor, he might appropriate it as a debt payment for the repartos and deny having received any tribute. Villahermosa sent Josef Talavera and twenty soldiers out to the ayllus supposedly to collect the tribute but with the actual mission of arresting and seizing the property of the hilacatas. They also grabbed the treasury receipts for the tribute delivered. Provoked by the violence of the soldiers, who were dispatched on three different occasions by Villahermosa, the Indians resolved to form a single force and directly confront the authorities.[34]

On December 22, a contingent of some one hundred community members commanded by Chuquiguaman descended from Collana ayllu down to the town. Initially they sought the corregidor to recover their tribute receipts, but Villahermosa, warned of the mobilization, had fled to La Paz only shortly before. They then headed to the residence of his reparto collector Solascasas to demand return of the receipts. When he denied them an audience, they made known their accusations against him and finally the exasperated official shot off his firearm, intending to end the unrest and disperse the hostile crowd. With some community members wounded by the attack, the crowd charged the house, broke in, and beat and stoned Solascasas to death. The Indians then reassembled in the plaza where, witnesses reported, they used their slings to stone the stores, circled about triumphantly, and rang the church bell in celebration. They broke down the jail door to free an hilacata detained for tributary debt as well as the other prisoners. Josef Talavera testified that he escaped with his life by hiding in the home of a townswoman while the Indians searched for other Spaniards to execute.[35]

After the uprising, Commissioner Castro continued his investigation in the midst of warnings that other towns in the province were at the point of revolting and that mere mention of the corregidor's name stirred unrest in some parts.[36] The origin of the Sicasica incident was attributed to the corregidor first of all because of his continual sallies to the provincial interior, against the court's dispositions, to collect his debts with the pretext of tribute. Deputy Josef Talavera was also held responsible because of his repartos, violence, and community weariness of his abuses. In the end, the indicted individuals were the corregidor, the deputy, the deceased collector Solascasas, as well as the insubordinate cacique Alejandro Chuquiguaman. Commissioner Castro reached the conclusion that there was no need for deputies of the corregidor in the towns, and the court deemed "well founded the clamor of provincial residents and the legal complaints presented in this Real Audiencia."[37]

Despite these apparently unambiguous findings, colonial justice and administration did not adopt measures suited to the seriousness of the moment. The audiencia admitted that individual excesses had been committed, but it did not recognize the structural nature of the conflict. After lengthy inquiries into the facts as well as reports and testimony presented in his defense by the corregidor, Villahermosa never received punishment. In July of 1770, the audiencia ordered the corregidor to return from La Paz to govern his province, procure public order, and collect his reparto payments without violence or price inflation.[38] Due to this negligence by the state when faced with an already critical situation, colonial power would be jolted by an even more powerful insurgency in Yungas soon thereafter.

When Commissioner Castro sought to enter the towns of Yungas in late 1769, he was impeded by the aggressive actions of Lieutenant General Juan Ignacio Larrea, who accused him of trying to stir up the population. Forced to withdraw from the area, Castro reported that the lieutenant general's intent was to cover up the iniquitous reparto. The commissioner remained convinced that in Yungas "there reigned the greatest tyranny and disorder in the reparto, and the people there were the most worn down with the severity of the debt collection." He submitted eight petitions containing the complaints of Chulumani Indians and indicated that many other Indians from communities in the area, who had caught up with the commissioner in Chupe, had their papers confiscated by Larrea.[39]

The general uprising of Yungas communities in 1771 brings to a close this first cycle of political conflict. In this reconstruction of the cycle from 1740 to 1770, we began with the towns of Chulumani and Chupe. Now in the culminating moment, let us return to them. The corregidor asserted that the communities of Yanacachi, Milluguaya, Irupana, Laza, Ocobaya, Chirca, Coripata, and others in Yungas participated in the insurgency, as did the Indians of the haciendas. According to another source, all of the Indians from the Yungas towns rose up with the assistance of other Indians from altiplano towns. The principal protagonists, however, were the two communities of Chulumani and Chupe.[40]

As all the participants recognized, the fundamental cause of the uprising was the corregidor and his system of repartos. Yet the second factor cited as a cause was the battle for the cacicazgo in the town of Chupe.

The corregidor and Lieutenant General Larrea attempted to impose Clemente Escobar Cullo Inga as cacique against the will of the community. Escobar was rejected for being the compadre of Larrea and favored by him in the reparto, for being "mulatto" or "zambo" and hence racially unfit, for seizing coca fields from peasants, and, above all according to Indian witnesses, for being "harmful" to them. When Prebendary Dr. Santiago de Querejazu together with the priest of Chupe admonished the principales in the presence of most of the community to obey Escobar, they answered that they would never accept him as cacique. They would only follow Simón González, "since González protected them and don Clemente Escobar did not."[41] Since at least early 1771, Simón González and the principales had waged a tenacious campaign in La Plata, sustained by the donations of the Indians, to have González recognized as the legitimate cacique. Different contingents of community members had traveled to the audiencia to present their case, and in retribution the corregidor had successfully obtained González's imprisonment at the royal court.

Several days after the visit of Prebendary Querejazu, rumors flew that the corregidor was preparing soldiers in Chulumani for a march on Chupe to grant Escobar possession of the cacicazgo. The principales instructed community members "that no one appear in town, so as to resist the cacique's reception and to avoid punishments since [Villahermosa] was coming with soldiers." They fell back into the hills and only later learned that Escobar's ceremony had taken place with no Indians present.

According to another source, the corregidor ordered some of them together and compelled them to render obeisance to Escobar. It was precisely at the time of this test of forces that the uprising in Chulumani occurred. Spanish witnesses later testified to having heard Indians say that Clemente Escobar was the cause of the tumult "because he insisted to the corregidor on a rupture *(rompimiento)*." We can imagine that the beleaguered cacique advocated wiping out, once and for all, the obstinate resistance and ungovernable effrontery of the Indians.[42]

At the same time the corregidor granted cacicazgo possession to Clemente Escobar in Chupe, he arrested two alcaldes, Lorenzo Apata of Chupe and Sebastián Coloma of Chulumani, because of the suit they brought against him in the Real Audiencia. This was the third cause of the uprising according to the testimony. During a general assembly at Río Yarija, Chupe Indians took the decision to forgo new legal proceedings in the distant city of La Plata, with undoubtedly delayed and possibly empty results, and to march directly to Chulumani to liberate the authorities from prison. Community member Diego Esquia testified that the Chulumani Indians invited them "to form a single body with them and go to war." A second contingent of thirty to forty people headed for the Chupe bridge to block the soldiers marching from Chulumani toward their community.[43]

For the Chulumani community, the jailing of the alcaldes was only the latest in a long series of provocations. As he had done in 1769 in the town of Sicasica, Villahermosa and his collectors repeatedly entered Chulumani to exact reparto payments through force, even though royal edicts, obtained with great sacrifice by the community, prohibited him from doing so. But in mid-1771, with the armed confederate movement headed by Juan Tapia, community struggle took on a new political nature. Besieging the town from the Alto de Guancané, the Indians would not settle for the deal offered by Villahermosa to free the alcaldes and withdraw himself from town in exchange for the withdrawal of the mutinied Indians. They captured the deputy of Coroico, Juan Calderón, and seized his arms as he approached town with a small guard. They played fife and drum, waved banners, and shouted loudly as they threatened to overwhelm the town.

Witnesses stated that the Indians raised gallows above the town and grew increasingly excited, "crying 'Thieves!' 'Scoundrels!' and other expressions against the Marqués [de Villahermosa], deputies, and allies, promising that now they would see who was who and would drink chicha in their skulls." According to the same witnesses, Tapia had affirmed before the movement began that "it was time to free themselves from the oppression of the Spaniards." In a demonstration of their confidence in their project, the Indians had named captains for the war and Juan Tapia as general as well as new authorities for the postinsurgency government: Mateo Poma, king; Juan Tapia, corregidor; Gregorio Machicado, lieutenant general; Juan Ordoñez, cacique. Given the degree of coordination and obedience to the leadership, it was assumed that the movement was premeditated.[44]

After a tense engagement over several days, the corregidor launched a counterattack. His soldiers erupted outside the town killing more than thirty Indians and wounding many more. Villahermosa ordered the death of some, including the alcalde Apata of Chupe, and hung the wounded. He had the cadavers quartered and displayed their members at symbolic sites to terrify the population.[45]

If the Chupe cacicazgo was a key factor in the mobilization, what role did the hereditary cacique of Chulumani, Dionicio Mamani, play during the uprising? Shortly beforehand, there had been an exchange of letters between Mamani and Juan Tapia that revealed just how removed the cacique was from his community. Mamani wrote to Tapia asking him why the Indians became so upset upon seeing soldiers. Tapia wrote to the cacique for his support, but it was denied him.[46]

During the confrontation, Dionicio Mamani and the second cacique of Chulumani, Sebastián Trujillo, together with the parish priest climbed to the Indian camp in an effort to dissuade the communities from descending upon the town. But in the end, the intermediary position between community and state that the cacique wished to occupy was lacking in political coherence. Under these historical circumstances, such a role might have been appropriate for a priest, yet for a cacique it represented a neutrality that was false in the eyes of community members. During the parley, which was destined for failure, "the Indians began to shout at don Dionicio Mamani that as their cacique he did not defend them." In his own defense later, the cacique maintained that "he had not proceeded against the Indians as they imputed, but rather he dealt diligently and effectively with the corregidor, deputies, and the priest, and with the Indians themselves, with the aim of pacifying the disturbances, which was his sole aspiration."[47]

The case of Dionicio Mamani serves to confirm that the crisis of legitimacy afflicting the cacicazgo institution involved both "blood" lineages as well as "intruder" caciques like Clemente Escobar, who were imposed by colonial powers above all for the conjunctural interests of the reparto. On this point, we may differ from the hypothesis that "the hereditary legitimacy of the post was undermined and that the entire cacique system red into crisis" due to the appointment of "intruders" named by the ...egidor.[48] The legitimacy of the post suffered not only because of external impositions but also because of the conduct of hereditary caciques themselves and their conflicts within the community.

Furthermore, the case of Dionicio Mamani, like that of others noted in this provincial cycle, yields the key criterion for understanding politically the problem of cacique legitimacy and its questioning by communities. It was not a matter, in this specific period and place, of the familiar historiographic criteria of "acculturation," or of private accumulation and economic reciprocity. Nor was it a matter of the lineage criterion, that is, "blood" inheritance or "ethnic" prestige. Rather, the decisive factor in the vision of Indians was whether the cacique fulfilled his obligation to defend the community or not. In the colonial context, polarized between communities and the regional apparatus of colonial power, the most urgent criterion of cacique legitimacy seen from below was that of practical political identification.

In order to clarify this argument about the political identification of caciques, we must look at the anomalies, those caciques who (unlike the majority who fell silent or collaborated and proved loyal to the colonial state in moments of extreme crisis) did stand in solidarity with their communities in the struggle against corregidores and the reparto. We noted above the case of Casimiro Andrade, the cacique of Palca who in the mid-1750s supported the legal struggle of his community. After holding out for a time, however, in the words of community members, "our cacique has become intimidated . . . so that now he does not want to act as our patron, as is his obligation." They added, "Since he is completely oppressed by the severe hand of General don Eusebio Yepes and his deputy don Francisco Xavier Avendaño, he has forsaken us."[49] It is likely that this type of solidarity in the legal protest would have been less of a risk while landlords and Spanish townspeople were also involved in the complaints and prior to the stage of greater polarization and violence. Obviously responding to pressure from below, various caciques signed petitions in the name of their communities to protest against abuses by the authorities, especially those of the new deputies who would have been superior rivals within the hierarchy of local power.[50] But in any case, caciques like Casimiro Andrade of Palca disappeared with the subsequent development of the conflicts.[51]

When we look at the cases of caciques whose commitment went beyond judicial action, it is notable that Marcos Santos Quinaquina, the alleged leader of the community reaction against Deputy Pardo de Figueroa in Mohoza in mid-1769, asked permission of the Real Audiencia to step down from his post immediately thereafter.[52] The cacique of Sicasica, Alejandro Chuquiguaman, preserved his freedom for a time despite repeated orders for his arrest, and he once escaped in Oruro when his captors were taking him to the royal jail in La Plata. However, after the 1769 uprising he did not exercise his post, and he was finally taken prisoner and sentenced to six years' labor in a textile workshop and an additional four years of exile from the province.[53]

The rival of Clemente Escobar and pretender to the Chupe cacicazgo, Simón González, was free of responsibility for the Chulumani mobilization in 1771, since he was in La Plata at the time. But after returning to his town, the acute conflict between the community and cacique Escobar, who was ritual kin of the lieutenant general, exploded in an incident that would have cost Escobar his life if it had not been for the intervention of the priest. The corregidor accused González of fomenting rebellion among Indians in Chupe, and finally he was sentenced by the audiencia to the same punishment as Alejandro Chuquiguaman.[54]

In synthesis, as the pressure increased upon the key post of the cacicazgo, the great majority of caciques, including hereditary rulers, adopted a stance of collaboration, whether willing or reticent, with colonial authority. While some independent caciques initially resisted the corregidor, their resistance set off a relentless campaign to co-opt them or, if this were not possible, to remove them and substitute others who would be properly subordinate. The few caciques who acted as defenders of the community eventually were forced to withdraw from their office or suffer the penalties of royal justice. We can imagine the influence exerted by their example: other caciques who might have wavered in their loyalties would ultimately be led to conclude that independence was untenable.

The process of political redefinition of caciques, deriving from the dynamics of reparto coercion and resistance from midcentury up until 1780, fed into the cacicazgo and cacique-community conflicts we have already examined.[55] It was this decisive conjunctural process that clinched the crisis of the cacicazgo and set the conditions for cacique "royalism" during the epochal insurrection of 1781.[56] Corregidor control over the post and the historical lesson of the earlier moments of extreme polarization substantially determined the fact that scarcely a single cacique participated in the massive mobilization led by Túpaj Katari in La Paz.[57] Many established caciques had reason to resent the challenge posed to their authority by rebels and radicals. Yet even potential sympathizers knew that no cacique could side with the community and survive retribution from the state. Hence many caciques elected to take up arms in defense not of their community but of the king. One decade after the Chulumani insurgency of 1771, hereditary patriarch Dionicio Mamani earned the recognition of Commander Sebastián de Segurola for his services to the Crown during the war.[58] Yet the acuteness of the cacicazgo crisis did not make royalism a secure option either. Dionicio Mamani died on the battlefield outside La Paz, just as other cacique governors and their families fell under the assault of their own communities.

Though we have followed the story only to 1771, the historical cycle examined in Sicasica is representative of the La Paz region as a whole. Its critical elements—the repartos and the transformation in the regional power structure, the growing wave of community mobilizations, and the political definition of caciques—were found throughout the provinces. The processes of politicization and polarization that culminated in the Chulumani insurgency and its project for a newly constituted Indian government matched the wider regional cycle that culminated in 1781 with Katari's radical anticolonial movement. The story may be concluded now with a glimpse at the rest of the region and the final decade of prolific and dramatic struggle.

The cycle elsewhere in La Paz also began to build in the 1740s. In Pacajes, several corregidor interventions in cacicazgo disputes provoked resentment, for example when Francisco de Sosa appointed one interim cacique said to be illegitimate and "of his [Sosa's] faction" in Jesús de Machaca.[59] We have already seen how cacique-corregidor alliances and the reparto were bound up with intracommunity struggles in Calacoto where Juan Machaca sided with Corregidor Zegarra, who intended to apply tribute payments toward the reparto debts owed to him by Indians.[60]

At the same time in the late 1740s, Francisco Sensano, the cacique of Zepita in Chucuito province, came under fire from his community for a series of abuses and for his complicity in the reparto. He was first named, and subsequently backed, by the corregidores precisely for his compliance and willingness to ensure their interests. They ignored edicts banning mestizo caciques like Sensano, who "has won the favor of the corregidores at the price of our sweat and labor." Among the accusations, Sensano was said to have donated a considerable sum to one corregidor to help him purchase a two-year extension of his term. With the corregidor's protection, Sensano could then take even greater advantage of community members. His immediate ally and patron was Miguel Indapuyana, the reparto collector of different corregidores. In exchange for Indapuyana's backing, the cacique supplied him with food and other gifts, including an entire ayllu, which was obliged to provide pongo servants in the Guacullani mining camp.[61]

In Yunguyo (Chucuito), the corregidor maintained Bartolomé Cachicatari as cacique for the purposes of his reparto, while others in the community backed the claim of his cousin Pedro Cachicatari and lamented "the ambition of the corregidores of these provinces, which is like an introduced plague." After hilacatas exposed the tribute fraud of the corregidor's client, they were arrested and, at another point, a pitched battle that ensued between the two factions left three dead and many others injured. In 1755, the Yunguyo case prompted Indian Protector Negreiros to denounce the "tyranny, insatiable ambition, despotism, and hostility with which corregidores routinely proceed in their provinces." He added, "There are clear proofs of this in a number of the cases brought before this Real Audiencia."[62]

The valleys of Larecaja were the site of especially notable struggles in the early to mid-1750s. They began in Ambaná, specifically in the estancia of Chuani, Anansaya moiety, where there lived an insubordinate "nation," estimated at some fifty people, said to be originally mitmaq families from near Marangani (Canas y Canchis province, in the Bishopric of Cusco) who remained there to escape the mita. In 1749, led by Diego Palli, the Indians dared to challenge Dr. Martín de Landaeta, parish priest, landlord, "perpetual tithe collector," and the most imposing figure in the local power structure. This quickly earned them the enmity of the Church, which accused them of rebelling against both civil and religious order: they refused to pay tribute, perform labor services in town, or recognize the authority of caciques and magistrates; they refused to offer tithes, attend mass and confession, pay parish fees, bury their dead in the church cemetery, or recognize and serve their priest.

In 1753, with Landaeta now a ranking canon in the cathedral of La Paz, the ecclesiastical investigation was resumed. But Chuani Indians filed a new suit of their own, this time against Diego Cristóbal Gemio, who had been appointed town deputy by the corregidor at the behest of Landaeta. At the same time, Gemio was now the acting, and often abusive, collector of local tithes. After returning from La Plata with an edict prohibiting further excesses by Gemio, community leaders Diego Palli and Diego Cutili became the object of implacable vengeance. Palli was beaten, "leaving him looking like a monster," when he would not consent to burning the papers from the audiencia. He was sentenced to one hundred public lashes and six years of forced labor in a textile workshop (the proposed sentence was later raised to perpetuity). Gemio also seized the subsistence resources of comrades and family, forcing them to flee the area. When his lackeys were unable to locate Diego Cutili, they captured his wife and two oldest sons.[63]

The Chuani struggle was inspired by the mobilizations and ambitious designs of Indian rebels in Azángaro in the late 1730s,[64] and it expressed a radical anticolonial project. The leaders were seen as "saviors" *(redentores)*[65] of the Indians, and they did in fact employ a discourse of emancipation. When they circulated from hacienda to hacienda to raise money, enjoying obvious local support, they assured laborers that "they could all recover the liberty necessary for themselves." They also nourished a vital historical memory of autonomy prior to the conquest, declaring that the movement's aim was to "restore to them their liberty." For the rebels, political liberty coincided with religious liberty. When Pascual Palli, Diego's brother and alcalde in 1750, stepped forth with his staff to prevent some Indians from going to mass, he asserted that they had been "liberated" from attending church ceremonies. In the same way, they considered themselves "free" from tithe taxation. Anansaya cacique Lorenzo Corina explained the aspirations of the Chuani Indians: they planned "to wipe out or dominate the Spaniards *(viracochas)*" and believed that "they are the saviors of the town and through force will overcome everyone, even those of the province, because it is their turn to rule."[66]

The Chuani Indians were seen as a genuine threat by local notables. Not only did Deputy Gemio react in self-defense, but Dr. Landaeta personally saw that they were prosecuted. Spanish landlords and townspeople united to present their case against the rebels. The cacique, who was helpless to control them and was blamed for their disturbances, also spoke out against the Chuani clan.[67] The concern over their influence was indeed justified. They had the support of other Indians in surrounding areas, and tithe resistance stirred the province of Paucarcolla at the same time. By the middle 1750s, Larecaja was caught in its worst bout of unrest. In an escalating, increasingly complex case of conflict, Indians in Italaque and Mocomoco protested against illegitimate caciques in each of their communities and joined together to oppose their lieutenant general who organized the local repartos and who manipulated the cacicazgos for his own ends. In 1755, the priest of Mocomoco, and uncle of Lieutenant General Diego de Torres, wrote in alarm that Indians had taken up arms to resist tithe collection. He appealed for urgent action, "before the hostility in this and other towns becomes generalized insolence."[68]

In Omasuyos in the early 1750s, we find typical cases of caciques under fire within their communities and maintained by a corregidor whose primary interest was reparto accumulation. The most prominent case of collusion was that between Corregidor Martín Vértiz Verea and the cacique of Laja, Tiburcio Fernández. When Indians from Maasaya Collana stood behind a rival to the cacicazgo, Bernardo Garfias, the corregidor, his scribe, and Fernández responded with litigation against Garfias and the insubordinate community members. The cacique was finally forced out of office, but when the corregidor sought to replace him with a close kin associate, it set off more community opposition.[69] In Guaycho, cacique Sebastián Nina cut a deal with the corregidor for more than five hundred pesos to suppress a decree against illegal repartos that he had obtained in 1753.[70]

The mid-1750s was a time of trouble for colonial authority in much of La Paz. We noted this already in Larecaja province, and Achacachi in 1755 was the site of an uprising against Vértiz Verea's reparto.[71] Concerned about the turmoil in nearby Laja and Achacachi and fearful of an outbreak of violence in his own province, the Pacajes corregidor refrained from punishing Indians in Viacha for their disrespectful conduct toward him.[72] The Crown itself felt compelled to address the abuses of Vértiz Verea, his son Francisco (who was responsible for the death of three Indians in Achacachi), and Deputy Diego de Torres in Larecaja, as well as the protection provided them by the magistrates of the Real Audiencia.[73]

The Omasuyos corregidores also came to be involved in a rash of disputes with provincial caciques that ultimately derived from the reparto distribution and collection system. Not only was Vértiz Verea under investigation for the Achacachi incident, but the colonial government held him responsible for provincial tribute arrears. He, however, passed the blame on to his own purported debtors, including caciques in Achacachi and Guaycho. Both Achacachi caciques, Pascual Arenas and Eugenio Verástegui, were jailed and had their property confiscated to pay off the corregidor's tribute debts. Arenas protested that he had duly met all tribute payments but that Vértiz Verea had embezzled the money for his reparto debts.

The corregidor claimed that the cacique was also personally responsible for the reparto money owed him: "He is the one who should pay it and not the [Indian] collectors, because that is the practice and custom in this province and all the others, . . . because these collectors are designated by Pascual Arenas." The cacique denied any financial obligation: "We caciques never assume the responsibility of paying off the value of those goods. They are only given to us in order to be distributed, with proper record taken, to the principales in each town according to their possibilities and the number of people under them. They then pay the corregidor or his debt collectors by installments. . . . I am nothing but a mere *mayordomo* or distributor of the goods. . . . I take on no individual obligation, nor am I fit to do so (as the royal laws stipulate, those of my condition are unable to contract substantial debts)."[74]

This instability in the provincial reparto system persisted under the new corregidor, Antonio Calonje. In 1759, a former interim cacique from Laja, Isidro Quespi, brought charges against Calonje for his excessive reparto and for not paying him the 4 percent commission on sales owed to caciques for distributing the commodities. That same year, the community brought a separate suit against Calonje for his reparto, and a riot resulted in the deaths of a court investigator and some of his company.[75]

In 1760, Laja cacique Ildefonso Fernández Chui challenged Calonje before the audiencia on behalf of himself and Carabuco cacique Agustín Siñani. After antagonism had mounted between Fernández Chui and the corregidor, Calonje allegedly misappropriated Laja tribute money and ordered the cacique's arrest for tribute default. The cacique fled to La Plata where he presented a list of illicit practices by Calonje that harmed Indians, caciques, and the Real Hacienda. The critical grievances were that the corregidor forced the caciques to distribute goods against their will and that he misappropriated tribute money for the reparto. He concluded by demanding that the corregidor pay him the 4 percent sales commission and that caciques no longer be expected to administer repartos. Calonje denied the charges and countered that the caciques bought the wares from the corregidor and distributed them at their own risk and for their own profit. They also used the money collected for their own commercial transactions before reimbursing the corregidor.

A year after the initial complaints filed by Fernández Chui, and shortly before the corregidor's term ended, the segundas personas and hilacatas from Carabuco directly accused Calonje of illegally overcharging them, thus leaving them in debt to their cacique. Agustín Siñani also now personally appeared before officials in La Paz to insist that Calonje should repay the excess amount as well as grant him his 4 percent commission. The corregidor could not prove that he had sold the reparto wares to Siñani, but he claimed that he owed Siñani no extra salary since the distribution was a "small service" rendered as "mere gratification." Siñani's reply was sharp: "General don Antonio has never been my benefactor that I should do his bidding in such an arduous task and proffer services without stipend. . . . The imperious corregidor coerced and obliged me to take up the reparto and the lofty collection of twelve thousand pesos in so small and miserable a town. The appeals of the powerful bring forced obedience, so one may not infer I would have done so gratuitously." The court eventually ruled in Siñani's favor and the retired corregidor, facing other legal charges for abuses and saddled with unpayable debts, fled the province in desperation.[76]

The situation in Omasuyos from the late 1750s to mid-1760s is particularly interesting since it suggests a relative contrast to the pattern of provincial power relations exemplified in Sicasica. In Omasuyos, caciques played a more important role as reparto collectors than in Sicasica, where lieutenants and deputies were more numerous and intervened more aggressively.[77] The Omasuyos corregidores controlled a less imposing apparatus and were apparently less successful at illicit accumulation (the material basis for accumulation was more advantageous in the coca-growing Yungas valleys). Undermined by debt, Vértiz Verea fell on the defensive by the end of his term, and Calonje absconded, taking his family with him. One hacendado, embroiled in a land dispute with Indians in Guarina, complained that the subsequent corregidor, Ventura Santizo, even indulged communities, "since the satisfaction of his reparto interests depends upon keeping the Indians and caciques content."[78]

It is true that in Sicasica there were also moments of breakdown in the corregidor's extractive apparatus, with internecine strife over debts and accounts ensuing between the corregidor and his agents. This occurred mainly in the 1770s when commercial capital relations became overextended as local markets grew saturated (despite the extent of their artificial and violent reproduction) and political disputes consumed the regional elite.

It would also be a mistake to exaggerate the boldness of Omasuyos caciques or their commitment to their communities. As reparto "mayordomos," to use the expression of cacique Pascual Arenas, they might have been able to prevent some of the egregious practices of reparto agents in Sicasica, and their legal challenges did help to undermine the position of the corregidores. Yet their relation to the provincial governor was one of interdependence and not without economic self-interest. Other business transactions aside, their 4 percent reparto commissions were worth approximately five hundred pesos to caciques Quespi and Siñani. Arenas entered the legal arena as a last resort, in self-defense and seeking individual salvation; in denying any personal financial responsibility, he only shifted the burden of debt to subordinate community authorities. Fernández Chui also acted after becoming a fugitive under threat of arrest. Siñani did not put himself at the head of the community's legal protest over reparto abuses, but sought primarily a private settling of accounts, including his share of the reparto profits, as the vulnerable Calonje was leaving office.[79]

In this phase then, Omasuyos was the scene of significant jockeying for local control. Corregidores applied strong pressure upon cacicazgos, while lacking fully consolidated power; caciques, accustomed to collaboration with their governors, reacted against the more direct threats to their personal wealth and position, without leading community legal protests or base-level mobilizations. In Sicasica, as we saw, there were isolated cases of caciques who resisted or challenged corregidores, but these were never enough to qualify the full force of the constituted provincial regime. In Omasuyos, the power of corregidores did not attain the same scale and consistency, and caciques were not so thoroughly co-opted, shunted aside, or crushed as were the occasional holdouts and renegades in Sicasica.[80] In this sense, Omasuyos in this period does not contradict the somewhat stark Sicasica case, whose features generally characterized the region and the time, but it does reflect Sicasica's limits as a model.

Elsewhere in the 1760s, there were ongoing, simultaneous conflicts between communities, caciques and cacicazgo pretenders, and state or other local authorities. We have already noted in Calacoto how community struggles involving caciques and repartos overlapped and intersected in the early part of the decade. The evidence for the rest of Pacajes primarily indicates community disgruntlement with caciques and fits our picture of limited cacique defense of their subjects.

New disturbances also rattled Chucuito province. When Corregidor Juan Joseph de Herrera sought to update tribute rolls and collect payment from the Zepita community, he proceeded to depose and jail cacique Pedro Sensano for lack of cooperation. His intervention provoked skirmishes and his designated substitutes met with sharp rejection. Bartolomé Cachicatari (who was previously embroiled in conflicts with the Yunguyo community) received repeated death threats and Joseph Chambilla fled town as collection time approached. Later in Pomata, Indians captured Bueno Mantilla, an official sent by the corregidor to collect tribute and reparto payments, and dispatched him to Puno. They apparently believed that they were no longer subject to the reparto and other burdensome exactions.[81]

The 1769 mobilization in the town of Sicasica, which ended in the death of the corregidor's agent Manuel de Solascasas, was followed by a new tide of insurgency in 1771. As we saw, the town of Chulumani was besieged by a confederation of communities whose leaders envisioned a new political order under Indian control. And finally, in November 1771, peasants in Jesús de Machaca killed their corregidor, Josef del Castillo, and the provincial capital of Pacajes, Caquiaviri, was taken over by Indian forces.

It was a time of turbulence in Pacajes. Recently, Indians in Curaguara attacked the cacique named for them by the corregidor. Also, Guaqui cacique Pedro Limachi had dared to challenge Castillo in the courts and had been jailed by him in retribution. When Castillo learned that Limachi had been freed and absolved of wrongdoing by the audiencia's commissioner, he set out toward Guaqui with the aim of seizing the cacique's property. On All Souls' Day (November 2), the corregidor and a small party found themselves in Jesús de Machaca and requisitioned mules for their journey from a tipsy festival celebrant. The woman did not prove submissive, however, and she began to berate him in anger. The governor responded by having her whipped, which in turn brought forth her husband, equally inebriated, to protest the violence. When the corregidor's lackey, an ex-cacique of the town by the name of Paucarpata, turned upon the husband, the woman continued haranguing the governor. Castillo began to strike the crowd with his staff and sword, causing greater numbers of Indians to join the fray. He then retreated to the cacique's house, but the furious crowd set fire to it. After breaking in through a window, they dragged their victims out for vengeance. They first smashed the skull of Paucarpata, beat the corregidor to death with iron bars, and dispatched several others in his band. The cacique's wife also perished from fright.

Word of the trouble spread quickly. The next day a contingent of sixty townspeople from Caquiaviri set out to assist Castillo and put down the mutiny. Before they arrived, however, they learned that the corregidor was dead and that the peasants were ready to do battle with them. Unarmed and alarmed, they turned back to the capital only to find that the community there was now in league with the Indians of Machaca. After taking the townspeople (including the cacica Nicolasa Sirpa, her children, and the son of the cacique from Viacha) as prisoners, the insurgents were faced with a major dilemma: what step to take next.

Over the following days, they cut off roads and communication with the city while debating the alternatives, including a massacre of all Spaniards and an armed march on La Paz. The corregidor in La Paz, Vicente Lafita, considered the "universal uprising" in Pacajes a calamity that threatened to spread throughout the rest of the district. His fear was founded upon the open and exposed geography of the city—surrounded by Indian provinces on all sides and by Indian parishes within the urban basin itself—and upon the memory of the sacking of the city in 1661. La Paz was also poorly prepared to engage in combat. The corregidor set about readying militias, yet weaponry was scant and he met with initial resistance. By the end of the year, order was still not fully restored in Pacajes and its capital.[82]

As in Chulumani earlier that year, events in Pacajes constituted a powerful experience that posed the prospect of radical social transformation. If the Pacajes communities were also caught somewhat unprepared by the turn of circumstances and their own sudden control, the episode was in some ways a rehearsal for 1781. It evidently galvanized consciousness and clandestine organization among a set of politicized and bold Aymara who would become future insurrectionary cadre. Túpaj Katari himself—a tributary of Ayoayo, the town next to Sicasica where the 1769 mobilization had taken place—was approximately twenty at the time, and in 1781 his wife acknowledged that his campaign had been conceived of ten years earlier. In his own testimony, Katari compared the unfolding of events and Aymara tactics during the siege of La Paz with the 1771 episode.[83]

The year 1771 was, then, a crucial moment in eighteenth-century struggles and one that left its mark upon the minds of Indians throughout the region.[84] Its significance was not lost upon colonial elites either. Corregidores in the region saw ominous signs and other La Paz authorities felt that only a major overhaul of the reparto system would avert greater disaster. Both treasury administrator Pedro Nolasco Crespo and Bishop Gregorio Francisco Campos recommended abolishing the system altogether and raising Indian tribute in order to provide corregidores with an adequate salary. Viceroy Manuel de Amat y Junient acknowledged that reparto abuses were the cause of the social unrest, and back in Madrid the magistrate of the Council of the Indies likewise recognized that desperation over the abuses and disillusionment with the courts were responsible for the threat to the kingdom of Peru. At every level, then, the reverberations of events in La Paz were registered, and a debate over the reparto was openly conducted through the 1770s. Yet the highest echelons of the colonial state stopped short of dismantling the lucrative reparto system until nearly a decade later when the general insurrection was already upon them. Substantive measures were never taken to modify the formal and informal mechanisms of exploitation nor to address the underlying and ongoing crisis of the political order.[85]

This review of the period from the 1740s through 1771 displays the central political dynamics that marked the age and set up the extraordinary experience of 1781. In the course of a specific process of politicization and polarization, a set of changes—in the regional political apparatus, the stance of intermediaries, and community strategies and tactics—brought on a heightening contradiction between communities and the sites of colonial power. These changes also moved Aymara peasants toward more radical anticolonial and autonomous Andean projects. This review also shows how the province of Sicasica represented, in a broad sense, the region as a whole. In effect, then, two orders of exemplification, one spatial and one temporal, have been considered: Sicasica reflected La Paz, and the culmination in 1771 rehearsed that of 1781. The latter parallel might seem improbable, since there lay ahead another full decade for specific new forces to unfold. Nevertheless, there would be little modification in the primary relations of conflict and struggle involving Aymara communities, their intermediaries and the regional political apparatus, and upper strata of the colonial state. That 1771 could anticipate so strikingly the insurrectionary conjuncture of a decade later attests to the unusual intensity and precocity of the process in La Paz compared to other southern Andean regions.

These last two chapters have examined the rhythms and dynamics of complex, multilayered struggles at the local and provincial level in rural La Paz. In the decade of the 1770s, the conflicts that have been identified did not abate, and there was even greater awareness in the countryside of the turmoil that engulfed not only the region but the southern Andes more broadly. Let us make a brief final survey of the provinces in the decade prior to the insurrection, taking care to note this enlarging regional awareness.

Many of the communities of Paucarcolla were engaged in major struggles against the abuses of the reparto regime. As leaders from one community commented: "These evils are so common and general that they plague not only this unfortunate, ruined province, but the rest of the kingdom as well." The political dynamic in Paucarcolla during the 1770s closely resembled that of Sicasica. The corregidores sought to extend their political control over the population by employing a "multitude of ministers," while using their influence to suppress legal protest. "When collusion is not at work, it is terror that runs things," observed one outsider. Their methods generated a ratcheting effect in the level of violence and polarization. As battles against caciques intensified, the communities attained an impressive degree of political coordination at the provincial scale. The provincial governor directly attributed the "insolence" of Indians in Paucarcolla to the example set by the uprisings in Sicasica and Pacajes.[86]

Colonial officials in Chucuito province were also beset with troubles during the 1770s. Corregidor Benito Vial attributed them to the weakness of state response and disciplinary action in 1771: "The Indians were led to this arrogance, I believe, by seeing no examples made to reestablish proper subordination to the authorities after the uprisings in the provinces of

Sicasica and Pacajes."[87] Communities became increasingly aggressive as they sought relief from the burden of exactions—reparto payments, tribute, and tithes—and greater control over the cacicazgos manipulated by corregidores. On more than one occasion, Indians stoned their corregidores and they repeatedly forced them to depose unpopular caciques and designate new ones of their own choosing. Vial put down one mobilization by opening fire on the crowd and he insistently requested military provisions from the viceroy. Yet, for fear of rioting, corregidores frequently acceded to community demands and refrained from applying punishment. In 1777, Corregidor Vial concluded, "I consider that the governor in this province enjoys only the faculties and authority tolerated by his natives and not those conceded him by the king and royal law."[88] In late 1780, even as the insurgencies in Chayanta and Cuzco were under way, Chucuito communities lodged new legal protests against the reparto abuses of corregidores and cacique complicity and blamed these problems for the turbulence throughout the kingdom.[89]

In Omasuyos and Larecaja, open confrontation was relatively less prevalent during the 1770s than in other provinces, yet there was keen awareness of ongoing conflict in the southern Andean district. We already noted the trepidation of the Omasuyos corregidor in the wake of the 1771 uprisings. Several years later, in the midst of a sharp cacicazgo battle pitting the corregidor against Indians in the provincial capital of Achacachi, community members revealed their familiarity with the Condocondo case of 1774. In that town, located on the altiplano of Paria to the south, Indians had risen up to slay their caciques, the Llanquepacha brothers.[90] In the Larecaja town of Ayata in 1773, the ominous tale of the Sicasica and Pacajes uprisings so recast the implications of local disturbances that one cacique, in fact a townsman appointed to collect the tribute, confessed mortal fear.[91]

The focal point of the struggles in Pacajes in the 1770s was Calacoto, the town whose conflicts between caciques and communities were the subject of the previous chapter. In this decade, Calacoto Indians pressed charges against successive corregidores for their reparto excesses and warned that the oppression, shared by communities throughout the province, could easily lead to a new uprising. In 1774, Corregidor Juan Ignacio de Madariaga reported to the audiencia, "The town of Calacoto is a perverse place, always reckless in litigation, with no fear of or subjection to their superiors, incorrigible, and most inclined toward immodesty. Whenever they assemble in their pernicious bands, inevitably persisting in their customary vices and drunkenness, they disobediently abandon all their obligations and invent complaints against the honor and conduct of their corregidores."

The "reckless and chimerical" Indians of Calacoto, he held, were unsettling the population, which showed a "strange" determination to live without subordination.[92]

The community's tenuous relationship with its caciques remained central to the dynamics of this decade. Among the cast of despised debt collectors, Calacoto cacique Agustín Canqui was singled out for his leading role in the local reparto regime. According to plaintiffs, Canqui took personal advantage of the corregidor's system of extraction and was rewarded for his allegiance with firm backing in his post. Community leaders argued not only that Canqui violated the recent legal proscription against his participation in the reparto but also that he was acting precisely at odds with his political obligation. They held that the cacique "consistently operates against Indians and meddles in affairs outside his purview, when exercise of his post requires, on the contrary, that he look to the relief of the community and its modest interests."[93]

The Sicasica communities were considered "pacified" after the disturbances of 1771, though colonial authorities remained on their guard for the rest of the decade. Caciques reported on the calm prevailing in the province, yet warned of the dangerous propensities of Indians in certain towns. They observed that communities could easily revolt once again if provoked by outside agitators.[94]

During the 1770s, much of the instability in Sicasica in fact stemmed from strife internal to the colonial state, regional elite, and provincial reparto regime. We have already noted the contention over political jurisdiction between forces located in Lima, the viceregal capital and hub of reparto commerce, and the audiencia in La Plata. Corregidores had always maintained ambivalent relations with other colonial elites in Charcas since their concentrated political power and notorious accumulation strategies could pose risks for social order and could clash with competing private interests. Yet from the 1760s on, they came under increasing attack. Secular and ecclesiastical officials in La Paz spoke out forcefully against the abuses of corregidores in the wake of 1771.[95] Finally, at the more local level, there was a rash of disputes over debts and recriminations involving the corregidor's reparto agents.

Corregidor Villahermosa's successor, Juan Carrillo de Albornoz, titled Marqués de Feria, came under fire from several directions simultaneously. Royal treasury officials in La Paz and their ally Francisco Tadeo Diez de Medina, a politically ambitious character from a prominent La Paz family,[96] charged him with numerous reparto abuses. While the prices of his goods were moderate, their quantity outstripped by far any previous distribution, in the view of Indians as well as other provincial residents. He employed both intimidation tactics and uncertified lieutenants-general to enforce the system, his accusers claimed, and his debt collectors directly confiscated harvested coca from peasants.

Marqués de Feria countered that the treasury officials sought to malign him, since he had denounced to the fiscal tribunal in Lima that they had embezzled fifty thousand pesos in tribute money. He also held them responsible for the 1769 uprising in Sicasica since they had issued decrees calling for caciques to deliver the tribute directly to the treasury, thus encouraging community disobedience toward Corregidor Villahermosa.[97]

The local apparatus of deputies and debt collectors also began to come undone. Diez de Medina produced the testimony of one of Marqués de Feria's own reparto collectors to support his accusations. Later, Francisco Cipriano de los Santos, a resident of Cavari who had served five years as reparto distributor and collector, testified about the corregidor's fraud. He calculated that Marqués de Feria actually distributed three times the amount allowed by tariff while formally reporting less than the allowed value. Santos also complained that he was paid only six hundred pesos annually, when his salary should have been proportionate to the reparto values and when other agents *(cajeros)* who executed the same arduous tasks in other towns earned two thousand pesos. The agent in nearby Yaco, he declared, had been equally prepared to denounce that the reparto exceeded the legal amount by an order of four, but his suit was successfully suppressed by the corregidor.[98] At the same time in the 1770s, disputes over debt corroded the hierarchy of Villahermosa's previous reparto regime. While the La Paz treasury pursued the former corregidor, his lieutenants and deputies owed him substantial sums. One local collector sought release from the financial demands made upon him by the deputy of Palca and Cohoni, Diego de Peón, on the grounds that he had been forced into the job, that the reparto was abusive and unjust, that community members were unwilling and unable to make their payments, and that, in any event, the Indians were the actual debtors.[99]

The antagonism between Marqués de Feria and treasury officials spilled over into commercial tax disturbances in La Paz. In 1776, under Visitador José Antonio de Areche's reform plan, the royal customs house began operating in La Paz and the ad valorem rate of *alcabala* duties (a tax on traded goods) was raised from 4 percent to 6 percent. This step had already caused popular protests in the city of Cochabamba in 1774, and almost immediately complaints were heard in the district of La Paz. In 1777, Indian and cholo traders from the urban parishes threatened to riot in opposition to the stringent controls over trade and the new financial burden. In 1778, new unrest spread in the city and Yungas valleys as the Marqués de Feria acted in support of Indian traders who complained that toll-house officers subjected them to abuses and that traditional tax exemptions were being denied them. Particular confusion surrounded the legal exemptions granted to Indians trading in "the fruits of their own industry" or in goods obtained through transactions with other Indians. Royal treasury officials, eventually backed by Areche himself, held that the corregidor's interpretation of the exemptions was so broad as to leave all Indian commerce untaxed. The result, they concluded, was to promote contraband by Indians (as well as Spaniards who surreptitiously employed them to evade taxation) and drastically to reduce royal treasury income.[100]

In March of 1780, following quickly upon the Arequipa revolt against its new customs house, open conflict was rekindled in the city of La Paz. Anonymous broadsides appeared threatening the life of customs house administrator Bernardo Gallo: "Pluck this thieving old cock *(gallo),* cut up some juicy morsels, and into the river with him. . . . Such a shame that many will pay for this thieving scoundrel." Another went even further: "Long live God's law and the purity of Mary! Death to the king of Spain and may Peru come to an end! For he is the cause of such iniquity. If the monarch knows not the insolence of his ministers, the public larceny, and how they prey upon the poor, long live the king and death to all these public thieves since they will not rectify that which is asked of them. . . . We will weep with grief since because of two or three miserable thieves among us many innocent lives will be lost and blood will run through streets and squares."[101]

After ominous new signs of violence and a final ultimatum appeared, colonial officials, cabildo representatives, canons of the cathedral, and prominent residents of the city called an emergency assembly and moved to close the customs house and lower the commercial duties to 4 percent in order to prevent the rioting of the plebe. Judging from the anonymous letters and broadsides as well as the testimony of witnesses, broad if unruly forces were amassed against the agents and institutions of "bad government." Bourbon commercial taxation and regulation were uniformly unpopular for distinct strata of society: creole landlords and merchants in prosperous La Paz, mestizo traders from the coast (who had recently proven their strength in the Arequipa riot), Indian and cholo muleteers and petty traders based in the parishes of the city, as well as community members from the provinces. In the tense days before the customs house was closed, bands of unknown men—a great many of foreign provenance, some disguised in masks and cloaks, often speaking Spanish and bearing arms—made the rounds of the city on foot and horseback. Travelers reported that hundreds of Indians and mestizos had arrived from Pacajes, Sicasica, and other provinces and that they were hovering on the rim of the altiplano and at the entry points to the city, awaiting "the uprising that there was to be . . . to remove the customs house." There is even evidence, such as the double-edged broadside conditionally calling for the death of the king, of exceptionally early conspiring by creoles against any form of Spanish colonial rule.[102]

As a decade earlier, the responses from higher spheres of the state once again revealed ignorance of the true conditions in the southern Andean interior and incapacity to remedy them. Visitador Areche, unwavering in his reform program, angrily condemned the decision of the La Paz assembly and futilely insisted upon its reversal. Intervention from the viceroy in Buenos Aires came too late. Fernando Márquez de la Plata, the emissary of the viceroy who later that year conducted the investigation into the causes of turmoil in La Paz, finally reported that he could not carry out his orders to reopen the customs house.[103] Emerging first in Chayanta and then in Cuzco, the pan-Andean insurgency was already underway. If no one knew what would ensue, state forces were clearly in disarray and colonial authority seemed an increasingly insubstantial or remote phantom to Andean subjects. In the countryside there was a palpable anticipation of momentous change.

The last two chapters have concentrated on the growing conflict and struggle in the eighteenth century at the local, provincial, and regional levels, especially as they involved Aymara communities. They have particularly emphasized the crisis of cacicazgo authority and legitimacy for two reasons: it was integral to the restructuring of the community political formation (as will be seen in chapter 7), and it had fundamental consequences for the operation of indirect colonial rule over the Andean rural population. My explanation for the eighteenth-century crisis and breakdown of the cacicazgo has centered around three interrelated problems. The previous chapter looked first at in-fighting among lineage descendants and contradictions internal to the institution, as well as at intrusion by illegitimate outsiders and erosion of the post due to state regulation and intervention. Second, it examined the sharp, pervasive conflict between caciques and the community base over the practices and power relations constituting local Indian government. This chapter has considered the third and decisive factor, the process of politicization and polarization that accompanied the consolidation of the provincial reparto regime and that undermined political representation and mediation by caciques. It has also filled out the picture of the unfolding, overwhelming crisis of colonial society with a final view of the hostilities in the urban setting over Bourbon fiscal and commercial reforms. These episodes engaged mestizo and creole sectors more fully than ever before, deepening even further the sentiment of disaffection with the colonial state and its privileged beneficiaries.

The conflicts treated in these chapters converged to bring about the definitive crisis of the cacicazgo, one from which the institution would not recover in the postwar decades. Chapter 7 will consider that last stage of the crisis and look at yet another very important dimension to the process: the shift of power to the base of the community that occurred simultaneously with the cacicazgo collapse.

In response to the historiographic problems discussed at the start of the previous chapter—the common profile of caciques as ambivalent mediators and the tendency to find cacicazgo crisis in every conjuncture of colonial history—I have focused on the political dimension of rural society in order to provide a more dynamic and historically specific view of the cacicazgo and its crisis. Insofar as the crisis involved a loss of legitimacy within the Indian community, we saw that the key criterion of legitimacy—one generally neglected in the historiography—was practical political identification. As colonial exploitation took on a new and increasingly ruthless aspect in the eighteenth century, Andean peasants expected their caciques not only to obey a moral code of economic reciprocity ensuring community material reproduction, the notion familiar in the literature on caciques, but also, as proper governors and political patrons, to "defend" and "protect" them from external aggression and abuse.

The story of how the cacicazgo institution (as a crucial instance of political representation, mediation, and power) was definitively riven over the course of our period offers an especially telling indication of the depth of crisis in the colonial social and political order. It reflects a breakdown of the instituted structures of control, the balance of forces and repertoire of strategies, as well as the cultural and symbolic practices all of which combined to constitute power and legitimation. This view fits with the hypothesis advanced by Steve Stern of a long-term erosion of paternal quid pro quos and pacts, native strategies of resistance and accommodation, and partial, fragile legitimacies that were negotiated through the first stages of colonial history and consolidated as part of what he terms "resistant adaptation." It is also possible to confirm Stern's proposal that an unusually aggressive strain of commercial capital, the more virulent for its tacit and later open sanction by the colonial state, was a leading cause of the reconfiguration of these relations. As this study shows, especially by its emphasis on the cacicazgo, the political consequences of the process reached to the most local level in the countryside. Not only did conflict recast the relations between communities and "external" forces such as state agents and institutions but it also consumed communities themselves with their established representatives, vernacular practices, and particular political culture.[104]

While Jürgen Golte's emphasis on the profound impact of the reparto de mercancías for eighteenth-century Andean society is quite justified, we have seen that its repercussions were as much political as they were economic. His thesis of a causal relation between economic ratios of exploitation and the propensity toward regional insurgency in 1781 not only suffers from the methodological shortcomings that scholars have noted. It also overlooks the reparto's actual role in the political crisis of rural society and offers no means to explain the regional articulation of an insurrectionary political movement. Without postulating that an intolerable threshold of exploitation had been reached, I have argued that community mobilizations in the eighteenth century in fact emerged, against the backdrop of changing forms of economic extraction, with changes in relations of regional political structure, community political representation and mediation, and political legitimacy.

A final comment is in order regarding the themes of political polarization and mobilization in this period. I have interpreted the peasant movements of 1771 as the culmination of a process that transpired over several decades and have framed the preceding decades in terms of the insurrectionary rupture of 1781. Yet we must keep in mind that the significance of the struggles throughout the century cannot be reduced to a reflection of the radical anticolonial moment in 1771 or to a foreshadowing of such a moment in 1781. Such moments were not directly arrived at nor were they sought by most Indian forces in the majority of the political engagements that we have considered.

The struggle against the corregidores did not immediately translate into a full-blown contradiction between communities and the colonial state. On the contrary, the communities took advantage of other sites and institutions of the state—especially the tribunal of the audiencia and its commissioners—in an effort to end exploitation under the regional political apparatus. Communities were aware of divisions within the upper levels of colonial administration and, whenever possible, waged their campaigns by setting dominant forces against one another. Likewise, they had recourse to colonial discourses of justice and of benevolent govern-ment by the sovereign king. Sicasica in 1769, under the independent com-mand of Alejandro Vicente Chuquiguaman, was not the only community that defied the corregidor in order to deliver its tribute as a sign of loyal vassalage. In these cases, communities implicitly presented themselves as seeking to reaffirm the pact or contract with the colonial state—in the final instance, with the king himself—that guaranteed them a measure of autonomy and that reprobate government officials had violated.[105]

Polarization must be appreciated, then, as a graduated process. Only in-frequently did community struggle have as its objective the overthrow of colonial state power as a whole and the constitution of fully autonomous Andean authority. Nevertheless, this was the radical pole of reference within a field of possibilities of which Indian leaders were aware. Depend-ing upon conditions, this alternative could be invoked or pursued in mo-ments of mobilization, especially after other recourse to the state had proven ineffective. By the same token, when the community-state contra-diction grew to supersede intra-elite divisions, state forces would close ranks to put down and punish insurgency.

To understand how a radical position or insurrectionary movement was articulated politically at those moments when polarization did reach maxi-mum proportions requires that we now undertake a deeper investigation of the more exceptional anticolonial projects that emerged over the course of this period and that would find fullest expression in 1781.

5

Emancipation Projects and Dynamics of Native Insurgency (I)

The Awaited Day of Andean Self-Rule

What did insurrection mean for Andean people in the eighteenth century? What were the historic possibilities perceived or imagined by those who followed the course of insurgency? Beyond the material conditions or structural forces that can be seen as causal factors moving them toward a radical break with the colonial order, what political motives or vision stirred them and sustained their efforts despite the risks and tremendous costs?

These are not novel questions, but they are fundamental ones. They provoked debate among eighteenth-century contemporaries and, since that time, have continued to exercise a hold over the minds of historians, artists, and intellectuals of different social spheres. The various ways in which colonial and national discourses in the Andes, as well as successive generations of academic historiography, have approached or sidestepped these questions constitute an intriguing, unexplored problem in itself.[1] Yet over the past two centuries, these approaches have revealed an ongoing fascination and provided clues as to the secular continuities and shifts in political and cultural perspective in the Andean countries.

In fact, nineteenth- and twentieth-century historians have rehearsed many of the very themes and interpretations first expressed by eighteenth-century commentators. Just as some contemporaries saw in the insurrection a yearning for the liberty (or "libertinism and irreligion," in colonial parlance) of the preconquest past, some historians today have considered the movement of the early 1780s as backward looking.[2] A colonial discourse about the cultural savagery of Indians, ostensibly confirmed by evidence of racial hostility (or what is known as "tribalism" in other colonial settings), ruthless cruelty, and physical violence, has found echo in the

horrified accounts of war by modern authors.[3] A notion of instinctive Indian reaction against an accumulation of abuses, often voiced by paterna-
listic churchmen and reformers, parallels the more recent social science assumption of subsistence thresholds and mechanistic reaction against
material exploitation. Likewise, the timeworn concept of a passive-
aggressive complex in colonized Indian peoples still circulates today.[4]
Needless to say, observations such as these have usually failed to go very far
in understanding Indian insurrectionary politics or culture. As we will see,
eighteenth-century stereotypes have specifically tinged the historiography
on Túpaj Katari and his Aymara movement in La Paz.

But the extensive academic literature on the pan-Andean insurgency
and civil war of the early 1780s, dating back especially to the monumental
labor of Boleslao Lewin and the influential work of Carlos Daniel Valcárcel beginning in the 1940s, has also posed a cluster of important themes
that address the questions stated at the outset.[5] These themes, which con-
nect up with original late-colonial debates as well at times, will be considered in the following analysis.

An initial political issue developing out of the early generations of
scholarship, by authors who were commonly marked by *indigenista* and
nationalist outlooks, concerns the loyalism, separatism, or protonational-
ism of Túpac Amaru's political program and movement.[6] This was in fact
a matter under discussion at the time of the insurrection, and in some ways
the problem remains a subtle one for us today. Another pressing problem
that was scarcely taken up by the early generations, however, consists of
how the native population as a whole looked upon the colonial state, the
king of Spain, and the political project of Túpac Amaru.

A more recent generation—schooled in the social sciences and drawing
from Marxist and Andeanist influences to expand the social, political, and
economic analysis of the movement—has also delved more deeply into its
ideological content, especially the millenarian, messianic, and utopian dimensions present in 1780–1781.[7] These authors have engaged in intriguing
speculation regarding a mythically charged notion of cosmic upheaval and
cyclical historical renewal *(pachakuti),* the symbolic significance of the
Inka and the anticipation of his return, and a powerful (at times unconscious) aspiration for collective identity as an ongoing motif in Andean
history.

The Christian religious elements in Amaru's program and in insurrectionary practice have also become important to an emerging debate over
"nativist" tendencies and the cultural stamp of colonialism upon Andean
peoples.[8] Here again we are faced with a colonial controversy that has

continued unabated in the scholarly literature. Did Indians seek to break with Christianity, a religion whose external imposition also involved the suppression of indigenous rituals, beliefs, and relations to the sacred? Does the evidence of Christian transgression and an eruption of formerly clandestine Andean religious practices suggest that Christianity was a superficial accretion that broke up at a time of profound social crisis, upheaval, and transformation? Or was the colonial stamp so deep that it made its impression not only upon public "transcripts" and ceremony, but even upon the most intimate material of spiritual life?

The historiographic themes identified so far—such as separatism or loyalism, millenarianism and utopianism, and religious inclinations in times of insurgency—will receive our attention in the next two chapters. Another topic that has received considerable attention is the content of the political programs of the insurgent leaders Tomás Katari, Túpac Amaru, and Túpaj Katari. This topic will also be taken up here, yet we will raise into view and investigate more closely some other issues less explicit in the literature. One limitation of the existing work is that the political outlook of Andean peasants has not been so extensively treated as the more formal programs of their leaders, particularly the Cuzco-based Inka Túpac Amaru. As a consequence, this work tends to see a breakdown of coherent political vision once community forces took the initiative during moments of mobilization. In what is perhaps a vestige of the early Cuzco-centric perspective on the great insurrection, the tendency is to consider peasant politics and the second phase of insurgency, after the Inka's defeat, in a "negative" manner, that is, in terms of nonidentification with the program of Túpac Amaru. Instead, what we need to appreciate is that peasants conceived of alternative political possibilities and debated them at times vigorously. Also, their views always existed in a complex, taut relation with those of their leaders. To assume that peasants simply opted to follow or abandon a formal, programmatic line articulated by a given leadership is to underestimate peasant political consciousness and agency. It also cuts off at the outset a prime path for historical analysis. This path—leading into the peasant political imagination—is precisely the one I have opted for here.

As the more recent research has suggested, there could also arise significant differences within the indigenous movement of the early 1780s that are critical for understanding of the prevailing insurrectionary motives, projects, and expectations. The questions surrounding the meaning of insurrection for Andean peoples are therefore not susceptible to simple or single answers. Historiographic discrepancies and the difficulty of reconciling separate lines of interpretation within a unified vision can be traced to a number of sources. To begin with, the political agenda of leaders could be ambivalent, shifting, or concealed for tactical reasons. Sectoral cleavages—for example, between Indian leaders and their social base, between Quechuas and Aymaras, between Indians and creoles or mestizo allies—could assume significant proportions. Regional distinctions, such as those between Cuzco and La Paz, raise other differences. Conjunctural timing, such as the suggested contrast between a first and second phase of the insurrection, as well as the sheer openness and fluidity of such an exceptional historical moment add another aspect that must be considered in analysis. Furthermore, the filters and biases of colonial observers and documents add another layer of complexity and contribute to modern misreadings and caricatures.[9]

Taking into account this variety of factors, which complicates and sometimes clouds interpretation, the next two chapters set out to answer the question of what insurrection meant to historical subjects. As in the preceding chapters, the emphasis here is political and cultural, yet greater attention will be paid to the religious dynamics that were so thoroughly bound up with the political movement and to the salience of spiritual power in its relation to political power. This chapter begins with a review of the distinct anticolonial options open to and debated by La Paz peasants in the eighteenth century, focusing especially on the events of the Caquiaviri (Pacajes) uprising of 1771. This will allow us to establish the extent to which the period of struggle prior to 1781 defined the political universe during the great insurrection. The analysis then moves up to 1780, considering the new and particular features of emancipatory projects in the southern Andes at that time as a way to situate the La Paz case. The comparative regional discussion of insurrection in Chayanta under Tomás Katari, in Cuzco under Túpac Amaru, and in Oruro, where creoles and Indian communities briefly aligned, makes it possible to go beyond a narrower regional focus and hence to reassess the specificity of the Aymara movement in La Paz.

The subsequent chapter is devoted to Túpaj Katari and the insurgent Aymara communities in La Paz. The discussion will there bring to the fore a set of themes that are commonly associated with La Paz in the literature on the Andean civil war—radicalism, racial antagonism, and violence, as well as the power of base-level community mobilization. When we explore more deeply, in cultural and political terms, the vision of insurgents and the nature of the movement in La Paz, we can overcome historiographic limitations, such as that of "negative" casting, and move beyond stereotypes that may be traced back to the late-colonial era. Together the two chapters will show how the political changes underway and the political perspectives of peasants earlier in the eighteenth century were connected to the experience and outlook of insurgents in 1781. Through the comparative approach, the analysis of the themes highlighted for La Paz will also illuminate fundamental political dynamics and consciousness in other regions and in the insurrection overall.

Surveying Anticolonial Options for Peasants Prior to 1781

The previous chapter's reconstruction of eighteenth-century community struggles revealed that peasant political forces were most commonly marshaled for recourse to the judicial sphere of the state, to end the abuses of overlords through collective direct action, and to pressure or control (in a sense, not so much exert control "over" as control "under") the instances of political power that mediated between the community and other outside forces. While all of these efforts can be taken, to one degree or another, as resisting, destabilizing, or modifying forms of colonial domination, at several exceptional moments we saw community organization and mobilization occurring as part of a more far-reaching anticolonial political project.

Anticolonial projects as conceived of here are ones that explicitly and self-consciously challenged the fundaments of colonial political order: Spanish sovereignty and Indian political subordination. The challenge to them could involve any of the following elements: (1) repudiation or displacement of the king of Spain (for instance, by an Inka king); (2) rejection of Indian political subordination (either through the subordination of Spaniards or the equivalence of the two peoples); and (3) assertion of Indian autonomy (through rejection of the Spanish crown or other Spanish authority in American, in this case Andean, territory). It is important to note that, by these criteria, anticolonial projects did not necessarily involve repudiation of the Spanish monarch. The agendas of eliminating or dominating Spanish colonists, granting Indians an equal standing, or dispensing with regional colonial authorities were not always accompanied by explicit antagonism toward or even reference to the crown. Also, while these projects could conceive of alternative postemancipation arrangements of political power, not all of them did so. In the cases considered here, such alternatives were formulated in different ways. Yet the annihilationist stance—elimination of Spaniards and Spanish symbols of authority without a positive vision of the alternative to colonial order—was also an instance of the anticolonial imagination.[10]

In the Chuani community of Ambaná (Larecaja), from the late 1740s to early 1750s, there surfaced a radical project inspired by the Azángaro conspiracy of the 1730s. Under their leaders the Pallis, the Chuani Indians rejected local civil and ecclesiastical authority, and they spread their message of "redemption" throughout the district. The movement's aim was to "wipe out or dominate the Spaniards (viracochas)," in order to restore liberty for Indians. It was their belief that "they are the saviors of the town and through force will overcome everyone, even those of the province, because it is their turn to rule."[11]

There are several points to be made about the political project present in the Chuani case. First, emancipation involved either the elimination of Spaniards or their subordination to Indians. The question of elimination or subordination of Spaniards was a key tension in eighteenth-century indigenous uprisings and, as we will see, one that acquired special importance in 1781. Second, the Indians displayed an evident confidence in historical destiny. Their leaders were "redeemers" who would secure the "restoration" or "recovery" of lost liberty, because it was their "turn to rule." The historical imagination here clearly envisioned a future salvation that was dialogically cast in distinction to the "memory" of the conquest and a former loss of autonomy. The idea of a new time and new "turn to rule" *(a ellos les toca mandar)* also came up in 1781 and was likewise expressed in the 1795 uprising of Jesús de Machaca (Pacajes). The leader in Jesús de Machaca proclaimed: "The present was another era *[Ya era otro tiempo el presente]*. . . . The cacique, his segunda, as well as the priest had to change, and . . . those that the community wanted had to take their place."[12] Emancipation, then, took on a profound historic dimension; it resembled a form of millenarianism, yet without the eighteenth-century Andean motif of renewal under the Inka.

Third, this was an exceptional instance of sharply defined and sustained opposition to existing Catholic religious authority. Chuani Indians refused to pay tithes or parish fees, to permit burial in the church cemetery, to attend mass and confession, or to recognize and serve the local priest. They established a sphere of practical religious autonomy, with the Pallis retaining tithe contributions and local charitable funds *(obra pía),* normally collected by the priest, for themselves. Political liberation was evidently imagined by them together with liberation from a Catholic cult presided over by abusive ecclesiastical representatives. The Chuani project differed fundamentally from the program of Túpac Amaru who would explicitly call for the preservation of Catholic worship and respect for the ministers of the faith. In other moments of uprising in the eighteenth century, as we will see, there is similar evidence—sometimes subtle, at other times overt—of an inclination to flout, disavow, or assail Christian worship, yet never did opposition attain the status of policy or become so concerted as in Chuani.

Was there a deep ideological counterpoint or alternative religious option conceived of by Chuani peasants? It is not clear that the Pallis were viewed as possessing or embodying sacred power, as we would expect the documents to indicate if this were the case. The term "savior" *(redentor),* which was applied to them, could have had an exclusively secular connotation; other community political leaders at the time (those engaged in the struggles against tithe abuses, for example) were also referred to as "redeemers" and obviously enjoyed the greatest respect from their fellows without acquiring messianic religious stature. On the other hand, the boldness of the Pallis in declaring peasants "liberated" from attending mass, for example, or collecting tithe and charity rents themselves, possibly suggests a spiritual self-confidence bound up with claims to alternative religious authority.

In any case, their radical religious position stemmed from a conjunction of local conflicts involving tithes and priests, including their formidable adversary the canon and potentate Dr. Martín de Landaeta, and a broader political consciousness left as a legacy by earlier Indian insurgents in Azángaro. While they did not repudiate Christianity as such, they went to extraordinary lengths, unmatched by other eighteenth-century Andean political projects, to evade abusive religious controls and to create their own relations of political and religious authority.[13]

The second exceptional moment when an identifiable anticolonial project emerged was in the siege of Chulumani in 1771. The uprising less than two years earlier in the town of Sicasica was similarly provoked by the reparto exploitation of Corregidor Villahermosa and his agents, yet there is no evidence that its leader, Alejandro Chuquiguaman, sought the overthrow of colonial rule or elimination of Spaniards as the objective of the ayllu mobilization. Even if he envisioned such an alternative or privately advocated it, which we cannot substantiate, the target of the collective actions that he coordinated was limited to the abuses committed by regional authorities. Chuquiguaman secured community tribute for the royal treasury, even when he refused to deliver payment to Villahermosa; and when the Indians assaulted and killed the corregidor's agent Solascasas, it was in self-defense, and the action was not followed by the sacking of property or violence against other townspeople.

The leadership and movement in Chulumani were of a yet more radical nature.[14] The Yungas mobilization was premeditated and a set of new community leaders—being neither caciques nor even formal ayllu authorities for the most part—stepped forth to organize and direct it. Juan Tapia, Mateo Poma and others in their circle of collaborators seem to have arrived at the conclusion that an armed uprising was the necessary response to the ongoing abuse of power by Villahermosa and Lieutenant General Larrea. Even if no full consensus existed within the communities about the need for mobilization, the radical designs of the leadership evidently had been divulged and were circulating prior to the uprising. Juan Tapia was soliciting funds from peasants, and on several occasions he visited Chupe. He exchanged provisions and correspondence with this neighboring community, and in one of his letters, which was read by the church cantor at an assembly by the Milluguaya River, Tapia announced that "it was time to free themselves from the oppression of the Spaniards."[15]

There were spontaneous, last-minute community decisions made about whether or not to carry out the mobilization, suggesting on the one hand that the uprising almost did not occur but also confirming that it was planned and promoted in advance. When the audiencia commissioner Peñaranda complied with peasant appeals to issue a suspension of reparto debts, the imperatives for mobilization temporarily dissolved. But, in a classic ratcheting effect leading toward greater polarization, Villahermosa successfully recused the commissioner, and community leaders realized that the corregidor would now return to collect his debts and was more likely than ever to seek violent retribution for the opposition against him. Juan Tapia claimed that it was Tomás Espinoza, hilacata of Yunca, who urged immediate action—they had to follow through on their original plan to rise up before the corregidor and lieutenant "finished them off."[16] After an assembly by the river Yarija, the community of Chupe ultimately determined to forgo further legal recourse against the colonial authorities and to march on Chulumani at the instigation of Tapia. While Chupe leaders would later claim they only sought to obtain the release from jail of their fellow community members, including their alcalde, they set forth with arms and were prepared for war. A separate contingent set out with the aim of cutting off the Chupe bridge in order to stymie the advance of the corregidor, who was said to be arriving with soldiers. After all Indian forces converged at the Alto de Guancané, a final assembly was held to decide whether or not to enter battle. The clinching influence was a rousing letter from the wife of Chupe leader Simón González who asserted that she could not agree with anyone who thought of pardoning the corregidor and his lieutenant.[17]

Once the siege of the town was under way, no one present could have failed to appreciate the challenge to regional colonial authority, the degree of racial polarization, and the Indians' ambition to assert political superiority. The radicalism and fervor of Indian forces in fact intensified over the course of the confrontation, which lasted several days. While his account obviously attempted to diminish his own role in inciting the communities, Juan Tapia later testified that he had acted out of fear of the masses and that he had tried to contain the many who sought to cast themselves headlong into battle and overtake the town.[18] They waved banners to give military signals, sounded their horns *(pututu)* and played drums and wind instruments (perhaps the *pinkillu*), and shouted insults, taunts and threats at the enemy. At one point, they moved up to the entrance to town and faced off with slings in hand, challenging the Spaniards to come out and fight. Just outside the town they also erected a gallows as a sign of justice—Indians were now prepared to issue judgment upon abusive authorities and to punish "thieves" and "scoundrels" for their crimes. Given the degree of polarization, they spurned their traditional political intermediaries, the caciques, because of cacique complicity with the corregidor.[19]

If the movement had sought only to obtain the release of the captive alcaldes and the corregidor's withdrawal from the valleys in accordance with audiencia decrees, it would have dispersed once these conditions were met. Instead, however, Indian forces rallied with each of the concessions made to them—first the community authorities were freed and then Villahermosa agreed to pull out—and they displayed renewed ardor. The communities' campaign, then, developed spontaneously and assumed increasingly ambitious political aims as the situation unfolded and appeared to confirm the Indian advantage. We cannot know for sure whether the corregidor, who counted upon significant firepower, really intended to withdraw as he promised; if he did, the most likely scenario would have been an Indian entrance into the town and at least a temporary takeover, with or without violence against town residents. In any event, such an outcome did not occur due to the arrival of the deputy from Coroico with his small force of recruits. After the men were stopped and disarmed, the corregidor—allegedly informed that the deputy had been executed—chose this moment to launch his bloody counteroffensive. Surviving peasants returned to their communities reporting that "the Indians had lost the victory."[20]

One of the most intriguing and significant bits of evidence from the case is the assertion that Indian leaders assumed honorific titles during the siege and were prepared to govern themselves in the wake of the uprising. Juan Tapia, acting as military general during the conflict, was to be the new corregidor; Gregorio Machicado would be lieutenant general; Juan Ordoñez would be cacique; and Mateo Poma would be king. We must be careful in addressing this evidence since it could have been a fabrication by Villahermosa to cast his enemies as open traitors to the Crown. But on inspection, it appears that Tapia was indeed addressed as "General" by the peasant militia who followed his orders and that his claim to the title of corregidor was widely known.[21] Also, in his legal defense of Juan Tapia, the audiencia's Indian protector implicitly accepted the evidence of parallel political titles when he attempted to absolve his defendant of responsibility by charging that the putative king, Mateo Poma, was the real ringleader and chief.[22]

A careful reading of the evidence, then, does support the notion that the movement in Chulumani, and coordinated throughout the surrounding Yungas valleys, involved bold anticolonial political aims that went beyond other organized community efforts to resist the oppressive hand of the corregidor. In contrast to the 1769 mobilization in the town of Sicasica, in which Indians ostensibly sought to recover the tribute receipts that had been confiscated by local colonial authorities, no legal legitimation for the movement was presumed, nor was there any claim to approval from higher levels of the colonial state, as for example in Chayanta prior to Tomás Katari's death. While there was no formulated political program in the Chulumani movement, there was the powerful aspiration to end Spanish oppression, categorically conceived, and the blunt purpose to replace existing colonial political power with Indian government. While more sophisticated conspirators might have looked for allies among local creole landlords or disingenuously pledged allegiance to the Crown, Chulumani insurgents overlooked such strategic and tactical considerations. Theirs was a keen, impatient rush to power, partly precipitated by the imminent threat of repression and escalated by the very development of the confrontation. At the same time, their actions reveal confidence in the belief that Spanish domination could not endure and that self-rule was the inevitable order of the day.

The third exceptional moment of a more radical, anticolonial nature occurred in early November of the same year (1771), when peasants in Pacajes rose up attacking their corregidor Josef del Castillo and seizing power in the provincial capital Caquiaviri.[23] The killing of the corregidor and several of his lackeys in Jesús de Machaca was a spontaneous reaction, on the occasion of the festivities for All Souls' day, against their violent treatment of the peasants congregated in the town. While there was certainly plenty of political significance to the confrontation, there was no peasant political project that prompted or oriented the attack. A more explicit engagement with distinctive political options and agendas was to emerge in the aftermath of the killing, as peasants in Caquiaviri suddenly encountered power in their own hands and were faced with the unexpected challenge of wielding it.

On Sunday, November 2, the day after the riot, the corregidor's men in Caquiaviri organized an unarmed auxiliary squad of townspeople to march to Jesús de Machaca. Believing that Castillo had found refuge in the church, they were horrified to learn, as they drew near, that he had been killed and that hostile peasants were massed and waiting to engage them in combat. After reversing their course, they arrived back in Caquiaviri where they were detained, some that very evening and others the next morning, by local community members now actively in league with those of Jesús de Machaca. When Caquiaviri Indians had seen the contingent of townspeople setting off to defend the corregidor and put down the uprising in Machaca, they had decided to mobilize themselves, declaring that "if they were going against the community [el común], then they would do the same thing against the soldiers who had gone."[24] Among those arrested on Sunday were the cacica Nicolasa Sirpa and her daughter, who were placed in the convent of Caquiaviri, as well as her son Esteban Herrera, who was shackled and sent to jail.

By eight in the morning on Monday, approximately one hundred Indian men and women from both moieties were rounding up, with much shouting and commotion, the Spanish and mestizo residents of the town, searching their homes and even seizing some of them in the priest's house. They began by taking the soldiers prisoner, crying, "Why did you go to Jesús de Machaca against the Indians?" As they captured the corregidor's closest collaborators, they remonstrated, "Why did you go to Jesús de Machaca if not to kill the Indians of that town?"[25] The interrogatory tone of the accusation put to the local residents ("Why did you go against the Indians?") seems to imply, as does the conditional tone of the original decision to mobilize ("If they were going against the community, then the peasants would go against them"), that the townspeople could and should have sided with the community against the corregidor. By supporting the corregidor's faction against the communities, the townspeople forced the Indians to take action against them.

According to another witness, the Indians proclaimed that "now that the corregidor was dead, there was no other magistrate for them; instead the king was the community for whom they ruled."[26] After finishing the rest of the search and posting sentinels on the outskirts of the town, so that no one could slip away unnoticed, they proceeded to drag other men out of the church where they had hoped to find sanctuary and out from under the canopy for the Eucharist which the priest brought forth in an attempt to pacify the crowd.

The next day there prevailed a tense, unstable mood with recurring, staccato bursts of violence.[27] The anger of the crowd became focused at one point on a mulatto who had been in jail prior to the uprising. He was overheard saying to the imprisoned soldiers that if they removed his shackles and furnished him with a knife, he would go out and slaughter the Indians like animals.[28] He was tricked into coming out of the jail, instantly dispatched, and then strung up from the *rollo* (pillar of justice) at the center of the town square. While Indians repeatedly threatened to kill all their prisoners and all those who refused to cooperate with them, the mulatto was apparently the first to die. We can imagine that Indians felt the greatest animosity toward the corregidor's accomplices, yet the mulatto may have been the most convenient target since he had already been detained for a crime, there was no one who would defend him, and he may have been perceived as less "Spanish" than other townspeople. To kill "Spaniards" was an extreme measure indeed, one that entailed the highest political risks and one that Indians were more likely to threaten than to carry out.

On several occasions, in fact, the insurgents stepped back from the brink of killing those who had proven themselves to be enemies. Town resident Francisco Garicano, perhaps the prisoner who attracted the most attention from the insurgents, was to be brought forth and executed at one point. Yet at the last minute, through a strange loss of resolve or coordination, the Indians did not take action. According to one report, "They forgot about him because of all the commotion and did not know what to do."[29] In the case of traitorous fellow Indians, there was a heightened moral tension. After the execution of the mulatto, they returned to the jail and withdrew a young man who had joined the soldiers in the march to defend the corregidor. He was the son of cacique Manuel Mercado from Viacha and he had been sent to Caquiaviri on an errand involving community tributary rolls. They tied him by his hands and feet to the rollo and whipped him "slowly but with great violence, . . . rebuking him at length between each of the blows."[30] We can imagine that it was community elders who chastised the young man so severely for his betrayal of the Indian communities. Finally he was "miraculously" saved and returned to jail when some Indians intervened on his behalf. Another Indian, the alcalde ordinario Valeriano Sirpa, was seized and his staff of authority taken from him after he tried to free the prisoners from jail. He, too, was dragged to the rollo and only escaped with his life by a "miracle of God."

But in at least one case, the crowd did not shrink from imposing the ultimate punishment against someone perceived to be more "Spanish." Their victim, Josef Romero, was one of the corregidor's sidekicks (a constable or *teniente de alguacil mayor*).[31] Amidst hue and cry, the community forces returned from an assembly and set upon the captive Romero. A few steps from the jail house door, he was beaten to death with rocks by men and women who then strung him from the rollo alongside the mulatto.[32]

The killings, violence, and threats of extreme punishment in Caquiaviri were not the sudden, spontaneous impulses of a rioting mob, like the one that rose up in Jesús de Machaca to kill the corregidor. On the contrary, during the days of the Indian takeover in Caquiaviri, the different paths of action followed by peasants were chosen after community assemblies and collective deliberation. In this sense, we can consider the killings, violence, and threats to be part of a radical political orientation or agenda that consciously envisioned the elimination or annihilation of significant features of colonial domination. While it was not the only political option conceived of by peasants in Caquiaviri—we will address others below—it did represent a powerful notion of social transformation that was also present at other moments of mobilization in the eighteenth century. This agenda was expressed more clearly and cogently in Caquiaviri than at any other time except for 1781, under the stark circumstances of war. Yet peasants were aware of this option at other times, even if historical conditions were less conducive toward its expression. We most commonly find it alluded to darkly and probably ironically, for example, to spook Spaniards, as when Indians threatened to drink chicha from the skulls of their enemies.[33]

This anticolonial violence was directed not only against people, but also against colonial institutions and their physical structures. The Indians became furious in one incident when Francisco Garicano attempted to leave the jail against their orders. They drew back a short distance from the jail and began pelting the door with stones from their slings. They cried that "they would do away with everyone inside because the jail had been built with their labor and therefore they would return it to nothing."

Taken abstractly, the implication of their words and actions is that they had both the power and the right to eliminate the subjects, structures, and signs of the colonial society that was oppressive to them and founded upon the very alienation of their labor, resources, and territory.[34] In another example of this radical tendency toward the outright destruction of the identified enemy, after a new pause in the events, the Indians descended upon the town once again late Tuesday night, vowing to raze the church, the priest's house, and the jail. They called for firewood and moved about lighting bonfires in the plaza.

The erratic shifts between aggressive mobilization and then tentative withdrawal by community forces corresponded in part to the counterinterventions of the town priest and to the overall dilemma of Christianity. As we can see in different ways during the uprising, the latter problem essentially consisted of deep ambivalence between a religion often identified with the oppressive political order, yet bearing undeniable spiritual authority for most peasants. In order to understand the nature of the political orientation and movement in Caquiaviri, we must note the manifestations of this ambivalence.

Once the uprising was under way, townspeople sought sanctuary in the local church and in the priest's residence. While peasants began by searching other houses, they did enter the priest's residence to remove the corregidor's accomplices who had taken refuge there. We can assume that some women and children may have taken shelter in the church throughout the uprising, yet peasants also finally entered the church to seize the more sought-after townsmen, most notably Francisco Garicano. Others of the soldiers were hauled out from under the canopy of the Eucharist when the priest brought it forth from the church to pacify the crowd. In the end, then, peasants showed some reluctance to violate Christian sanctuary, yet political imperatives overcame this hesitancy.

When Corregidor Castillo was killed, the priest of Jesús de Machaca (who was under threat of assassination himself) fled immediately to La Paz with his assistant. By contrast, the priest of Caquiaviri, Vicente Montes de Oca, confronted the insurgents in an attempt to avert violence and temporarily succeeded in defusing the mobilization. The priest, clearly cognizant of the extreme circumstances, drew upon the most forceful means available to dissuade the peasants from their enterprise. By producing the Eucharist itself *(nuestro amo el señor sacramentado),* he challenged them with that most sacred and mysterious aspect of Catholic ritual and spiritual power. With his invocation of the Christian Lord and manifestation of Christ's miraculous transubstantiation, peasants were faced with the choice of subordinating themselves to God's minister or pursuing their course of mobilization against the apparent will of the Christian God.

The first time that the priest presented peasants with the Eucharist on Tuesday, in the morning at the door of the church, they withdrew to hold an assembly. Later that afternoon, over five hundred returned with much commotion to execute the corregidor's officer, Josef Romero, and with the aim of killing Francisco Garicano. Montes de Oca came forth with the Eucharist yet again, this time to the rollo itself where he proceeded to parley with the Indians for an hour and a half. After dialogue was exhausted, the priest removed his robes and threw himself to the ground, saying that they should kill him rather than the poor prisoners, who were without blame. After this last-ditch, dramatic step, the Indians settled down, approached in order to kiss the monstrance, and withdrew once again.

Another witness reported, however, that not all the insurgents showed such respect for Christian spiritual authority during this episode. A group of them, among which may have been some of the acting leaders, told the others that "those who wanted to obey should go ahead"; they, meanwhile, stood by irreverently at the door of the jail, without even removing their headgear.[35] As we saw above, that night the Indians returned to the town with new enthusiasm, threatening to burn not only the jail, but the priest's house and the church.

There can be no doubt that the priest's bold, forceful interventions frustrated the movement to a significant degree, dividing it internally and causing it to withdraw and regroup repeatedly. Clearly Christian religious belief and authority posed a major dilemma for insurgents in Caquiaviri. For how could they go up against domination by Spaniards or the colonial political order that was protected and sustained by religious powers many Indians feared, revered, and felt compelled to obey? And yet peasants did challenge the priests in Jesús de Machaca and Caquiaviri. They threatened to tear down the local site of worship (having built the church themselves, as they had the jail), and some spurned reverence to the Eucharist.

Some of the religious tensions found in the Pacajes uprising in 1771, such as those involving Christian sanctuary or obedience toward priests, also arose at other times and in other places during eighteenth-century peasant mobilizations. Yet the depth of religious ambivalence during such moments—involving the vacillation between reverence toward and repudiation of Christian authority (the latter being reminiscent of the Chuani movement)—was demonstrated more dramatically in Caquiaviri than at any other time, with the exception of 1781. As we will see, the issues of religious definition and spiritual power reemerged to acquire crucial significance during the great insurrection.

Let us return to the topic of the political options conceived or debated by Caquiaviri peasants. Community authorities circulated throughout the surrounding countryside to convoke Indians, not only from the ayllus of each moiety but from the haciendas, for their political assemblies (cabildos). The mayordomo of the Estancia Comanchi reported, "Tuesday night, three Indians came to the estate in order to persuade the Indians there to join with those from other areas in the town of Caquiaviri to see what was to be done with the prisoners. . . . Wednesday morning an Indian alcalde from Caquiaviri arrived at the estancia to convene the Indians. They brought nine peons [yanaconas] before this witness who delivered them over because there was nothing he could do to prevent it."[36] We know, then, that decisions about "what was to be done" were discussed in the community assemblies and, over the course of the uprising, Indians repeatedly returned to the town from their meetings fired with new initiative.

We have already seen that one radical political option or agenda, loosely conceived, was the annihilation of Spaniards and the institutions of colonial society. A second radical view was expressed in the striking proclamation: "Now that the corregidor was dead, there was no other magistrate for them; instead the king was the community by which they ruled." This fascinating claim seems to have been a local interpretation of Spanish political ideology, with its origins in medieval scholasticism, which held that God had vested political power in the people, who then delegated it to their legitimate monarch. In exceptional cases, for instance if the throne were vacant or the king's power were abused tyrannically, the people were justified by natural right in recuperating that power.

Such ideas of popular sovereignty were in circulation in South America during the colonial era, as witnessed in the creole-led neo-Comunero revolts in Paraguay in the 1720s and 1730s and New Granada in 1781 and the independence stirrings during the Napoleonic invasion of Spain in the early nineteenth century. In the little-known case under examination here, these ideas were apparently adopted by Andean peasants in an ambivalent formulation of two notions. First, the community (el común) was said to represent the king, ruling in lieu of the absent (defunct as well as illegitimate) colonial authority. Second, the community was said to be the king. Sovereignty, in other words, had devolved upon the people. This second sense may even have effectively displaced the king, without renouncing him overtly. The formulation thus hovered between autonomy without separatism on the one hand and explicit communal sovereignty on the other.[37]

Another conception involved a novel sense of corporate integration with other non-Indians under Crown sovereignty, yet without traditional racial/ethnic hierarchy. One witness testified, "After having threatened all the prisoners that they would kill them, the nearly two hundred unruly Indians went to the estate of secretary don Josef Rivera. They later returned saying that they would not kill them after all, because the Secretary had told them that all were vassals of the king." In the given context, the idea that "all were vassals of the king" is an intriguing one whose meaning is not explicitly clarified by any other evidence from the case. Even the figure of Secretary Rivera remains obscure to us; he was most likely a creole landowner who held the respect of community members, perhaps since he was not an ally of the corregidor.[38]

To begin with, the idea stood in contrast to the option of killing the enemy, and it did not imply a rupture with colonial political authority in the final instance, since the king retained lofty political prestige. It therefore diverges from the notion that "the king was the community for whom they ruled." But what did peasants mean when they said they would not kill the prisoners since all were vassals of the king? It would be superficial to pass over this comment as a meaningless excuse to avoid the grave consequences of killing, or as a straightforward, conventional upholding of legal or political norms. In the extraordinary circumstances of the uprising, Indians clearly understood more than this by the idea. It is also worth noting that no Christian moral reference served to justify their reversal of position; instead they were articulating an explicit political criterion.

The idea that "all were vassals of the king" as it was understood by Rivera himself may or may not have coincided with the gloss given it by Indians. For both, it presumably entailed coexistence of Indians and non-Indians within a unified body politic, that is, a certain kind of political integration that would have also preserved the relatively distinctive spheres of the collective social subjects (Indians and Spaniards) constituted over the course of colonial history. For insurgent community members, it may well have also contained a powerful subversive significance. First, it suggested an equality between all the king's subjects, whether Indian or non-Indian, and hence a dismantling of colonial caste hierarchy. Second, it superseded any reference to lesser regional instances of colonial political authority (such as the corregidor, audiencia, or viceroy). In this respect, it can be seen to complement the cry at the start of the uprising, "Now that the corregidor was dead, there was no magistrate for them." Even if the concept of corporate integration and equality under the king did not posit an absolute break with colonial political authority, or a renunciation of its ultimate expression (the king himself), the peasant notion did leave open the possibility of strikingly new and different political and social relations in the region. And insofar as the Indian sphere was conceived of as separate, equal, and not subject to the impositions of regional colonial authorities, we are really confronted with an Indian vision of substantial autonomy. In this sense, autonomy did not simply indicate separateness; even if the distant king and his great symbolic power were not repudiated, it meant effective self-rule.

How were these strikingly new and different political and social relations in the region imagined? The same account we have been considering goes on to report: "They later returned saying that they would not kill them after all, because the secretary had told them that all were vassals of the king, but that they must dress like Indians, with woven mantles and tunics, to unite with them *[mancomunarse],* and that they had to go to Jesús de Machaca for the same purpose." What emerges then is an important new idea of association and fellowship, defined on Indian terms, that was distinguished from the idea of annihilation of the enemy. It is not entirely clear whether the notion of "vassals of the king," to which we have no further allusions in the documents, lost its hold over Indian political consciousness after the decisive meeting with Secretary Rivera or whether it might have subtly merged with this new notion of corporate integration and unity—referred to in this discussion as *mancomunidad*—that oriented and organized the actions of insurgents in the following days.

Let us consider more of the evidence about the Indian project for mancomunidad. Perhaps as early as Monday, the insurgents had a list of the townspeople that one of the town residents, Gregorio Hinojosa, had written up under threats from his captors. From the door of the jail, as they played fife and drum, Indians called the townspeople by name to come forth and make up with them *(hacer amistad)*. On Wednesday morning, a group of townsmen who had fled to the Comanchi estate received word from their wives that the Indians were summoning them for a reconciliation *(para hacer amistad)*. If they did not return to the town, the Indians threatened to seek them out, hacienda by hacienda, and to hang them like dogs, burn their houses, and destroy their flocks of livestock. Fearing retribution, the majority of them set out for the town.

In the town that same morning, the community confederation held a massive assembly. The insurgents concluded by ordering that all townspeople had to take a vow of residency and swear their obedience to the

Indians. They also had to don Indian mantles, tunics, and headgear, and their women had to wear the same wrapped dress as Indian women. If they did so, their lives would be spared and they would be freed. The orders were then carried out, and townspeople were brought forth from the jail dressed in the prescribed fashion.[39]

In response to the challenge of how to remake political and social relations in the wake of uprising, it is worth noting the remarkable cultural inventiveness of the solution proposed by Caquiaviri insurgents. This solution would be implemented once again in 1781, yet this is the first case on record of a peasant political policy for community domicile, ethnic cross-dressing, and the assimilation of non-Indians.[40] Within the bounds of what they saw as their own territory and political sphere, Indians were willing to incorporate outsiders as new members of their community, rather than eliminate them outright, on the condition that they adopt Indian social codes, norms, responsibilities, and, in a sense, Indian identity. The coercive aspect of this mancomunidad was by no means inconsistent with accustomed practices. Within community political culture, coercion could be a standard part of the process of negotiating consensus, or achieving a hegemonic arrangement of forces, out of conflictual conditions.[41] This can be seen in other cases of mobilization, for example during the siege of Chulumani when reluctant peasants were persuaded to join their companions under the threat of losing their community lands. Belonging to the community, and partaking of its collective rights, benefits, and ties of solidarity, brought with it the serious moral obligation to respect negotiated consensus and to act in accord with community resolutions, while to do otherwise would provoke censure. In a sense, the townspeople were being incorporated into the community as forasteros, and like Indian forasteros they were required to be relative subordinates who followed the directives of elder and established community members. This forastero analogy further highlights how the unprecedented political and social relations established in Caquiaviri followed from an Andean cultural template for community.[42]

After the prisoners were released from jail, the ensuing episode rendered even more explicit the community terms of the new social relations established by insurgents and exposed another important political agenda for peasants. From among the prisoners brought forth now in Indian garb, insurgents seized Manuel Uriarte and carried him off as their captain. A fight then broke out between the two moieties over which of them he would belong to. Uriarte was dragged from one corner of the square to the other, with each corner representing the ritual space or jurisdiction of one of the rival moieties. In the midst of the dispute, they took him to the rollo with the intention of killing him, but then the superior strength of one moiety allowed its members to carry him off again and swear him in, with flute and drum, as their captain. They proceeded to name Francisco Garicano and Gregorio Hinojosa as secretaries (presumably Garicano knew how to write, as did Hinojosa), one for each moiety. The ceremonies continued, again with the accompaniment of flute and drum, as the "new community" of Spaniards (*"machaca común' que quiere decir nuevo común de españoles"*) was ordered to arm itself with slings, poles, and clubs. In preparation for the war that Indians were to have with the soldiers from the city of La Paz, insurgents also ordered that rocks be stockpiled in the town square.[43]

In this process—so extraordinary in its creativity, it bears repeating—of conscious constitution of new social subjects and relations, the final outcome of mancomunidad between Indians and non-Indians was a new community of Spaniards subsumed within the greater, overarching community political formation. If we recall the vertical segmentation of Andean social organization and the associated multivocality of community (see chapter 1), we can explain how the identity of non-Indians was simultaneously reproduced and transformed through cultural incorporation. At a "higher" level of social organization and signification, the townspeople, having adopted the political and cultural codes of community, assumed "Indian" identity. The figure and texture of their lives became part of a single patterned fabric that was, so to speak, designed, woven, and worn by Indians. Yet at another relatively "lower" and "internal" level, incorporation did not mean annihilation of previous identity, for the new community was composed entirely of mestizos and creoles. The situation of the new members of the greater community, then, was analogous to that of an ayllu of forasteros distinguished from the ayllus of other originarios.

It was the cultural and political hegemony of Aymara peasants, under the exceptional circumstances of the time, that allowed for this solution of mancomunidad with cultural incorporation as well as a final, very important political agenda we could call "rule from below." With this final element, political relations in Caquiaviri did indeed come to resemble the initial exclamation of insurgents—"Now that the corregidor was dead, there was no other magistrate for them; instead the king was the community for whom they ruled." Political decisions were discussed and made in community councils with the participation of Indians from all the ayllus and haciendas. Townspeople were physically seized, ceremonially inducted as authorities and officers (namely, captain and secretaries), and coerced by the loosely coordinated community base. It seems, of course, especially striking that mestizos and/or creoles should be placed at the head of an Indian movement. While they were identified as Indian through cultural incorporation, no one could deny their simultaneous Spanish identity. If their authority was not seen as at odds with Indian political strength, it was because the relationships of authority and power were being reshaped at this time within the community political structure and political culture. It was the developing community notion of rule from below (involving control "under," so to speak, as opposed to control "over") that made it plausible for Uriarte, like the secretaries, to be designated to "serve" as an authority.

The Caquiaviri case also allows us to see a certain practical and historically novel divergence between political authority and political leadership, which formerly would have been unified in the person of the cacique. The cacique family did not side with the community and was in fact detained by Indians. Designated Captain Manuel Uriarte was put at the head of insurgent forces, and he undoubtedly held a place of honor as foremost community authority. Yet he was subject to the determinations of the community, and actual power to direct the campaign was not concentrated in his hands. We also noted the presence of two Indian alcaldes during the insurgency: one circulated about the rural district summoning Indians to the community council; the other had his staff of authority taken away and was nearly executed at the rollo for acting against the community. These references to the captain and alcaldes show common characteristics of the community authorities: their symbolic prestige, their service and fulfillment of established functions, and their accountability to the community base. (See chapter 2.)

Neither the cacique family nor the authorities (Captain Uriarte and the alcaldes) exercised real political leadership in Caquiaviri. A leader was one who could take the initiative to define the political agenda, decide a course of action, and, obviously within given limitations, control the collectivity. Thus, a political leader held actual power over others, as the cacique had done traditionally and as new figures were now doing in other exceptional moments of mobilization. These leaders could be respected and experienced elders, such as Pascual Escobar or Felipe Ali who assumed prominent roles in the Chupe mobilization in 1771, or dynamic new, even youthful, figures such as Juan Tapia in Chulumani or Túpaj Katari himself. These issues of rule from below and changing political representation lead to an important conclusion: the question of political authority and power in the reconstituted Caquiaviri community was worked out in a fashion that revealed an emerging new political culture in the age of cacicazgo crisis. (See chapter 7.)

The actions and declarations of insurgents in Caquiaviri reflected a set of conscious political orientations and options that, singly or in combination, could attain the status of an agenda: annihilation of the enemy; racial equality and autonomy as vassals of the king; fellowship with non-Indians (mancomunidad); community cultural incorporation; and rule from below. Caquiaviri presents an especially interesting case since these orientations, with their strong communitarian and democratic thrust, were clearly base-level initiatives conceived of by ordinary peasants, in the absence of established individual leadership or top-down hierarchy. Of the different options we encountered, some must have been less developed than others. The idea that "all were vassals of the king" is the one we have the least evidence for. It seems to have engaged insurgents less than the idea of local mancomunidad. It could also be suddenly overridden by antagonism and the inclination toward annihilation. As this last possibility indicates, there could be alternation from one position to another, however contradictory.[44] These elements, though we have separated them analytically, could also be combined in different ways. The idea of all being the king's vassals may have merged with the notion of mancomunidad, while mancomunidad ultimately came to involve cultural incorporation and rule from below.

It is unclear whether a single agenda prevailed, since there is little evidence of how events unfolded after that Wednesday. Indians were not immediately subjugated, and they continued to receive reports from spies in the city and to anticipate a clash with Spanish militia from La Paz. In the town itself, the project of reconstituted social and political relations involving the cultural incorporation of local residents and rule from below does appear to have persisted (perhaps in conjunction with the threat of annihilation). On Friday, Indians released Manuel Tilas from jail, in native dress like other townspeople, and gave him the assignment of guarding the jail.[45]

The objective actions of the Pacajes uprising, with the killing of the corregidor and takeover of the provincial capital, went beyond those of any other peasant mobilization in eighteenth-century La Paz, save the general insurrection. Yet the limits of the movement in Caquiaviri in 1771 were also significant. Different political visions were present and under debate, as was not the case in Jesús de Machaca at the same time, but Indians found it difficult indeed to arrive at a consistent stance that was equal to the challenge before them. The movement was marked by vacillation, tentative advances and withdrawals, and a juxtaposition of sometimes incompatible elements. The ambivalence toward Christian spiritual authority reflected the overall political uncertainty. Caquiaviri was not so sudden and spontaneous a mobilization as many others in the eighteenth century, yet there was a sense in which peasants were indeed unsure how to proceed once local power was theirs. This difficulty in forging a consistent political program was connected to the absence of any outstanding leadership to coordinate and direct community forces. The very experience of such power in the hands of Indians, and of the inability to wield it more effectively, may have spurred a number of committed and farsighted Aymara peasants to engage in new organizing efforts and preparation for a future political opening. This was probably true of Túpaj Katari himself.

By the late 1770s, historical circumstances, both political and cultural, were moving toward an even more charged conjuncture of crisis. The peasant political agendas worked out over earlier decades would retain their relevance, and Túpac Amaru would forcefully articulate a consistent political program and consistent position regarding the religious dilemma, as a reference for different sectors of Andean colonial society. Leadership, too, would emerge to take up the task of social transformation. And finally there would be another dramatically important new factor—the mystique of the Inka's final return as king of Peru.

In Ambaná, Chulumani, and Caquiaviri, we can identify a central set of anticolonial political options prior to 1781: radical elimination of the colonial enemy; regional Indian autonomy that did not necessarily challenge the Spanish Crown; and racial/ethnic integration under Indian hegemony. They entailed no fixed or single religious position, but the challenge to the Catholic cult in Ambaná was unusual for the eighteenth century, while the ambivalence evident in Caquiaviri was more common during times of mobilization. The importance of these different political agendas and projects is that they express a range of views of what was possible in a new and transformed society: they are eighteenth-century peasant visions of Andean utopia. These political views were also present during the great insurrection, but it should now be apparent that they were not present for the first time in 1781. Rather, they had surfaced earlier and evolved during the important, protracted process of struggle in the eighteenth century. Although they have received limited attention in scholarly literature, their existence reveals not only a complex political culture and rich political imagination that took form in opposition to colonial oppression but also a vast political horizon stretching beyond it.

Surveying Regional Insurrectionary Projects in 1781

To understand the specific nature and aims of Túpaj Katari's movement in La Paz and to examine the predominant historiographic thesis about La Paz as a region within the overall revolution, the movement must first be situated in relation to other regional projects and experiences in 1781. Laying out the comparative cases of Chayanta, Cuzco, and Oruro, this section will focus on key points of strategy and on the political program of insurgents. The colonial institutions identified as most objectionable, the higher sites of colonial authority, and the attitude toward creoles, or American-born "Spaniards," form a set of concerns that will receive particular attention. At the outset, however, we should note one other fundamental feature of Indian political consciousness on the eve of the insurrection.

Any analysis of a revolutionary conjuncture must consider the broader outlook that sparked and sustained popular commitment. In order to break with the past and openly renounce existing conditions and in order to risk the retribution of established authority, an alternative vision must emerge to capture the collective imagination. In the time of the pan-Andean insurrection, it was a millenarian vision that afforded a logic to the course of history and a confidence in the future. It was thus crucial to making insurrection seen by large parts of the populace as an appropriate and viable course of action.[46]

In none of the earlier peasant political mobilizations in La Paz do we find the motif of emancipation under the Inka. This possibility would have been familiar to those critical of colonial domination, since the claim for Inka political sovereignty had emerged in 1739 with the conspiracy led by Juan Vélez de Córdoba in neighboring Oruro, as it had in Juan Santos Atahualpa's midcentury movement in central Peru; yet it never materialized in the La Paz region even during the radical anticolonial moment of 1771.[47] It is extremely important to recognize, however, that by the late 1770s a new millenarian mood with the presentiment of Inka restoration was building in the southern Andes. The convergence between notions of Andean utopia and neo-Inka political authority would contribute to an overall insurrectionary conjuncture more dramatic than any yet witnessed.

In 1776, rumors already circulated about an imminent time of major upheaval (with famine, illness, and tribulations for Indians), when the Spaniards would be expelled from Peru and the Inka would rightfully regain his throne. In one Cuzco tavern, for example, it was predicted: "All the Indians of this kingdom would rise up against the Spaniards and kill them, beginning with the corregidores, alcaldes, and other pale-skinned blonde people. There was no doubt about this, because the Indians in Cuzco had named a king to govern them." This epochal shift, initially expected to occur in 1777 ("the year of the three sevens"), was foretold by the prophecies of Santa Rosa and San Francisco Solano.[48] It is easy to imagine that the political turmoil between 1777 and 1780—including the unrest in La Paz in 1777, 1778, and 1780 over Bourbon reform measures—was interpreted as confirming the prophecies of cataclysm.[49] In La Paz, as we will see, Túpaj Katari placed great faith in such prophecies of historic transformation.

Another influential idea in this period, and one that could combine with millenarian expectation, was the view that Spaniards had acquired the kingdom illegitimately and that the heirs to the Inka dynasty remained the rightful rulers.[50] In Huarochirí (Lower Peru), a conspirator against the colonial government affirmed: "The prophecies of Santa Rosa and Santo Toribio would be fulfilled, meaning that the territory would return to its former owners since the Spaniards had conquered it wrongfully *[la habían ganado mal]* and through a war brought unjustly against the natives who had lived in peace and quiet."[51] Túpac Amaru himself, in his coronation edict, proclaimed that "the kings of Castile have usurped the Crown and dominions of my people for close to three centuries."[52] In La Paz, leaders urged on Indian combatants with assurances that the king of Spain "had conquered the kingdom wrongfully, and that the time had come for the fulfillment of the prophecies."[53] Insurrection therefore was seen as bringing to a close one age, dating from the Spanish invasion in the sixteenth century, and issuing in a new one in which justice would be restored. It was in this sense that one of Túpac Amaru's colonels, Diego Quispe the Younger, wrote of the war in 1781 as a "new conquest."[54] In the previous section of this chapter, the evidence revealed that peasants already anticipated a historic turning point, a moment of political transformation and end to colonial rule. In Ambaná, they declared it was "their turn to rule," while in Chulumani they were stirred with the announcement that "it was time to free themselves from the oppression of the Spaniards." But the astonishing appearance of Túpac Amaru gave a new power to peasant expectations, as it seemed to confirm prophecy and the prospect of political transformation.

Chayanta: Autonomy and Loyalty to the King

The movement of Tomás Katari in Chayanta would have added to the sense that a new era was dawning. Katari's battles against abusive local and regional officials began in 1777, and after returning from a remarkable overland journey to the court in Buenos Aires, he proclaimed: "I now bring from the viceroy a new government, which will no longer be sheer thievery."[55] Under Katari's command, Indian autonomy seemed to become a reality by 1780: the communities forced from office illegitimate caciques who were in league with the corregidor; they deposed the corregidor Joaquín Alós himself and acted to prevent his designated successors from taking over; and in the absence of other effective colonial control, Katari governed the province virtually on his own.[56]

As his political stature and informal jurisdiction continued to grow among communities, not only in Chayanta but in surrounding provinces, Katari was evidently looked to as a savior invested with spiritual as much as secular power. One cacique rival called him an "idolatrous Indian, a sorcerer." According to other reports, he was venerated while alive—his followers addressed him as king and by other "divine" titles, they kissed his feet and clothing, and sought his judgment as they would an oracle—and after his assassination, rumors suggested that he had resuscitated.[57] Katari's renown extended as far as Sicasica in the early stages of the La Paz insurrection.[58]

Chayanta is conventionally taken as one of the primary regional theaters of the great insurrection, yet the objectives and significance of Tomás Katari's movement have not been entirely clear in the historiography. Considering that, on one hand, Katari firmly stood up to provincial corregidores and their agents as well as the Real Audiencia itself, while, on the other, he consistently demonstrated his loyalty to the viceroy and the Crown, can we say Katari led an anticolonial or politically subversive movement? His commitment to the higher manifestations of colonial authority was matched by his emphasis on legal politics and his efforts to assure compliance with the state's tribute and mita requirements. At the same time, however, in the absence of effective colonial authority at the regional level, Katari assumed political functions and a political jurisdiction that clearly exceeded his legal attributions as tribute collector and cacique in Macha.

Indian tribute became a key issue of dispute in Chayanta. Katari's enemies cast him as a "rebel" against the Crown by claiming that he seduced Indians with the promise of a lower tribute. Katari countered that corrupt and disobedient officials were the ones who had misappropriated tribute income and who refused to follow legal orders, such as those issued on his behalf by royal treasury officials or the viceroy. As proof of his sincerity, he made sure that his community satisfied the correct amount of tribute, which was in fact a higher figure than had been paid in the past. While Katari maintained his commitment to meet tribute and mita demands, he did take a stand against reparto payments to the corregidor and he sought to influence the official appointment of the provincial magistrate. He also insisted on legitimate representatives for Indian jurisdictions, meaning an end to the abuse of mestizo interlopers occupying the cacicazgos as well as the allegiance of other local Indian authorities. But despite Katari's demonstrations of loyalty and regional authorities' self-interested distortions of his intentions, the underlying question was who held power in the region, and there could be no doubt that state control had receded. His political power, symbolic authority, and the practical autonomy he secured for Indian communities through his astute and untiring campaign represented a serious challenge to colonial order.[59]

Even after the armed confrontation in Pocoata in August of 1780, in which Corregidor Alós was taken captive by Indians and then exchanged to gain the release from prison of Katari, the Indian leader continued to claim that there was no uprising going on in the region. But, as the polarization increased, it became increasingly difficult for Katari to contain community animosity toward hostile authorities and to put off demands for relief from colonial exactions, including tribute to the Crown.[60] With Katari's assassination in January of 1781, the new leadership openly adopted an anti-Spanish stance and turned to Túpac Amaru as their native king.

Within the insurrectionary context of 1780–1781, the singularity of the Chayanta case is that, in its genesis, it was not an irradiation of Túpac Amaru's movement. It originally developed independently with dynamics that more closely resembled those we saw in the preinsurrectionary phase of struggle. It grew out of the conflict with the regional political apparatus of colonial domination and out of the breakdown of community political mediation and representation. In contrast to Túpac Amaru who harbored effective separatist aspirations from the start, Tomás Katari maintained good faith toward the Crown and went to great lengths to fulfill his perceived commitments. Yet over the course of a remarkable struggle to see that justice was done, regional colonial authority came undone and Katari's project became one of unprecedented Indian political power and autonomy under the Crown. We saw that a strong move toward autonomy was also made in 1771 in Pacajes; but the Chayanta experience, under the exceptional leadership of Tomás Katari, went far beyond it in clarity, coherence, and practical realization.

Cuzco: Restoration of the Inka

On November 4, 1780, José Gabriel Túpac Amaru seized the corregidor of the province of Tinta, Antonio de Arriaga, and launched his movement as heir to the throne of Peru's native kings. Though he did not publicly announce his separation from the Spanish Crown, he conducted himself as only a monarch would and the populace immediately recognized his royal ambitions. Túpac Amaru began by securing military victories and the adherence of Indians, mestizos, and creoles in the district south of the city of Cuzco. His initial momentum, apparently confirming the overwhelming superiority of Indian forces and the providential nature of his movement, was so great that it may have bred a certain complacency about prosecuting the war.[61] He was unable to capture the strategic capital city, but the southern provinces fell to Indian troops loyal to the Inka. Eventually his political sway would extend to Arica, Tarapacá, and Atacama on the coast; the valleys of Charcas such as Larecaja, Yungas, and part of Cochabamba to the east; and as far south as Jujuy and Salta, with echoes in Mendoza in the new viceroyalty of Río de la Plata. The movement also won sympathies in the central and northern highlands of Peru, and repercussions were felt even further to the north in the viceroyalty of New Granada.

In Túpac Amaru's words, "The time had come to shake off the heavy yoke that for so many years they had suffered under the Spaniards."[62] In late 1780, it certainly did seem that the millenarian promise of revolution, redemption, and justice was being fulfilled.[63] Though communities in La Paz would not join the insurrection until February of 1781, by late 1780 there were signs of enthusiasm for Inka sovereignty in the region. Indians in Sicasica requested that their corregidor, Ramón Anchoríz, return a portion of the tribute he had collected from them; half the amount could remain with the corregidor to be paid to the king of Spain, they held, but the other half was due to their Inka king.[64]

Just as Tomás Katari's political intentions were disputed by his eighteenth-century contemporaries and have been debated by scholars today, there have been discrepancies over whether Túpac Amaru remained loyal to the Crown or harbored separatist tendencies.[65] In the years prior to the insurrection, while serving as cacique in the towns of Surimana, Pampamarca, and Tungasuca (Tinta), Amaru had gone to great lengths to gain the audiencia's recognition of his legitimate descent from the original trunk of the Inka dynasty that ruled Peru in the sixteenth century. He also headed a petition by the caciques of the province that outlined the intolerable burden of the Potosí mita for their subjects and requested its suppression. This campaign before Visitador Areche and Viceroy Guirior, however, eventually came to nought. While quite familiar with the internal workings of the colonial courts and state administration, it is likely that Túpac Amaru, conscious of his distinguished historical inheritance and sensing a duty to defend the people of Peru, grew increasingly frustrated with the difficulty of colonial reform in the 1770s. Yet even when he took the irreversible step of executing Corregidor Arriaga and announcing his royal heritage, he claimed to be acting as the commissioner of superior colonial authority. He repeatedly yet falsely declared that the king had issued royal orders authorizing him to extirpate "bad government" in Peru.

There were several reasons for this duplicity. Túpac Amaru understood the profound respect that much of the Indian peasant population felt for the king of Spain, who was, after all, commonly joined in colonial discourse with the Christian God, as one of the "two Majesties." As their sovereign lord, to whom they duly rendered tribute, he was perceived as the supreme patriarch and final guarantor of justice and of their rights to community political and economic reproduction. As we saw in the previous chapter, community mobilizations in the eighteenth century were primarily directed against the abuses of local and regional government officials rather than colonial authority as a whole; for Indian peasants, it was perfectly believable that if the distant king in the unfamiliar land of Spain were only aware of his ministers' wrongdoings, he would naturally intervene to prevent them. So instead of directly challenging the notion of the king of Spain's power, with its benevolent and fearsome aspects, Túpac Amaru preferred to assume it for himself by posing as the king's agent. Furthermore, as the previous chapter also suggested and the case of Tomás Katari confirms, it was by no means uncommon in polarized political settings for higher colonial authority to emit decrees in favor of Indian community representatives and political leaders that were denied, suppressed, or resisted by regional officials. Amaru's claims to royal authorization, which were sustained after his death by his leading officers, Diego Cristóbal and Andrés Túpac Amaru, were indeed a plausible fiction.

Nor did Túpac Amaru wish to alienate other sectors of colonial society, especially creoles, by an abrupt, categorical repudiation of colonial authority.[66] Such a stance would have effectively equated sympathy for his movement with outright treason against the Crown. By publicly acknowledging the king in a large portion of his proclamations and correspondence, or by not directly asserting his own claims to sovereignty even when he made no mention of the Spanish monarch, Amaru left open a margin of ambivalence that would have made it easier for the hesitant to give their support. It also preserved the political option of greater autonomy without the finality of separatism and provided a credible basis, Amaru hoped, for negotiation with Spanish forces. Hence, for example, he demanded abolition of the reparto, Indian alcaldes mayores in the place of corregidores, and a new audiencia in Cuzco (headed by a new viceroy) that would be more responsive to the needs of Indians, while at the same time reassuring the besieged population of the capital that he wished to leave direct rule over the land to the king of Spain.[67] The official Amarista stance that the Inka sought to eliminate "bad government" and that the corregidores were the ones who had rebelled against the king by their lawless and sacrilegious exploitation—an argument reminiscent of Tomás Katari's position—gave insurgent leaders, faced with the threat of state punishment, a measure of self-justification within the terms of Spanish colonial discourse.

Túpac Amaru's strategic cautions were enough to mislead some twentieth-century historians, who concluded that his manifestations of loyalty to the Crown made him but a precursor, rather than authentic advocate, of Peruvian independence.[68] Nonetheless, as Boleslao Lewin understood and lucidly argued, Amaru's ultimate objective was indeed to found a new Peruvian social order under uncompromised royal Inka command.[69] This view is supported not only by careful textual analysis of Amaru's written documents, but also by his conduct during the war. When entering provincial towns, for example, local priests received him with the ceremony due to kings. And just as in political and military practice Amaru governed as the supreme lord of a vast Peruvian territory, evidence from throughout his sphere of influence reveals that his followers treated him as monarch and his contemporaries, whether adherents or adversaries of the movement, understood its radical implications.

Finally, the clinching evidence of Amaru's underlying project for full political independence is the coronation edict, a copy of which was found in his pocket at the time of his capture. Bearing the title "Don José I by the grace of God, Inka king of Peru, Santa Fe, Quito, Chile, Buenos Aires, and the continents of the southern seas," he declares in the edict, "The Kings of Castile have usurped my crown and my people's dominions for close to three centuries, burdening my vassals with unbearable levies, tributes, commutations, customshouses, commercial duties, monopolies, property taxes, tithes, royal fifths, viceroys, audiencias, corregidores, and other ministers, all of them equal in tyranny."[70]

Túpac Amaru's program involved a major overhaul of colonial political and economic institutions, and the abolition of a long list of exactions affecting different sectors of Peruvian society.[71] Corrupt and abusive government officials would be eliminated, especially corregidores, who would be replaced as provincial magistrates by Indian alcaldes mayores. With the abolition of repartos and state monopolies, restrictions on trade were to be lifted, and the universally unpopular customshouses and commercial taxes (the alcabala in particular) would be removed. There would be an end to forced labor in the Potosí mita, and textile shops (another despised symbol of bonded Indian labor and infernal laboring conditions) would be closed. Yet another remarkably advanced measure granted liberty to slaves.

Túpac Amaru made no pronouncement on the delicate subject of landed property. This was evidently a priority for peasants and we may assume he favored the restitution to Indians of wealthy estates held by Spanish proprietors. Yet the prospect of large-scale expropriations may well have been too threatening for the creole sector he sought to court. Also Amaru never intended for tribute to be abolished, though he did, under community pressure, suspend payments during the war. This was not part of a strategy to feign allegiance to Carlos III; rather, for Amaru the principle of tribute rendered by vassals to their king was simply not in question. According to the coronation edict, tribute as well as the royal fifth *(quinto)* would continue to be paid to the sovereign lord, who was none other than "don José I," or Túpac Amaru himself.

Against enemy accusations that he sought to return to pagan idolatry, the Inka leader consistently presented himself as a loyal Catholic and insisted that his movement was not directed in any way against priests or the Church. Though he did denounce the abuses by priests of their Indian parishioners, and despite his own excommunication and the militant opposition of the Church, Amaru maintained a clear policy affirming Christianity. Under restored Inka rule, the Christian cult would be respected, and the population would continue to meet ecclesiastical exactions, paying tithes and first fruits *(primicias)* to local priests.[72]

The question of racial/ethnic relations was critical to Túpac Amaru's program. Echoing the manifesto of Juan Vélez de Córdoba in 1739, he called for Europeans to be eliminated from the kingdom and espoused a common cause between creoles and Indians, all of whom were born on American soil and suffered the tyranny of the peninsular Spaniards. Rather than an ethnic nationalist project, joining Indian peasants and nobles in opposition to all whites, whether creole or European, his was a cross-racial Peruvian nationalist project. He envisioned that all native-born subjects—

Indians, creoles, mestizos, and zambos—would "live together like brothers and congregated in a single body, destroying the Europeans."[73] This evidently implied the dismantling of the colonial caste hierarchy and an unprecedented racial egalitarianism, though not a dissolution of racial identity as such nor all forms of racial difference. Amaru obviously needed to court creoles as strategic allies in an anticolonial movement, but he was earnest in his overtures to them and in his aspirations for the harmonious order to come. His vision also would have been accessible to the Indian masses: it resonated with the kind of peasant conceptions of social reintegration within a new unified polity that we encountered in Caquiaviri in 1771, and Dámaso Katari far to the south in Chayanta, for example, retained the Inka's notion of Indians and creoles joining forces within a single "body."[74] It was a bold proposition uncertain of success, however, since it meant that ultimately creoles would be politically subject to an Inka monarch and because peasants commonly identified creoles with peninsular whites, with both groups falling under the category of Spaniards.

In early April 1781, Spanish troops captured Túpac Amaru after the battle of Tinta. On May 18, the Inka leader was executed in a public ceremony along with others of his collaborators and family members. Military command thus passed to his first cousin, Diego Cristóbal Túpac Amaru, whose headquarters were in the town of Azángaro to the north of Lake Titicaca. While the Spaniards reconquered the Cuzco region, the lake district and the highland plateau and valleys reaching far to the south remained largely under the control of insurgents.

Quechua forces from the north, under the leadership of Andrés Túpac Amaru, moved down through Larecaja and Omasuyos all the way to the besieged city of La Paz. An impressive, proud, and astute eighteen-year-old, Andrés Mendigure was the nephew of the Inka José Gabriel. After his three-month siege, the town of Sorata, capital of Larecaja province, fell to Indian troops in August. He was subsequently joined by Miguel Bastidas, nephew of Túpac Amaru's wife Micaela Bastidas, for the second phase of the siege of La Paz, now waged jointly between Quechuas and the Aymaras under Túpaj Katari.

Oruro: The Failure of Indian-Creole Coalition

At the time of Amaru's call to arms, political conditions in the mining city of Oruro were quite precarious. Economic production had gone into a tailspin from which it would not soon recover and this exacerbated a long-standing rivalry between creoles and peninsular Spaniards. While creoles owned most of the local mines, they were dependent upon European merchant-financiers for the credit lines so necessary in the volatile, capital-intensive industry. In this time of decline, even the most powerful of Oruro's miners were saddled with debts and resentful that loans were not forthcoming.[75] Furthermore, in January 1781 the peninsular corregidor of Oruro had successfully arranged the election of his own European clients to the municipal council after decades of political control by creoles like the members of the Rodríguez and Herrera families. That same month, insurgency swept the countryside as Indian communities in the surrounding provinces of Paria and Carangas rose up to kill their corregidores.[76]

Violence broke out in Oruro on February 10, amidst panic and a flurry of rumors that the corregidor and his European faction intended to attack creole militiamen and kill off their adversaries. After a confused incident, a plebeian mob of creoles, mestizos, and cholos rioted and burned the house of one peninsular merchant where a number of Europeans had taken refuge with their wealth. By the next morning, eleven Spaniards and five slaves had died as a result of burns and severe beatings. At an improvised assembly, the crowd proclaimed its will that the prominent creole Jacinto Rodríguez be the new corregidor and that the Europeans leave the city at once or be killed. As the day went on, thousands of Indian community members converged on the city to support their comrades, or "brothers" in Túpac Amaru's language, and defend the new corregidor. Indians and creoles were seen embracing in the streets.

There can be no doubt that this unprecedented interracial alliance was built upon mutual expectations of Túpac Amaru's approaching government. Creoles and plebians, as well as Indians, knew that the Inka had risen up and gone to war in Cuzco. Rumor had it that he was nearing La Paz and before long would arrive in Oruro. Over the following days, creoles and plebeians shouted cheers for Túpac Amaru and at one point a creole tore down the Spanish royal coat of arms that hung above the postal building. Initial animosity toward Europeans and subsequent fear of the Indians in their midst combined with anticipation of Inka rule to produce a favorable creole disposition toward the coalition.

For Indians in Oruro as elsewhere, the coming of "their king" seemed to fulfill a long-awaited promise. In the words of community leader Santos Mamani, "The time had come for the relief of Indians"; as another Indian put it, "It was now the time in which the government of Spain came to an end."[77] Clearly, Indian communities had taken the lives of their provincial corregidores following the Inka's own example in Tinta. In the city, they sought out and struck down Europeans in fulfillment of Amaru's orders and gave backing to Jacinto Rodríguez in preparation for the new political order that the Inka would lead.

At the start of the uprising, their conduct in the city was also carefully guided by Túpac Amaru's distinction between European and creole Spaniards. On a number of occasions, Indians brought white captives before Rodríguez to ascertain whether they were creoles, who should be freed, or European enemies, who should be executed.[78]

What were the relations of power between the two parties in this alliance? On February 14, thousands had paraded through the city streets on the way to the plaza to hear an edict from Túpac Amaru. As Indians passed before the home of the wealthy creole Manuel Herrera, they signaled their obedience to him. Herrera, dressed in an Indian tunic *(unku),* offered them embraces and addressed them as "brothers, friends, comrades." This anecdote shows, first of all, that the ostensible regional political authorities were creoles like Herrera and the Rodríguez brothers. They enjoyed the popular support of urban plebians and the formal recognition of community members.[79] We can also see, however, in Herrera's donning of Indian dress, that Indians exercised enormous power as they occupied the city.

In fact, all creole residents of Oruro were effectively obliged to wear Indian clothing and chew coca. The rumor circulated that any whites found in Spanish dress would be killed. The men wore ponchos or tunics and sometimes carried headgear, a coca pouch, and a sling; women wore wrapped dresses known as *axsu.* Jacinto Rodríguez himself wore a special tunic similar to those of Túpac Amaru. According to one account of a meeting at Rodríguez's house, he held up two tunics, one of black velvet trimmed with gold and the other purple with fringe and silver ribbon, saying: "They brought me this to wear. What do you think?" Manuel Herrera, speaking for everyone, answered: "It would be quite in season to wear such an outfit." So Rodríguez put one on, and the others followed his example, though they would later claim that they did so to save their lives.[80]

In Oruro, expectation of Inka rule provided a new context for power relations and hence, by extension, for cultural norms. In Caquiaviri in 1771, as we saw, ethnic cross-dressing was also a sign of Indian power. Yet now, despite threatening rumors, there was clearly more room for cultural maneuver by creoles and they feigned voluntary adoption of Indian dress. Their leaders could joke ironically about it among themselves, all the while maintaining an outward display of intercultural fraternity. Thus, cross-dressing in Oruro was not so unilaterally imposed as it had been with prisoners in Caquiaviri and as it would be with prisoners in Sorata later in 1781.[81] While community mobilization in Oruro brought forceful political pressure from below and "Spanish" authorities were obliged to accede to base-level initiatives, as had been the case in Caquiaviri, power relations were not so one-sided in 1781 as they had been in 1771. Creoles retained a real and effective leadership role locally, and rural communities respected their authority to govern the city in representation of the Inka. Indians were following the interracial political agenda of Túpac Amaru in good faith, and they took creole gestures as signs of genuine partnership.

It was a remarkable alliance to occur in a colonial society so deeply stamped by racial/caste segregation and hierarchy. It was also a tenuous one, however, and would not stand the test. Within a week, the powerful forces unleashed proved overwhelming. Simultaneously, the limitations upon revolutionary social reorganization, like the boundary markers found at the edge of peasant fields or at the far margin of a community's territory, came into view.

Indian demands for the suppression of tribute and the turnover of money held in the royal treasury provoked an initial altercation with creoles on the night of February 13. Significantly, this ended in the death of Sebastián Pagador, the creole firebrand who had incited the urban population to arms against the Europeans the night before the uprising. After Pagador, acting as a treasury guard, smashed the skull of one peasant trying to gain entry to the building, a crowd of Indians seeking justice brought him before Jacinto Rodríguez. In an effort to calm the throng, Rodríguez ordered his arrest, yet Pagador was killed in retribution before he reached the jail. As the insurrection proceeded, community members interpreted creole refusal to meet their demands over tribute as a violation of the will of Túpac Amaru.

Another key demand of peasants was for redistribution of land. Free communities sought to extend their holdings in the face of hacienda encroachment, while hacienda peons wanted estate property turned over to them directly. During the first phase of the alliance, they did in fact obtain concessions from priests, Europeans, and creoles including Jacinto Rodríguez. Indians and creoles could easily agree on the abolition of the reparto de mercancías, since Europeans monopolized this commerce; yet, since many landlords were creoles, the threat of expropriations could not fail to pit them against each other. The land question was so sensitive it even divided Indians. Poor, landless hacienda peons were less interested in the creole alliance and more radical in their aims and actions. Those from Rodríguez's own estate Sillota, for example, eventually organized their own assault on the city and were the last to surrender when the insurgency waned.

Discrepancies also developed over the treatment of Europeans. Creoles became increasingly uneasy as Indians continued to search out and kill peninsular Spaniards. Here again, Indians interpreted creole reticence to wipe out the enemy as evidence of lack of loyalty to Túpac Amaru and lack of resolve to prosecute the war. On one occasion, Indians brought a fugitive European, Manuel de Bustamante, before Rodríguez to obtain permission for an execution. When Rodríguez ordered only his imprisonment, it provoked the ire of one of the captors: "You have called us to kill *chapetones* [Europeans], and now you only want them to go to jail. Well, it does not have to be this way." Shouting "Community! Community! *[Comuna! comuna!]*" they finally put the man to death.[82]

Thus the breakdown of alliance followed from the divergent tendencies of the two parties. Indians were quite correct in identifying an underlying lack of creole political commitment. For the creole elite, it had been initially expedient to call for community mobilization within the city against a common European adversary. Once plebeian and community forces had risen up, however, prestigious leaders such as the Rodríguez brothers saw it as their task to bring them to bay. Having quickly established control over the city, their participation in the alliance derived from expectations of the Inka's imminent arrival, fear of greater Indian violence and expropriations, and diplomatic strategy to assuage their militant comrades. The conduct of creole leaders, then, was calculated, pragmatic, even cynical.

On the 15th, the creoles attempted a deal to persuade Indians to withdraw from the city. They took twenty-five thousand pesos from the treasury and offered to distribute one peso to every Indian. The act of disbursement lapsed into strife, however, and more radical groups refused to leave the city afterwards. Many community members felt the payment was inadequate and resented creole treatment. They maintained their demands and even began to loot creole stores. At this point, creole leaders decided to eject Indians by force. On the 16th, creoles and mestizos drove them from the city and, in the absence of any higher authority to arbitrate between the contending parties and to enforce a truce, the phase of interracial alliance effectively came to an end. The communities took the turn of events to mean definitive betrayal, and one bystander heard the fleeing Indians cry, "We will take revenge!"[83]

The succeeding phase was one of greater political and racial polarization. While communities would launch new attacks in March and April against all the city's residents, creole leaders would join forces with the remaining Europeans and support the royalist cause. Indian objectives were now more radical than ever. They intended to tear down the royal treasury building and raze the entire city, thereby eliminating tribute, ending all opposition to Túpac Amaru, and securing their own liberation. Claiming what was rightfully theirs, all lands as well as all mines and mills were to be redistributed to the greater community of Indians (el común).

Elderly Antonio Ramos Chaparro of Challapata (Paria) frankly declared to his interrogators the aspirations that he and other Indians shared:

> To obtain possession of the lands that intruders usurped many years ago, because long before they had belonged to the community of his town. They took them under the pretext that they were surplus lands sold off by the king [a reference to the colonial *composición de tierras* by which purportedly excess community lands were sold by the state to private buyers], and they have been divided up among so many owners that they harm his people. This motivated him to be free of them [the intruders], and hence he advised the members of his ayllu how to achieve his desire, and because it is in the interest of all of them to take advantage of what is theirs. . . . This is my only crime, and having believed that once this city was destroyed we would pay no more tribute or other taxes, and that my community would be the owner of everything. . . . Unfortunately, it has all come to nought.[84]

The familiar ambivalence toward the established figures of Christian spiritual authority gave way, after the rupture in relations, to more pronounced hostility on the part of radicals. In Paria, before the fatal clash with their corregidor, communities first sought the mediation of the town priest. But after the corregidor rejected negotiation and opened fire on Indians, they ignored the entreaties of the priest and even berated him when he attempted to intervene to save the life of the magistrate.[85] When Indians first occupied the city, they respected the lives of creole and European priests and did not require them to wear native dress, yet they paid no heed to Bishop Menéndez when he tried to subdue them with exhortations or the Eucharist. This evidence recalls the religious ambivalence of communities in other earlier moments of mobilization. In the final stage of the insurrection, however, the radical peasants from Sillota threatened to destroy existing religious forces, which they identified with the political power of the enemy. While they were not repudiating the Christian cult as such, they vowed to decapitate the icon that they clearly saw as the spiritual patroness and protector of the city. In their view, the Virgen del

Rosario de Santo Domingo was a witch whose evil powers worked against them.[86]

After their expulsion from the city, Indians came to identify the enemy not as Europeans exclusively, but "Spaniards" of either peninsular or American origin. As they saw it, this shift away from the interracial program of Túpac Amaru was forced upon them by the disloyalty of creoles. If there was an admirable boldness, generosity, and vision on the part of leaders like Amaru who advocated alliance between Indians and creoles, there was, at the same time, a clarity on the part of peasants who ultimately recognized that creoles participated in their political subjugation and economic exploitation. Santos Mamani, the leader of the Challapata community, held out as long as possible for a reconciliation with creoles, yet in the end he led his forces into battle against all *qaras*. Explaining his outlook to a priest at one point, Mamani inquired whether "he had not heard that the time had come for the relief of Indians and the annihilation of Spaniards and creoles whom they call *qaras,* which in their language means naked, because without paying taxes or laboring they were the owners of what they [the Indians] worked on, under the yoke and burdened with many obligations. They obtained the benefits, while the Indians spent their lives oppressed, knocked about, and in utter misfortune."[87]

This approach to Indian political visions has considered not only prominent insurgent leaders and formal political programs, but also the overlooked, less familiar ground of political options conceived of by peasant community members in times of uprising. The Caquiaviri case is of great value in revealing the debates going on within the community and the shifting terms and tones of peasant agendas. In both Caquiaviri and Chulumani, there were at times tentative or erratic rhythms, at other times consuming momentum. Moments of mobilization required improvisation, even on the part of experienced, strategic leaders; in all the community uprisings considered here, we find bold initiatives along with instability. Indian peasants and leaders demonstrated extraordinary creativity in working within or borrowing from existing guidelines, in reinterpreting them, or in imagining unprecedented social arrangements.

In crystallized form, three principal projects emerged from the experience of anticolonial uprisings in La Paz prior to the general insurrection — radical annihilation of the enemy, regional autonomy that did not challenge the king of Spain, and racial integration under Indian hegemony. It is important to reiterate that these were specifically peasant agendas, not formal programs designed by outstanding individual leaders such as Juan

Vélez de Córdoba in Oruro in 1739, Juan Santos Atahualpa in the central Peruvian highlands in the 1740s, or Túpac Amaru in 1780.

The vision of Tomás Katari and its evolution over the course of political struggle in Chayanta was closer to the peasant experience in La Paz. His initial aims to retake the cacicazgo and reestablish political order where it had been distorted by local and regional authorities led him to take exceptional measures to see that community tribute payments reached the royal treasury. In this regard, he bears a resemblance to Alejandro Chuquiguaman, who claimed the cacicazgo in the town of Sicasica, challenged the corregidor and his agents over the reparto, and eventually led the local uprising in 1769. But, from what we know, Chuquiguaman's campaign cannot be construed as representing a fundamental challenge to colonial order. Like Tomás Katari, he conscientiously saw that tribute was delivered to the La Paz treasury; and the uprising developed spontaneously out of a showdown between the community and the local colonial authorities, who later punished them for their insubordination and seized the treasury receipts.

The most subversive aspect of Tomás Katari's campaign was the way in which it created, for the state, a growing political vacuum in the countryside, one which Katari himself filled. His movement came to acquire de facto autonomy, even as he earnestly insisted on his allegiance to the Spanish Crown. In this respect, his project can ultimately be likened to the option of autonomy with loyalty to the king that emerged during the Caquiaviri uprising in 1771.

The millenarian and utopian outlook that recurred in these anticolonial movements contained an important Indian conception of time and history. In the eighteenth century, conspirators and insurgents confidently expected the time of Spanish domination, issued in with the conquest, to come to an end. Even if one could not be sure precisely when this epochal change would occur, it was understood that a historical and political renewal was imminent. In Ambaná, this millenarian vision was accompanied by a radical challenge to the existing Catholic cult, while in the late 1770s the prophecies of social upheaval and transformation showed a conspicuous Christian influence. In both cases, however, the evident belief that time and history played themselves out in successive stages implied a significant pattern of destiny or providence. This mythic aspect undoubtedly contributed to the reverence with which Indian community members treated the leaders of the anticolonial movement in Ambaná as well as Tomás Katari and Túpac Amaru. More exalted than regular patriarchal protectors, we can assume they received the title of "saviors" or "redeemers" for their role in the collective historical emancipation.

The project of Inka restoration led by Túpac Amaru in Cuzco was the single most important addition to the political panorama at the time of the great insurrection. While a small sphere of educated, urban-based critics of Spanish colonial government sustained the idea of legitimate Inka authority during the eighteenth century in Peru, there is no evidence of any political agenda for Inka sovereignty in the region of La Paz until late 1780. So far this analysis has emphasized the millenarian figure of the Inka as well as the ambiguities of Túpac Amaru's own separatist project. In the following chapter, the view from La Paz will allow us to explore further his political significance for local peasant insurgents.

At first glance, the initial days of Indian-creole partnership in Oruro suggest similarities to the situation in Caquiaviri. In both places, creoles held posts of authority during the uprising while accommodating to community forces, most overtly through ethnic cross-dressing. The project of racial integration under Indian hegemony was thus tried out, however briefly. And when the alliance broke down in Oruro, there emerged the agenda of annihilating the enemy, as it had in the earlier anticolonial mobilizations in La Paz. The resemblances between Oruro and Caquiaviri derived from the strength of base-level community forces (with a corresponding absence of prominent, charismatic, or visionary leadership) in both cases.

Yet, as we have seen, the dynamics in Oruro were profoundly shaped by the general anticipation of Inka rule and the concrete agenda set by Túpac Amaru. His program determined the interracial alliance, and creoles did not emerge from jail to enter into political relations with Indians, as they had in Caquiaviri. In both cases, creoles were forced to accede to the greater power of Indians, yet in Caquiaviri this power was located below in the community, while in Oruro it was ultimately located above in the Inka king.

An initial finding in this chapter is that a key set of Indian options, agendas, and expectations of emancipation had been worked out in the conflictual, politicized period prior to the full-scale revolutionary conjuncture. But it has also been established that from 1771 to 1781 there emerged a major new element in the insurgent imagination. With Túpac Amaru, the peasant vision shifted from the model that "the king was the community for whom they ruled" to a utopian project of Inka sovereignty. In turning next to the Aymara movement and its leader Túpaj Katari, we can more fully examine the fundamental question of how Indian community forces—seasoned by decades of political struggle yet now under the command of visionary leadership—perceived, participated in, and shaped the pan-Andean insurrection of the early 1780s.

6

Emancipation Projects and Dynamics of Native Insurgency (II)

The Storm of War under Túpaj Katari

Building on the discussion of insurgent projects and political practices in the previous chapter, how does the La Paz case enhance our overall understanding of the pan-Andean insurrection of 1780–1781? In addressing the insurrection from La Paz, the point here is not simply that regional differences are important within the broad categories used to analyze the movement.[1] It will not be my purpose to show how regional or local particularities can corroborate or add nuances to an established macrolevel view. Nor will I be concerned to prove that the perspective from a "peripheral" area, with dynamics of its own, can correct for a traditional bias in the literature that assumed the insurrection as a whole could be characterized by the patterns prevailing in Cuzco. For instance, the absence of cacique participation in La Paz can be taken to show that the insurgency was not a "rebellion of the caciques," a notion that is at times still encountered in references to 1781. By the same token, a comparison between the social origins of the leadership in La Paz, where there was primarily an Indian peasant command structure, and Cuzco, where there was greater creole representation, shows that the movement overall was not so racially heterogeneous as the Cuzco profile might suggest.[2]

Of course, the leading work on the great insurrection was never confined by a narrow Cuzco-centric scope. The panoramic coverage of Boleslao Lewin and subsequently that of Scarlett O'Phelan have drawn upon abundant archival materials for Upper as well as Lower Peru.[3] A new body of unpublished or only recently published regional monographs will further advance the historiographic appreciation of local and panregional dimensions to the Andean insurgency and civil war of 1780–1783.[4]

With regard to La Paz and its particular importance, there is no justification for considering it in any sense a peripheral region. The two prolonged sieges of the city, which spanned from March until October of 1781 and brought together both Aymara and Quechua forces, made La Paz one of the two foremost theaters in the war, the other being the city of Cuzco and its hinterland. In terms of the duration of the campaigns in the region, the intensity of the combat, the quantity of material and human resources expended by both sides, and the strategic importance of control over the city and its resources, La Paz may even be considered the primary military theater.

Furthermore, the literature recognizes that there were essentially two stages to the insurrection and holds that the second stage had sharply distinctive features.[5] The initial stage unfolded mainly in the Cuzco district and lasted up until the capture of the Inka in the town of Langui. In the later stage, military command passed to Túpac Amaru's relatives and other regional leaders, and the locus of the insurgency shifted to the southern Aymara provinces. The first point that bears emphasis in our approach here is that La Paz was the core region in the second stage. For coming to terms with the meaning of the latter phase of the insurrection and war, La Paz offers the best possible place to begin.[6]

The previous chapter treated some of the distinctive features of other key regions in the insurrection: Chayanta, Cuzco, and Oruro. What are the crucial issues seen as marking the second phase of the war and distinguishing the region of La Paz? In the more recent historiography, mobilization in La Paz, especially under Túpaj Katari, has taken on the following set of associations: it reflects the most radical, racially antagonistic, and violent aspect to the war; and it represents the supersession of Indian leaders and their formal political program by the self-determining momentum of peasant combatants.

These associations are not always explicit, but they can be extrapolated from the literature as a whole. In the following summation by Alberto Flores Galindo, who saw the epicenter of events shifting over time to the southern altiplano, we may consider La Paz to be the regional expression of the peasant project: "In the Tupamarista revolution there were two forces that wound up at odds with one another. The national project of the indigenous aristocracy and the class (or ethnic) project that emerged out of rebel practice. At first, all appeared to accept the 'political program' of

Túpac Amaru. The divergences arose with the very unfolding of events, at the same time as the violence developed. It was thus evident that while the leaders envisioned a revolution to break with colonialism and modernize the country, . . . peasants understood that they were called to a pachakuti [cosmic upheaval and transmutation]."[7]

According to Scarlett O'Phelan's appraisal, which ultimately suggests a strong democratic quality in the Aymara movement, leadership in La Paz was less determined by kinship ties within a small circle and less marked by a vertical command style than in Cuzco. Túpaj Katari relied more upon a community base of support, leaders were designated from below, and "Indians overwhelmed their leaders' guidelines for action." For María Eugenia del Valle de Siles, corroborating another judgment of O'Phelan, the movement in Upper Peru displayed "not only a rural and popular character, but a marked indigenous accent," which contrasted relatively with that of Lower Peru.[8] The view, also sustained by O'Phelan, that a more radical antiwhite and anticreole position developed within the Aymara army during the second stage of the insurrection was taken further by Leon Campbell, who distinguished between the "kataristas' capricious racism" and the "tupamaristas' fragile ethnic coalition." Campbell also spoke of a "virulent Aymara nationalism" vis-à-vis not only whites but Quechuas from the north. René Zavaleta Mercado also conceived of the Aymara wing within the overall insurrection as a mass movement whose democratic content was vitiated by its ethnocentrism, reactionary violence, and radical messianic fervor.[9]

The prominent or distinctive features of La Paz that emerge from the literature—features that will be interrogated rather than immediately assumed in this chapter—are often predicated upon a contrast with Cuzco. In fact, the nature of the movement in La Paz is sometimes and in some ways seen as antithetical to that of Cuzco. Therefore, the issues that have been identified—radicalism, racial antagonism, and violence, as well as the strength of base-level forces—suggest some of the most significant differences within the movement overall and can help to answer the questions posed at the start of the last chapter as to the meaning of insurrection for Andean people.

Once those features associated with La Paz in the literature have been specified, however, it is possible to take the analysis one step further. For, in other ways, La Paz was not utterly distinct from other regions. There were, after all, comparable dynamics in the northern district, and the questions of radicalism, racial antagonism, and violence as well as the thrust of base-level forces do arise elsewhere. Eschewing a regional essentialism that fixates on supposed contrasts between different areas and a cultural essentialism regarding the people in those areas, the dynamics in La Paz can be seen to reflect questions of prime importance in other regional theaters of the insurrection. By the same token, to take a pair of examples from regions also formerly treated as peripheral or secondary, the conclusions to the previous chapter established that the issues associated with Chayanta—Indian autonomy without abandoning the colonial pact with the Spanish king—or Oruro—where cross-racial alliance was tried out—are pertinent for understanding La Paz. Beyond its military and conjunctural importance, then, La Paz in 1781 is a valuable site to address the meaning of Indian insurgency throughout the southern Andes in the "age of insurgency."

In the death-sentence of Túpaj Katari, Oidor Francisco Tadeo Diez de Medina, a creole from a prominent La Paz family, condemned the Aymara leader as an "infamous, perfidious traitor, mutineer, assassin, and ferocious man or monster of humanity in his shamelessness and abominable and horrible ways."[10] The images of Katari as a beast, monster, or barbarian have continued to surface over the past two centuries. A sense of horror yet fascination with the violence of 1781 remains barely below the surface in much of the literature dedicated to the Andean civil war and in the profiles of the Aymara commander.

Just as La Paz has come to represent in some ways an antithesis to Cuzco, Túpaj Katari, who is often seen to embody representative characteristics of the regional movement in La Paz, figures as the antithesis of the Inka José Gabriel Condorcanqui, better known as Túpac Amaru. Julián Apaza, who later took the name Túpaj Katari, was born in the jurisdiction of the town of Sicasica, and after transferring to the neighboring town of Ayoayo he became a tribute-paying forastero resident in Sullcavi ayllu.[11] A mistaken rumor had it that he was the illegitimate son of the Ayoayo sexton and that he served for a time in the same occupation.[12] According to other unsubstantiated reports, he labored in the home of a mestizo notable in the town of Sicasica as a lowly bread baker and at a creole-owned ore refinery in the same area. By his own account, he was a trader *(viajero)* in the La Paz commodities of coca and baize cloth.[13] José Gabriel Condorcanqui was also a trader circulating along the southern Andean routes that connected Cuzco to the great mining center in Potosí. But Apaza would not have owned a large train of mules like his political counterpart; in all likelihood, he would have been a typical petty Indian trader from the Sicasica highland district. Indian community members from the area had longstanding trade ties with the Yungas valleys, where they obtained coca leaf in exchange for highland goods such as woven cloth and jerky. They then circulated widely, along the royal highway that passed through the Sicasica towns, spanning out over the altiplano, and down to other eastern valleys or to the Pacific coast, for coca in particular was ever and everywhere in demand. This petty mercantile activity was presumably intense in the eighteenth century as the La Paz regional economy expanded vigorously.

Unlike Condorcanqui, Apaza was not an Indian noble nor was he accustomed to intercourse with members of the creole and European upper class. He was illiterate and spoke no Spanish. Neither did he cut an impressive figure, as Condorcanqui did, for his Spanish interlocutors. The Augustine friar Matías Borda, who spent six weeks in the El Alto rebel camp, estimated his age at thirty and described him as looking "quite ridiculous" as a political and military chief.[14] The scribe Esteban de Loza, who encountered him after his capture, gave this rough sketch: "The said Julián Apaza was a native of Ayoayo, an Indian of very low condition, who had labored in the lowest occupations, being one of the poorest of people during his life. He was of middling stature, with an ugly face, somewhat deformed in his legs and hands, but his eyes, though small and sunken, along with his movements demonstrated the greatest astuteness *[viveza]* and resolution; of slightly whiter color than most of the Indians from this region."[15]

In the literature, Amaru and Katari are also contrasted politically. Zavaleta put the distinction this way: "In effect, two wings or tendencies can be discerned in [the general movement]. On one hand, a political line that we might call peasant or ecumenical for all of colonial society (an Inka program for all Peru), incarnated by Condorcanqui himself but also by the Rodríguez brothers and even their forerunner Tomás Katari. On the other hand, a millenarian, militaristic, and ethnocentric wing, which is expressed directly and rather ferociously in the figure of Julián Apasa. . . . If Katari was more bloodthirsty, extremist, and terrible than Amaru, the latter held a project for all, a utopia that was not merely utopian."[16]

The image of Katari as an irrational, superstitious impostor given to drunkenness and carnal excess comes in large part from the account of Fray Borda. According to the common version, Julián Apaza justified his leadership of the movement after intercepting a letter from Túpac Amaru meant for Tomás Katari. He falsely claimed to have received the Inka's approbation himself, fabricated the new appellation "Túpaj Katari" by combining the names of the Cuzco and Chayanta leaders, and pretended thereafter to be viceroy. He engaged in arbitrary violence and incredible, "absurd" ritual or magical performances.[17] The colonial judgments have been echoed, until the present, by other writers. Ridicule and repulsion mark the commentary of Campbell: "Katari established a virtual monarchy in Pampajasi overlooking the city of La Paz, living there with his queen and court, consulting oracles and mawkishly behaving as a sovereign. . . . During the months which passed prior to the arrival of Colonel José de Reseguín and the Spanish forces from Buenos Aires in October, . . . Katari had grown more irrational and capricious, ordering anyone who was not demonstrably Aymara put to death and consulting oracles for guidance."[18] If Katari's ritual and religious practices were incomprehensible to colonial elites and remain so for later historians, the same could be said for his correspondence. While one nineteenth-century scholar remarked on the "barbarous Indian orthography," a century later another prominent historian found the correspondence "unintelligible": "The confusion in his letters is incredible."[19] Even the one scholar who has specialized in the siege of La Paz, María Eugenia del Valle de Siles, found it difficult to overcome the "confusing, contradictory, and incoherent language." Rather than exploring the letters in their own light, she concluded that they only impoverished the political and ideological content of Túpac Amaru's project.[20]

The work produced in Bolivia varies somewhat from the literature addressed so far in this discussion, since it is less concerned with the insurrection as a whole or the specificity of La Paz within the larger Andean context. Compared to the Peruvian literature on Túpac Amaru, it is notable, first of all, that Túpaj Katari has never fit so neatly within the Bolivian nationalist pantheon, even as a precursor of independence.[21] There is a body of work, which could be considered *paceñista* urban history, that attempts to honor the heroes and martyrs of both camps in 1781. Rather than pass judgment against Aymara forces, it recognizes the oppression borne by Indians under Spanish colonial rule as well as the valor of Indian leaders and troops in battle. It also empathizes deeply with the suffering of the urban populace under siege. This paceñista current fixates its attention on the 109-day siege itself and has relied for its accounts primarily upon the diaries produced by creoles and Europeans who lived through it.[22]

Just as Katari finds no convenient niche within the nationalist political imagination, it is difficult to embrace the siege as an episode of regional/urban history since it leads to no affirming regional/urban identity. Perhaps avoiding the uncomfortable conclusion that 1781 was a race war, various authors have ultimately acknowledged it to be a story of "the countryside against the city."[23] Unsurprisingly, this work does not probe deeply into Indian perspectives or provide much insight into Túpaj Katari. The Aymara leader is evoked rather blankly or rhetorically, for the most part, as an audacious and astute caudillo. As a whole, this literature presents a powerful image of unresolved confrontation and social trauma, though it does not explore their roots or seek to explain them.[24]

The foremost scholar of the insurrection in La Paz, María Eugenia del Valle de Siles, emerges from this same paceño tradition. Drawing upon lengthy, dedicated investigation and thorough familiarity with the abundant archival materials, Valle de Siles has accomplished the major task of reconstructing the narrative of events in the region at the time of the war. Her deep immersion in the empirical evidence affords sound judgment on many historical matters that surface in the pages of her study. She has transcended the paceñista emphasis on the city to include the rural hinterland within her scope, and she has dealt sympathetically with the Aymara forces as much as with creoles and Europeans.[25]

Her work is, at the same time, limited conceptually—she spends little time on matters of theory, historiography, or thematic discussion about the nature of the historical moment she is covering. Nor does she pretend to provide an original interpretation of the indigenous vision of the war. Her treatment of Túpaj Katari is the fullest available; she assembles the most important evidence and takes cognizance of the biases and filters in the colonial documents. Yet in other ways her portrait is lacking. She finds, for example, Katari's written communications to be without "logic and sense" and she blurs his profile in her effort to fit Katari within the homogenizing typological categories of a messianic leader. She also makes the misleading assertion that he was the "messianic caudillo" of a separate Aymara nationalist movement.[26]

The Manifestations of the "Resplendent Serpent"

By early 1781, we can imagine that Julián Apaza, at the mature age of thirty, was a man seasoned by years of personal hardship and wide experience. As a common forastero from a rural ayllu of the altiplano, he was brought up and lived in the poorest, most demanding of circumstances. He suffered from a physical infirmity, perhaps childhood poliomyelitis, that left his legs and hands somewhat twisted. His physical energy was not diminished, however, for it clearly matched the intensity of his character. He undoubtedly developed self-reliance from early on. If he did work in an ore mill, as rumored, he would have known firsthand the creole economic power and the rigors of colonial proto-industry. As an itinerant trader he would have been exposed to the rough conditions of the road. He was surely accustomed to brusque dealings with the other Indians, cholos, and mestizos who led their llama caravans or packs of mules along the same routes and must have met strangers and heard stories about distant corners of the realm. In his travels, he would have learned a great deal about the lives of people residing in the rural highlands and valleys and may have visited other colonial cities besides La Paz. He would have acquired an extensive knowledge of the engrained, everyday modes of colonial domination, as well as the common suffering of Indians, their fears and resentment, and the yearning for release from the "heavy yoke."

Julián Apaza's political formation clearly derived from the acute phase of community struggle (while he was still in his teens) that culminated with the uprisings in the town of Sicasica in 1769 and in Yungas and Pacajes in 1771. In 1781, Apaza's wife, Bartolina Sisa, stated that he had contemplated the movement for ten years.[27] As a trader, he would have also been very familiar with the unpopular commercial reforms being introduced in the 1770s. These measures affected Indian traders, as they did mestizos and creoles, and Apaza would have known about the customshouse and tax disturbances in Yungas and the city of La Paz in the late 1770s. If he was not present at the 1780 riot in the urban center, he may well have been among those Indians seen converging upon the city from Sicasica and Pacajes while it was underway. (See chapter 4.)

Bartolina Sisa had a falling out with her husband and on no less than five occasions was jailed because Apaza had not made his tribute payments. She had not seen him for two years prior to the insurrection, during which period Apaza was presumably especially active in organizing the movement. He would later acknowledge having "traveled to a great many towns and places and made enormous efforts to persuade and mobilize the Indians." Túpac Amaru made a trip to Cochabamba and Oruro in April 1780, only months before the outbreak of insurgency in Cuzco, yet there is no evidence that the two ever crossed paths. With his forceful personality and clandestine efforts, Apaza did succeed in forming a small nucleus of people, a number of them relatives and reliable contacts from Ayoayo, who were committed to his project from the start. When the time for mobilization came, Julián Apaza was prepared and Túpaj Katari came forth to assume command in full view of the La Paz communities.[28]

When considering the identity and conduct of Túpaj Katari as a leader, it is important to keep in mind that he was faced with a tremendous political challenge. It was his task to motivate, mobilize, and guide tens of thousands of peasants from around a vast area, who possessed no regular military training and no preexisting political vehicle that unified them on such a broad scale. It is also critical to regard Katari in a new light, outside the shadows of colonial stereotype and prejudice. With these considerations in mind, we will look at three questions that are fundamental for understanding Túpaj Katari: his political identity and legitimacy, warrior culture and violence, and spiritual power and identity. From this approach, a more palpable and intimate, a more human and even more remarkable figure begins to emerge.

First, then, is his political identity. By late 1780 and early 1781, the political influences of Tomás Katari to the south and Túpac Amaru to the north were converging in the Sicasica area to produce an exceptional state of affairs. Tomás Katari, increasingly in need of outside support, sent word that he had obtained a reduction in tribute payments. Twelve of his followers traveled to the province, presumably to extend his political connections.[29] The Sicasica corregidor Ramón Anchoríz also reported that Indians were asking for a return of their tribute payments, because half the amount was due to Túpac Amaru.[30] In the southeastern area of the same province, bordering on Cochabamba and Oruro, Indians circulated about, mobilizing communities with edicts from Túpac Amaru, "their king and redeemer," and with large wooden "medals" portraying the Inka and his consort.[31]

In February 1781, as the insurgency was underway in nearby Oruro and at the start of the insurrection in Sicasica, the figure of Tomás Katari assumed prominence. As Gregoria Apaza testified: "The motive for rising up was the repartos of the corregidores, the customshouses, the commercial monopolies, and other exactions that were charged them. They intended to abolish them, taking the lives of corregidores, Europeans, and other employees who collected these taxes. The Indians declared that there was a decree from His Majesty to this effect, and its executor was one Tomás Katari who came from up there and from Spain."[32] The specific political program here and the pretense of being a "commissioner" of the king of Spain clearly reflect the project of Túpac Amaru; and we know, as the Oruro uprising demonstrates, that the Cuzco leader's designs were familiar to Indians in the region at this time. But the report also draws on the stories about Tomás Katari, who had indeed traveled as far as Buenos Aires and obtained a state decree in his struggle against local and regional misgovernment. Rumors circulating in the countryside told of Tomás Katari journeying all the way to Spain and holding a private interview with the king.[33]

Gregoria Apaza went on to add: "With this news [of Tomás Katari's commission from the king of Spain], the Indians of Calamarca and

Ayoayo were stirred up and resolved to prepare for him with the atrocities and destruction that they wrought in Sicasica, Sapahaqui, Ayoayo, and Calamarca."[34] Such peasant anticipation of their redeemer, reminiscent of the situation in nearby Oruro during the same month of February, evokes the coming of Túpac Amaru. Another source attributed the community attacks that took place during carnival in the highland and valley areas of Sicasica, as well as those of neighboring Cochabamba, to an order of Túpac Amaru.[35] Yet Gregoria Apaza explicitly cited Tomás Katari as the mysterious figure awaited by the population in Sicasica province.

This overlap and possible confusion of identities in local peasant perceptions, as well as Tomás Katari's prominence, may have resulted from the initial clandestine operations of Julián Apaza himself. The Sicasica region was the home ground for Apaza's organizing and the evidence suggests that he strongly identified with the Chayanta leader during the early stages of the movement. Reports of Tomás Katari's resuscitation surfaced immediately after his assassination in mid-January, and Apaza, according to one story, subsequently declared himself to be Katari's reincarnation. Another story told of Julián Apaza intercepting a letter from Tomás Katari, sent before his death, to Túpac Amaru. The correspondence allegedly contained papers documenting Katari's lineage and ancestry, and Apaza seized them to stake his own claim to the deceased Katari's authority.[36]

Julián Apaza's own testimony under captivity appears to support the idea that he directly identified with Tomás Katari and that he claimed to possess documents establishing his political ties with the Chayanta leadership. He acknowledged that, after the peasant attack on Sicasica on February 24, he took command of the movement "by the faculty granted him *by a Katari,* by certain papers he gave him in the town and hills of Sapahaqui, which conferred on him the title of Viceroy."[37]

The identification with Tomás Katari persisted after Julián Apaza revealed himself to the Indian population and assumed public command of the insurgency in La Paz.[38] Indian followers addressed him as "Tomás Túpac-Katari" in their correspondence and when cheering him in his El Alto headquarters overlooking the city. He also demonstrated his political succession when he designated authorities and issued orders for the town of Coroma, far to the south in the province of Porco, where Tomás Katari's influence had previously been in effect.[39]

Yet Julián Apaza also explicitly identified with Túpac Amaru and Inka authority, most obviously in the names and titles he declared.[40] When he presented himself as "Tomás Túpac-Katari, Inka king" in some earlier moments of the uprising, he sought to project Inka noble preeminence while retaining political autonomy from the Cuzco leadership. At this stage in the insurrection, the La Paz commanders and his circle of advisers even entertained the idea that the movement could develop beyond regional hegemony and, by defeating Túpac Amaru himself, secure uncontested rule over the realm.[41] It was especially common for Túpaj Katari to refer to himself as "Viceroy" and for his consort Bartolina Sisa to be addressed as female "Viceroy" *(Virreina)*. Though Diego Cristóbal Túpac Amaru grew indignant upon hearing this self-attribution, it was an acknowledgment by Katari of Inka sovereignty.

As the war drew on and the Cuzco leaders consolidated formal superiority within the political hierarchy, Katari dropped the assumed name "Tomás," linking him directly to the Chayanta leader. He retained his original name, "Julián," while maintaining associations with Inka authority. He thus referred to himself simply as "Julián Túpac-Katari Inga," or, adopting the military-political title granted him by Andrés Túpac Amaru, as "Governor." In one honorific formula—"Governor don Julián Túpac-Katari, descendant and principal trunk of the royal armies that governed these kingdoms of Peru"—he echoed the noble genealogical discourse of Túpac Amaru and framed his own military status in terms of the preconquest authority of the Inka state.[42]

As eighteenth-century contemporaries observed, the very name "Túpaj Katari" was a compound that drew upon the redemptive figures of Túpac Amaru and Tomás Katari. In both Aymara and Quechua languages, according to the trilingual Oidor Diez de Medina, "túpac" meant brilliant or luminous, while, coincidentally, the Quechua term "Amaru" and the Aymara term "katari" both signified "serpent."[43] Yet it also worth noting another point about this appellation. "Tupacatari" was, in fact, a real surname of principales in the town of Sicasica where Julián Apaza was born.[44] This could appear to be another curious yet irrelevant coincidence, but it may not have been insignificant to Julián Apaza when he took his adopted name. Apaza—who was not only a peasant commoner but a forastero at the bottom end of the community tributary scale—may have been symbolically laying claim, in taking this name, to the elevated ethnic, community, and patriarchal prestige of local Indian nobles.

Naturally, this claim would not have been well received by other Indians of higher state than Julián Apaza. Fray Borda laid out this dilemma of political and patriarchal legitimacy for Apaza: "There were many who disputed the government of said Katari. They said, if an Indian with the minimum family obligations, the son of an unknown father—and at best the illegitimate son of so-and-so Apaza, the Ayoayo sexton, an occupation he was trained in—as well as being by nature very rude, since he didn't even know how to read, and someone whose marriage with the said queen is even disputed, if he had himself crowned or made chief, why shouldn't they do the same, given that they were principales and legitimately worthy of respect?"[45] For rivals such as these, especially ones familiar with the prevailing dynastic hierarchy in Sicasica, Apaza's noble pretensions would have provoked special irritation.

Katari also relied upon Inka certification to back up his authority. He requested various commissions from Diego Cristóbal Túpac Amaru so that Indian troops would respect his command. On one occasion when furious community members threatened to kill him and the Quechua colonel Juan de Dios Mullupuraca, they "satisfied" the troops with a decree from José Gabriel Túpac Amaru. In some cases Katari also continued to maintain Amaru's fiction of the commission from King Carlos III, and in a clear parallel to the claims of caciques in the eighteenth century, he held that the king had recognized his noble Inka status.[46]

One episode during the war brings together a set of the issues we have considered so far: the importance of Tomás Katari's figure in the Sicasica area during the early phase of the insurrection; Túpaj Katari's compound identification with Tomás Katari and Túpac Amaru; and the problem of political legitimacy vis-à-vis local community members and nobles. In late April, two letters written in the name of the Sicasica community announced that Indians refused to obey Túpaj Katari. They held that he lacked any title granting him the right to govern and that he was of a low social sphere. Any legitimate authority had to be transferred from the insurgent in Chayanta, "Tomás Túpac-Katari," who had in fact maintained correspondence and ties with the primary leader José Gabriel Túpac Amaru of Tinta. They called for an end to the siege of La Paz and warned of the approaching Spanish auxiliary troops.

Túpaj Katari then set forth to win over the recalcitrant community of Sicasica. When he reached Ayoayo he produced a copy of a letter from Túpac Amaru, written to Visitador Areche, in which the Cuzco leader laid out his justification for the uprising. According to the Spanish report at the time, Amaru had dispatched the letter to his collaborator in Chayanta, the "real Tomás Túpac-Katari," but it never reached him because the messenger died en route in Omasuyos. The letter fell into the hands of the impostor Túpaj Katari, the story went, who declared that it was a royal decree *(cédula)* addressed to himself. Though he did not succeed this time in gaining the adherence of the Sicasica community, Katari finally called for three days of "royal festivities" in El Alto to celebrate the content of the letter.[47]

Túpaj Katari's engagement of plural sources of identity and authority were as mystifying to observers then as they have been today. Indian politics were, indeed, not transparent and straightforward; yet when Indian political conduct is seen as strategic, it does point toward underlying interests and stakes. The profusion and confusion of names and titles, the adoption of different political identities, and the claims to possess legitimating documents were part of Katari's tactics to establish his own political power in the region and his legitimacy as an organic peasant leader in a hierarchical setting. They should not be seen as the peculiar ruses of an impostor but as a more common recourse within colonial political culture.

Katari's symbolic tactics recall those of caciques and Indian nobles who drew on multiple sources of authority as political governors and mediators in colonial society. His creative attempt to generate a lineage identification of his own—as "Katari," "Inka," or "Tupacatari"—resembled the efforts of Indian nobles who asserted, and sometimes reinvented, their genealogical lines for political purposes. (See chapter 2.) Tomás Katari, Túpac Amaru, and other Inka leaders during the insurrection also relied on improvised or calculated tactics involving assumed identity and documentary claims. Miguel Bastidas, for example, presented himself as the Marquis of Alcañises and Andrés Túpac Amaru released fabricated letters from José Gabriel after the latter's death. To the great frustration of colonial authorities, in the aftermath of the insurrection new leaders would continue to emerge and claim the Inka mantle.[48]

The importance of controlling official documents had been proven in the local battles, such as those over cacicazgos and repartos, that were ongoing in the eighteenth century. Politics surrounding the production, circulation, and semantic consumption of colonial documents were of course present, for Indians as well as for other colonial subjects and agents, throughout the colonial period. Yet the increasing politicization of the countryside in the late-colonial era raised the stakes for communities, for scribes and other rural intermediaries, and for colonial authorities.[49] It was a time when caciques were less and less reliable as community representatives who could be entrusted with the tasks of obtaining, guarding, and interpreting such critical written media of authority. Documentary politics—involving the pursuit of power and legitimacy flowing from real or imagined written texts emitted by higher spheres of political authority—thus became just as important for the projects of nonliterate peasants as they had been for Indian governors and nobles or colonial elites in the past.

Let us turn now to a second aspect of Túpaj Katari, his warrior persona, and to the problem of violence. The conventional discourse among eighteenth-century elites cast Katari as a "bloodthirsty Indian butcher or ferocious beast." For Fray Borda, who had firsthand experience of the Aymara commander, Katari was "tyrannical, wild, and inhumanly carnivorous." Borda's profile of Katari and his "barbarous cruelty" resulted not only from his aggression against the residents of La Paz but also from his conduct within the insurgent camp and vis-à-vis other Indians. The friar told of Katari ordering frequent corporal punishment and executions not only of captives and deserters but of his own Indian troops and cadre as well. His violence was intimately associated, for Borda, with regular drunkenness and lasciviousness.[50]

The testimony of other leaders within the Aymara and Quechua camps also pointed to Katari's "homicides and enormous violence." Miguel Bastidas, the Quechua commander and brother-in-law of Túpac Amaru, reported that Katari's "fury" and desire to "kill all whites and Spaniards" prompted the Cuzco leaders to move into La Paz and take charge of the regional insurgency. He reported that Katari acted spontaneously because of his "fierce, ardent spirit and drunken abandon." "The colonels generally professed hatred for Apaza," he added; "they feared him and looked upon him with terror because of the liberty with which he, prompted by his energy and boldness, dispatched so many Indians when they opposed him." Katari himself acknowledged killing a number of Indians, usually by hanging and in one case with the body being dismembered and then tossed down the mountainside. By his own account, most of these victims had either spoken against him, stolen his property, acted in overweening fashion, challenged his authority, or humiliated him.[51]

Among the various reasons for Katari's use of violence, it is evident that he sought to reinforce military discipline and political order within an insurgent movement that had limited organizational cohesion. As a leader, he not only encouraged his soldiers with the conviction that they enjoyed divine favor, he also urged them to "give their all," pushing them to fight day and night without respite. With strokes of his saber, he drove forward those troops that held back from full combat with the enemy.[52] At times, he blamed the successful resistance of the city on the indolence of his own captains and soldiers: "Because [the city] was not already taken and destroyed, he would suddenly flog, as many times as he wanted, the captains and hilacatas, sometimes fifty or one hundred lashes. He [inflicted] other cruel and tyrannical punishments and sometimes executed those who did not demonstrate sufficient courage and formal acceptance of his ideas, which were to be inviolable."[53]

He was also obviously striving to impose his own authority, which we have already noted was somewhat fragile and lacking in ascriptive, "natural" foundations, over that of rivals or independent agents. He supposedly ordered the death of Marcelo Calle—a high-ranking Aymara leader who was his old comrade from Ayoayo and one of the earliest collaborators in the movement—for having carried out executions without Katari's authorization. He hung another Indian for a homicide he committed while acting as a military recruiter for the Inka leader Andrés Túpac Amaru.[54]

The cacique of Tiahuanacu was another victim at the gallows for his attempt to bypass Katari's command and avoid military obligations through recourse to wealth and ethnic prestige. After showing initial support for the campaign, he used it as an opportunity to conduct trading business in Yungas. He traveled to Diego Cristóbal Túpac Amaru's headquarters in Azángaro to donate coca and cash; and he returned with special dispensations allowing him to live at ease with full privileges in the town, for one son to hold the post of corregidor, and for the other to act as lieutenant in Tiahuanaco. In another case, Katari was summoned by an Indian calling himself the Qolla Qhapaq, the preconquest lord of the Aymara provinces. He warned Katari to present himself with an escort of only six men and to respect his authority, for otherwise he would draw upon his faculty for "lowering the sun from its hemisphere" through the manipulation of two mirrors. Katari, fearing the possibility of such magical faculties, appeared instead with a large force of troops. After a brief encounter, he seized the purported Qolla Qhapaq as a sorcerer, stabbed him repeatedly, and had him shot.[55]

It is also clear that Katari had a keen sense of personal honor, and this was at stake, for example, when he ordered the death of the one of the colonels in the Quechua army, Faustino Tito Atauchi. Challenging the Aymara commander's jurisdiction in La Paz, Tito Atauchi took Katari prisoner and stripped him of his wardrobe, coca, and silver and gold. He then delivered him, dressed only in an old shirt and undershorts given to him by Indians, before Andrés Túpac Amaru in Sorata. Andrés reproved Tito Atauchi for his unauthorized action and freed Katari with the new title of Governor. Upon returning to El Alto, Katari avenged this humiliation by hanging his enemy.[56]

This code of honor points toward another facet of Katari's personality and conduct, which ultimately involved Andean cultural and gender norms for violence. He took pride in the signs of rank—such as the fine dress, the store of coca that was symbolically important for the reciprocity of the patron, or the precious metals confiscated by Tito Atauchi—yet he entirely lacked the cultural refinement and nobility of José Gabriel or Diego Cristóbal Túpac Amaru. His sensitivity to humiliation and deadly reactions to challengers, as well as his "fierce, ardent spirit" *(genio ardiente, bravo),* revealed a warrior rather than a prince or statesman.[57]

Katari's fearlessness was also reason for his fearsomeness. Miguel Bastidas astutely noted this point when he declared that Katari's lack of hesitation in imposing corporal or capital punishment struck "terror" in the hearts of his followers. The unrelenting pressure upon subordinates and physical violence did breed resentment, but his intention was to instill profound fear and he succeeded in doing so—"he made their spirits tremble." Psychological intimidation was also central to his military campaign against the besieged Spanish population of the city. His letters to the Spanish authorities contained stark threats—for example to "return [the city] to dust and ashes" or to cut the throats and string up those who held out against him. He hung captives from the gallows in full view of the city. When he discovered that the creole artilleryman, Mariano Murillo, had been secretly corresponding with Spanish officials, he lopped off his arms and sent him back to the city.[58] He directed his troops to keep up their shouting and din throughout the night so as to keep the population permanently unsettled. The common conception of Túpaj Katari as an atrocious savage and the trepidation of the besieged urban residents indicate that he was quite capable of instilling horror in his Spanish enemies as well.[59]

Besides the functional political and military purposes of violence, which Spaniards also relied on, how can we understand Katari's conduct? According to Olivia Harris's contemporary ethnographic fieldwork, Andean peasants in northern Potosí view physical force and violence with striking ambivalence. Manifestations of physical force can be seen as admirable or as disturbing, legitimate or excessive, depending on the circumstances, yet they are ultimately associated with vital and even sacred powers. Violence is considered "other" or apart from "normal" social order, but in contrast to some bourgeois Western conceptions, it is "a necessary alternative state rather than a breakdown of normality."[60] The use of physical force in the form of fighting takes place on exceptional occasions when daily life has been suspended. In such liminal situations, which are lubricated by alcohol consumption as in other ritual performances, individuals manifest the dangerous and sacred forces of the earth, the mountains, and the ancestors.

In northern Potosí, the ambivalence of physical force and violence are metaphorically represented in the form of unpredictable, dangerous, fearsome animals. The fighting ability of the bull, for example, is admired, while its tremendous strength is also harnessed for the purposes of household and community reproduction. The condor, by relative contrast, is a wild predator identified with destructive, asocial powers, yet also worshipped because of its link to the mountains and ancestors. As part of the overall multivalency of masculine identity in Andean culture, men in particular are associated with these animals and their violent potential. The animal symbolism thus reflects the connection between virility and violence. Ritual combat during festivals *(tinku)* is one occasion when men are expected to express this potential, and open warfare *(ch'axwa)*, though even less frequent, is another.

These cultural and gender coordinates for violence provide a point of departure for understanding eighteenth-century Aymara warfare, Túpaj Katari's culturally specific conduct and identity during the campaigns, and differing peasant and elite reactions to him. Given the exceptional circumstances of the insurrection—a clearly differentiated time of war—Túpaj Katari's ruthless and implacable treatment of his enemies was entirely consistent with the ambivalent norms of Andean peasant culture. His violence, which was intended to horrify and awe, was appropriate for a brave masculine warrior, and he expected his followers to display similar fierceness and tenacity in battle.

He was unpredictable, dangerous, and menacing like a wild animal, and here again his name identified him with powerful, and potentially malevolent, underground forces that were now aroused. According to Bertonio's Aymara dictionary of 1612, "katari" signified "large snake"; while twentieth-century ethnographers have identified the katari as a "rattlesnake" or as an aquatic monster considered to be a malignant spirit. This creature can cause illness in people who come across it and hence offerings are sometimes made to propitiate it.[61] The snake's magical force in battle was also summoned by other Aymara leaders. A snake-rattle talisman "for the successful outcome of his malicious intents" was found among the implements of war possessed by one of Katari's officers.[62] At another early point in the war, he called himself "Julián Puma Katari," taking the name of the Andean mountain lion that is venerated in certain contemporary Aymara ritual contexts.[63]

Katari's symbolic identification with fierce and powerful wild animals recalls Guaman Poma's account of Andean warriors and chiefs in the warring age before the Inka's rule: "They were great captains and valiant lords of unalloyed courage. It is said that during battle they became lions and tigers and foxes and vultures, falcons and mountain cats. Thus, to this day their descendants are named *poma* [lion], *otorongo* [jaguar], *atoc* [fox], *condor, anca* [falcon], *usco* [wild cat]; and wind, *acapana;* bird, *uayanay* [parrot]; snake, *machacuay;* serpent, *amaro.* Thus the names and arms that came from their ancestors were of other animals; they won them in the battles they fought." Guaman Poma stressed, besides other pious and ethical features of their society, the fierce *(bravo),* cruel, and violent manner of these warrior lords when they fought. He further noted that they made ritual use of purgative and hallucinogenic plants to develop their physical strength and, we can infer, to transform themselves into tutelary animal spirits during battle.[64]

The evidence of Katari's drinking must also be understood within the Andean cultural frame. In the colonial period, alcohol consumption by Indians continued to be part of ritual performance and the demarcation of liminal circumstances in which one stepped outside the bounds of everyday life and made contact with sacred powers. Not only was such drinking appropriate for ceremonial religious occasions, such as Catholic festivals that Indians scrupulously celebrated in El Alto, but it was appropriate generally during a time of war. This Indian ritual practice was completely ignored by Spanish witnesses who observed condescendingly that Katari would be inebriated when he headed military processions on the outskirts of the city and parleyed with the enemy over the surrender of the city.[65]

Drinking was also especially important for a military chief who had to show that his own personal and physical power was unmatched. Here again there were parallels with the Aymara lords of the preconquest past whose valor was demonstrated by drinking copiously without losing their faculties.[66] The evidence from the war shows that Katari himself moved very capably between, on one hand, public drinking that involved the appropriate loss of self-control in ritually significant moments and, on the other, public drinking in which Katari retained full self-control. The night before his capture, he gave an example of his energy, astuteness, and even intuition while under the influence of alcohol. As part of a trap to delay Katari and give Spanish troops time to apprehend him, Tomás Inka Lipe sponsored lavish festivities in the town of Achacachi (Omasuyos) and plied the commander with alcohol throughout the evening of revelry. But suddenly, at one o'clock in the morning, Katari angrily announced that there was a plot to betray him and he immediately set out with a small group of loyal associates to evacuate the area.[67]

Finally, one other element in the colonial portrait of Katari's "savage" violence should be addressed. According to Fray Borda's report, when Katari made his regular rounds to oversee and encourage his troops, he would abduct Indian women from their families, with no regard for the scandal raised, in order to have sex with them. The women and their families attempted to resist these assaults, yet fear of Katari and the threat of punishment were overpowering. Such sexual predation, which took place when Katari was inebriated, followed established, yet once again ambivalent, codes in Andean peasant culture. Here again, Katari's conduct evoked the wild, terrible aspect of the carnivorous condor that seizes vulnerable sheep from Indian flocks.[68]

Considering the reactions to Túpaj Katari, we can see how peasant ambivalence toward violence could mean a mixture of sentiments. Mobilized community members could feel fear of the Aymara commander, as well as resentment and fatigue if they were directly subject to his exercise of physical force. Yet, under the circumstances of war, there would also have been shared, organic cultural assumptions and respect for a military leader acting in accordance with peasant norms of virility.

At the same time, the evidence points to striking contrasts between Katari and Indian elites who shared many common cultural and gender norms with "civilized" Spanish elites. Not only royalist caciques in 1781 but even some leaders of the insurgency recoiled before the peasant violence that Katari exemplified. This was most evident in the case of Miguel Bastidas, the somewhat reluctant Quechua commander who held maximal authority in the La Paz theater in the late phase of the war. When Bastidas, through Spanish interpreters, described Katari as bravo, we can imagine he had in mind the attributes of fearlessness, fierceness—with implicit animal connotations, though these would have held a distinctive resonance and not a pejorative significance for Andean peasants—and rage that Katari did in fact manifest as a leader. As already noted, Bastidas explained that the Cuzco leadership had intervened in La Paz precisely in order to control Katari's "fury." Bastidas himself maintained strained relations with the Aymara leader, found the "deaths, robbery, and devastation" repellent, and lived in "horror and fear" of the peasant troops.[69]

Túpac Amaru exemplified a patriarchal mode of political and gender authority distinct from the warrior figure and wild power of Túpaj Katari. He primarily projected a paternal image of benevolence and protection and a dignity befitting royalty. To avoid oversimplifications, we should note that Amaru also backed up his public decrees with clear warnings for those who should disobey him, and he did lead his forces to an early military advantage. By the same token, Katari also sought to assume the hierarchical prestige of his renowned political contemporaries, their paternal tone, ascribed nobility, or putatively commissioned rank. But the general profiles retain their contrasts. Unlike Katari, the scourge of the city of La Paz, Amaru displayed limited prowess or ardor on the battlefield. For example, he expended valuable time on political and administrative affairs and symbolic displays of governance in the southern provinces when he needed to move his troops against the capital Cuzco, as his consort Micaela Bastidas urged him to do. When he finally did reach the city and found it would not promptly surrender, he withdrew rather than risk sustained military engagement.[70]

Just as, in important respects, he and his circle followed colonial political and military codes during the war, he did not stray from colonial moral codes such as Christian sexual prescriptions. There were no accusations against him for indulging in "lasciviousness" or encouraging sexual violence, as against Katari; nor did he take an extramarital partner as Katari and other Quechua leaders did, an act that was, after all, within the parameters of colonial patriarchal practice. Again unlike the Aymara chief, Amaru rarely became inebriated, a threatening sign of Indian unruliness for colonial elites and one that caciques were supposed to control.[71] In the end, then, the issues surrounding Túpaj Katari and the expression of violence illuminate important cultural differences responding to ethnic, class, and gender identity in colonial society.

The religious aspect of Túpaj Katari represents a third key to interpretation of the Aymara leader. In historiographic accounts, as we have noted, he has been ridiculed as an irrational and superstitious primitive or sociologically typed as a "messianic" leader. The cliché of Katari as atheistic, heretical, sacrilegious, or idolatrous, which was sustained by eighteenth-century elites, also assumes new significance in light of the emerging debate over the nature or degree of "Christianization" among Andean peoples in the colonial era. Our initial point here is to establish how religious forms of different cultural and historical provenance came together for Túpaj Katari in a meaningful fusion (rather than confusion) and to further specify the models for his ritual conduct.

For elites, of course, the religious cult in El Alto clearly operated outside ecclesiastical purview and made a mockery of Christianity. For his part, Katari asserted in a letter to Segurola, "I am as Christian as anyone else." The Indian chapel, approximately twenty yards square and roughly assembled out of poles with a ceiling of textiles, was furnished with ritual articles, icons, and even an organ taken from churches in the area. While he was often held responsible for the looting of churches, in fact Katari took scrupulous care of the religious objects in his custody. After transporting the Virgin of the Litany with him to do battle in Sicasica, for example, he safely returned the icon to its sanctuary.[72] Contrary to the accusations that he sponsored attacks against priests, he went to great lengths to see that clergymen, among them the Augustinian Fray Borda from Copacabana, were brought in to celebrate mass, administer the sacraments, lead processions, and otherwise maintain the cult throughout the war. Túpaj Katari held some of them in high esteem and was undoubtedly responsible for the fact that so few lost their lives in La Paz.

The story of Father Antonio Barriga's death is particularly revealing of the religiosity of Aymara peasant troops and that of their leader. Barriga was a Franciscan who had gone up to the Indian camp in El Alto on Monday of Holy Week in order to perform religious services. In the aftermath of a disastrous day of fighting on Wednesday, Indians determined that the clergyman had cursed them during his morning mass. They pointed to the fact that he had worn purple adornment, that he delayed in giving the ceremony, that he prayed toward the city from the edge of the plateau above it, and to other potential signs of treacherous sorcery. On the next day, while Katari was absent, they stabbed him to death and hung him along with other captives in view of the city.[73]

Katari became enraged when he returned to discover the killing. He severely punished those who had participated and called them excommunicates. He personally carried the body to the chapel, where he conducted a series of rites and grieved for the dead man. At one point he took the communion table from the portable altar, placed it upon the man's chest, and set the Sacrament from the church of Achocalla on top. Later, he removed the Eucharist from the monstrance, threw it upon the corpse, replaced it, and then carried the monstrance off with Bartolina Sisa as if they were going to enter the city. He was stopped in midroute by a crowd of Indian women and men who begged him to return.

There was clearly much more at stake for Katari than merely obeying Túpac Amaru's orders to respect priests. Other witnesses told Borda that Katari removed the Eucharist and, clutching it to his chest with one hand while wielding his sword with the other, he stormed about the plain, "letting everyone know that he had not been an accomplice of the disastrous and tyrannical death of Reverend Father Fray Antonio Barriga, so that he would receive no punishment whatsoever, much less meet defeat at the hands of the Spaniards."[74] Katari was extremely upset because he believed, as others would have had reason to believe as well, that there would be heavy spiritual retribution for the death. He sought to avoid culpability himself and to convince others, especially in the wake of the unexpected, crushing military losses of Easter week, that the movement would not be hurt as a consequence. The killing of Barriga did not indicate an anti-Christian religiosity on the part of peasants; rather their religious conception, according to which Christian spiritual forces occupied a fundamental place within a wider, animated field of the sacred, did not conform to ecclesiastical orthodoxy. By the same token, what contemporaries considered Túpaj Katari's "profanation" of the Eucharist was actually a sign of his own Christian imagination and convictions.

Other Christian references, with their charismatic tone or extraecclesiastical implications, have been taken as symptomatic of his messianic tendencies. The clearest evidence was his declaration that, "I am sent from God, so that no one has the power to do anything to me, and thus it seems to me that all I say is the work of the Holy Spirit."[75] He also carried with him a small silver box that "he opened slightly, looked inside, and then closed. Once in a while, he put it up to his ear, demonstrating to others that because of what was communicated to him by means of the box, he knew everything and was incapable of making a mistake in the pursuit of his aims. He even went so far as to profess that God Himself spoke into his ear." Other reports coincided with this account of Katari's "monkey business" *(monerías);* in one case, it was said that he told his followers that an image of the Virgin spoke to him from the box.[76]

When he emerged from the chapel, he extended blessings to the throng of Indians who cheered him in unison, "Tomás Túpac-Katari, Inka king!" They repeated this exclamation as they followed him to his "palace," with many of the officers kneeling to kiss his hand. This points once again to the connection between Túpaj Katari and Tomás Katari.[77] The Chayanta leader was venerated by his followers who addressed him as king and by divine titles, kissed his feet and clothing, and considered his word to be oracular wisdom. According to rumors, Katari persuaded his followers that they would resuscitate three (or five) days after their death in battle. This idea of resurrection was also associated with Túpac Amaru—he allegedly promised Indian combatants that they would be revived after three days—yet it specially resonated with Tomás Katari who, according to rumors, had been resuscitated himself.[78]

On Holy Thursday, prior to the celebration of Christ's resurrection, Katari washed the feet of twelve poor people and gave them food to eat. Yet this was not a case of Katari posing as a messianic Jesus. It was rather a Christian liturgical practice in itself appropriate to the Catholic calendar and scandalous to Spaniards only insofar as it was normally performed by royalty or other eminent personages.[79]

A number of other elements in Katari's religious repertoire were at a further remove from orthodox colonial Christianity or were of clear pre-Christian Andean origin. The sacred box by which he received divine guidance—possibly the sort of container used to transport the sacrament for administering the last rites—may have been similar to the small boxes which Uru Chipaya people of the southern altiplano used to hold *champi*. Champi are pieces of unworked bronze used in the Chipaya cult for chthonic divinities known as mallkus. While few are found today, they used to act as guardian spirits, associated with the ancestors, that could be consulted by their owner, and they could even be intermediaries for communication with a mallku. They also had malignant powers and could be used to curse an enemy. These functions, most explicitly the divine consultations and communication, fit with the accounts of Katari's use of the sacred box. The champi also resemble the protective amulets or stones known as *illa* that are kept with great secrecy, for example by the Laymi of northern Potosí. It seems safe to speculate that the silver box that Katari so mysteriously consulted could have contained similar talismans.[80]

Within the Indian chapel, Katari and Bartolina Sisa sat on a special dais along with other high officials. While mass was being celebrated, which was also the time he would consult his silver box, Katari looked in a small mirror that was set before him, and he continually made faces and gestures that Fray Borda considered "laughable" and utterly incongruous for celebration of the mass. At the critical moment when the officiating priest lifted the host and the chalice, Katari gazed in the mirror and then exclaimed: "Now I am seeing. I know everything that is happening everywhere in the world."[81] What was the meaning of this conduct?

Mirrors and, by homology, metals have had a rich, multivalent significance in Andean ritual and cultural representation. One basis for their importance is that they are reflectors of light.[82] Bertonio's Aymara dictionary reveals the semantic associations between mirrors *(lirpu* or *quespilirpu)*, resplendent objects such as glass or crystal *(quespi)*, and redemption or liberation (*quespiatha* meaning to free or redeem, *quespiyri* meaning redeemer).[83] We can see, therefore, the emancipatory or redemptive connotations in the very name "Túpaj," which according to Diez de Medina signified "brilliant" or "luminous" in both Aymara and Quechua.

But Bertonio also gave an added religious gloss to the Aymara verb "quespiata," with its associations to mirrors and luminosity. In Spanish translation, the term could mean "redeem from the hands of the Devil." According to contemporary ethnography, mirrors are considered to have a protective effect, like the coins or metals they resemble, by warding off the destructive forces of devils and the dead.[84] Thus, Katari's "mysterious" and "superstitious" behavior during mass involved recourse to Andean ritual articles (both his silver box and mirror) that assured spiritual protection and guidance at a time of intense spiritual warfare against demonic enemies.[85]

But what of Katari's claims to "see" and "know" what was happening in other places, while gesticulating and making faces? Once again, ethnography provides an answer. Among the Laymi, mirrors are identified with eyes; and in the Aymara area of Chucuito, coins, which are minted metals associated with mirrors, are also called "eyes" during ritual ceremonies. In these ceremonies, ritual specialists have these "eyes" set out upon a table in order "to see and think more clearly."[86] We can thus infer that when Katari looked into the mirror, he was not looking at himself, absorbed in his own image. Rather he was seeing other people and places, and reacting expressively to what he saw.

According to one full description of his actions during mass, "This idolater begins looking at himself in the mirror and then he declares, 'Now I am seeing. I know everything that happens everywhere in the world.' He continually takes his box (robbed from some church) out of his pocket, he looks at it and puts it up to his ear and to his eyes. Then he repeats the same thing, that he knows and understands everything. With this trick, the Indians are left full of admiration and very satisfied with his knowledge and power."[87] Katari was, then, demonstrating not only spiritual power but supernatural knowledge like that possessed by Andean ritual specialists. In La Paz today, the generic Aymara term for one of these specialists is *yatiri,* meaning "one who knows." The exceptional abilities, shown by Katari, to communicate with spirits and to clarify matters that are obscure through such communication are proper to the shamanlike specialist known as a *ch'amakani,* meaning "master of darkness." He is, as Katari himself was, an ambivalent figure both feared and respected for his powers, which can be used for black magic as well as for health and good fortune.[88]

The story of the purported Qolla Qhapaq—"who once governed these provinces," in Katari's account—confirms the use of mirrors in the generally clandestine practices of eighteenth-century Andean ritual specialists. And it supports the idea that Katari sought to establish his own sphere of spiritual power. As we noted above, Katari took quite seriously the Qolla Qhapaq's claim that he could "bring down the sun from its hemisphere by means of two mirrors." When Katari encountered the man, speaking in a falsetto voice from behind a curtain in the manner of a ch'amakani, he immediately killed him ostensibly as an evil sorcerer but also as a political and spiritual rival.[89]

Finally, it is interesting to note that Katari also summoned on his behalf the forces of the gentile ancestors *(chullpas)*, who were associated with the underworld and the dark age prior to the advent of Christianity. He approached their ancient tombs, scattered across the landscape, and cried out in a booming voice, "Now is the time to return to the world to help me!"[90]

So far then, we can see that the religiosity of Túpaj Katari involved the active, creative conjunction of forms and beliefs flowing from dual traditions and was meaningful for Katari and for those peasants who were "full of admiration" for him (just as it was heretical, idolatrous, or absurd for colonial elites). During the critical moment of war, which was charged with intense spiritual energy and significance, Katari had recourse to all the sacred resources at his disposal. Normally clandestine religious practices emerged into public view as Katari drew upon extraecclesiastical references and sources of power. His religious persona was probably inspired in the beginning by the cult surrounding Tomás Katari, with whom he originally identified and who was reputed to be a sorcerer. His own religious conduct, so inscrutable to observers then and now, was undoubtedly modelled after that of Andean ritual specialists, particularly the ch'amakani.

Katari was clearly concerned to assert (even defiantly) his identity as a Christian, as Túpac Amaru felt the need to do as well in his public declarations. Within his own camp, Katari also sought to demonstrate his spiritual powers, for example clairvoyance and communication with divinities and dominion over demonic forces. Yet when colonial observers treated Katari's religious conduct as histrionics—he "affected . . . much religion, with violent gestures and genuflections"[91]—it says as much about elite attitudes as it does about the Aymara leader. They would not take his religious expression seriously, and the effect was to reinforce notions of him as aberrant and primitive or as a charlatan. It would be a mistake to think that Katari was disingenuously improvising an eclectic religious identity or affecting a messianic style in order to secure his command. There was more to his conduct than instrumentalist theater, the display of cult and psychopomp to obtain legitimacy as a leader.

Katari was indeed aware of the contours of Andean peasant religiosity and he moved within them as a leader seeking to unify his movement. Yet the importance he placed on ritual revealed a personal preoccupation that must be understood given the conditions of intense spiritual warfare. Katari knew he needed spiritual power to hold ascendancy, and his military forces needed such power in order to triumph. Thus, it was not only personal but collective ritual that concerned him. Celebration of mass before ranking authorities, clergymen in their vestments, and peasant troops was the most important instance of this. Yet he also encouraged singing and dancing by Indians at the chapel and fasting by the priests in his camp as an act of devotion and purification.[92] At the same time, Katari believed that the outcome of the war depended ultimately on God. To understand more fully his religious outlook, and simultaneously the political vision of insurgents, we need to look at his letters.

In early 1781, Túpaj Katari was convinced, as was Túpac Amaru, that an epochal social transformation was underway. The prophecies circulating about the Peruvian coast and Cuzco highlands since the late 1770s had also been heard in La Paz and insurgent leaders referred to them confidently. During the political assemblies held in El Alto, officers repeatedly insisted: "They had to continue unto death in the effort to free themselves from the many burdens and taxes that the king of Spain's ministers, like the officials and corregidores, so arbitrarily imposed. These tyrannies had obliged them to rise up, as well as the fact that the time was up for the fulfillment of the prophecies that this kingdom would return to its own" *(volviese a los suyos)*.[93] These prophecies were echoed in the correspondence sent from El Alto and they help to understand the key declarations that historians have found so incoherent in Katari's discourse.

In his letter to the bishop of La Paz, Katari stated: "In the end, God above all else. We are following this judgment: what is God's to God and what is Caesar's to Caesar." To the head of the Franciscan order, he wrote: "You can forget your illusions. Now it comes from on high that everything be in its place, what is God's to God and what is Caesar's to Caesar." A letter to Segurola written in the name of all the communities of four provinces asserted: "Our aim is to die killing because this whole time we have been subordinates, or better yet like slaves; and in this assumption the Sovereign Legislator has awarded us this relief, because they were exceeding the law of God, and that is why now what is God's returns to God and what is Caesar's to Caesar."[94]

The scribe who penned the letters of Katari and the one attributed to the communities was probably the secretary Bonifacio Chuquimamani. He was described by Borda as an Indian who had lived for years in the city and worked as a clerk in the ecclesiastical tribunal. Over the course of the war, several such secretaries served Katari and had his consent to compose edicts and correspondence. But Chuquimamani was one of the most radical and influential of all Katari's counselors. According to Borda: "He wrote letters to La Paz full of a thousand follies, proposing in them that our king and lord had obtained this kingdom unjustly, that it was time for the fulfillment of the prophecies to give to everyone what is his, and what is Caesar's to Caesar. He also explained this to the Indians in their language, so that they would not falter in their campaign to take the city, and so forth, exaggerating the advantages they would enjoy in the future when they ruled."[95]

The prophecies told that each party would be "given" what belonged to it *(lo que es suyo)* and, in the sense of restoration, that what belonged to each would be "returned." The injunction to render unto Caesar the things that are Caesar's and to God the things that are God's was not associated with any of the reported prophecies in Lower Peru, and it was evidently lifted rather freely and creatively from its New Testament context (Matthew 22:15–22). When the Pharisees asked Jesus if Jews should pay taxes to Caesar, trying to force him to choose between sedition or repudiation of anticolonial Jewish groups, Jesus's clever response contained an ambivalent political message: it could be taken to mean sanction for the established order, or as a subversive challenge to secular authority by religious authority. It is unclear whether this Biblical allusion was in wider circulation and subject to popular exegesis at the time or whether it was Chuquimamani himself, drawing from his proximity to the ecclesiastical sphere, who introduced it into insurgent discourse; nor do we know precisely how he or Katari explained it to peasant troops. Yet the particular twist in the interpretation of this message for anticolonial Aymara leaders in eighteenth-century La Paz was that Caesar did not mean Carlos III, the supreme colonial authority, but the Inka king who was the rightful ruler of Peru. The broader implication was that the kingdom, and the things of the kingdom, would be given or returned to the Inka king and Indians, to whom they properly belonged.

The ideas expressed involved a fundamental reordering of social relations, or more exactly, the arrangement of a new harmony where disorder and injustice ("bad government") had prevailed. Because the king of Spain's representatives had violated the laws and exceeded the limits established by God or, in the explicitly radical version, because the conquest by the king of Spain was originally unjust, things now had to be put back "in their place." Ownership, rights, and law would be restored to what was appropriate or proper—in the sense of correct and also in the sense of belonging to or "one's own" (lo suyo).

The notion that everyone or each party would be given what was "suyo" (his or hers/its/theirs) paralleled the idea that things would be in their proper place *(cada cosa esté en su lugar)*. In other words, there was a correspondence drawn between property and place. In the latter phase of the war, Katari demanded the return of his captive wife and offered a truce in which "each party will go to its place" *(cada uno irá a su lugar)*.[96] For the insurgents, then, each of the contending parties had a place that was appropriate to it; that is, property and place also corresponded to distinctive subjects.

In one dispatch, Katari announced, "Thus, I will send all the Europeans on their way, so that they move to their lands." In another letter, he made the same offer: "They can all go safely to their country; they will be given an open path."[97] Explicitly, therefore, Europeans belonged in Europe, which was their land and their country; implicitly, Indians belonged in Peru, which was their own land and country. Here again, the idea of restoration and restitution involved a historical dimension referring to the changes that occurred with the conquest. Europeans would go *back* to where they were from or *return* to where they belonged, and Indians would recover the lands that once had been theirs.

The idea of rendering unto God what was God's displayed a religious conviction that came forth again and again in Katari's correspondence, underscoring his keen spiritual preoccupation and open acceptance of God's will. His letters were studded with expressions such as: "In the end, God above all others"; "this is from on high"; "all this is permitted by God, for without his great will nothing occurs"; and "with the favor of God." More than epistolary formula or the rhetorical additions of scribes, these were central to his thinking and reflected his personal views on the war. Hence, for example, he declared that strength of arms mattered less than having God on one's side.[98]

Katari was buoyed by his belief that divine providence favored him. His astounding rise from obscurity to power appeared to confirm this and justify his political and spiritual authority. The early circumstances of the war also seemed to indicate that the prophecies were true and that his movement would triumph. But this confidence was only one aspect of an underlying, radical acceptance of divinely determined fate. He believed that his forces would prevail, yet he consistently recognized "God above all others." In response to a letter from his collaborators, he wrote, "It seems to me that this is heaven-sent, that everything will fulfill our desires, from what we can tell. But everything depends on the will of the Supreme Legislator." He understood that without God's favor his forces would fail and acknowledged that both sides could be destroyed if God so willed it: "But if it comes from heaven that we both be wiped out, the will of God will be fulfilled in all things, because as they say, cut the bad fruit from the roots, thus we will all be wiped out."[99]

It was this religious attitude that explains Katari's conduct at the end of his life. After his detention at Chinchayapampa on November 9, 1781, he did not hold out as a defiant warrior against his captors. Nor did he show a supine acquiescence, like Miguel Bastidas, in the hope of being pardoned. He was first made to participate, along with the other insurgent leaders and community representatives, in a mass ceremony of repentance at the Sanctuary of Peñas in the district of Guarina. Then, over two days, Spanish interrogators with a scribe and interpreters took down his "confession" (or sworn testimony), in which he acknowledged that "he knew he must die."[100] On November 14, 1781, Katari was given the last rites and, when he reached the plaza where he would be quartered by four horses, he stopped to address the crowd of thousands of Indians who had come to Peñas to receive the king's pardon. He declared that they were not to trust in the Amarus, that their leaders had misled them, and that they should accept the pardon. He added that he now deserved to die because of his deeds.[101]

During the insurrection, Katari had acted as a fierce military commander, in accord with Andean peasant expectations and with the exigencies of war. He had also appeared as a distinguished political representative, within the terms of legitimacy established during the colonial era and during the phase of emancipation. After his capture, the time of war had effectively ended and, in terms of culture and gender identity, there were no longer the appropriate conditions for reckless, arbitrary, or fierce behavior. Nor could he present a prestigious political persona. In his final moments, he stood before the assembled body of Indians and, though he was now stripped of all signs of hierarchy, he spoke to them one last time with the dignity and authority of a true leader. According to Loza, the one observer who left an account of the scene, "they were astonished to see such a punishment applied to an Indian whom they had so respected."

Katari's words prior to the execution did not indicate that he was reconciled to the injustices of colonial government or Spanish occupation. They showed his practical realization that the insurgency was over and there was no purpose to further resistance. The Quechua leaders in particular were targets of his ire because, he believed, they were two-faced liars who had betrayed him while seeking pardon for themselves. He may have imagined that the anticipated historical and political transformation would come to pass in the future, but clearly he did recognize that the time spoken of in the prophecies would not come about in 1781. God had not, after all, favored the forces of the Inka king and his followers. The outcome of events proved that he had been mistaken in his initial confidence. He now openly accepted the divine will and was ready to give up his own life in repentance before God.

The energy that had always characterized him was undiminished to the end. But it was also Katari's perfect equanimity that so impressed Loza. In a passage that clearly broke from any predictable colonial discourse and that contradicted the conventional notion of Katari as a religious heretic or idolater, the scribe felt compelled to remark: "This tyrant, who during the course of the rebellion had committed such atrocious crimes, merited from Divine Clemency the greatest succor in the hour of his death, as he showed with his great repentance. He went forth to the execution staring intently at a crucifix, while making the most vigorous exclamations, and he preserved absolute tranquillity up to the very instant of his death." His bearing remained that of a man sustained by a deeply rooted religious outlook and one who faced his fate without doubt or hesitation.

In relation to the existing historiography, the foregoing study of Túpaj Katari's identity and conduct offers a more probing and intimate portrait of a figure who has usually been demonized or ridiculed within the terms of colonial (including neocolonial) discourse, or consigned to a hazy rhetorical existence as heroic caudillo because his life and politics are felt to be too contradictory, even explosive, today. The political, military, and spiritual aspects of Katari have been seen in light of the key problems that he faced as an organic peasant leader: namely, the difficulty of building legitimacy for himself and achieving a unified, coordinated movement of local community forces from around an extensive geographical area. The image that emerges is one of an extremely dynamic, creative revolutionary struggling to find—at an exceptionally fluid moment amidst a set of tremendously challenging conditions—the right stance before Aymara peasants, other Andean insurrectionary leaders, and their colonial adversaries, as well as before diverse sacred forces, ministers, and divine providence.

La Paz: The Community Groundswell

When peasant troops descended upon La Paz from the rim of the plateau overlooking the besieged city, as they did morning after morning, they commonly whooped and shouted, often with the accompaniment of drums, flutes, the pututu horn, and mortars used for firing salutes. It was with this same hue and cry, and the reports of rifles, that they acclaimed their leader Túpaj Katari. Their cheers were a cry of victory *(haylli)*, like the song traditionally sung by triumphant warriors as they entered a town after battle *(hayllitha)*. Just as the masses of warriors approaching the enemy resembled menacing dark storm-clouds, their outbursts were, within the terms of Aymara culture, like the thunderous, driving tempests *(hallu hayllisa huti)* that wreak havoc on peasant fields and crops.[102]

The main features of the Aymara war in La Paz, as they appear in the historiography of the 1781 insurrection, were identified at the start of this chapter: radicalism, racial antagonism, and violence, as well as the power of base-level mobilization. Building upon the study of Túpaj Katari, we turn now to these overlapping issues in order to interrogate and elucidate them further and to explain them, insofar as they do reflect actual historical dynamics rather than the superficial stereotypes of colonial discourse. This analysis will involve situating the issues within eighteenth-century Andean political culture and the conjuncture of 1780–1781 and understanding the "storm of war" from the Aymara vantage point.

Generally speaking, the radical orientation within the Andean insurrection can be thought of as practices and ideology going beyond the political stance laid out by the Túpac Amaru leadership in the first phase of the war. This refers especially, but not exclusively, to the identification of creoles and mestizos, alongside Europeans, as the colonial enemy and to the general deployment of violence, outside the regular military context, against the subjects and structures that were perceived by insurgents as representing colonial oppression.

While these features are normally identified with Túpaj Katari, there were in fact other agents associated with radicalism in La Paz. First were the communities themselves. According to Fray Borda, some of the Indians in Katari's camp were aware that he had led them into a doubtful situation from which they could not easily extricate themselves, but the communities "felt it was better either to die or defeat the enemy." The letter attributed to the communities of the four provinces declared: "The edicts issued by Sr. Gabriel Túpac Amaru have not been declared; they have all been covered up. That is why we are now motivated to see that all of us be wiped out, so that there be absolutely no more mestizos. For us the issue is to die killing, since all this time we have been subordinate, or better put, like slaves. . . . Though our viceroy proposed to us that we be humble, this is impossible. Inevitably we will finish you off because we have determined to do so."[103] The letter identified all non-Indians as the enemy and threatened to eliminate them entirely. It also corroborated Borda's report that community members firmly intended to fight without quarter against the enemy, without regard for their own life, in order to achieve domination. This idea was not an incidental one or merely confined to La Paz. After Tomás Katari's assassination, a report from the southern territory stated, "There is a single opinion that is heard: 'Since our king Katari died, let's all die killing.'"[104] The similar political discourse points once again to the links between the Chayanta and La Paz insurgencies.

The second agents of radicalism were certain advisers of Túpaj Katari. Perhaps the most notorious was one-eyed Pedro Obaya, who arrived from Azángaro falsely claiming to be Túpac Amaru's nephew. He took the honorific name of the historical Inka ruler Guayna Cápac and was commonly known as "the little king." His influence was most evident in the clever battle stratagems employed by insurgents. Obaya apparently sought to cultivate his own effective political power, rivaling that of Katari, through direct relations with the insurgent communities and by agitating among them. He also advocated the elimination of creoles.[105]

But Bonifacio Chuquimamani, the Indian or cholo secretary who had worked as an official scribe in the city, was an equally if not more important figure.[106] He had taken a leading role at the start of the uprising in the province of Sicasica and acquired the title of *oidor* as one of Katari's closest collaborators and highest counselors. Katari himself later testified that Chuquimamani, out of all the leaders, was "the most rebellious."[107]

As we noted above, he penned Katari's letters expressing the notion that all would receive what was theirs, and Caesar what was due to Caesar, and he expounded these ideas to Indians in their native language. He asserted that the Spanish sovereign had obtained the kingdom unjustly, and he incited the troops with the prophecies and the promise of material rewards when they governed. He was also the probable redactor of the letter, with its radical terms and tone, from the communities of the four provinces.

The massacre on March 19, 1781, in Tiquina is one episode that historians have commonly cited when referring to radicalism in La Paz. It was undoubtedly also the kind of occurrence that disturbed Inka leaders to the north and moved them to send in their own forces to establish political control. When Túpaj Katari's messenger, Tomás Callisaya, first arrived, he made three trips around Tiquina, an annex of Copacabana (Omasuyos), summoning the local population to an assembly. He then stood at the cabildo with a noose around his neck (indicating he should be hung if he did not tell the truth) and holding a knotted cord that represented an edict from the La Paz leader.

He solemnly declared the new laws: "The sovereign Inka king orders the execution of all corregidores, their ministers, caciques, tribute collectors, and other dependents, women and children without exception for sex or age, and anyone who is or appears to be a Spaniard, or who at least is dressed in imitation of Spaniards. And if they are favored in any sanctuary, and any priest or anyone else impedes the primary aim of executing them, they will be completely overcome, the priests being executed and the churches burned down. Neither should there be mass, confession, or adoration of the Holy Sacrament."[108] According to Fray Borda who, was the priest in Tiquina, Callisaya went on to add that Indians should not hold meetings anywhere other than on hilltops, they should not eat bread or drink water from fountains, and they should completely abandon all Spanish customs.

Callisaya then undid the knot—meaning that the threads or ties that formerly existed had come apart, the old problem had been resolved, and the new law was now in force[109]—and the crowd broke out in an uproar with general rioting. They moved toward the church to remove the townspeople and the Indian agents of the corregidor who had taken refuge there, but Borda warned them they would incur God's wrath if they violated the sanctuary. At this, they hesitated and regrouped to decide whether or not to proceed. After resolving to do so, the men attacked the "Spanish" men and the women attacked the "Spanish" women, slaying one hundred people in all. When the priest proposed that, at the very least, they should bury the dead bodies, the Indians rebuked him sternly, saying that the Inka king had ordered that they be left in the fields to be eaten by dogs and birds, for the Spaniards were excommunicates and devils.

During the Caquiaviri uprising of 1771, Indians only posed the threat of radically eliminating the perceived enemy; in this instance, ten year later, the agenda of annihilation was carried out. While the violence appeared indiscriminate—a blood bath without mercy for women, children, or the elderly—it was in fact preceded by ritual formality and coded communication; it was politically directed, religiously sanctioned, and consciously carried out after collective deliberation. Borda described it as a "formal tumult"; amidst all the mayhem, the orders were followed exactly, without the least deviation.

The Tiquina episode indicates that nativism—the outright rejection of Spanish customs—and repudiation of Christianity were present as a radical political option at the time of the insurrection, but the other available evidence suggests that they were rarely expressed. Katari did order that only Aymara be spoken in the camp in El Alto, but by the time Fray

Borda arrived to serve as chaplain, still during the early stages of the siege, Katari had given up using knotted cords and "other ceremonies," relying for his communications only on what was "properly written" in Spanish by his secretary Chuquimamani.[110] As we have seen, he adapted political elements from the model of colonial state administration, he dressed at times in Spanish garb, and he instituted the Christian cult in El Alto.[111] Nativism and anti-Christian positions, then, were not defining or essential features of political radicalism.

But to what extent does Túpaj Katari merit his historical reputation as a radical in contrast to Túpac Amaru? Despite the personal differences between them, Katari derived many of the political and cultural guidelines for his identity and movement from the Cuzco leader. He sometimes donned the same dress as Túpac Amaru—with the tunic, solar pendant, and golden masks on the shoulders and knees—to establish his Inka persona. He adopted the same rhetorical style and elements, in one case even composing a letter in the name of José Gabriel Túpac Amaru. The military command structure of his movement was Spanish in origin, but at least partly assimilated through the example of the Cuzco movement.[112] Of most importance for assessing radicalism, he generally followed Túpac Amaru's political program in his formal and public pronouncements throughout the war. In his letters to the city, he reiterated that the movement was directed primarily against corregidores and other state officials, due to their exactions and "bad government," and that, while Europeans had no place in the kingdom, he would respect creole compatriots. In practice, he also assured the safety of Catholic priests and the preservation, though on terms that were not acceptable to ecclesiastics themselves, of the Christian cult. The Tiquina episode, therefore, as well as other evidence connecting Katari to the radical tendency to eliminate "Spaniards" categorically, should not cause us to overlook a significant degree of political complexity and ambivalence to Katari.

The mobilized Aymara communities also implicitly accepted the terms of Túpac Amaru's program, as well as his political authority and right to rule. Inspired by their leaders, they eagerly anticipated his coming and the fulfillment of their emancipation aspirations. Pedro Obaya testified that Indians expected his arrival within three years, and that if he did not arrive by the time the city had fallen, they would march to Tungasuca to render homage to him.[113] Even after his death, which insurgent leaders denied to the troops, they saw it as their task to follow and fulfill his orders. The son of Isabel Guallpa (who as the widow of Carlos Silvestre Choqueticlla led the holdouts in the southeastern valleys of Sicasica until July 1782) was asked what the motive for the uprising was and if idols or superstition prompted it; he replied that there was no particular "superstition" and no motive other than the decrees of Túpac Amaru.[114] Given this recognition of Túpac Amaru's authority and program, what accounts for the evidently more radical tendencies of Katari and the communities in La Paz?

The first part of the explanation is conjunctural. The movement in La Paz was underway in late February as peasants in Sicasica province rose up and took over various towns with general assaults against "Spanish" towns-people. Katari's public operations began in early March of 1781, with his forces spreading into the Yungas valleys and Chucuito province. His forces laid siege to La Paz on March 14 and the Tiquina uprising, which in its violence was not an exceptional incident, followed shortly thereafter.

This entire wave of peasant mobilizations came precisely in the wake of the breakdown of the creole-community alliance in Oruro. On February 15, creole leaders had expelled Indians from the city, and in early and mid March communities launched counterattacks, one of them only a day before the Tiquina episode. The new mobilizations in Oruro were directly articulated with those in Sicasica: there were fluid ties between the highland communities in both places as well as those in the adjacent valleys; there were efforts to coordinate a unified offensive; and in the late stages of the war, there was a recognition among Oruro communities of Túpaj Katari as the viceroy of Túpac Amaru.[115] Radicalism in the La Paz theater thus corresponded to a phase of polarization set off by the prior developments in Oruro. The cross-racial alliance there had proven unsustainable in practice and Indians loyal to Túpac Amaru ended up identifying American-born "Spaniards," including mestizos, as well as Europeans as a generic enemy in the war of emancipation. While Túpaj Katari did not abandon the formal program of Amaru set forth at the start of the war, by March of 1781 Indians did not pursue it so scrupulously as they had originally in Oruro, and their leaders concluded from immediate experience that it would not be realized.

The issue of racial antagonism—usually conceived of as a polarization between Indians and whites that superseded Túpac Amaru's program for Indian-creole alliance—is one of the crucial aspects of radicalization that the historiography has associated with La Paz and the second phase of the insurrection. To what extent does the historiographic conception hold up and how was this question perceived by Indian insurgents?

From the constitutive moment of the conquest, there was a historical foundation in colonial society for "racial" distinctions defined narrowly in terms of hereditary physical traits. The subjects of colonial society were aware of these distinctions, and they formed part of general colonial discourse about collective social identities.[116] One of the prophecies circulating about Cuzco prior to the insurrection warned: "All the Indians of this kingdom would rise up against the Spaniards and would kill them, beginning with the corregidores, alcaldes, and other pale-skinned blonde people" *(gente de cara blanca y rubios)*. In 1781, Túpaj Katari derisively referred to "whiteys" *(señores blanquillitos)* in his public correspondence.[117] There was, therefore, in this era prior to more reductive biological and phenotypical categorization of social groups, a general "racial" characterization based on observable physical attributes that distinguished between Indians and "white" people of Spanish birth or descent. And this distinction emerged sharply at points during the insurrection.

Yet there was also much more social and cultural complexity to the question of polarization and antagonism in the war. Beyond a narrow definition of race based on hereditary physical attributes, it is appropriate to think of a second ample sense of the term "race," a notion with the broader social connotations of distinctive peoples or nations. We are broaching here the open question of collective identities and distinctions in eighteenth-century Andean society.

During the war, this ample sense of race emerges with the radical identification of Spaniards, rather than exclusively European-born subjects (known as chapetones), as the enemy of insurgents. The term "Spaniard" was, on one hand, a caste category jurally constituted by the state in contradistinction to the category of Indian. But in rural society, it was also a complex ethnic category whose boundaries could be, within certain important limits, culturally fluid, permeable, and whose content could encompass a wide range of elements all relatively set off, once again, from the constitutive elements of Indian ethnic identity. The broad ethnic (rather than narrowly defined racial) nature of the polarization during the war can be seen in the Tiquina proclamation that called for the execution of "anyone who is or appears to be a Spaniard or who at least is dressed in imitation of Spaniards." It is also evident from the fact that all manner of mestizos—who were seen as "mixed-bloods" by whites and Indians—came to be identified with the Spanish enemy. Hence the letter attributed to the communities of four provinces in La Paz declared the objective that "there be absolutely no more mestizos."[118] This identification by insurgents of mestizos and others who were culturally distinct from Indians as Spanish enemies was radical in relation to Túpac Amaru's original program but it coincided with the prevailing criteria of social identity and distinction in the colonial Andes.

For Indians, the cultural category in Aymara language that coincided with Spaniard was q'ara, meaning naked, bald, or barren.[119] Spaniards were naked insofar as they lacked belongings of their own; they were bald like a patch of earth without vegetation or a field that bore no crops. Applied to people, like town residents, the conception implied antagonism— such an infertile, unproductive class of people did not maintain itself but lived parasitically off the labor and resources of Indians. The term encompassed Europeans, creoles, and mestizos and it was used throughout the Aymara territory during the war. Both Fray Borda and Diez de Medina registered the use of the word in La Paz, but the most explicit historical gloss came from Santos Mamani, the leader of the Oruro insurgency, who shared the common belief that "the time had come for the relief of Indians and the annihilation of Spaniards and creoles whom they call 'q'aras,' which in their language means 'naked,' because without paying taxes or laboring they were the owners of what they [the Indians] worked on, under the yoke and burdened with many obligations. They obtained the benefits, while the Indians spent their lives oppressed, knocked about, and in utter misfortune."[120]

Thus, there was a racial/ethnic principle of polarization that identified Spaniards as the enemy. A second principle was more explicitly political and it identified the enemy as all "traitors" to Túpac Amaru. In this sense, the response to Jan Szeminski's question about antagonism and violence in 1781—why kill the Spaniard?—is that Indians killed Spaniards—that is, mestizos and creoles as well as Europeans—because the majority of them had refused to join the Inka king and had situated themselves politically in the opposite camp. This political criterion of discrimination, found not only in La Paz but across the insurrectionary territory, was central for leaders as well as a key to the intensive political discussions sustained among peasant community members at the local level.[121]

In his correspondence, Túpaj Katari mainly hewed to the line set by Amaru, promising to pardon and protect all creoles and mestizos who joined him, but threatening to destroy them along with the other Europeans if they spurned him. After discovering that his creole artilleryman and confidante Mariano Murillo had secretly been in communication with the enemy, Katari wrote to the city, "Out of pity for the creoles I have not until now engaged in full combat; but in view of their betrayal, I have resolved to reduce all of them to ruin." Even many of the creole, mestizo, or cholo soldiers who did desert the city were executed upon reaching the insurgent camp. In spite of his promises of protection, Katari often concluded that these deserters could not be trusted. Even if they were not spies sent to reconnoiter in his camp, they could all too easily return later, with valuable intelligence, to the side of the traitors.[122]

Ultimately, Indians, too, were targeted and killed as enemies if they did not side with insurgents. The category of traitor, then, was to a large degree equivalent to that of Spaniard, but it also exceeded it. From the beginning of the war in La Paz, caciques and their families and property were frequent victims of attack. Though their ethnic identity was somewhat blurred, particularly by acculturation and mixed-race ancestry, their betrayal was keenly felt by peasants since community norms required their political leadership and protection. Over previous decades, caciques had consistently lined up with corregidores and regional elites in a general process of political polarization, but they renewed their alien political identity when they rejected the overtures of Túpac Amaru and their own communities in 1780–1781.[123]

When the insurgency initially swept through the province of Sicasica, armed and agitated community members in Ayoayo assembled before the home of their cacique Felipe Alvarez. They believed that he had received an edict from Túpac Amaru calling him to bring an end to the "thieving of corregidores, priests, and other authorities that so afflicted the Americans." They vociferously demanded that "as their cacique and the descendant of the ancient Inkas and lords, he had the obligation to stand up as their leader and face all the adversities that were brought against them, adopting the ideas of the rebel [Túpac Amaru]." Alvarez instead tried to calm them, appealing for obedience to the king of Spain. He then fled to join up with other Spaniards, and when Túpaj Katari arrived in the town they destroyed the property and papers of the cacique. Alvarez soon organized a royalist military contingent, and he died fighting when insurgents took the town of Caracato.[124]

As the war wore on and colonial military forces slowly regained the advantage, some communities sought the pardon offered by the Crown and even turned in their former leaders as a demonstration of loyalty to Spanish authorities. For other Indian insurgents, however, these acts were traitorous and called for the same ultimate punishment due to all Spaniards. The forces of Carlos Silvestre Choqueticlla, for example, sent letters to the town of Sicasica and its Indian population, threatening to kill the creole leader from Oruro, Juan de Dios Rodríguez, whom they knew to be in the town along with all other Spaniards and Indians there. In this case, Indians in the town of Sicasica were deemed traitors because they had resisted Túpaj Katari from the start of the uprising, and they retained their ties to the turncoat creole leaders in Oruro.[125]

Thus political-military considerations were fundamental to the terms of polarization. Antagonism during the insurrection did not derive immediately from an essentialist racial view on the part of Indians, nor did it arise exclusively from engrained cultural criteria. Nevertheless, Szeminski's analysis, which missed this political principle of polarization in the war, did recognize another important principle that was defined by religious criteria—the Spanish enemies were identified as spiritual adversaries. Túpac Amaru had initially denounced European officials for their "heretical" and unlawful actions that went against God and king. Motivated by what he considered to be true Christian sentiment and obligation to God, he sought to reestablish religious as well as political order by eliminating such officials and Europeans in general. By contrast, the Tiquina episode showed that, for insurgents in La Paz, "all the Spaniards were excommunicates and devils" who should not receive Christian burial. They thus adopted a more radical conception: all Spaniards, not just ministers or even Europeans, were targeted; and they were cast not only as morally reprobate but also as expelled from the Christian community and as evil beings peripheral to or outside the human sphere of existence.[126]

Beyond the formal ideological pronouncements or directives of leaders, other evidence gives us more of a sense for peasant views on this question. Between midnight and dawn on April 24, an estimated seven to eight thousand insurgents mounted an all-out attack on the city. They confidently expected the defenses to collapse, but Indian losses continued to mount up throughout the night. Frustrated and perplexed that the enemy could withstand their full forces, which probably included the deployment of magical power, peasants drew the unanimous conclusion that "the Spaniards were sorcerers and devils."[127] According to their interpretation, Spaniards must have manipulated (as sorcerers) or embodied (as devils) black or evil magical forces in order to successfully resist the Indian offensive. In this instance, the demonization of Spaniards was the product of a war that was saturated with ritual and spiritual content.

By Diez de Medina's report, Indians shouted to the besieged city that they had decapitated the statues of Christian figures and saints and that since the Spaniards could no longer put themselves under their religious protection, they would be vanquished. Diez de Medina understood that if Spaniards worshipped certain images, then Indians viewed those same images with hostility. But this overt religious antagonism did not mean that Indians categorically repudiated Christianity, as Diez de Medina also thought. Rather they conceived of a battle between good and evil spiritual forces, with certain religious figures, such as Christian saints, positioned on one side or the other. This vision diverged from a more orthodox understanding, such as that of Túpac Amaru and other insurgent leaders, in which religion was somehow beyond or outside the political conflict. Here again, for peasants practically engaged in war, religious polarization and opposition approximately coincided with racial/ethnic and political polarization.[128]

There was also a socioeconomic or class principle of polarization present for insurgents in La Paz. Túpac Amaru had originally refrained from challenging the colonial property regime, except for the odious institution of the textile workshop, which relied on forced Indian labor. In striking contrast, Túpaj Katari at one point included landed estate owners along with the usual set of malefactors and culprits—"the present and past corregidores who were in the city, their deputies, priests, helpers and substitutes, royal officials and their dependents in the customshouse, Europeans, and *landlords*"—whom he demanded be turned over in order to end the siege. Diez de Medina, a prominent landlord himself, confirmed the radical character of this demand when he commented that the list "effectively included everyone."[129]

The class principle was also manifest in the Indian takeover of Sorata, where Andrés Túpac Amaru ruled that women, children, and the poor were pardoned, but that the rich and the Spaniards, both Europeans and creoles, had to die. After bringing the captives into the plaza, Indians dispatched "all the people with rank, wealth, distinction, and official posts."[130] At the same time, this principle was present implicitly in the widespread pillage of haciendas and seizure of goods, crops, and livestock held by creoles and mestizos, cacique families, and townspeople.

Just as the peasant insurgent identification of Spaniards as the enemy coincided with fundamental criteria of cultural identity and distinction in eighteenth-century rural society, this factor of class antagonism matched the prevailing structure of socioeconomic hierarchy. And both these cultural and class principles were contained and conjoined in the native Aymara conception of the q'ara—non-Indians who lived parasitically off of community labor and resources. Finally, in the radicalization of the conflict in 1781, peasants came to identify Spaniards, traitors, and wealthy subjects in colonial society as their enemy and these racial/ethnic, political, and class categories of adversaries acquired a general, if approximate, equivalence.[131]

Turning next to the issue of Indian violence during the insurrection, which was broached above in relation to Túpaj Katari, it is necessary at the outset to put the matter in context. Violence was integral to colonial society generally, and the constant threat of its application—against Indian subjects—sustained Spanish colonial domination. As one corregidor of the city of La Paz expressed it: "The Indian has a propensity toward disturbance, novelty, and movement. But this only persists in a system while he does not see the threat of punishment, or, simply put, the arm raised over him. It is the threat that keeps these people in order."[132] Furthermore, during the war itself, Spanish violence was merciless, implacable and strategically calculated to terrify the enemy into submission.

In some cases, Indian violence may in fact have responded to or been modeled after that of their adversaries. Túpaj Katari stated that the siege of La Paz was only launched after Indians saw Spanish forces massacre hundreds (including women, children, and infants) in Viacha and raze the town of Laja.[133] When insurgents in Sapahaqui quartered various captives, including a cacique who was tied to the tails of four spirited mules and torn to pieces, they clearly styled the execution after the Spanish method. If Túpaj Katari authorized ritual executions in El Alto, Segurola regularly held them in the main plaza of the city. Two Indian women who went foraging for firewood outside the city, for example, were accused of communicating with the enemy and killed as spies. On another occasion, Diez de Medina noted in his diary, "This Sunday, the Lord was sanctified by the execution of an Indian woman who carried coca from the city to the rebel camp."[134]

Nevertheless, if Indian violence during the insurrection was not exceptional, it did have its own specific sources, and, given the importance of this theme for the historiography, these sources require examination. As we have already noted, one factor in the explanation for violence is conjunctural. In February and March, in the wake of the rupture between Indians and creoles in Oruro, violence increased across the altiplano as part of a process of radicalization. When Andrés Túpac Amaru moved into the La Paz region in May 1781, in part to establish political control over Katari's movement, he continued to promote the Inka's original program for interracial alliance; yet the traitorous conduct of creoles and mestizos caused him to maintain a practice of radical violence, which was exemplified by the mass executions after the conquest of Sorata.[135]

This points to the political and military factors in the explanation for Indian violence. Returning again to Szeminski's question, a primary political reason why Indians "*killed* the Spaniard" was that they understood that Túpac Amaru had himself indicated this course of action. In fact, not only did Amaru's political program involve the elimination of colonial officials and Europeans generally, but in his letters to the city of Cuzco, for example, he warned that all who resisted him would suffer violent consequences. In his public declarations to the city of La Paz, Andrés Túpac Amaru, speaking for the Inka, repeatedly threatened to wreak havoc upon the city if it persisted in its "rebellion."[136] Túpaj Katari also consistently promised to reduce the city to dust and ashes, enforcing Túpac Amaru's punishment for betrayal.[137] The agenda of annihilation then, was seen as the fulfillment of Túpac Amaru's orders to destroy all traitors to his emancipatory movement.

In studying Túpaj Katari, we saw how violence served him politically to intimidate the enemy during the siege, as well as to establish effective command internally and impose discipline in a peasant army that suffered from limited organizational cohesion. Mobilized peasants and other insurgent leaders also relied upon this instrumental and exemplary violence. In Caracato, for example, reports described how rampant killing by Indians, which left pools of blood in the church, the streets, and the plaza, was designed to "shake the loyalties of the Spaniards." Diego Quispe the Younger, one of the Quechua colonels operating in La Paz, recommended the preliminary hanging of one or two Indians in each town as a method to ensure the mobilization of local communities.[138]

Important cultural factors for understanding Indian violence also emerged from the profile of Túpaj Katari. Within the cultural context of Andean peasants, the war was an appropriate moment for the expression of wild, dangerous, and terrible forces associated, in gender terms, particularly with one aspect of masculine identity. As colonial authorities noted at times with admiration and local elites noted with horror, regular peasant combatants could display the same fury, ferocity, and fearsomeness that were shown by Katari.[139] The association of physical force and violence with wild animals was only one way that Indians conceived of war in terms of metaphors of nature. Aymara linguistic evidence also suggests an overlapping set of semantic correspondences between battle and domination of an opponent, on the one hand, and the destructive power of, for example, storms, hail, torrential floods, and earthquakes, on the other.[140]

Certain forms of Indian violence—such as when they beheaded their victims, extracted their hearts, drank their blood, or otherwise mutilated their bodies—were ritual acts that symbolized radical destruction of their adversary. Szeminski has emphasized a religious aspect to this violence— this was the treatment appropriate for alien Spaniards seen as demons and antisocial nonhumans outside the Christian community.[141] Yet such ritual actions may have also been traditional practice during ethnic warfare within Andean society. In a study of Aymara conceptions of politics, power, and conflict, Platt provides an analysis of the semantics of destruction and domination in Aymara warfare (ch'axwa) that is helpful for understanding the cultural categories underlying the annihilation agenda in eighteenth-century peasant mobilizations. Yet his model of warfare between Andean ethnic groups has only partial applicability for the clash between Indians and Spaniards during the great war of 1780–1781. According to Platt's notion of complementary antagonism, violence is culturally channeled toward a future unity, domination moves toward domestication, and a new equilibrium is ultimately sought between former adversaries. Though Túpac Amaru spoke of ridding bad government and reestablishing the social order with proper obedience to the Spanish king and his laws, which can be seen as an attempt to renegotiate a ruptured traditional pact, the insurrection in its radical dimension implied the dismantling of the colonial pact and the categorical, final elimination of Spaniards. Seen from the radical vantage point during the war, the colonial situation involved the illegitimate presence of Spaniards within Andean territory and this conflict called for a resolution that was relatively distinct from those worked out traditionally for ethnic tensions within Andean society.[142]

Regional socioeconomic structure provides a final factor—which must be posed as an hypothesis here—for understanding Indian violence in the second phase of the war. The southern altiplano hinterland, the core area for the second phase of the war, contained an unusually dense cluster of free communities and its growing indigenous population was the largest in all the Viceroyalty of Peru. Compared to valley regions in Cochabamba and Cuzco, for example, there was relatively less penetration in the form of haciendas, markets controlled by colonial elites, and mestizo settlement in Indian towns. The altiplano was thus marked by sharper racial/ethnic segregation and predominant Indian presence. Thriving interregional trade revealed an important degree of Indian economic power, but within the peasantry itself, market forces had not brought about significant new levels of class differentiation of the kind that would undermine communal institutions.

In a structural sense, these demographic and socioeconomic characteristics may have made the region one in which Indians, whose community struggles evinced an increasing political assertiveness from midcentury on, could more easily imagine the elimination of alien Spaniards and the attainment of community autonomy and hegemony. Such a prospect would have seemed less viable to Indians elsewhere, such as those in the valleys where community structures were weaker and where there were long-standing socioeconomic conditions of a more heterogeneous sort.[143] This hypothesis fits with the evidence that Indians hoped to recuperate the territory and resources that properly belonged to them (lo suyo) and to govern themselves. As we saw, this idea was propagated in La Paz by leaders like Bonifacio Chuquimamani, and Indians in Oruro, which had comparable regional characteristics, also expressed similar expectations.

Looking at the question as a whole, this discussion demonstrates that Indian radicalism, defined in contrast to the initial program of Túpac Amaru in Cuzco, was not an intrinsic or essential tendency of Aymaras or peasants in general, as the lingering colonial discourse suggests. Radicalism—involving especially a set of antagonisms primarily structured around the poles of Indian and Spanish identity as well as the deployment of extreme, terrible violence outside the regular military context—was based both upon indigenous cultural categories and structural material conditions, but it ultimately emerged during the insurrection due to conjunctural political circumstances.

The other outstanding issue for understanding the insurgency in La Paz, in relative contrast to Cuzco, is the power of base-level mobilization. One of the keys to this issue is the relationship between insurgent communities and leaders, and before examining the evidence of community power during the insurrection, it is appropriate to start by establishing the virtual absence of leadership by caciques, the traditional community representatives.

The late-eighteenth-century documentation for La Paz reveals only one relatively clear case of active cacique participation in the insurrection. Incriminating evidence, including twenty-five slings and correspondence written to Túpaj Katari, turned up in the home of Cayetano Cruz, cacique in Santiago de Machaca, and an inquiry found that the cacique had traveled about Pacajes and to El Alto fomenting the insurgency. Cruz's own son acknowledged that the cacique was a captain of Katari, though, the son feebly protested, he had been forced to accept the role. Cruz was apparently an interim governor and not a member of the local lineage with hereditary claims to the cacicazgo.[144]

The cacique of Tiahuanaco, possibly a hereditary lord of the Paxipati lineage, seems to have gone along with the insurgency initially, while trying to avoid an active military role. He sought to take economic advantage during the war, engaging in trade to Yungas, and then curried the favor of the Amarus in the northern district. When he returned to Pacajes, claiming to have Inka sanction not to join in the war and local political appointments for his sons, Túpaj Katari angrily issued a death sentence for circumventing his authority. In a third case, the cacique of Mitma moiety in

Chulumani, Sebastián Trujillo, was also said to have been a notorious insurgent leader in his district. However, a family descendant disputed the story, which surfaced in the documentation twenty-five years after the war, maintaining that Trujillo had been taken prisoner to El Alto and immolated there on Katari's orders.[145]

There were, then, remarkably few exceptions to the rule that caciques were identified with the Spaniards and as traitors to the movement. In some cases, such as that of Felipe Alvarez of Ayoayo, Dionicio Mamani of Chulumani, or Agustín Siñani of Carabuco, who were all hereditary patriarchs, caciques fled their towns after overtures that they join the insurgent forces.[146] Of those who took refuge in the Spanish-controlled cities, most frequently La Paz, Sorata, or Cochabamba, many obtained titles as royalist military officers at the head of loyal Indian troops, and they marched forth to engage and subdue their anticolonial adversaries. Those who successfully escaped had their local patrimonies ransacked and pillaged in retribution by insurgents. And many caciques, along with their family members, simply did not escape from or survive peasant attack. One witness, a town resident from Sicasica province, described the fate of Felipe Alvarez to be typical: "The Indians killed him and removed all his chattel property and livestock, leaving his offspring with nothing but vacant estates, a bare shell of lands, as they did with all the other caciques and Spaniards." Juan Tomás Balboa Fernández Chui, another eminent dynastic heir and cacique of Urinsaya moiety for the towns of Laja and Pucarani, lost his haciendas and two young children before participating in the military repression of the uprising. He later wrote of the consternation felt by all as the insurgents descended upon them, intending to destroy the lives and property of Spaniards and caciques as they had throughout the northern lake district.[147]

Those who did assume leadership roles in the movement also found themselves subject to strong pressures from below and often unable to control the communities when they seized the initiative and acted autonomously. Both Aymara leaders, like Gregoria Apaza and Túpaj Katari, and Quechua leaders testified to the irrepressibility of community troops and their tense, unstable relation with authorities in La Paz. Miguel Bastidas admitted dispatching summons and titles to rural towns as the noble Inka kin of Túpac Amaru, but he stated that he did so at the urging of Indians who came to him for the purpose, "since he had no way to deny them because of the horror and fear that he felt toward them." Mariano Túpac Amaru, who took up the insurgent leadership in Omasuyos in December 1781, wrote: "Though I and my colonels have often reprehended them, the Indians were uncontainable. . . . Once they come together in community, they cannot be brought to reason. They do not cease until they obtain their ends." If young Andrés Túpac Amaru's conduct was more radical than that of the statesman Diego Cristóbal or the reluctant Miguel Bastidas and if his character was "fierce and proud," he may well have been responding consciously or unconsciously to the political, cultural, and gender expectations of peasants in La Paz. After Bernardo Gallo, the notorious customshouse official in La Paz, voluntarily turned himself over to the besieging forces, Andrés had him hanged at the urging of the Indian troops.[148]

Túpaj Katari himself declared that "often he could not restrain the Indian communities, in their pride and arbitrary manner, due to his fear of their fury and ferocity." He held that they sometimes acted on their own, disregarded his orders, or exceeded the policy in effect, as for example when they killed the priests in his camp or attacked certain towns. They also demanded that he kill Spanish prisoners in retribution for the executions of Indians on Holy Wednesday. On one occasion they nearly attacked him and the Quechua colonel Mullupuraca, and in order to avoid other such challenges, he was obliged to scourge and execute those Indians whom the communities wanted to see punished.[149]

Of course, such statements by Indian political leaders might be taken as transparent attempts by compromised political representatives to downplay their own responsibilities. Yet such testimony holds fundamental significance. To dismiss it could cause us to underestimate the strength of the demands and autonomous initiative of peasant communities in this period, a conclusion that other evidence independently corroborates. The letter attributed to communities of the four provinces, for example, suggested a similar dynamic between peasants and the leadership in El Alto: "Though our viceroy [Túpaj Katari] proposed to us that we be humble, this is impossible." When Katari and Bartolina Sisa set out for La Paz in the wake of the killing of Father Barriga, they were detained by a multitude of Indians, "who encircled him, with excessive boldness in their shouting and deprecations, so that he should not abandon them." This entire episode, with Katari on the verge of entering the city, might seem theatrical, but peasant capacity to control the movement of insurgent leaders was again confirmed at a later stage when Indians prevented him from withdrawing from Pampajasi before oncoming Spanish troops.[150] These forceful challenges and control from below, and not only the relative disorganization of peasant militias, provoked in turn rigorous, severe measures on the part of Katari. In an ongoing test of his authority, he did need to discipline troops that could turn unruly or exceed themselves, but he also felt compelled to meet their strength and match their challenges in order to demonstrate the unwavering quality of his leadership and his adamantine nature as a warrior chief.

Recent historiography has pointed to other evidence of popular, communal, democratic content distinguishing the movement in La Paz. Katari, or in his absence Bartolina Sisa, consulted the other Indian advisers, officers, and representative political bodies in large war councils. He also had twenty-four tribunals distributed across the heights overlooking the city. These would have been court sites each with their own gallows and rollo, yet they may have also acted as independent political-judicial organs. In one case, a cabildo ignored Katari's policy when it ordered the execution of the priest of Songo. It would be an exaggeration to say that these were the governing institutions in El Alto, but collective assemblies were part of the political organization in the Aymara camp, and evidently there was a certain degree of distribution of power between Katari and these representative bodies.[151]

Not only were the leaders of the movement principally of community origin, but communities had a role in the designation of some leaders. Valle de Siles showed that, in fact, this occurred only rarely in the case of higher-ranking authorities. It was generally true that communities named their own local militia heads, though they, too, required Katari's approval.[152] In liberated towns, new authorities were also designated through a mutual agreement between local communities and high-level insurgent leaders. Bastidas, like Katari, regularly issued titles for authorities at the request of community members. Andrés Túpac Amaru's representative would call together the communities he visited in order to elect a new cacique; and hilacatas in Ancoraimes called for Miguel Bastidas to name a new cacique in lieu of the one previously selected by him.[153] A similar process occurred with the priests who were summoned to serve in the Indian camp—some were chosen by Katari and others by the communities. The Indians even felt so bold as to propose that the priest of Calamarca replace Bishop Campos as the ranking prelate.[154]

There was, in the end, a significant contrast between the La Paz and Cuzco movements in terms of the power relations between leaders and communities. While the higher-ranking Aymara officials were indeed almost always Katari's kin or old cohorts, and he did exercise hierarchical authority like the Quechua leaders, the vertical relation did not involve merely a top-down flow of power. There was also an important degree of control from below and a visible, dialectical negotiation over power that were not matched in the northern theater. Finally, these dynamics must be understood as emerging from the local political processes and changing political culture that marked the age of crisis and insurgency.

The crisis of Andean rule, entailing a breakdown of the colonial structures of control, mediation, and legitimacy at the regional and local levels, set the conditions for community mobilization in 1781 and for the unforeseen manifestation of Túpaj Katari that have been examined in this chapter. The Aymara leader stepped into the vacuum left by the caciques, as an organic if relatively novel sort of peasant political representative. In relation to the communities themselves, he did seek to invest himself with the traditional prestige and the concentrated, hierarchical, and patriarchal authority of native lords that involved top-down impositions. Yet in relation to colonial society as a whole, the historical importance of Túpaj Katari and his movement was in the vigorous, powerful upward thrust that battered the rotted beams, boards, and mortar of the colonial edifice.

These two chapters have explored the meaning of Andean insurrection and the political vision and consciousness that stirred and sustained anticolonial Indian insurgents in the eighteenth century. By taking a longer-term look at anticolonial projects in La Paz, it becomes obvious that the political imagination in 1780–1781 did not burst forth spontaneously. Recent scholarly contributions have already established a utopian tradition in the colonial Andes that envisioned a new Inka-led social order. This study suggests that, even outside the core areas of noble Inka culture and among the subaltern rural strata of colonial society, there was a polyfaceted collection of emancipation projects and agendas that had been practically elaborated by peasant communities during decades of local and regional struggle. Like an accumulated reservoir of alternative political-ideological positions and directions, this political culture oriented Indian insurgency during the fluid new historical moment of the insurrection. This point also allows us to appreciate that peasant political conceptions were not simply positive or negative reflections of the formal, programmatic lines of their leaders, such as Túpac Amaru in 1780–1781. In fact, through the power of base-level mobilization and the dynamics of control from below, insurgent leaders, both Aymara and Quechua, found themselves having to accommodate to peasant community forces and expectations.

We have also taken a broad-scope view of the southern Andean territory during the great insurrection. As this chapter has shown, the full significance of the Aymara insurgency of 1781 in La Paz cannot be understood in isolation from the other regional movements during the insurrectionary conjuncture. As a historical event, the regional movements flowed into one another, influencing and altering each other through ramifying causal processes. At another level of analysis, the distinctive content of the other individual regional movements helps to make sense of the dynamics of insurgency in La Paz. In order to explore the meaning of insurrection, distinguishing features and key political projects have been identified for:

Chayanta—Tomás Katari's initial struggle for autonomy while retaining loyalty to the king of Spain;
Cuzco—the aspiration toward Inka sovereignty; and
Oruro—cross-racial alliance between Indians and American-born creoles.

These features and projects either surfaced in analogous form in La Paz during the previous moments of mobilization, as discussed in the conclusion to the previous chapter, or they arose directly as primary political references in La Paz in 1781.

The distinctive historical features of the movement in La Paz in 1781, and the character of its leader Túpaj Katari, have likewise been examined, while simultaneously engaging in a critical effort to expose and highlight the radiating elements of colonial discourse within the primary sources and secondary historiography. Dispensing with essentialistic and colonial supremacist assumptions about Aymara culture, this chapter has dealt with the questions of radicalism, racial antagonism, and violence, as well as the power of base-level mobilization in the insurrection. And just as the features and projects of other regions were relevant for thinking about anticolonial mobilization in La Paz, the analysis of La Paz with its specific features turns out to be of value for conceiving of other regions and the insurrection more widely.

The questions of radicalism, racial antagonism, and violence were actually quite alive in Cuzco during the first phase of the war. Túpac Amaru's own policy and experience in the north contributed toward the mandates to destroy the colonial enemy and eliminate traitors. Also, the military clash in Sangarará, when local residents refused to side with the Inka, and Amaru's victory there represented an early breakdown in the promise of creole alliance. Sangarará did not decide the matter for the rest of the insurrectionary territory, as events in Oruro proved, but it meant that the central problem of racial antagonism was already manifest.[155] If polarization and violence did increase in the latter phase of the war, particularly in the La Paz theater, this was due most immediately to conjunctural and political factors rather than an intrinsic tendency of Aymaras or peasants. The contrasts between Aymara leaders and Quechua commanders from the north were not always clear-cut, and Andrés Túpac Amaru and his colonels in La Paz, for example, also often assumed the radical stances usually attributed to peasants.

The radical agenda of annihilation during the war derived from a set of different sources, as we have seen, and while it appeared undiscriminating, it was actually culturally framed and set within a conscious political vision. As polarization sharpened, there were growing tendencies to essentialize the adversary, for example as a demon, and to pursue the enemy's elimination, yet such tendencies were politically constituted and relative. In 1781, as in 1771 in Caquiaviri, the agenda of annihilation existed as the counter-option to incorporation of the cultural and political other.

This was certainly true for Oruro, where Indians moved to destroy the city after the abortive union with creoles and mestizos, but it also arose in the La Paz theater. Before the defenses of the provincial capital Sorata collapsed, some two thousand mestizo and creole men, women, and children surrendered to Andrés Túpac Amaru in the mountains above nearby Ananea. He then forced them to dress in Indian clothing and, in a parallel to the Caquiaviri case, he named the reluctant creole Antonio Molina as a ranking political authority, the new magistrate of Larecaja. When Indian forces finally took Sorata on August 5, Molina, dressed like Andrés in an Inka tunic, stood alongside the young commander and his consort Gregoria Apaza as they held court in the plaza.

What justice did the conquering Inka dispense to residents of a town that had held out against him, despite all his assurances that only the Europeans and colonial officials would be punished if they surrendered? Annihilation was the fate of all those men who, unlike Antonio Molina, had rebelled against the Inka, yet women and children were spared. The women were made to remove their Spanish skirts and shawls, their hats and footwear, and to don the clothing of Indian women. They were also given coca to chew and they were called "Qollas," as native residents of the Inka's realm. This cross-dressing and identity transformation was another expression of the alternative of cultural and political incorporation under Indian hegemony.[156]

In Caquiaviri ten years earlier, the incorporation of townspeople prevailed as an option over the threat of annihilation, but in 1781 the categorical annihilation of Spaniards came to the fore when the alliance with mestizos and creoles proved unsuccessful. Though this chapter has dwelt at length on the problems of antagonism and violence, because they are the principal features associated with La Paz, this focus should not cause us to overlook the counteroption that Indians continued to hold open.

The comparable practical autonomy of the Indian communities in Caquiaviri in 1771 and in Oruro ten years later was expressed in explicit fashion, with insurgent discourse revealing a self-conscious community political identity. Just as Caquiaviri peasants declared, "The king is the community [común] for whom they rule," Oruro forces shouted "Comuna! Comuna! Comuna!" as they overtook the city and carried out actions of retribution. According to one witness's account, "Comuna!" indicated "all for one." By another version, "In the name of the community and ayllu even the least of them took their side, and the part became the whole and the whole the part, as they supported their cause." In both mobilizations, peasants imagined political solidarity and identity in community terms—"the mere name of community was of great veneration and respect for them."[157] Though the Inka was also a strong political reference for Indians in Oruro, the community reference significantly shaped peasant interpretations of the insurrectionary objectives especially after the breakdown of the creole alliance. Hence the expectations of community members, who claimed for themselves the lands and mines in the hands of Spaniards, diverged from and superseded the original program of Túpac Amaru.

The term "común" meant ayllu, as the above citation suggests, yet it is interesting to note how Indians appropriated and incorporated the Spanish term for community into Aymara-language discourse. The new community of cross-dressing Spaniards in Caquiaviri was *machaq común*. The Spanish term "comuna," meaning residents of a municipal unit, would also have been equivalent to an Aymarization of the Spanish term "común," with the nominal form in Aymara being created through the linguistic addition of the suffix "-a." As part of the sociolinguistic explanation for this phenomenon, the importance of the Spanish term "común" undoubtedly stemmed from the ongoing community struggles in the colonial period. These struggles were waged in relation to a colonial state that defined a major sphere of negotiation (primarily the courts) and a crucial (legal) discourse. Thus, in particular situations Aymara communities had reason to identify themselves using Spanish nomenclature, and the very intensity of the political struggles they engaged in gave power to this identity.

The explicit articulation of the community reference in Caquiaviri and Oruro can be attributed to the great autonomy of the community mobilization in each case. Though the Inka king provided another fundamental reference for political identity in Oruro, he was a relatively remote, transcendental figure; in the absence of any prominent hierarchical authority after the betrayal of Jacinto Rodríguez, the community reference retained its immediacy. For La Paz in 1781, the available documentation provides no such explicit community reference for political solidarity and identity. Though base-level forces, challenging and overwhelming the insurgent leadership, were stronger in La Paz than in Cuzco, Túpaj Katari's presence did distinguish La Paz from Oruro in its radical phase.

In the age of crisis for Andean rule and the new moment of cacique alignment with the colonial state, Túpaj Katari stepped in to fill the vacant space left by traditional community representatives and to lead mobilized peasant forces. Faced with difficult organizational limitations and strong pressures from below, Katari displayed remarkable political creativity and resourcefulness, and he exercised a vigorous command drawing upon multiple sources of power. His charismatic, visionary leadership—infused with the venerability of Tomás Katari and the supreme authorization of the Inka sovereign Túpac Amaru—carried community mobilization to a new level in eighteenth-century La Paz. And ultimately, among the assembly of anticolonial Indian leaders in Andean history, Katari himself, in all his intensity and ambivalence, represented the most concentrated expression of insurgent peasant political energies.

As Bartolina Sisa acknowledged, Túpaj Katari encouraged Indians with the promise that "they would be left as the absolute owners of this place, and of its wealth"; and Indians themselves spoke expectantly of the no longer distant time when "they alone would rule."[158] Beyond the regional distinctions in 1780–1781—involving in each case a specific balance between community mobilization, regional leadership, and overarching Inka authority—there was a shared anticipation of an imminent epoch bringing a new arrangement of social relations and power. For Andean peasant insurgents, the double prospects of greater community power and Inka rule coincided in a vision of Indian emancipation, self-determination, and hegemony.

7

The Aftermath of Insurgency and Renegotiation of Power

The war had laid waste to the countryside, leaving hamlets reduced to rubble, crops and herds of livestock decimated, and families in mourning. In the wake of Katari's ritual execution in Peñas, a few isolated Indian leaders and rebel bands sought, with little success, to reignite the movement, while counterinsurgency forces swept the provinces to remove all traces of resistance. Against a backdrop of loss and desolation, there were tentative, halting efforts to put life back on an ordinary footing in Guarina and to rebuild the Andean political order.[1]

In May 1782, the aged and ailing patriarch Matías Calaumana, accompanied by a train of community authorities, delivered twenty-two hundred pesos for the royal treasury in an attempt to persuade colonial authorities of his ability to rule his local dominions as he had in the past.[2] For skeptical Spanish officials, the old cacique's loyalties were not in doubt, in fact he had gamely obtained military title as a commander of Indian troops to collaborate in the "pacification" of the provinces once he, along with other refugees in the city of La Paz, had been liberated by royal auxiliary troops.[3] What did concern officials, however, was future stability in local government, and in the eyes of almost everyone, Calaumana's time had come to an end.

The man who emerged to challenge Calaumana for local authority was a peasant community member named Gaspar Guanco. When warfare first burst upon Guarina, Guanco, a tribute-paying forastero from Hilata ayllu of Anansaya moiety, was temporarily serving as a modest alcalde ordinario subordinate to Calaumana, his lord and governor. Once the insurrection opened up a local political vacuum, Guanco became a leader of peasant forces in Guarina and received official title as magistrate (*justicia mayor*) from the insurgent Quechua colonel Juan de Dios Mullupuraca. Later, when the tide of the war turned, he skillfully managed to switch sides, bringing the community around to collaborate with newly arrived Spanish troops and dispatching captive rebels to prison in La Paz.

With Matías Calaumana racked by illness and lacking a male successor, Guanco even made so bold as to propose himself as the new cacique in Guarina. This predictably infuriated Calaumana, who cried out against the younger man's low birth and denounced him as a "wretched Indian" *(indio ruín)* unfit for such office. However, for Ignacio Flores, the military commander-in-chief for Charcas and new president of the Real Audiencia, the interests of governability made Guanco a better candidate. Not only was Calaumana on his last legs, but he was notorious for his harsh character and unloved by the Indians in Guarina. If he returned to govern, there was even risk of a revolt. Guanco, despite his earlier disloyalty to the crown, had the backing of community members and could be counted on to control them. In other words, he had proven himself indispensable as an effective new political intermediary who could serve in reestablishing local order.

Therefore, in August 1782, Flores appointed Guanco interim cacique to govern and collect tribute in Guarina. While Flores recognized the ancestral rights and privileges of the Calaumana family, Matías Calaumana himself was forbidden to reenter the town. By the end of the following month, the bedridden patriarch had drawn up his last will, and shortly thereafter he passed away.[4]

The new governing arrangement thus came to involve a tacit compromise between state authorities and community forces, but also the noble Calaumana family. The cacique's creole widow, María Justa Salazar, agreed to have Guanco govern and collect tribute until her eight-year-old daughter, Juana Basilia Calaumana, came of age and could claim her cacicazgo inheritance. This arrangement seems to have functioned initially, but in 1783 the widow came forth to request that she, as mother and tutor of the rightful heir, should assume full responsibility for community administration. After all, she argued, not only her past experience governing the community when her husband had been absent, but her recent participation alongside Guanco in the collection of tribute and the dispatch of the mita prepared her for the post. Moreover, she had landed wealth that would allow her to meet any tribute arrears. Above all, she was moved by fear that Guanco's power, given his support from the community, would effectively blot out the memory of her family's traditional role and dim any hope of future influence.[5]

It is not clear from the available documentation that the widow was immediately successful in her appeal, but in subsequent years, Gaspar Guanco did yield his formal authority, and other local "Spanish" notables stepped in to assume the post of interim cacique and collect tribute. While they had the official backing of the new provincial governors, known as subdelegates, their actual influence and legitimacy were limited. Juan Bautista Goyzueta acted as interim cacique in Guarina before moving on to Carabuco where he obtained the cacicazgo through marriage and became embroiled in a protracted struggle against hostile community members and other noble Indian rivals. Next Silverio Torres, a local hacendado who only recently had been engaged in a land dispute with the community, succeeded Goyzueta as cacique–tribute collector in Guarina. Then, in 1789, the widow herself took charge temporarily, and this turnover of "Spanish" caciques continued on into the first decades of the nineteenth century.[6]

Yet, in this same period, colonial rulers were aware of an important new phenomenon, namely that ordinary community members had worked out their own forms of self-administration in Guarina. In one case, involving communal regulation of household land tenure and tribute payments, treasury officials commented on the "government that the tributaries, with the hilacatas and segundas, run amongst themselves."[7] Significantly, it was now Indian peasants and their formerly subaltern authorities, rather than cacique elites, who actually managed the *internal* affairs of community government.

In the 1780s and thereafter, the community was acephalous and vulnerable to *external* threats. There was no outstanding, highly skilled Indian political representative to take the place of Matías Calaumana, and the constant turnover of nominal caciques made it more difficult to fend off hacienda encroachment. Nevertheless, different peasant authorities and principales took the lead in defending the community, and they gained increasing experience in dealing with their landed adversaries, local brokers, and the courts. Among them, Gaspar Guanco reappeared prominently in a successful suit in defense of the community in the early 1790s. It was the community itself that elected him, as a former cacique who understood Spanish and was familiar with documentary politics, and proposed to judicial authorities that he be empowered as its legal defender and agent *(protector* and *apoderado)*. As such, one of Guanco's concerns was to recover the land titles that had been lost due to the "continuous mutation among proprietary or interim caciques," thus facilitating encroachment from outsiders and even illicit land sales. In the late 1790s Guanco was still on the scene as a prominent elder and political representative, now working in conjunction with other community members including potential younger leaders such as his son Hildefonso.[8]

There was then an emerging division of functions that once had been united in the Guarina cacicazgo. Tribute collection turned over among members of the local non-Indian elite, whose political authority was legally nil and whose legitimacy in the eyes of the governed was limited or minimal, yet who often still assumed the title of Cacique. Hereditary status was mostly symbolic, vestigial, and debilitated as neither the widow nor underaged daughter could make a substantive bid for power. Community government (internal administration and external relations) fell into the hands of community members themselves, especially their rotating authorities, principales, and elders. In the end, the cacicazgo had shattered, a new community political formation was replacing the old, and state and community were seeking new terms of engagement.

There are elements of heightened drama or special poignancy in the Guarina story recounted episodically in this book. One was the great power of the native lord Matías Calaumana and the remarkable timing of his death. A second was the insurrection's denouement at the Sanctuary of Peñas, within Guarina's jurisdiction. Yet another was the unexpected rise of an obscure commoner, Gaspar Guanco, to community leadership. And yet Guarina's local history was in keeping with the general processes unfolding throughout the region. If the timing and circumstances of these processes involved myriad local variations, many of the actors and their historical challenges and political conflicts were the same. Also, as this final chapter will show, the overall outcome of the tensions, struggles, and ultimate transformations in Guarina resembled that of the entire highland Aymara district.

Perhaps the most striking aspect of the Guarina narrative is its precise dramatic timing: the epochal shift in community power relations occurred in the immediate aftermath of the Andean civil war. The Guarina events thus hold a narrative appeal, but they also can deceive in their simplicity. In most towns in the highland district, the crisis of Andean rule did not occur so fatefully in 1780–1782, and the transfer of authority from traditional Andean lords to commoners did not take place so abruptly. The process, as earlier chapters have shown, in fact involved a longer unraveling. The strife over the cacicazgo and cacique-community conflicts, which had proliferated for decades prior to the great conflagration, would persist into the waning decades of the colonial era.

Yet in the early 1780s, this was not a foregone conclusion. In the postwar period, the Bourbon state introduced a new administrative model in the provinces of the highland Andes, as it did throughout the American viceroyalties, as part of its overall program for imperial reform in the latter half of the eighteenth century. Designed to update and facilitate colonial rule, it is important to evaluate the significance of this new model, the intendancy regime, for the accumulation of local political conflicts. We must also assess the effectiveness of state reform in addressing the crisis of late-colonial society, which I have argued was deepening over the decades prior to 1781. This chapter considers the last stages of the breakdown of Andean rule, examining the ways in which the refurbished colonial state apparatus and different colonial subjects responded to the crisis or contributed to it. It will focus particularly on the stratum of political mediation between communities and the state and its renegotiation in this period. At issue were the age-old strategies and mechanisms of indirect colonial rule through native elites.

The other theme that this chapter takes up is the reconfiguration of power relations within Aymara communities as the crisis unfolded throughout the eighteenth century. The aim here is to discern what new political structure and political culture were coming into being as the inherited structure of ethnic authority gradually broke down. This crucial problem is one that has only rarely and recently drawn the attention of historians and has most often been the subject of conjecture rather than sustained empirical investigation.[9] The evidence for late-colonial La Paz suggests that as the cacicazgo collapsed, there was a simultaneous process in which power shifted to the base of the community. The result was a substantially democratic political formation, an internal order in which, as in Guarina, ordinary community members "ran the government amongst themselves." Emerging along with the new structural distribution of power, an attendant political culture emphasized broader participation, service to the community, consensus decision making, control from below, and the accountability of authorities. There were limits and costs to this communal democracy, but as the product of historical struggles it also represented politically significant gains for Aymara peasants. Though the radical anticolonial projects to recuperate political power throughout the Andes had failed to come about in 1781, the impulse toward autonomy was kept alive at the local level and contributed to the emergence of a new community polity.

Reconquest and Reform

Predictably enough, circumstances after Katari's death were tenuous and fraught with the fear and reality of ongoing violence. While tens of thousands of Indians had converged on the Sanctuary of Peñas in November 1781 to appeal for and receive the king's pardon, and communities throughout the region had similarly professed their loyalties to the Crown, Indians accepted pardon in some areas only strategically, waiting to see if the balance of forces would shift once again. Spanish military commanders Sebastián de Segurola and José Reseguín continued to wage brutal pacification campaigns until mid-1782, especially in Omasuyos and across the entire swath of highland and semitropical valleys from Larecaja down to Yungas, Río Abajo, and eastern Sicasica (Inquisivi).[10] By this time, most communities only dreaded the prospects of more war and repression, yet on occasion new conspirators emerged and attempted to revive the Indian cause. Such was the case, for example, with the new Inka Esteban Atahuallpa in Pacajes in 1782.[11] In Lower Peru, a new uprising shook the highland district of Huarochirí in 1783, shortly after Diego Cristóbal Túpac Amaru and his nephews Andrés and Mariano were finally put under arrest.

If some authorities were still edgy about further outbreaks of rebellion, Segurola was particularly obsessed with crushing the lingering threats he perceived around him. He zealously pursued Túpaj Katari's missing son, Anselmo, until the ten-year-old boy turned up in the custody of the Inka's mother and relatives in Cuzco. Feeling vindicated in his prosecutorial methods, Segurola insisted on the need to "cleanse the country of all vestiges of such iniquitous kin of people who with their perverse deeds were newly infesting the kingdom. It is remarkable we have not experienced, as I feared, the repeat of trials equal to or greater than those past."[12] Another plot in Sicasica, Oruro, and Cochabamba that he investigated relentlessly in the mid-1780s proved a ghostly fabrication.[13]

Segurola, then, seemed to seek the tonic for anxiety in military and criminal retribution. By the same token, local elites (who were undoubtedly marked by the trauma of the war yet also seizing the opportunity for political advantage in its aftermath) engaged in a civil counteroffensive against Indian society generally and community forces locally. La Paz resident Juan Bautista Zavala's recommendations reflect the hysteria and yearning for racial vengeance: "The Indian will be good if he is continually punished, not allowing them [sic] to be indolent, much less to have money, which only contributes to their drunkenness and rebelliousness. Henceforth they should pay double tribute to the king. He should eliminate the communities, sell these lands to the Spaniards, subject the Indians to the Holy Office of the Inquisition, because they are now more malicious than we are, and burn the Laws of the Indies."[14] Another revanchist scheme from the time proposed a comparable series of measures: caciques and Indian governors should be eliminated (along with corregidores and repartos); caste hierarchy should be redefined and reinforced through control over Indian and plebeian labor, geographic mobility, sexuality, language, dress, and religion; regional military force should be built up; and the fiscal regime should be restructured, especially through radical expansion of tribute collection.[15] An alternative plan under discussion involved reducing the entire Indian population to the status of forasteros, seizing community lands, and then renting them out to Spaniards to compensate for the drop in tribute income. The objective was to "end their assemblies and communities, which are sources of unrest."

Fearing Indian reactions, however, the authorities were hesitant to follow through on such revanchist schemes. With regard to the last plan mentioned, Sicasica officials deemed "very grave the difficulties we face in promoting such measures due to the inevitable disturbance of the peace."[16] The proposal to expropriate Indian lands was therefore not taken up officially by authorities, though a de facto expansion of haciendas did take place in and around the urban core of La Paz.[17]

In the countryside, the elite offensive took a variety of forms. We do not have evidence that elites launched a general hacienda expansion or reduced the overall wages or terms of trade for Indians. However, at the same time that church and state were attempting to rationalize tax collection to raise tithe and tribute revenue, local tax collectors often did introduce arbitrary and onerous new charges. For example, in the context of a long-term struggle over the terms of tithing, local landowners who collected tithes frequently took advantage of postwar circumstances to ignore customary exemptions for communities and increase their rates.[18]

There were cases of a local settling of scores, though these typically involved individual conflicts and claims to power and property rather than a unified onslaught to reduce community resources. In local disputes, elite intimidation commonly involved accusations that an enemy had collaborated with rebel troops, or dark intimations that "rivers of blood" would be made to flow anew.[19] Local authorities, including caciques, affirmed the need for a severe, harsh hand to govern and sometimes claimed royal authorization to crush dissent.[20]

At the same time there was a bid by local notables to concentrate political authority, and where possible economic control, in their own hands. These were most often mestizo or creole townspeople who had taken over as interim caciques or tribute collectors and who sought to bolster their power by simultaneously acting as local judicial officials (usually *alcaldes pedáneos*) and tax collectors (of the alcabala, tithe, or other duties). A case in point is the cacique of Carabuco, Juan Bautista Goyzueta, who entered office in 1782 and held it for decades thereafter despite strong community opposition to his abuses. He was also simultaneously alcalde pedáneo, tithe farmer, and administrator of church resources *(mayordomo de fábrica)*. "Since in Carabuco we have no other king or judge to whom we can turn," Indians protested, "Goyzueta strives to finish us off with his harsh abuses."[21]

The office of alcalde pedáneo—a cross between town judge *(juez de prevención)* and sheriff—was a new post that proliferated during the intendancy period.[22] At precisely the same time that Spanish caciques were multiplying faster than ever, the alcaldes pedáneos became the first non-Indian state officials to exercise judicial authority within Indian towns. The justification for this was taken from one article of the Ordinance of Intendants of 1782, which stipulated that such an official be named in towns with many Spanish residents. However the Ordinance did not intend to contravene the Laws of the Indies, which prohibited Spanish residence within Indian towns—the new judicial post was presumably intended instead for Spanish towns and apparently only introduced into Indian towns through the conniving of colonial bureaucrats. After 1789, with the death of Segurola who had been named the region's first intendant, La Paz became one of the most notoriously mismanaged and corrupt of all the intendancies in the Andes. According to one exposé, it was Segurola's lieutenant and legal counselor *(teniente letrado* or *asesor)* Dr. José Pablo Conti who began to issue these petty judicial titles at a fee, with provincial subdelegates also receiving a cut. The proliferation in the countryside of this Spanish judicial post had the effect of challenging indigenous administration of justice and violating the legal autonomy and integrity of Indian towns.[23]

In sum, two new developments can be distinguished in the immediate aftermath of the great insurrection. On one hand, a tense climate of suspicion and hostility, the recent memory and occasional reignition of overt violence, and various forms of elite offensive marked the local postwar context in the countryside. On the other hand, it was precisely at this time in the 1780s that upper levels of the state launched new initiatives to restructure colonial administration and revamp the social order.

The Bourbon reforms of the eighteenth century have often been viewed, especially in older textbooks and traditional historiography, as an impressively vigorous and coherent program, born of a new enlightened and rationalist thought, which sought to cast off the baleful legacies of Hapsburg misrule and usher imperial Spain into the modern era. Gathering momentum beginning about midcentury, especially during the reign of Charles III (1759–1788), the state reform agenda was multipronged, concentrating on commercial, fiscal, administrative, and military organization. A particular stimulus to reform was the threat of a rival power in England, which called for tighter Spanish regulation of transatlantic trade, higher Crown revenues, and greater military preparedness. Since imperial reform was to be founded on more efficient management and extraction of American resources, it required more centralized state authority and loyal colonial officials. Peninsular Spaniards were, therefore, generally preferred when it came to the appointment of administrative offices.

An important body of scholarship, which we might call revisionist in relation to the traditional vision, has in recent decades come to question a number of the assumptions about the ambitiousness, lucidity, coherence, and effectiveness of the reforms in the Latin American colonies. In the light of this work, Bourbon policies often appear to have evolved in a more dilatory, vacillating fashion, plagued by internal contradictions, often unapprised of local conditions and needs, and when not superficial in their impact, sometimes leading to disastrous results. Even when considered in terms of their own objectives, scholars have found the record of reform to be very mixed if not an outright failure.[24]

During the 1770s, Bourbon reform was clearly a factor critical in leading Andean society toward political polarization, anticolonial aspirations, and ultimately insurrection in 1780–1781.[25] My interest here is in assessing the importance of state reform in the postinsurrectionary phase known as the intendancy period. Usually the reforms have been analyzed from the panoramic levels of the metropolitan or viceregal administration and regional markets, or in terms of their cumulative effect in destabilizing colonial society. What I wish to do here is return to the fundamental questions of the intent and impact of the reforms, yet addressing them at the local and rural level, which has often been bypassed in the historiography.[26] After reviewing the reform impulse in broader social terms, I am interested in focusing on the problem of colonial political order and the extent to which imperial reform from the 1780s on managed to address and resolve the political crisis underway since the mid-eighteenth century.

The intendancy regime established throughout the colonies in the 1780s had been originally adopted by Bourbon officials from the French model. After its midcentury consolidation in Spain and a phase of design and experimentation in Cuba and New Spain, the full system would have its debut in the Viceroyalty of Río de la Plata, recently founded in 1776 as a key innovation to secure imperial interests. The guidelines of the new system were first laid out in the 1782 Ordinance of Intendants and the titles of the new officials were issued the following year.[27]

At the head of the new administrative structure a superintendant was based in the viceregal capital Buenos Aires.[28] Under him, a set of new officials, the intendants, wielded centralized authority over large districts, known as intendancies. In the Viceroyalty of Río de la Plata there came to be nine intendancies: Buenos Aires; Paraguay; Córdoba; Salta; La Plata (covering the district of the archbishopric of Charcas, except for Cochabamba and Potosí); Cochabamba (including Santa Cruz de la Sierra); Potosí; La Paz; and, after 1784, Puno.

The intendants in turn oversaw at the subdistrict (partido) level subdelegates who replaced the corregidores. (The term "province" that formerly applied to the corregidor's jurisdiction was now officially reserved for the higher-level jurisdiction of the intendant.) In La Paz, the partidos of Pacajes, Omasuyos, and Larecaja remained identical to the former corregimientos of the same name. The vast and restive corregimiento of Sicasica had recently been subdivided into two: its altiplano territory and southeastern valleys retained the name Sicasica, while its rich coca-growing valleys to the east of the city formed the partido of Yungas, or Chulumani. Since Viceroy Juan José Vértiz determined that the Collao region to the north of Lake Titicaca was too extensive to be governed by the intendant of La Paz, the intendancy of Puno was designed to administer Puno, Chucuito, Lampa, Azángaro, and Carabaya.[29]

While the introduction of the model had followed a lengthy process of formulation at the highest levels of the imperial state, the timing of its implementation in the region was very significant. It was received by colonial bureaucrats at the viceregal level just as they were in the process of studying the causes of the recent social conflagration and the remedies required to prevent another similar experience. Alongside the other fiscal, commercial, and administrative objectives of Bourbon policy, the abolition of abusive corregidores and repartos, identified as the prime causes of rebellion, were perceived as the essential elements of sociopolitical reform.

There were, however, critical problems with the model as a new and improved form of governance. The new intendancy system in Río de la Plata ultimately offered little to address the abuses and conflicts within rural society since there was no clear change of policy regarding the native population. In administrative terms, the Ordinance itself was mostly concerned with urban life, industry, and commerce, and most intendants were content to neglect rural affairs and to treat Indian communities only as sources of greater tribute revenue. In the viceroyalty of Peru, colonial bureaucrats were acutely aware of the social crisis in the highlands and more actively engaged in coming to terms with the flagrant problems of provincial government. Under pressure from regional authorities, Minister of the Indies José de Gálvez modified the original Ordinance, with its prominent focus on finance, to address these specific problems when the intendancy system was launched in the Peruvian viceroyalty in 1784. Nonetheless, even in Peru, these political-administrative reforms proved largely unsuccessful. There was jurisdictional tension at upper levels of the viceroyalties and particular rivalry between audiencias and the new intendants. Even more problematic proved to be the post of subdelegate. Historians have called it the "Achilles heel" of the reforms, and it was recognized as such by Ignacio Flores, President of the Audiencia and Intendant of La Plata, and other perceptive contemporaries.[30]

A nuanced appraisal of the new subdelegates could identify certain distinctions between this authority and his predecessor the corregidor. The corregidor benefited from advantageous conditions for private economic accumulation. He also wielded a more autonomous provincial political power since he was subject only to the distant audiencia rather than a regional authority like the intendant. Yet the homologous character of corregidores and subdelegates was clearly perceived by Indians and other colonial observers. Subdelegates were ruling virtually identical jurisdictions, with the same political apparatus. They, too, exercised authority in the four branches of administrative, judicial, fiscal, and military power. Finally, they came to be regularly accused of the same abuses that corregidores, whom Viceroy Amat had once described as "dipthongs of merchant and magistrate," had committed before them.

The reparto was abolished and hence in principle there was no longer a powerful economic incentive to occupy this post. However, the new laws did not correct the flaw of the old system, namely an inadequate salary for provincial governors. The absence of any stipend was precisely what had previously led corregidores to concern themselves first and foremost with lucrative commercial enterprise. Since the subdelegate post held no new advantages to attract professional bureaucrats who might prove judicious governors, it drew instead undistinguished and often unscrupulous creoles from the region who perceived ongoing opportunities for personal gain. The outcome was a renewal of despotic control *(autoridad omnimoda)* and extraeconomic extraction: neoreparto practices; extensive and monopolistic trading; prestations and personal services by Indian community members; clientelism involving caciques; manipulation of Indian authorities and cruel punishment of community members; private commercial and mining investment of appropriated tribute funds or rents that should have been allocated to community treasuries; and other widespread forms of corruption and influence peddling.

In many parts of the Andean highlands, then, the status quo ante was effectively reinstated. But if corruption and abuse of authority on the part of intendants and subdelegates were widespread, such problems proved especially ingrained in La Paz. The frequent turnover and sale of offices prevented a stable and transparent bureaucracy from forming. The previously noted proliferation of alcaldes pedáneos in Indian towns serves as only one example of how new political developments in the countryside could actually derive more from venality and manipulation by local and regional elites than from rational designs for administrative efficiency and centralized control. Inveterate fraud particularly plagued the intendancy during the 1790s and 1810s, and the bilking of treasury revenues left La Paz with huge fiscal deficits. Higher-level interventions to bring La Paz finances and officialdom under control were met with insurmountable local resistance. These intractable problems, compounded by jurisdictional tensions between intendants and the audiencia, nullified or mitigated the effects of reform efforts at the regional and upper levels of the intendancy system. [31]

One of the few historians to probe in greater depth the effects of administrative reform at the local level, Brooke Larson has examined the important case of Cochabamba, which was governed by an exceptional figure, Francisco de Viedma. The intendant of Cochabamba stood out among his contemporaries as an unusual example of a vigorous, perceptive, and forward-looking official, the perfect image of the purportedly "enlightened" and "modernizing" Bourbon administrator. Viedma set out to revitalize village society in his district through a process of agrarian reform. The Ordinance urged intendants to take an active role in managing community resources, specifically in administering town treasury funds *(cajas de comunidad)* and redistributing land to those villagers who lacked it. In fact, this sort of state penetration to reorganize village society was not a novel idea. As Larson has argued, it harkened back to Toledo's reforms in the sixteenth century, and in a readaptation of the earlier colonial model, it sought to reconsolidate a stable community base that would allow for colonial economic extraction. Yet even in the case of Cochabamba, where an unusually talented and conscientious governor was in place, the reform experiment brought about few real changes and wound up in failure. The substantial mortgage returns earned from community loans *(censos de comunidad)* could not be collected and land redistribution was modest.[32]

Reference to the sixteenth century and Viceroy Toledo is also helpful for understanding La Paz in the immediate aftermath of the insurrection. In a region torn apart by civil war, the early 1780s were a time of both reconquest and reduction *(reducción)* in the minds of colonial authorities. Segurola and his collaborators were concerned not only with reconquest in the sense of military subjugation (or pacification according to the contemporary euphemism) of Indian communities. They were also seeking to reincorporate the population within the colonial social order. The protector of Indians in La Paz, Dr. Diego de la Riva, spoke of this process in terms of "postliminium," a term drawn from Roman law that refers to the social reintegration and reacquisition of citizenship of people who had been outside the political community, such as those captured by the enemy during warfare. Of course, the term could be applied only in an ambiguous fashion in the Andes at this time since there was no real difference between the population being reabsorbed (Indians) and the foreign or enemy population (also Indians). This fact was acknowledged by the protector, who noted that Indians had voluntarily broken away from the "civil body," or "body politic," and ungratefully assumed the condition of "infidelity." He evidently understood this infidelity as a repudiation of "both Majesties," in the conception current at the time, that is, a lack of spiritual faith in the Christian God and political disloyalty toward the Spanish monarch.

The protector proffered this opinion in late 1781 as urban authorities were seeking to reactivate petty commerce by Indian women. The purpose was not only to facilitate the supply of food and lower prices for consumers, since monopolistic intermediaries were allegedly preventing market women from returning to the city plaza, but more importantly to reestablish necessary social "communication and conversation." "The aim," he asserted, "is to submit [Indians] to the former society and engagement that they shattered." Thus within the city of La Paz, commercial and interethnic exchange were perceived as means to social reunion and reincorporation.[33]

At the town and local rural levels, postwar reconstruction also meant subjugating, containing, and "reducing" the Indian populace to the desired civil order. Thus under the intendant rule of General Commander Sebastián de Segurola, a reconquest mentality and Spanish civilizational reform would converge. If new intendancy laws provided the blueprint for this "reduction," the irony was that, in significant ways, this late-colonial reform agenda would essentially reinaugurate sixteenth-century colonial projects, such as Viceroy Toledo's scheme for forcing Indians to settle in European-style municipal towns.

In October 1784, Segurola, as the new intendant of La Paz, personally appeared in Caquiaviri, in the presence of the subdelegate, caciques, and Indians, to hold a public assembly and promote the reforms intended for the Indian towns of Pacajes: Indians should henceforth build their homes in the town center since their isolated dispersion throughout the countryside bred misery, mistrust, and "brutish life." Town residence was favorable for spiritual indoctrination, political relations, education in Spanish, instruction in the arts and trades, and in "drawing them to the customs and manners of Spaniards." The streets in each town should be kept paved, clean, and straight, as in cities, so that "under these principles, people are stimulated toward society and the appropriate civil relations." New houses should also display the same rectitude and order. Secure jails and adequate wayside inns (tambos) needed to be built, with signs posted to facilitate transit between towns. Schools should be built for Indian education in reading, writing, the arts and trades, with community lands set aside to fund a local schoolteacher. The authorities should be informed of any delinquency or mishandling of the Crown's fiscal interests. The intendant should be notified of the existence of all community treasuries in order to regulate them properly and of any lapse in the payment of rents owed to the community (for loans or property). The intendant should also be informed of the existence of any town stores (pulperías), in order to collect the required state revenue from them. The cause of the decline of mining in the district should be studied, as well as the possible means for its revival. Finally, as the official document from the occasion attests, the intendant noted that the viceroy and the new laws emphasized the need for Indians to devote themselves to their agricultural, manufacturing, and livestock-raising activities, and "he referred at length to many other points concerning public order and justice." Segurola then had testimony of his proposals written up, particularly so that the subdelegate could properly inform the caciques and obtain their assistence.[34]

The design of Segurola's proposals, drawn from the Ordinance of Intendants and early-colonial legal precedents, was evidently less innovative than Viedma's in Cochabamba. It is also noteworthy that many measures were limited to gathering information, rather than introducing new institutional forms or practices. The real significance of the proposals lay in the state's newfound initiative to control a local rural stratum of society in which state power had completely lapsed. The documentary account of Segurola's visit to Pacajes is clearly only a partial one, since the points of "public order and justice" *(policía y justicia)* were left out by the scribe.

Nonetheless, it does provide a sense for the wide range of local issues on the mind of the new intendant.

Economically, Segurola displayed a standard concern to secure the Crown's fiscal interests, assess potential natural resources, and encourage Indians in their labor. There was also the express intent to assist Indians by monitoring and regulating community resources *(bienes de comunidad)* and the municipal treasury *(caja de comunidad)*. This institution had been established by Toledo in the sixteenth century and the lending of community funds *(censos de comunidad)* to the state or private landowners had always been brokered by state officials.

Yet this economic assistance failed in La Paz, as it had in Cochabamba. The occasional reports on community resources tended to be incomplete and unenthusiastic. In the partido of Chulumani in 1786, community resources existed in only one out of fifteen towns. In Omasuyos, there was an attempt under Segurola to have community members pool livestock that could then be rented out for communal benefit. But in some towns peasants failed to cooperate, and in others the initial stock soon dwindled away. Lands used for communal agricultural and livestock production were inadequate. Also, communities seem to have gained no greater access to the interest due them from outstanding loans.[35]

The cultural dimension of the intendancy reforms, and the Bourbon reforms more generally, have rarely been explored by historians yet are of particular interest. The urbanizing aims pursued a classic agenda for exercising vigilant disciplinary control over colonial subjects and converting them to European norms of sociability. Segurola's proposal for the countryside, like the legal orders to reestablish commerce in the city of La Paz, reflected an assumption of classic colonial discourse that urban interaction and civic order following the European model would contribute toward the cultural transformation of Indians.

This cultural project, however, came to very little in the end. Similar Bourbon reform efforts had been repeatedly proposed going back to the 1760s. When the colonial administration previously inquired throughout the southern Andes about cracking down on Indian assemblies and festivals, drinking and religious ceremony, a number of local officials expressed pessimism about the possibility. It would be too difficult to carry out in practice, they feared, and could even provoke more harmful consequences such as rebellion. Earlier legislation had also sought to establish schools for instruction in Spanish language within Indian towns, with the aim of abolishing native languages. Yet this proposal was stymied, among other reasons, due to the lack of community resources required to pay the salary of a schoolteacher.

The neo-Toledan call for urban order and civility went largely unenforced by rural authorities and ignored by town residents. In practice, then, the intendancy reforms proved one more superficial and unsuccessful attempt at the cultural assimilation (and hence elimination) of Indians.[36]

If other economic and cultural initiatives were frustrated, the one area in which the Bourbon and intendancy reforms met with striking success (in La Paz and more widely in the Andes) was in the collection of tribute. Despite the notorious fiscal corruption in La Paz, tributary revenue rose dramatically in the region throughout the eighteenth century, remaining high until independence mobilizations upset collection efforts. From 1750 to 1800 alone, tribute income rose sixfold (from 54,379 to 320,755 pesos). At the end of the century, La Paz rose nearly to the level of Potosí, still a major mining and commercial center, as the leading regional source of revenue within Upper Peru. La Paz's own overall income was overwhelmingly drawn from the tribute payments of its burgeoning Indian population. At this time, the intendancy of La Paz had the highest Indian population anywhere in the Andes, and it ranked with Cuzco and Lima as the most important sources of tribute for the Crown.[37] Thus, due to strong demographic expansion and more efficient regulation of the tributary apparatus, the state achieved fiscal success at the expense of the Aymara communities it was in other ways unable to subdue and control adequately.

Yet how effective was Bourbon reform in addressing the protracted rural political crisis in the late eighteenth century? Curiously, at Segurola's public assembly in Caquiaviri, the triumphant commander and newly inaugurated intendant apparently made no mention of the war that had just come to an end. Also, his scribe's record simply passed over the intendant's prescriptions for juridical and political order. This did not mean, however, that political reconstruction was a minor concern for the authorities. It may have indicated, rather, that the new regime had few substantive political reforms to announce. In a sign that the postwar order would be erected upon old and now faulty foundations, Segurola's entire mandate was written up so that the caciques—who had just proven their loyalties to the Crown, yet whose power and legitimacy was deeply eroded within the communities—could collaborate in putting it into effect.

The Final Downfall of the Cacicazgo

After decades of local conflict and then full-scale war, political order in the countryside hinged on the unresolved problems of community political representation and mediation with the colonial state. Since caciques were closely identified by both Indian community members and many local elites with Spaniards and with the ruling regime in the provinces, their crippled condition reflected the precariousness of colonial authority more generally. In 1782, as Spaniards sought to regain their hold over the devastated region to the north of Lake Titicaca, the corregidor of Azángaro described the terrible plight of the caciques: "Many of them have died, others are fugitives, and yet others deposed, because *that entire order has been overturned.*"[38] Having already explored in earlier chapters the onset of its crisis in the eighteenth century, we can take up the issue of the cacicazgo once more and follow it through its last stage of decline.

We previously reviewed a body of Andean historical literature that sought to explain the legitimation crisis of caciques in terms of the "lineage criterion," Hispanic cultural assimilation, or class differentiation. The first of these hypotheses—that legitimate Indian caciques with hereditary rights to their posts were replaced by non-Indian intruders, especially appointees of regional colonial officials—has been most prevalent in studies of the final decades of colonial rule. It is often associated with the notion that the Bourbon state—through intendancy reforms or postwar repression—was responsible for abolition or effective dismantling of the institution.

Such views do have the merit of entering into important political terrain, yet they can be misleading for two reasons. They tend to assume a one-way, top-down process of causality in the collapse of the cacicazgo. The needs of the state—either in suppressing potentially subversive ethnic leadership or in controlling posts of authority at the community level—are seen as initiating the political transformation and dictating its terms. The roles and perspectives of Indian community members are thus taken for granted, and the intracommunal conflicts of hereditary lords are overlooked. Second, insofar as they focus on the post-1780 period, they tend to ignore the tensions and contradictions accumulating over earlier decades, many of which set up those of the later period.[39]

To reiterate my own view of the evidence from La Paz, the cacicazgo crisis was underway beginning in the 1740s. While conflict surrounding this institution was present going back to the sixteenth century, and its local features in the eighteenth century were not always qualitatively different, the cumulative effect of frequent and widespread local conflict was unmatched in previous eras and it distinguishes this period as one of crisis. The explanation for the process involves a set of factors, including institutional and intracommunity tensions. It is particularly worth recalling here that the institutional problems with cacicazgo intruders, among them non-Indians and the clients of regional colonial authorities, were common prior to the intendancy period. Yet the critical conjunctural factor provoking the crisis was the politicization and polarization bound up with the struggles over the reparto. Usually linked to structural economic forces, the reparto's implications for the cacicazgo must be understood in terms of political coercion and resistance involving different state institutions, local authorities, and communities. The decisive criterion for cacique legitimacy within communities proved to be a political one: whether or not the cacique stood up for his subjects in the face of hostile outside forces. Since caciques as a whole failed to protect their communities, their legitimacy and authority were undermined internally. The crisis, then, stemmed as much from within as from without, from below as from above.[40]

Insurrection itself struck a powerful blow against the cacicazgo, thinning the ranks of many Andean noble families. This shock was followed by a deepening of the crisis in the decades prior to independence. Though the Andean cacicazgo was not ultimately dismantled due to the state's counterinsurgency campaigns in the early 1780s, there was a challenge mounted against it from above at this time. As part of a general reassessment of ruling strategies, the deliberations among colonial administrators during this reconquest recalled early colonial debates among Spanish elites. Visitor-General José Antonio de Areche, reviving the classic argument that caciques held too much sway over Indians and treated them tyrannically, spearheaded the drive to abolish the institution.[41] Even prior to the war he sought to separate caciques from tribute collection, so that henceforth it might be carried out by elected governors and alcaldes, as in New Spain. The Inka-led insurrection only confirmed his suspicions of native lords and led him to advocate more radical measures. Besides imposing harsh sentences upon the political circle of Túpac Amaru and cracking down on diverse manifestations of Inka culture and lineage, he ruled that the future of the cacicazgo succession throughout the viceroyalty would be left up to the king's discretion. While those caciques loyal to the Crown would be left in office, even they faced the prospect that their descendants would no longer be permitted to inherit the title.

Areche's designs in the early 1780s seem to have been based on a serious misunderstanding or misrepresentation of the political situation in the countryside. Areche emphasized only the subversive symbolic and political potential of the cacicazgo, magnifying the role of Túpac Amaru and his relatively small number of cacique followers.[42] He did not acknowledge the predominantly loyalist tendencies of caciques throughout the region and the fact that they had been instrumental in putting down the uprising. Other colonial officials, however, held a different view from that of Areche. Peru's Viceroy Agustín Jaúregui, for example, did believe that caciques were useful to the crown as political intermediaries and enforcers of order. Such confusion and discrepancies demonstrate the lack of a coherent, clear-cut political vision at the level of the colonial state.[43]

In the Viceroyalty of Río de La Plata, colonial authorities were also debating the problem of Indian disaffection and postwar restructuring. The viceregal attorney (fiscal) in Buenos Aires, Dr. Pacheco, weighed the proposals of Areche in Lima and collected the reform recommendations of General Commander Ignacio Flores (now president of the audiencia of La Plata), those provided by Oidor Francisco Tadeo Diez de Medina in his sentencing of rebels in La Paz, and those of other ecclesiastics and cabildo authorities within his jurisdiction. A review of Pacheco's report, which was dispatched to Spain by Viceroy Vértiz in early 1783, helps to understand the terms of the debate and the tentative solution—a mix of radical cultural reform and pragmatic interim preservation of the cacicazgo—that was being elaborated at the upper level of the viceregal administration in Buenos Aires.[44]

Dr. Pacheco began by noting two antithetical approaches to the problem. First was a revanchist scheme, such as the one advocated by the members of the city council (cabildo) of Cochabamba. According to these local officials, Indian towns should be converted into large private estates, or *encomiendas,* as at the time of the conquest; cacicazgos should be "exterminated"; Indians should be "reduced to pure subjection and obedience"; and militias should be stationed in all city and provincial capitals. For Pacheco, this plan amounted to turning Indians into serfs, who were by nature "separable from the common society of the nation and general society of peoples." It would mean strict punishment for the recent crimes and blasphemies, but would go against the body of royal and ecclesiastical legislation concerning Indians. Pacheco preferred instead a second more paternalist scheme, one which would be in harmony with existing law and display "extreme indulgence, exemplary gentleness, and reputable equity." While it, too, sought obedience, this was to be combined with "the most perfect union possible."[45]

To achieve this larger goal, it was necessary initially to remove the most obvious sources of revolt. Among the immediate issues addressed, including the reparto, customshouses, the mita, and tribute, Pacheco strongly advocated exiling Túpac Amaru's remaining family and proscribing future reference to Inka genealogy. At the suggestion of Diez de Medina, he also recommended banning Indians' use of horn instruments and seashells, whose haunting sound summoned up not only the preconquest past but the recent memory of warfare.

The next task was to instill the loyalty of true Catholic vassals in the hearts of Indians through religious and political instruction and assimilation. This involved an ambitious project for cultural extirpation of "the vestiges that they have preserved of their gentile past and, with them, the aversion to the Spanish name." At the same time it called for cultural homogenization: "Indians are to become uniform with the [conquering] nation, . . . with detestation for the ancient customs and memories of gentility."

The first priority here, and key to other forms of cultural conversion, was linguistic. Instruction in the dominant colonial language—"the consequence of the political system for all conquering nations"—would permit proper religious indoctrination and the banishment of gentile superstitions from Indian memory.[46] Priests and provincial magistrates were jointly to guard against witchcraft, drinking, and unlicensed gatherings or festivals. Native dress, decoration, and imagery were also to imitate Spanish norms. Representations of the Inka, for example, which would stir up dangerous sentiments, should be replaced by Christian holy images and portraits of the Bourbon kings.[47]

The subject of Indian nobility and the cacicazgo was more contested. Some of Dr. Pacheco's informants shared Areche's view that the cacicazgo should be abolished, and the more radical among them advocated taking this step immediately. Ignacio Flores, however, held a contrary position. As General Commander of Spanish troops during the counterinsurgency campaigns in Upper Peru, Flores had seen firsthand the valor and sacrifices of Indian nobles and had relied upon them to achieve victory. He therefore proposed awarding medals to them for their demonstrations of love for the king and heroic military conduct. Rather than challenge the cacicazgo as an institution, Flores argued it should remain exclusively in the hands of Indian lords. Other informants, including Diez de Medina, made no pronouncement upon the subject, implying that no reform was called for or no alternative evident to them.[48]

In formulating his own opinion, Pacheco began by taking the elimination of ethnic difference as the final aim of state policy, yet he asserted there were major obstacles to achieving it. The difficulty was not that caciques had established legal rights, for the laws were susceptible to change if the state required it and caciques could always be compensated for any alteration of their legal standing. The crux of the problem was Indian deference to caciques. With Túpac Amaru in mind, Areche had argued that this was what made caciques a threat. Yet, seen from a different angle, this very same deference was cause for preserving caciques, since they could control the Indian masses and persuade them to admit civilizing instruction. It was, after all, precisely this strategy that Church officials had settled on to evangelize Indians in the Second Council of Lima in 1567 and that the Crown had long employed in order to rule. Ultimately it was this approach, in spite of the recent abuse by some caciques of their status and privileges, that Pacheco believed was best suited to the current program for reconstruction and assimilation.

Pacheco reiterated his commitment to the goal of bringing Indians into conformity with the norms governing other vassals of the Crown. Yet Areche's plan of substituting alcaldes for caciques had several drawbacks. There was no guarantee that alcaldes could command the same following as caciques, and furthermore, caciques had shown greater loyalty to the Crown during the insurrection than had Indian community alcaldes. Also, given the deference shown caciques, it was quite possible that any attempt to unseat them would lead to popular unrest. As recent events demonstrated, he argued, Indians were capable of the most irrational conduct, following their leaders with reckless abandon rather than submitting out of fear to a superior force. As Pacheco saw it, cacique political authority, though at odds with Spanish norms, could actually be an effective instrument for inducing Indians to adopt Spanish ways. They could successfully encourage their subjects to send their children to school and abandon their pagan customs and costumes. The elimination of native cultural signs, practices, and memories—any and all elements of Indian identity—would also ultimately undermine the basis upon which cacique authority rested. In Pacheco's words, it was "necessary to use an antidote of something harmful in order to prevent other sorts of harm, and by preventing them exterminate it."

Though his position was less radical than that of Areche, Pacheco was not averse to the gradual disappearance of the cacicazgo. He argued not only that loyal caciques should be kept in office but also that those who had received a pardon for their complicity in the insurrection should be retained, provided that they had been adequate governors prior to the war. In cases where the cacicazgo post was vacant, legitimate successors should be solicited, yet interim community government could pass into the hands of elected alcaldes. Pacheco assumed that Indian nobles and principales would be content with this arrangement, since they could take over the post of alcalde and thereby maintain their authority over other community members. Awarding them with medals for their conduct in the war could further stimulate them to accept this new status. In such cases in which caciques were absent and alcaldes received state backing and local prestige, the authority of caciques would shift almost unnoticeably to alcaldes. Not only would local political office thereby be brought into line with Spanish municipal norms, but these short-term rotating officials would be much easier for colonial authorities to manipulate than seasoned, cunning caciques. The entire process relied on a "political game, whose aim may not be easily understood by Indians." Caciques in office would have no cause to join in any protest over the gradual decline of the institution. Those with some cacicazgo claim would come to see that the office of alcalde carried with it the same prestige and authority formerly enjoyed by caciques. The colonial state would therefore achieve its aim of Spanish political uniformity, while Indian nobles and their followers would become accustomed to the idea that the shift involved no real change.

Pacheco went on to suggest another peculiar possibility, first raised by Flores. If Indian noblemen did receive such praise from the king and retain posts of authority, it would encourage more Spaniards to marry into prestigious Indian families and gain access to the local exercise of power. Though existing laws prohibited the "confusion of other peoples" in Indian towns because of the vices and tensions it could breed, a stronger rationale favored ethnic intercourse. This process would create a mixed-race stratum that would dilute the "aversion" of Indians to Spaniards and increase commitment toward colonial authority. In the end, mestizaje would contribute toward the long-term subordination and Hispanization of Indian towns.[49]

Dr. Pacheco's reflections fit within a long tradition in which colonial thinkers and administrators advocated transforming the cultural identity of Indians and generating new Hispanic Christian subjects in their own ideal image. While the two were ostensibly antithetical, the project of homogenization had coexisted with the policy of ethnic or caste segregation since the sixteenth century. At the time of Bourbon reform in the late eighteenth century, early colonial references still figured significantly in the debates of colonial elites. Pacheco, for example, explicitly rejected the neo-encomendero agenda, voiced by revanchist local Spaniards, that was predicated upon caste segregation.[50] His own call for radical cultural reform, like the intendancy ordinances announced by Segurola in Pacajes province, can be seen in many ways as a continuation of Toledo's initial civilizational project for Indians.

Yet it is also possible to detect a new tone in Pacheco's analysis. Viceroy Toledo himself had participated in the subordination of feudal encomendero interests in Peru and the establishment of Indians, like other Spaniards, as vassals directly subject to the crown. Nonetheless, Toledo's political order also maintained an explicit jural distinction between the social spheres, or republics, of Indians and Spaniards. By contrast, Pacheco now spoke of social "uniformity," a condition in which "the natives [would] live under the very same laws as other vassals in general." Though expressed tentatively and hypothetically, without direct repudiation of the code of dual republics, the discourse of homogenization was framed here in more ambitious terms than in the past.

Beyond the common reiterations of the need for cultural reform and the lament that previous efforts had been lacking or gone for nought, there are actually few indications that such reforms were actively pursued in practice at this time. As has been noted above, Segurola's ordinances apparently led to little substantive change in the La Paz countryside. The continual failure to achieve the expressed goal of cultural reform can be understood in terms of different factors, such as the limitations of state power to transform local life, the discrepancies among colonial elites, and the resistance or threat of resistance by Indian communities. Given actual conditions in the Andean highlands, then, the discourse of homogenization appears either naïve or disingenuous. Those who articulated it were seemingly quite removed from local realities, or speaking with little conviction. If equality were pursued in earnest, and if it were achieved, it would have eliminated the fundamental cultural distinction that shaped the forms of colonial discourse and hierarchy. It would have undermined the vision that the colonizers had of their world and of themselves. And it would have meant an end to the material structures of exploitation—such as mita labor and tribute—upon which colonialism as a social order rested. As it was, the racist and paternalist assumptions behind the repeatedly invoked plan for homogenization acted to reinforce the sense of hierarchical difference between Spaniards and Indians. With its emphasis on legal equality, the discourse would only acquire concreteness (while retaining its contradictions in social practice) during the nineteenth century in the form of liberal projects for republican citizenship.

As for the cacicazgo specifically, it is interesting to note that both Dr. Pacheco and Areche based their relatively divergent views on the classic assumptions that caciques were abusive and that they were followed blindly by their Indian subjects. Neither of them perceived a potential contradiction here—why would any political subjects show loyal obedience to despotic authorities? Pacheco simply attributed deference to the ignorant nature of Indians; with their limited rational faculties, it was to be expected that they would follow their leaders "in the manner of sheep."[51] Given the intensity of the conflicts between caciques and communities in the southern Andes in this period, once again it bears commenting that these high-ranking vicere-gal administrators were either very uninformed about local and regional conditions or disingenuous in their reports. Ignacio Flores appears to have been a more knowledgeable observer of rural conditions than Areche or Pacheco and an astute counselor. Flores knew that in practice the great major-ity of caciques had shown themselves to be loyal to the Crown and that their services were needed for political governability. It was his pragmatic influ-ence that led to Pacheco's clever solution: caciques ought to be preserved, at least on an interim basis, as the best available instruments for colonial cul-tural conversion.

Other of Pacheco's concrete ideas for change were contradictory and superficial. Intermarriage between Spaniards and Indian nobles still pre-served the institution of cacicazgo, while caciques' conversion into alcaldes was in many ways a nominal step. His comments also showed little under-standing of what such issues would mean at the local level. Intermarriage was already going on, and the phenomenon of intruders marrying into the cacicazgo was one that often raised the ire of communities. Government by alcaldes and other community authorities was also emerging, as will be seen below, but it looked quite different from the system envisioned by state officials. Rather than a readapted form of state control through In-dian elites, it rested on such principles as the rotation and accountability of authorities and high communal participation. In the end, lacking a coher-ent alternative for political reordering, Pacheco settled for an interim solu-tion in which cacique loyalism was rewarded and cacicazgo succession and the rights of Indian nobles were reconfirmed.[52]

A special council, which met in Spain to address the issues, agreed with Areche about the need to erase all signs that could evoke the memory of the preconquest past. Since the presence of Inkas and hereditary lords re-minded Indians of their former liberty and sovereignty, the council rea-soned that cacicazgo succession and the very term "cacique" ought to be banished. Yet even Areche believed that immediate abolition would pro-voke antagonism and that gradual, less perceptible reform would be more prudent. Ultimately, the Crown opted not to take more immediate and drastic steps, such as stripping caciques of their tributary or political func-tions or barring the principle of hereditary succession. In royal decrees is-sued in 1782 and 1783, the Crown confirmed loyal caciques in their posts, while reserving for itself the right to name any future caciques.[53] At this juncture, the Crown was indeed following Areche's lead, though it was not overt about its underlying agenda. It sought gradual extinction of the caci- cazgo through passive regulation—by not naming any new caciques when a successor was lacking, the lineages would eventually die out naturally.

Like so many other Bourbon cultural and political reforms in this pe- riod, the agenda to abolish the cacicazgo was never pursued effectively. Given the discrepancies among state officials and the fear of provoking In- dian unrest, the Crown's policy was not only covert, cautious, and gradual- ist, but also expressed in vague and tentative legislation. Whether inten- tionally or not, it failed to clarify the future status of those cacicazgos that were not Inka lineages, that were loyal to the Crown, or that were outside the radius of the uprising. After all, these made up the vast majority in the southern Andes, and even in Cuzco most caciques had supported the Spanish forces. This bred confusion in the Peruvian courts for the remain- der of the decade. Eventually the viceregal attorney in Lima, referring back to the Laws of the Indies and the opinions of the seventeenth-century jur- ist Juan de Solórzano, brought attention to the inconsistencies between the postwar initiatives and preexisting legislation on cacicazgo succession and the traditional rights of hereditary lords. In response, the Crown reached a new decision that thwarted the intent of the recent initiatives. The royal decree of 1790 confirmed not only loyal caciques in their post but also those caciques located outside the radius of the insurrection, and it guaran- teed the succession of their offspring.[54] Ultimately then, the legal chal- lenges to the cacicazgo in the early 1780s had limited impact on local con- ditions in most of the southern Andes, though they can be taken as a sign of the worsening fortunes of the institution.

While effective new political and legal initiatives for the cacicazgo were not forthcoming from upper echelons of the state, the crisis of the institu- tion persisted at the local level in the countryside. The sharp political pola- rization that occurred with the reparto diminished somewhat after its for- mal abolition, yet other institutional conflicts were accentuated. Problems of cacicazgo succession, for example, continued as rival pretenders waged fierce, and in some cases ceaseless, battles over proprietary and political rights. (Recall the protracted strife in Chucuito, sketched in chapter 3.) The phenomenon of encroaching sons-in-law in this period also revealed the same community dynamics of intrusion and axes of illegitimacy that were present earlier in the century.

In the immediate aftermath of the insurrection, a new conjunctural sit- uation spawned more institutional conflict and cacicazgo intrusion. Faced with the vacuum left by caciques who had fled or expired during the war, colonial military and political officials designated interim authorities in many towns to ensure local order and the prompt collection of tribute. Political loyalty to the Crown thus emerged more immediately than ever as a criterion of eligibility for community government. Ambrosio Quispe Cabana, for example, was displaced from his cacicazgo in Cabanilla (Lampa) by the subdelegate yet granted the cacicazgo of Pomata and Pisancoma (Chucuito) because its interim cacique had died at the hands of rebels. Quispe was a descendant of Inka nobility, yet he had no proprietary right nor prior status in Pomata. He earned the confidence of colonial officials and hence his new post solely due to his record of political service. In some cases, the arbitrary appointments of officials provoked the resentment of others with a prior claim to the cacicazgo. Also, given their lack of communal legitimacy, many postwar appointees often came under fire from their own subjects. In Guaycho (Omasuyos), for instance, community authorities successfully unseated Pedro Guachalla who had been named interim cacique by the inspector of the Viceroyalty of Lima in 1782.[55]

Institutional conflicts over tribute collection posed an even more important set of problems. Among these were new forms of legal confusion and manipulation linked to the intendancy regulations. In the past, corregidores had sometimes named interim appointees when no legitimate cacique or legally "competent" (that is, adult male) blood heir existed to collect tribute, and these appointees were put in a position to arrogate the powers of caciques. In the 1780s and 1790s, with regional authority now in the hands of subdelegates, the problem became rampant. The Ordinance of Intendants contained a mixed set of guidelines for tribute collection that facilitated the opportunistic practices of the subdelegates. The Ordinance recognized either caciques or collectors (cobradores) in standard local tributary operations, while also allowing a greater role for Indian alcaldes. At the same time, it granted subdelegates substantial discretionary power to designate collectors where they saw fit. Subdelegates seized upon this to name men who were beholden to them, often mestizo or creole townspeople. The tributary function, once firmly controlled by caciques, was now slipping out of their grasp.[56]

At the same time, these local agents of the subdelegates often took the opportunity to usurp a share of the traditional governing powers of caciques. The appointed tribute collectors simply stepped in as de facto community governors, becoming known as "caciques cobradores." The practice and the term were not legally sanctioned, since subdelegates had no power to name caciques, yet colonial authorities often took them for granted as they became widespread. Subdelegates and even higher-ranking intendancy officials sometimes also engaged in illicit sale of such appointments, and this means of enrichment gave rise to an increasing turnover of cacique–tribute collectors. Unsurprisingly, communities objected to this "continual mutation" of "caciques" as an intolerable source of local political instability.[57]

By the mid-1790s, the persistent confusion over caciques and tribute collectors and the rising tide of community legal protests against abusive authorities led the Real Audiencia and the viceroy to issue orders to the intendancies. Drawing on the Ordinance of Intendants and the royal decree of 1790, the audiencia ruled that tribute collectors named by subdelegates could not assume the functions of caciques, that Spanish and mestizo caciques or governors were illegal, and that hereditary caciques who had been displaced from their rightful position should be restored.[58] These orders were received with joy by Indian communities, yet they exacerbated tensions between the audiencia, especially its attorney Victorián de Villava, and the intendants and subdelegates of the district.

The viceroy in Buenos Aires therefore intervened next in an attempt to resolve the problems surrounding the cacique–tribute collectors. According to the viceroy, if the subdelegate did not wish to assign tribute collection to Indian alcaldes, as the Ordinance of Intendants allowed, he could name collectors who might better secure the fiscal interests of the state. These collectors were essentially auxiliary commissioners of the subdelegate, and therefore they could act as required not only to ensure tribute collection but also to resolve any other problems involving the mita, land, labor services, and public order. They were not, however, to disturb the ordinary jurisdiction of alcaldes or legitimate caciques. The subdelegate could also place legitimate hereditary caciques in charge of tribute collection. While they were due special consideration, tribute collection was not automatically attached to the cacicazgo, and hence caciques could be removed from tributary operations if they proved unsuitable. The viceroy enjoined subdelegates not to abuse their right to appoint tribute collectors, either by naming a variety of individuals or unreliable ones. To prevent a multiplication of authorities who might cause harmful consequences, alcaldes and hereditary caciques should be the preferred candidates for collection. With the audiencia continuing to oversee the hereditary cacicazgos and intendancy officials running the tributary apparatus, the viceroy concluded that "disputes will be avoided, with all resulting in admirable harmony."[59]

The viceroy's optimism was unwarranted. Though he recommended that Indian alcaldes and hereditary caciques be preferred as collectors, subdelegates had no real motive to do so and their discretionary powers went unchecked. If anything, the authority of the subdelegate's non-Indian clients was strengthened since they were allowed to act for their superior not only in tributary but also in a range of other local affairs. Rather than "admirable harmony," the result was ongoing pressures from the regional state apparatus, protest from communities, and tensions within the governing institutions.

In 1798, the audiencia drew the attention of the Crown to the "deplorable" state of the intendancy of La Paz: "They have invented the granting of annual titles from the intendancy to the caciques and alcaldes pedáneos of the province. They charge twenty-five pesos for each of them, which comes to over six thousand pesos. If anyone wants to get rid of a cacique or alcalde, a gratuity is given to Don Fermín Sotes and the intendant, and a new title is issued even if the person was not in office more than two weeks. Hence in one year there have been ten caciques in two towns, and at this rate there will be ten thousand."

Conflicts were sharp in Larecaja, where one town alone (Chuchulaya) had seen four caciques in ten months. Pacajes was also in an uproar because of Sotes, the confidant of Intendant Antonio Burgonyo, and the subdelegate had been forced to flee to the city. Indians throughout the region had ample reason to fear or despise the new appointees who lorded it over them with the intendant's authorization. At the same time, the constant replacement of caciques and alcaldes pedáneos went against the wishes of the audiencia, making La Paz in recent years "the reef upon which its authority had shipwrecked."[60]

The tensions surrounding tribute collection by Spanish appointees continued on beyond the turn of the century. The abuses and insistent protests finally prompted the colonial administration, once Ferdinand VII reassumed the throne and a temporary liberal project stalled, to restore collection exclusively to Indians. A new tributary code, dictated in Lima in 1815, prohibited Spanish or mestizo involvement and turned collection back over to caciques. Where no cacique was in place, collection fell to a member of the rightful family or a principal, or otherwise to Indian town alcaldes. The measure was predictably controversial. The subdelegates of La Paz opposed it on the grounds that Indians could not be counted upon to guarantee the revenue in case of a shortfall. Yet fiscal authorities noted that where communities had been collecting their own tribute without other intermediaries for some time, conditions were the most stable and payments the most regular.[61]

Along with these specific postwar institutional conflicts, there were ongoing local cacique-community conflicts due to a host of other familiar abuses of power. As they had done for decades before the insurrection, then, communities continued to challenge illegitimate political representatives and intermediaries, and they did so employing many of the same legal resources. One of the notorious cases of conflict in the region occurred in Jesús de Machaca. After playing a role in the repression of the insurgency, Pedro Ramírez de la Parra took over the cacicazgo, exercising despotic power and engaging in myriad excesses and abuses that were registered by community plaintiffs. Apparently, the situation nearly gave rise to an uprising in 1795.[62] In Carabuco, community members brought suit against cacique Juan Bautista Goyzueta, described as a poor cholo from Lampa who also came to power during the reconstruction immediately after the war. At the same time, rivals claiming hereditary rights to the cacicazgo sustained litigation with Goyzueta for over forty years, in a lawsuit lasting longer than a person's normal life span.[63]

Yet the community challenge to caciques was not only directed against such postwar carpetbaggers and interlopers. Taken as a final refrain, the story of one hereditary patriarch, Pedro Limachi, will serve as a reminder of the acute, at times intractable contradictions that marked cacique power over the larger period of this study. As cacique of Guaqui (Pacajes), Limachi held power for longer than any other community governor in the region. A young successor to his father, he took over the post in Urinsaya in 1745. In the late 1760s, adversaries within the community challenged his authority and unleashed a complex power struggle that Limachi barely survived. The case was replete with all the elements of conflict previously noted in cacique-community battles, including a rival bid to the property rights of the cacicazgo and extensive accusations of abuses against community members. (See chapter 3.) Among other charges, the cacique was said to be the close collaborator of the corregidor and favored by him in his transactions, since Limachi served as collector of his reparto debts and other private interests. At one point during the investigation by the Real Audiencia's commissioner, the cacique was forced into hiding as a multitude of peasants came close to storming his residence.

Limachi's defense was not entirely consistent. He said that the adversaries who initially brought the suit against him were a resentful, self-interested pair who did not represent the community at large. He also accused the judicial commissioner of bias and blamed him for inflaming community members against their cacique. And finally, he attributed community hostility to the uncivilized condition of Indian peasants and their chafing at his paternal efforts to correct their moral, civil, and spiritual waywardness. One witness testified on Limachi's behalf: "The majority of the brutish and pusillanimous Indians see things to the contrary of the zealous cacique, and for this they abominate him." In April 1771, the tribunal in La Plata ultimately upheld Limachi's authority.[64]

During the Pacajes uprising in November of that year, no caciques participated in the mobilization, and in fact they were the targets of attack along with other mestizo and Spanish townspeople. Interestingly, however, Pedro Limachi's name became associated with the origins of the affair. The cacique had entered into a legal dispute over the reparto, and Corregidor Castillo had responded by imprisoning him under false charges. At the time of the clash in Jesús de Machaca, Castillo was on his way to seize the property of Limachi and his wife in Guaqui. Are we to make of this that Limachi was now aligned with restive community forces in the province? This seems improbable. It is more likely that Limachi had run into some of the same problems that other prominent altiplano caciques, especially in Omasuyos, had faced in the early 1760s. As the collector responsible for reparto debts, Limachi's relation with the corregidor probably collapsed under financial strain, and hence Castillo's scheme to claim the cacique's personal resources as collateral. Rather than leading community grievances, Limachi would have reacted against the corregidor and sought to impugn him out of tactical self-defense. The audiencia once again vindicated Limachi in the new litigation involving the corregidor.[65]

Pedro Limachi cuts an especially intriguing figure as the most prominent cacique patriarch—in fact one of the only ones—to endure into the postinsurrectionary era. While there is no positive evidence of his whereabouts in 1781, his survival attests to his political intelligence, luck, and loyalty to the Crown at the moment of maximum mobilization. Nevertheless, his authority remained subject to attack as the century drew to a close. In 1792, an anonymous text written in the name of Indians in Pacajes and Sicasica denounced the excesses of caciques including Limachi who was described as an "eternal thief." In 1799, the members of Guaqui's ayllus vented their frustration with their seventy-year-old cacique. According to them, Limachi was responsible for abuses "over many years." He had stifled their complaints and "cast a pall upon the truth." Since he controlled all the magistrates in the province and even those in La Paz, they lamented, they could never expect justice to be done.[66]

Caciques did not disappear altogether until the first laws of the new Bolivian republic legally abolished them, yet abolition was only a formal measure confirming their prior de facto loss of political control. In the sixteenth century, native Andean lords had proven themselves too powerful to be eliminated by Viceroy Toledo in his overhaul of Indian social organization

o valuable for the project of Spanish colonial domination. In the early
enth century, however, they held no such power themselves and no
such value for the nascent creole state. Their practical authority was by then
deeply eroded and they lacked the formerly substantial, naturalized legitimacy that they had enjoyed during their colonial heyday.

The Takeover of Ayllu Authorities

What were the implications of this general crisis of In-
dian government, affecting hereditary as well as interim authorities, for the
community political formation? With the breakdown of a long-standing
arrangement of power in the eighteenth century, what new balance of
forces was emerging within the community?

Generally speaking, I believe a transfer of power from the apex to the
base of the political formation was taking place. This was most pronounced in cases where authorities actually took over cacique responsibilities. During conflicts with caciques, in their absence, or during terms of
ineffective caciques, subordinate authorities and lower-level ayllu representatives and principales began to assume new or broader functions. Also,
despite the reduced role or effectiveness of caciques as administrators at the
town and moiety level, the dynamics of interayllu coordination continued
to structure the organization of the larger community.

In challenging the colonial authorities allied with local caciques or in
confronting caciques themselves, these subordinate authorities, especially
hilacatas, and principales stepped forth in a more prominent position as
community political representatives. They were charged with the tasks of
contacting scribes, producing petitions or denunciations, and guarding
valuable community documents. They met with the commissioned agents
of the colonial state and spoke up for the community in local disputes.
They also traveled to the provincial capital, the urban hub of the region, or
to the distant court in La Plata to plead their case and obtain decrees from
the audiencia.[67]

These subordinate authorities also proposed to take over, and in numerous cases did take over, the critical task of community tribute collection,
normally the primary function of caciques. Segundas, hilacatas, and (at
state behest from the 1780s on) alcaldes handled tributary registers, secured
payment from peasant households, and delivered the aggregate sums to the
provincial governor. On some occasions, they offered collective financial
guarantees for community tribute.

In Laja in 1753, community members were engaged in a campaign to unseat Tiburcio Fernández from the cacicazgo. Bypassing their cacique, hilacatas and alcaldes delivered the tribute for the semester directly to the authorities in the provincial capital Achacachi. Objecting to the corregidor's claim that the cacique was needed to guarantee the money in the future, the community declared that "all the Indians of the town" had ensured it. The cacique was superfluous to tribute collection, they held, since the hilacatas effectively did all the work themselves. In another case in 1756, Indians in Mocomoco objected to having unsuited caciques named to govern their moiety. Given the inadequacy of the previous cacique, Xavier Arias, the segundas had taken charge of the collection and delivery of tribute, and Arias had played no role in this or in any other governing affairs.[68]

Beyond tribute collection, then, this last example shows how subordinate authorities proposed to perform, and sometimes did perform, other services of government and administration as well, relying upon established traditions and principles of social organization. In Ulloma in 1779, the hilacatas and principales who sought to rid themselves of their interim cacique–tribute collector asserted, "If we had not taken the trouble to sustain order *[el buen regimen]* and governance, everything would be lost today." In Curaguara after the turn of the century, Indians complained that the subdelegate capriciously named and then replaced caciques, though he lacked the authority to do so. In lieu of a newly designated cacique–tribute collector, the community proposed that two principales acting as segundas should stand in until a legitimate hereditary successor to the cacicazgo came forth.[69]

Among the particular tasks they handled, the hilacatas oversaw the designation of civil authorities, festival sponsors, and donors for community expenses from their individual local ayllus. They also coordinated labor service turns and distributed communal lands. To take one example from the town of Sicasica in 1796, the hilacata of the ayllu Collana Hiluta was responsible for nine different cargo appointees and their cash contributions. They included an alguacil and festival sponsors (one *prioste* and two *fueras*) and three people reserved for the captain of the Potosí mita. These three resembled colquejaques and marajaques, with two donating sixty-six pesos and the one known as a *halaya* making his prestation in cash, kind, or herding labor.[70]

The transfer of power to the base of the community was partial and uneven, varying from place to place and from one moment to another, but it was a process that went on of necessity with the unraveling of cacique authority beginning around midcentury. It also had irreversible consequences for community political culture and consciousness. Elders accumulated and transmitted valuable experience and awareness as leaders. Even after the severe repression of the insurrectionary movement and despite the drive by local elites to concentrate power in its aftermath, communities continued to show political self-confidence and assertiveness, and they did not submit meekly to forceful new pressures from above. At the same time, colonial officials began to take notice of the fact that community members were now starting to "run the government amongst themselves." Realizing the viability of this, some recommended doing away with other intermediaries appointed by the subdelegate, such as Spanish tribute collectors, who only generated conflict. In the midst of one dispute in 1807, for example, the Protector of Indians in La Paz declared that community members would be better off governed by a segunda authority, rather than a cacique, tribute collector, or other such boss, and that the royal treasury would also benefit as result.[71]

The political transformation can be seen not only in the proposed or actual takeover of cacique functions, but in the active efforts of communities to propose their own candidates to fill a vacant office or replace an unpopular cacique. Sometimes these candidates were principales who were considered qualified representatives. For example, in order to lessen the vulnerability of their town, which had gone for a year without a cacique and which lacked any legitimate heirs, hilacatas in Calamarca proposed that the viceroy choose a cacique for them from among three principal candidates who were members of the community.[72] Other times, Indian candidates were nobles with hereditary claims to the post. In Laza, for example, authorities and principales requested that the daughter of a former cacique, who was also the widow of a man killed in 1781, replace the Spanish cacique–tribute collectors named by the subdelegate. As the cacica Felipa Campos Alacca herself explained to the viceroy in 1796:

> The height of my misfortune was to have my cacicazgo usurped because of the new dispositions and mutations in government at the time of the new intendancy administration. My loss lasted for sixteen years until your highness in his pity emitted a royal provision ordering that caciques of legitimate descent be restored to their cacicazgos and where there be none, that three Indian principales be put forward so that one be confirmed from among them. The subdelegates are to retain only the faculty to name tribute collectors who should in no way intervene in the proper functions of the Indians due to their repeated complaints and petitions. Impoverished and fed up with the mistreatment of the Spanish caciques who have

governed them provisionally, they motivated your highness, after consultation with the attorney-general for Indians, to order the restoration of the usurped caciques.

After another cacica was restored to the post in Irupana, large contingents of Indians from Laza besieged the subdelegate with complaints against their caciques. They descended upon him repeatedly and pressured relentlessly until he finally restored Felipa Campos Alacca. Campaigns such as this one were ebullient and relatively successful initiatives to exercise greater control over the highest level of community political representation.[73]

Community members clearly came to believe they had a right to be governed by caciques, usually Indian caciques, *of their choice*. This was expressed in striking fashion in Palca around the same time when Indians, led by their hilacata, rioted before the possession ceremony of a hereditary successor to the cacicazgo, Martín Romero Mamani. While earlier in the eighteenth century such ceremonies were routine political rituals conducted by state officials with little community participation, by the end of the century entirely new circumstances prevailed. One town resident overheard the Indians declare that "they were the ones who had to elect a cacique to their will and satisfaction." They rejected Mamani, the son of patriarch Dionicio Mamani of Chulumani, and sought the appointment of another individual who was to their liking.[74]

A bitter Martín Mamani subsequently wrote: "Ever since the first discoveries of America, the foxy spirit of the Indian has been detested. As soon as he finds a crack of protection from superior authorities, he manages to work his way in completely with offensive imputations until he annihilates the reputation of his immediate rulers."[75]

Caciques and their subjects had indeed been negotiating the balance of power within communities over centuries. Yet at the end of the eighteenth century, Martín Mamani was personally and painfully witnessing the end of a once more stable Andean colonial relationship and with it the loss of a once steadier patriarchal control. In the past, caciques had normally enjoyed the stature of noblemen with paternal rights and obligations, while their subjects were expected to respect and obey them as would children. But the patriarchal position, which had been so compromised by the forces of colonial domination, was now scarcely viable. It is symbolic of the changing relations of power that in the towns of Irupana and Laza, communities mobilized to install the female progeny of earlier caciques. Likewise, in Ayoayo, Indians called for the appointment of Melchor Alvarez, the son of a cacique lord killed in 1781, whom community members announced "we have raised" and who would therefore treat them well.[76] The old gender, generational, and kinship metaphors of power were inverted here—in figurative terms, these caciques were dependent women and children, protected by the elders and authorities of the community and therefore owing it sexual, filial, and kin allegiance.

Such examples indicate that the cacicazgo crisis did not involve a repudiation of the cacicazgo institution or hereditary authority as such. Seen from below, as the struggle for political autonomy continued to be waged locally in the aftermath of the insurrection, the practical aim for communities was to ensure accountable political representatives and to control the stratum of mediation with outside forces. In principle this could mean restored caciques who were worthy of trust. However, with the increasing absence of such legitimate caciques, it more often came to mean ordinary authorities already serving within the ranks of the community.

Seen from above, the state's overriding interest was in preserving local order, and considering the threat of disturbances, it was inclined to respond to many community demands. Despite the contrary position of its own subordinate officials, in a number of cases it recognized the cacicazgo candidates proposed by mobilized communities. Colonial authorities also began to take note of the fact that community members were starting to "run the government amongst themselves." Realizing the viability of this, some recommended doing away with other intermediaries who were clients of the subdelegates and who continually generated conflict. In 1807, the protector of Indians in La Paz declared, "If His Majesty knew about the excesses and tyrannies [of the tribute collectors], . . . there would be no caciques, tribute collectors, or other bosses *[mandones]*. They would be better off governed by an Indian segunda, and there would be greater, more advantageous benefit for the Royal Patrimony."[77] It was this very same outlook that eventually led authorities to ban unpopular Spanish tribute collectors in 1815. These forms of state accommodation to community political pressures contributed to the overall process by which power was transferred to the base of the communal polity.

Beginning in the latter half of the eighteenth century, power shifted away from the traditional maximal authority within the community political formation, devolving downward and dispersing into a constellation of other political agents and sites. The dynamics of ayllu organization continued to structure community political, economic, and ceremonial life, and subordinate authorities, appointed in representation of local ayllus, took

on a larger role and responsibility. Elders and principales provide
ship and experience from outside the sphere of state-regulated auuu...,.
In times of mobilization, other charismatic or talented leaders, including
younger men lacking principal or elected authority rank, could also
emerge to direct the community (as for example Juan Tapia, leader of the
Chulumani siege in 1771, or Túpaj Katari himself in 1781). Finally, the
community assembly acquired greater prominence as the space for political debate, elaboration, and decision making. Community forces at large
could now demand more from acting governors, control them more
closely from below, or they could well up to displace them altogether.
While wider visions of emancipation and self-rule were frustrated with the
defeat of the insurgents in 1781, Indian communities continued to fight te-
naciously for local spheres of autonomy. The result of these struggles
throughout the late-colonial period was a democratized communal formation that is still recognizable in the southern Andean highlands today.

In the aftermath of the great insurrection, the overall balance of power
at the local level was shifting and unsettled. The reconquest offensive of
local elites met with resistance from Aymara communities, and its gains
were uneven. Indian forces were still to be reckoned with for a number of
reasons. While both groups had suffered losses in the war, the native population was rapidly increasing and it overwhelmingly outnumbered that of
Spaniards. Indian communities were benefiting economically from dynamic participation in the expansion of regional and interregional markets. The communities had gained formidable strategic and organizational
experience in their legal and political struggles over preceding decades.
Also, the political and especially the military apparatus of the colonial state
was still weak in the countryside. Given the threat of ongoing upheaval,
colonial authorities perceived that a stable new political order needed to be
built with community acquiescence. A set of revanchist schemes were
therefore discarded and more ambitious reforms postponed.[78]

The shifting power relations within communities were also bound up
with the unresolved relationship between local forces and the colonial
state. The cacicazgo crisis and the devolution of communal power involved a many-sided struggle to control the stratum of political mediation
in the countryside. Andean noble families managed to retain their hold
over a bundle of rights and privileges associated with their entailed property yet saw their other functions and authority wither away. Other community members took the tasks of collective self-government increasingly
in hand yet found themselves continually beset by intruders. Non-Indian
townspeople insinuated their way into influence as tribute collectors and

petty justices yet were operating between quasi legality and illegitimacy. The colonial state was caught between a reformist tendency to eliminate cacicazgo and the practical aim to achieve stability based on established customs, laws, and institutions. Ultimately, no cohesive new articulation between the colonial state and local forces would come about in the wake of the insurrection. There was instead a clotted mixture of obsolete rules for power, faltering reform initiatives stemming from upper spheres of the state, improvised strategies advanced by opportunistic local elites, and the perseverance of retrenched Aymara communities. With neither anticolonial Andean insurgents nor Bourbon authorities able to impose their will successfully, the larger crisis of colonial rule proved insuperable. The region would now enter into the wars of independence and then reemerge unsteadily, in the faint light of the republican dawn, only to discover a similarly troubled state of affairs.

8 Conclusions

And Continuations

I have sought in this book to give greater insight into the Andean political world of two centuries ago. Above all I have been concerned to convey a more intimate sense of the local and interior sphere of Aymara politics and to reflect on its significance for the age as a whole. This undertaking has led to a particular historical vision and three sets of findings.

In the eighteenth century, a concatenation of conflicts shook colonial society at every level. The conflicts upset local social relations and institutions, regional regimes, and the upper echelons of the colonial state. As existing structures of colonial rule were breaking down, a deep transformation and remaking of the Andean community took place, with political power relocating from the apex to the base of the community polity. Aymara peasants themselves brought about this re-creation of community through a process of struggle against colonial conditions of domination, and the outcome had lasting implications in the nineteenth and twentieth centuries. At various points throughout this period, the accumulating struggles of peasant communities in the countryside found expression in projects and movements that radically challenged Spanish political control. This emerging anticolonial political imagination and practice eventually culminated in the Andean insurrection of 1780–1781.

These two concurrent and interconnected developments in the eighteenth century—colonial crisis and internal community transformation— helped set the stage for the great insurrection. If the eighteenth-century Andes were one of the most turbulent regions anywhere in the Atlantic world, the southern Andes and La Paz were at the center of those colonial convulsions. In La Paz, the groundswell of peasant community forces in times of mobilization as well as the new flow of power from the bottom up in local political relations distinguish this period as an "age of insurgency."

Indirect Rule Comes Undone

The eighteenth-century political crisis involved an unraveling of relations of authority and mediation not only between Indians and their colonial governors and overlords, but also within Indian society itself, at the crucial community level of social organization. My conception of the Aymara community as a specific political formation has not relied upon assumptions of a seamless social fabric, social equilibrium and collective harmony imagined according to normative ideology, or sheer egalitarianism within a discrete communal unit. On the contrary, though indigenous cultural survival is often cast in terms of resistance to antagonistic external forces, such as landlords, the market, or the state, this study reveals that much of the extraordinary Aymara political vitality in the eighteenth century was also bound up with and revealed through acute internal tensions and conflict.

By treating the community as a specific political formation, this study has emphasized a major structural aspect of community politics and their historical change. In this approach, political norms, functions, and institutions have been framed in terms of underlying relations of power. There are empirical, methodological, and analytical reasons for dealing with the cacicazgo institution in greater depth, as I have done here: the cacicazgo occupied a central position in the arena of social conflict; it generated an abundance of documentation; and it offers special insight into internal community dynamics.

The crisis of the cacicazgo—that strategic instrument of indirect Spanish control over the Indian population—was the result of multiple, often crosscutting forms of local conflict. Accumulating over decades, these conflicts brought peasant community members, descendants of Indian lineages staking claims to cacicazgo property and authority, and a range of local and regional state agents into wrenching struggles throughout the countryside. Antagonism over cacicazgo succession and intrusion by outsiders to the community eroded the institutions of community government. Battles over community resources and reciprocity arrangements as well as abuse of authority frayed the relations between caciques and their subjects. The overriding cause of the internal political breakdown was the polarization that ensued as colonial magistrates manipulated the regional apparatus of the state to intensify extraction through the forced distribution of commodities. The political legitimacy of caciques thereby came under fire as never before. Taking these elements together, the study has provided a historically grounded and dynamic account of the colonial cacicazgo and explained its crisis in fundamentally political terms.

The World Right Side Up

A vision of autonomy and self-determination, imagined at varying levels of projection, grew out of the more common mobilizations of the period and characterized the anticolonial movements we have surveyed. As the crucial strata of colonial political representation and mediation came under fire and the inherited structures of Andean rule entered into irremediable crisis, the intense struggles over Indian community government ultimately connected up with a range of notions about social justice and political reordering that defied Spanish colonial rule. The political consciousness of Aymara peasant insurgents was not defined solely in terms of the agendas of leaders and elites, nor did it take a single, set form of expression such as ethnic extermination.

In Ambaná in the late 1740s and early 1750s, community leaders believed it was "their turn to rule," imagining not only local but provincial autonomy. In Chulumani and Chupe in 1771, after conflicts with the corregidor that included the jailing of alcaldes and the imposition of an illegitimate cacique, insurgents named their own new hierarchy of authorities, including a cacique, lieutenant general, corregidor, and king. In Caquiaviri, Indians proclaimed, "The king is the community for whom they ruled," and they too put in place new authorities. At the time of the great insurrection, Tomás Katari led his movement for regional autonomy in northern Potosí, challenging illegitimate caciques and Spanish officials. In Cuzco, Indian hegemony took the form of an Inka king for all Peru. In Oruro and La Paz, insurgents imagined Indian rule as the convergence of Inka sovereignty and community power. In the variety of emancipation projects that were identified—the alternatives of annihilation or incorporation, autonomy under the king, and Indian hegemony with control from above or below—self-rule was the recurring, core aspiration.

The specific dynamics of the war in La Paz—radicalism, racial antagonism, violence, and base-level mobilization—were not the result of atavistic impulses on the part of Indian insurgents, nor of other putatively prepolitical sorts of anticolonial nativism, peasant utopianism, or subaltern class fury. What came to be seen by elites at the time and historians thereafter as "race war" in La Paz emerged most immediately from conjunctural political conflicts, especially the failure of Indian-creole alliance in the earlier stages of the insurrection. The potential for this polarization was present under Túpac Amaru in Cuzco as well, and followed from insurgent as well as counterinsurgent military strategy attacking "traitors" throughout the war. Thus, the historiographic distinctions commonly drawn between La Paz and Cuzco, as theaters in the insurrectionary war, can lead to oversimplification of the complex historical processes in each region.

In the end, the character of insurgent imagination, mobilization, and leadership in La Paz during the insurrection was shaped not only by the course of struggle in preceding decades, but by the concurrent regional movements in Chayanta, Cuzco, and Oruro in 1780–1781. The controversial figure of Túpaj Katari, for example, an Indian commoner striving to establish his authority over autonomous communities, drew heavily on the prestige of Tomás Katari and the Inka Túpac Amaru to consolidate his political identity and legitimacy. At the same time, the projects and dynamics present in La Paz resonated with those in other regions, and hence the focus in this study casts light on the late-colonial political crisis and insurgent political culture more generally in the southern Andes.

After panregional anticolonial forces receded in the early 1780s, the concern with self-government, expressed in ongoing struggles over political authority and mediation, persisted at the community level through the early nineteenth century. In the 1795 movement in Jesús de Machaca, the leader Juan Cuentas, backed by hilacatas, alcaldes, and community members from the twelve ayllus, reportedly announced that: "The present was a new era. . . . The cacique, his segunda, as well as the priest had to change, and . . . those that the community wanted had to take their place." The community subsequently denied that it had mutinied, accusing the cacique Pedro Ramírez de la Parra of fabricating the story in order to punish Indians for having brought a legal suit against him and for seeking to depose him. Whatever the veracity of the contradictory versions, the meaning of the entire episode could not be missed. It exposed anew the critical problem of illegitimate authority and the ongoing community struggle to define and determine itself politically.[1]

Community Power Reconstituted

As the established modes of Indian government and colonial mediation collapsed, a transformation occurred that would have enduring consequences for the political structure and political culture of

Aymara communities in the modern age. While the cacicazgo crisis was central to this transformation of the community polity, it also derived from a second, longer-term dynamic involving Indian nobility, principal status, and the cargo system. In order to explain the contradictory late-colonial evidence, I suggested that as the noble stratum slowly declined over the colonial period, subordinate authority posts were taken over by peasant community members, and principal status was assumed by those elders who had fulfilled a career of community service turns. As cacique control eroded and subordinate authorities assumed a primary political role, the loosely arranged civil cargo system, structured by the principles of ayllu organization, acquired greater salience. This phenomenon thus contributed to the devolution of power to the base of the community.

With the downfall of Indian nobility and cacique authority, power dispersed to other community political agents and sites: subordinate authorities acting in representation of local ayllus; elders and principales; spontaneous leaders in times of mobilization; and collective assemblies at which the majority of landholding peasant families were represented. Political power, formerly centralized and concentrated at the apex of the political formation on a permanent basis, was redistributed in a more diffuse pattern on a rotating, temporary basis. The overall political transformation thus had two clear consequences. First, as the hereditary patriarchal elite declined, there was a reduction of ascriptive authority, that is, authority deriving from conditions of estate, class, kinship and gender into which individuals were born. Second, there was more direct and broader political participation for community members.

All families with full community membership were expected to contribute to collective decision making, and a common will or consensus—even if it was achieved through difficult negotiation and a contest of pressure and resistance—was required for the community to take action. All families with full membership were also expected to exercise authority on a rotating annual basis. Rotating and temporary officeholding was coordinated in accordance with the principle of egalitarian representation for the diversity of local ayllu units. Officeholders viewed the exercise of authority as obligatory service that would leave them materially impoverished if symbolically enriched. While community members held respect for the person and position of local authorities, the effective control from below meant that authorities had to follow and enforce the common will.[2]

Finally, the decline of the cacicazgo involved a reduction in political power that was constituted and situated at a remove from the ayllus, which were the basic cells of the broader community. The cacique's role as community representative was brought into question during the process of political polarization as, from the peasant perspective, the cacique increasingly defined himself in practice as alien to the community. The failure of caciques to identify with the community in critical political conjunctures brought on the challenge to this specialized, fixed, permanent site of higher-level representational authority. The political transformation served to circumscribe such representation and replace it with scaled-down, less independent representation as well as greater direct participation by community members in civil affairs. Whereas the differentiation between higher representative political authority and the basic nucleus of the community had proven conducive to exploitation of peasant political subjects, the new exercise of authority by peasant community members themselves promised a higher degree of political integrity and more consistent self-government. In objective terms, therefore, the eighteenth-century community transformation meant a greater democratic content in social relations and a wider margin of political autonomy.

This democratization was not unlimited, of course, nor did it mean that all axes of hierarchy were removed.[3] If one prominent form of patriarchal power diminished, male domination continued to characterize other aspects of gender relations. Peasant women (addressed as *mama t'alla*) did share the authority post and decision making with their spouses, although usually as the subordinate partner in the couple. They did sometimes exercise direct, effective leadership, but this was usually in temporary substitution for their partner; under normal circumstances, their authority was mainly symbolic. They also played active roles in community mobilization and occasionally intervened decisively in collective assemblies, yet men remained the principal combatants and the usual, formal representatives of the household in political assemblies.[4]

Generational hierarchy also persisted although, by definition, it was not ascriptive. Younger couples were expected to hold authority posts, and over the course of their lives, by following the path of cargo obligations, all were expected to attain prestigious principal status. If we compare the symbolic conceptions of caciques and hilacatas (the key representatives of the local ayllus) in terms of their metaphoric kinship associations, the cacique was cast in a parental role (as father) while the hilacata (meaning "older brother" in Aymara) had a sibling role. It is true that generational and gender notions placed the hilacata in a hierarchically superior position relative to other siblings. Nevertheless, compared to the categorically *vertical* relations with the cacique, *horizontal* relations with authorities were strengthened by the community transformation.

Socioeconomic hierarchy also remained within the community, although ascriptive class power was not so pronounced beyond the sphere of noble cacique families. Landless peasants—usually unmarried youths and nonkin dependents—were not considered full community members and therefore were excluded from full community rights and obligations. Originarios enjoyed a property advantage and greater prestige than agregados or forasteros. Insofar as originario status was inheritable by children, we can recognize a degree of socioeconomic ascription. But the categories of originario, agregado, or forastero could also be permeable and mutable. Changing land tenure conditions within a family and tributary reform by the colonial state could cause households to move from one category to another. Agregados and forasteros possessed of land could also be called upon to serve as authorities if the community required it.

We should also note that community members did not reject ascriptive authority as such. Inherited originario or principal status (where the latter carried a noble association among its multiple connotations) and the privileges they conferred continued to be valued by Aymara peasants. Even in the late stages of the crisis of Indian community government, peasants sometimes attempted to reconstitute cacicazgos as long as they would be responsive to the community at large. Also, classic patriarchal authority could still hold legitimacy when identified with Indian communities, as it did in the case of Túpac Amaru during the great insurrection.

There was, then, a significant degree of democratic content in the political formation as it developed out of the struggles in the eighteenth century. At the same time, specific limitations to membership and participation remained, and ascriptive authority was not repudiated in and of itself. The emerging political formation also brought with it risks and disadvantages. Operating at a higher level within the segmentary organization of the community, the cacique was in a position to facilitate interayllu coordination and territorial cohesion. If he followed traditional codes of moral economy and reciprocity, he could play a useful role as an economic benefactor and guarantor of community subsistence. As a permanent economic and political administrator and intermediary vis-à-vis outside forces, he could develop specialized skills and knowledge, and could accumulate valuable experience and outside contacts that would redound to the benefit of the community. The failure of cacique authority thus contributed toward potential fragmentation and more precarious conditions for community reproduction.

But given the specific historical process of struggle in the late-colonial period, the new distribution of power was a logical outcome that held clear advantages for community members. Above all, there were fewer possibilities for despotic abuse of authority and manipulation from above by colonial elites or state authorities. In fact, as we have noted, there was no significant rearticulation between communities and the state in the waning years of Spanish rule. Colonial authorities did not name or regulate hilacatas and segundas; and state attempts to increase formal control over alcaldes, who did have to answer to the ayllus that put them in office, were of limited success. Principales and elders also exercised influence outside state purview, and colonial officials conducted no formal surveillance of communal assemblies.

These findings not only help us to rethink the late-colonial Andes, but to begin to broaden our conception of the revolutionary Atlantic world. In the eighteenth century, native American peoples nourished their own ideals of liberty and self-determination. While indigenous communities did not mobilize with "democracy" as their aim, their struggles against the domination of an Old World empire brought about effective and enduring practices of communal democracy and sovereignty that differed from Western liberal principles.

Turning our sights to the present, the late eighteenth century was a "constitutive moment" (Zavaleta) for the community political formation and political culture as we know them today in the heartland of the Aymara indigenous population. Rural social and political relations did, of course, undergo considerable alteration over the course of modern Bolivian history. Processes of local administrative and territorial fragmentation, and at times recomposition, have continued to unfold. Changing state policy, hacienda expansion and contraction, and a series of internal community dynamics, revolving around demographic, resource, and jurisdictional matters for example, have reshaped the social landscape since the colonial period. Nevertheless, there have also been important structural political continuities. In nineteenth-century La Paz, the new administrative unit of the canton, composed of local ayllus grouped in moieties, was homologous with the colonial town unit. Today, there remains in many areas, despite atomization and increasing institutional-jurisdictional superimposition, a basic level of coordination among local communal units that makes up an integral, overarching social space. While the traditional town center, performing administrative and ceremonial functions, has recently become less significant, the constellation of local communal units is still integrated around a center (oftentimes a municipal center) that provides key services.

In this similar structural context, we find many of the same political forms and principles that existed in the late-colonial period. Cyclical rotation among the ayllus or local communal units defines collective participation and representation. The commnual assembly, marked by a high degree of direct participation and consensus decision making, forms the core of community political power. The cargo system, headed by elders who have accrued prestige by following the path of authority posts, continues to operate. Many authority posts are identical to those from the colonial period and are similarly held as obligatory service. Authorities themselves remain subject to the tight surveillance and control of the community base.[5]

Contemporary political anthropology and sociology has drawn attention to the striking democratic nature of the Andean community in Bolivia. The concepts and models in circulation include that of the community as a "ministate" or as a "local republic" (Albó); the ayllu as "polis" (Rivera); and "Aymara democracy" (Albó) or "ethnic democracy" (Rojas).[6] This study has traced the historical roots of this democratic political structure and political culture to the late-colonial struggles of Aymara communities.

If the community transformation in the eighteenth century left a political legacy that persists to the present, its full significance will only emerge once future work clarifies the nineteenth- and early-twentieth-century history of political structures and power relations in the countryside. We should not assume, for example, that the late-colonial breakdown of community political representation and mediation carried over unmodified until the conjuncture of the 1953 Agrarian Reform. Just as communities and the state tested new political strategies in the aftermath of the great Andean insurrection, they did so over the course of republican history. There were certainly new and conflictive cycles, even if they lacked the full scale and intensity of the eighteenth-century process, that entailed the construction and dismantling of strata of political representation and mediation.

The insurgents under the command of Pablo Zárate Willka in 1899, for example, sought (in the words of one contemporary) the "reconstitution of the autonomous communal system" and asserted that in the future all officials should be Indian since they would "no longer tolerate the authority of whites."[7] The story of Faustino Llanqui, community leader in Jesús de Machaca in the early part of this century, provides an even fuller illustration of the new variations as well as the enduring features of local political dynamics. In 1919, Llanqui came forward as cacique principal to protest against the corregidor, or canton-level agent, of the Bolivian government:

> Having reliable information that Sr. Lucio T. Estrada is to be named corregidor of my canton Jesús de Machaca, all the cabildo members have charged me, in representation of them, with the responsibility of advising this authority that said Estrada cannot be corregidor, since he is a town resident of notorious antecedents and an abusive person who mistreats the community members and charges excessive fines and is finally the scourge of the town.

> Because of these antecedents, Sr. Prefect, I ask of you that the indicated Sr. Estrada not be named. I am opposed to it in the name of all the hilacatas of Jesús de Machaca. Being an authority who does not fulfill his obligations and is abusive, it is not possible to have a perverse authority in our town, because it would cause our poor and unfortunate indigenous race to wail and suffer.[8]

In the republican period, the corregidor, whose title linked him to the discredited provincial magistrate of the colonial period, was a town-based non-Indian official who had taken over the colonial cacique's local coercive and surveillance functions on behalf of the state.[9] As for Faustino Llanqui, he was one of those Indian leaders in the early twentieth century who resuscitated, without state certification, the maximal authority post of the colonial cacique. Llanqui, who was evidently constructing a new identity based upon references he found in colonial documents in his possession, claimed descent from a sixteenth-century native governor in Jesús de Machaca. In the 1920s, he and other *caciques-apoderados* led an important Indian campaign for territorial and educational rights in the face of despotic power wielded by the local and regional landed elite and state officials.

The case of Llanqui and other caciques-apoderados is noteworthy, first of all, because in a new political cycle, they attempted to recuperate and reconstitute a legitimate higher-level political representation for their communities. They did so through a conscious and creative reworking of the colonial past, with its lasting legacy and ongoing implications. The figure of the cacique, once thoroughly withered in La Paz and finally sloughed off by Bolivarian decree, did not remain permanently obsolete, nor did communities repudiate the reintroduction of higher-level authority.[10]

At the same time, Llanqui's story shows how fundamental concerns of Indians in the late-colonial period, especially the abuse or legitimate exercise of authority, remained present and pressing. It demonstrates, furthermore, that the eighteenth-century processes set primary terms and parameters for the later swings in community political representation and projection in the national period. While he stepped forth as a new manifestation of cacique leadership—a blood heir to the noble lords of the past and representative of all the ayllus of the canton—Llanqui was also very aware of the mandate from below. The eighteenth century laid the terrain as well for state initiatives to establish new hegemonic forms of control over the rural population. After the breakdown of indirect colonial rule through caciques, the republican state turned to mestizo and creole townspeople to exercise coercive and paternalist authority over communities. The full historical irony of the reappearance of the corregidor and cacique in this episode—in a relationship of confrontation rather than complicity—emerges from our understanding of the eighteenth century.

This glimpse of the cacique and the corregidor of Jesús de Machaca in 1919, in light of eighteenth-century history, matches up with Rasnake's view of the change in the traditional authority system in Yura from the colonial era to the present. Rasnake conceives of a shift from internal to external hierarchy (in other words, from indirect to direct state rule at the town level), and a shift from authoritarian to egalitarian ethnic representatives. Though distinctions between the cases of Yura and the region of La Paz can be cited, for "traditional" authority systems in the national period show pronounced regional and even subregional diversity, my analysis of the transfer of authority to the base essentially accords with Rasnake's interpretation. But while Rasnake emphasizes 1781 as the crucial moment when the system changed—given the fact that the hereditary cacique of Yura and his three sons were killed at that time—our treatment of La Paz reveals that the political rupture and violence against caciques in 1781 expressed a broader late-colonial situation of crisis for community and state political structures and a transformation unfolding over decades before and after the insurrection.[11]

This exploration of Indian politics and the late-colonial crisis in the Andes has shown how peasant community members in the Aymara highlands of La Paz brought about important historical change through their own agency. It has also sought to recover their motivations and visions as they engaged in political and insurrectionary action. At the turn of the twenty-first century, the richness, vitality, and intensity of Aymara peasant politics go unabated, and historical memory continues to stir and direct Aymara political initiatives. Authorities and community members in

Jesús de Machaca today recall Faustino Llanqui and the community campaigns led by him in their own efforts to rebuild local authority structures and to recuperate communal integrity and autonomy. At a time of new cultural and political ferment, the secular struggles of the ancestors, against colonial and neocolonial conditions of domination, are present in conscious as well as unconscious ways. Some Aymara leaders like Llanqui or, before him, Túpaj Katari, Bartolina Sisa, and Gregoria Apaza, have regained their prominence in recent decades. Others who played a decisive role—such as the unnamed woman who urged Yungas community members into battle from the Alto de Guancané over Chulumani or old Francisco Marca who journeyed back and forth between his altiplano home in Calacoto and the colonial court in La Plata—can be remembered because, often in spite of themselves, they left a trace in the written record. Yet even those who moved so silently or invisibly as to leave no documentary trace also made their historical mark and the consequences of their accumulated actions are with us now. Together Aymara peasants and their leaders in the eighteenth century made history, remade community, and passed on a legacy for present-day struggles.

Abbreviations

Notes

Bibliography

Index

Abbreviations

Archives

AA   Archivo de la Curia Arzobispal de La Paz. La Paz, Bolivia.

ABUMSA   Archivo de la Biblioteca Central de la Universidad Mayor de San Andrés. La Paz, Bolivia.

AC   Archivo de la Catedral de La Paz. La Paz, Bolivia.

AGI   Archivo General de Indias. Seville, Spain.

AGN   Archivo General de la Nación, Buenos Aires. Buenos Aires, Argentina.

AHN   Archivo Histórico Nacional. Madrid, Spain.

ALP   Archivo de La Paz. La Paz, Bolivia.

ANB   Archivo Nacional de Bolivia. Sucre, Bolivia.

RAH   Archivo de la Real Academia de la Historia. Madrid, Spain.

Other Abbreviations

ACI   Actas del coloquio internacional: "Túpac Amaru y su tiempo."

CDIP   Colección documental de la independencia del Perú.

CDRTA   Colección documental del bicentenario de la rebelión emancipadora de Túpac Amaru.

Notes

Chapter 1. Contours for a History of Power and Political Transformation in the Aymara Highlands

1. Quechua leader Diego Quispe the Younger wrote of it as "the new conquest by Sr. Governor José Gabriel Túpac Amaru Inka" (Archivo General de Indias [AGI] Buenos Aires 319, "Cuaderno No. 4," fol. 39). Ignacio Flores, appointed military governor of the district of Charcas during the insurrection, described the war as a "new conquest," adding that "surely it is more difficult to bring these provinces under control now than it was to win them at the time of the Inkas, because the Indians have lost their former simplicity" (AGI Charcas 595, Carta de Ignacio Flores a Vértiz, La Paz, 9/VII/1781 [7 fols.], fols. 5–5v). Dr. Diego de la Riva, the Indian protector for La Paz (a colonial attorney charged with the legal representation of Indians), spoke of a "reconquest" (Archivo de La Paz [ALP] EC 1781 C. 101 E. 14).

2. Mestizos were people considered to be of "mixed" Indian and Spanish ancestry. Creoles *(criollos)* were Spaniards born in the Americas, as distinguished from those born on the Iberian peninsula *(peninsulares)*. See chapter 2, n.6, for further discussion of terms of collective identity.

3. In most instances, I have opted not to update the orthography of personal names and place-names found in the colonial sources. The case of the three great insurgent leaders, however, calls for special consideration. Their overlapping names and the variability in common spelling today means that any option can be only partly satisfying. Based on orthographic systems for the Aymara language, "Katari" is increasingly used in Bolivia for the colonial spelling "Catari." I employ it here to refer both to the leaders in northern Potosí (Tomás Katari and his brothers) and La Paz (Túpaj Katari). If the nominal similarity between them seems confusing at times, that was, after all, the intent of Túpaj Katari when he adopted Tomás Katari's surname. "Túpaj" is a contemporary Bolivian rendering, again based on Aymara orthography, of the colonial "Tupa" or "Thupa," and hence I use it for the La Paz leader. Since "Túpac" is more commonly found in Peru, I refer to the Cuzco leader as "Túpac Amaru." Note also that "Inka" is increasingly common usage for the colonial "Inca" or "Inga."

4. See Palmer (1959, 1964); Hobsbawm (1962); and Langley (1996).

5. On the Haitian revolution, see James (1963) and Fick (1990). See Trouillot (1995) on the inconceivability of the revolution, and the general problem of historiographic "silencing."

6. The Latin American historiography addressing rural rebellion is voluminous, and the literature on late-colonial resistance and the wars of independence is itself extremely rich. Generally speaking, however, this work has not provided a full or intimate view of anticolonial politics at the local level among subaltern subjects. With some notable exceptions (e.g. Fick 1990; Ferrer 1999; Van Young 2001), even the work on independence movements has focused more on creole projects and leadership than on subaltern political agency and consciousness. For the most encompassing literature review on rebellion in Latin American history, see Coatsworth (1988). Cf. also McFarlane (1992, 1995) on rebellion in seventeenth- and eighteenth-century Spanish America. The classic village revolt is described by Taylor (1979) for Mexico. For more on the Mexican region, see Katz (1988) and Van Young (1992). Bourbon reform and the resistance it provoked in New Granada and the Andes are treated in J. Fisher et al. (1990). For more on New Grenada, see McFarlane (1984), as well as Phelan (1978) and Loy (1981) on the important 1781 Comunero revolt. The Andean bibliography will be discussed more extensively below. An initial set of Andean references for the period would include Flores Galindo (1976); O'Phelan (1988); Stern (1987); Sala i Vila (1996b); Walker (1996); and Serulnikov (1998).

7. My approach to peasant politics shares affinities with different bodies of work in history and social science. Peasant studies, combining political economy and historical perspectives, has produced sophisticated analyses of peasant rebellion. There have also been important critiques of the peasant studies literature on agrarian resistance. In a critique of key assumptions in the literature having to do with peasants as political actors, and drawing out the implications of research in the field of Andean studies, Stern (1987b, 3–25) advanced a set of methodological suggestions whose value is confirmed in this study of La Paz. Peasant community members are treated here as political agents moving and negotiating within a wide field of power relations, even when they do not engage in overt, collective, or violent action. This study likewise shows that peasant consciousness cannot be summed up as narrow, defensive, misoneist, or "prepolitical," and that it creatively reflects culturally specific visions. The study pays particular attention to the central and complex dimension of ethnicity that has been largely overlooked in the comparative analysis of peasantries. It also considers longer-term cycles and multiple levels of conjuncture that help to situate episodes of conflict. In a critical reflection on the "agrarian question" and its literature in Latin America, Roseberry (1993) points to the same issue identified by Stern—the nature of peasant political practice and consciousness—as the foremost problem for analysis.

Within peasant studies, the landmark work of Scott (1976, 1985, 1990) on moral economies, quotidian resistance, and peasant political discourse has been absorbed in this study, although it is worthwhile to note here one limitation of his approach that emerges from consideration of the eighteenth-century Andean case. In moving beyond narrow social science views that circumscribed peasant politics to intermittent uprisings and formal relations with national political forces (states and political parties), Scott privileged instead everyday, informal, isolated, petty, and covert acts of resistance. He sought to vindicate "resistance without protest and without organization," and argued that such resistance is more effective than collective mobilization that risks reprisals from above. This tendency in Scott's work itself diminishes the full scope of peasant political agency and downplays an important aspect of peasant community experience. This problem stems from an ahistorical and static notion that peasants occupy a permanent position of "weakness" vis-à-vis the dominant group. Eighteenth-century La Paz provides one striking example of how power relations shift historically in ways that can favor peasants, who may opt to seize the initiative in concerted, overt actions and even cast off previously negotiated pacts with overlords or the state. This point is specifically illustrated by comparing tithe resistance in the colonial Andes, where collective mobilization came to play a central role, with the cases of early modern France and contemporary Malaysia, where religious taxation slowly eroded due to peasant foot-dragging and passive opposition. Cf. Barragán and Thomson (1993) and Scott (1987).

Important work has also been forthcoming from the Indian school of Subaltern Studies. In particular, Guha's methodological reflections on counterinsurgent discourse and his paradigmatic approach to insurgent consciousness (1988, 1999) have influenced my own analysis. Finally, within Andean historiography, Roberto Choque, Silvia Rivera, and a generation of young Aymara historians have led the way in writing peasant political history from within, adapting multidisciplinary research methods to represent the vision of Indian political actors and deploying the historical memory of resistance within the context of contemporary Aymara cultural and political organization. (See n.17, below.)

8. Cf. Mallon (1995), who elaborates a framework, drawing from Gramscian and poststructuralist sources, for explaining how hegemonic arrangements within communities are constructed out of differentiated and conflictual conditions involving gender, generation, ethnicity, and class and how these changing internal conditions can shape regional and national political configurations.

9. This project is consonant with a new body of research on peasant politics and political culture in Latin American historiography. For the "age of insurgency" in the Andes, the new work has focused specifically on internal community conflicts and the transformation of indigenous authority systems; community-state relations and anticolonial peasant projects; and the form and content of indigenous political discourses. For examples, see the special forum in *Colonial Latin American Review* 8, no. 2 (1999) and the following monographs: Penry (1996); Robins (1997); Sala i Vila (1996b); Serulnikov (1998); Stavig (1999); Thurner (1996); and Walker (1999).

10. Despite the wealth of multidisciplinary research into peasant communities and ayllus, Andean studies has lacked explicit and developed *political* analyses of the community as a whole, its internal dynamics, and its structural transformation over time. An important early contribution is Fuenzalida (1970). Cf. also Bonilla et al. (1987).

11. One primary theme within Andean studies that is relevant here is the nature of Andean social organization and its reproduction or transformation over time. After an initial focus on the long-term continuities in social organization, ethnohistorians have increasingly concentrated on the important problem of the colonial breakdown of precontact ethnic kingdoms or federations and the emergence of the local peasant communities that are present today in the Andes. The problem has been sometimes cast as one of ethnic destructuration, with external colonial forces and impositions seen as leveling or decapitating the successive layers of hierarchically segmented social organization. But as recent work has recognized, this structural analysis was limited insofar as it failed to examine the dynamics internal to Indian society and the ways in which Andean people themselves contributed to historical change through their own actions.

I will not address this overall trajectory or Andean social organization as a whole, but this study does examine a key aspect and a key moment of this process—the specific political transformation that occurred in the eighteenth century. It also emphasizes, through structural and historical analysis, the way that Indian people, acting in response to colonial domination, transformed the late-colonial Andean polity and shaped the process of ethnogenesis. See Murra et al. (1986); Barragán and Molina Rivero (1987); Segundo Moreno and Salomon, eds. (1991), especially the contributions of Urton (1991) and Saignes (1991); Wachtel (1992); Powers (1995); and Abercrombie (1998).

12. AGI Buenos Aires 319, "Cuaderno No. 4," fols. 60v, 77.

13. On this working definition and a brief historical and linguistic sketch of the Aymara people, see Albó (1988, 22–34). For more on Aymara identity recently, see Albó (1979b); Albó et al. (1981–1987).

14. Bouysse 1987. Saignes 1986.

15. Albó 1988, 22–34.

16. For a variety of sources and interpretations regarding Aymara ethnic resurgence and political movements today, see Rivera (1984); Hurtado (1986); Albó (1987, 1991a, 1991b, 1993); Cárdenas (1988); Pacheco (1992); Calla (1993); Tapia (1995); and Ticona (2000).

17. Bandelier 1910, 19, 34–35. Cf. Forbes (1870, 199, 227); and La Barre ([1948] 1969). Bolton (1973, 1976) sought the cause of perceived Aymara aggression in a medical problem, hypoglycemia.

18. Saavedra 1903, 174–175. Cf. Paredes 1906, 110–112.

19. Since the 1970s, Aymara ethnography and ethnohistory have acquired significant dynamism and largely abandoned the earlier discourse about Aymara

character. This work will be engaged and cited throughout this study, but for a wide-ranging introduction see the contributions and materials in Albó (1988). The literature addressing Aymara democracy is cited in chapter 8. Young Aymara anthropologists and historians, a number of whom have been associated with the Taller de Historia Oral Andina (1984, 1986), are building on the pioneering contributions of Silvia Rivera (1978, 1984, 1991, 1993) and a first generation of Aymara scholars such as R. Choque (1979, 1986, 1988, 1991, 1992, 1992, 1993a, 1993b, 1996 [with Ticona]). See, for example, Huanca (1984); C. Mamani (1989, 1991); Santos (1989); M. E. Choque (1992, 1995); Ticona et al. (1995); Fernández (1996, 2000); Ticona and Albó (1997); Ticona (2000); and M. E. Choque and C. Mamani (2001).

20. O'Phelan (1988). Stern (1987a). Coinciding with Rowe (1954) and O'Phelan, Stern (1987a, 72, 82) acknowledges that the presence of earlier insurrectionary threats permits an extension of the period back to the 1730s.

21. Cf. Barragán and Thomson (1993) for a study that periodizes the proliferation of social conflict over tithes in colonial Charcas.

22. R. Arze 1979.

23. Archivo General de la Nación, Buenos Aires (AGN) IX 5-5-3, "Plan de la división de la provincia de Sicasica," 1779, fols. 5, 7v–8. On the important circulation and production of coca, grown in the Yungas valleys of La Paz, see Lema (1988).

24. On the late-colonial demography and economy of the region of La Paz, see Klein (1993). For more on eighteenth-century economy and society generally in Charcas, see Santamaría (1977, 1989); Klein (1982, 64-86; 1998); Tandeter and Wachtel (1984); Larson (1988); Wachtel (1990); Tandeter (1992, 1995). On the late-colonial city of La Paz, see Barragán (1990); Crespo et al. (1975).

25. The distribution described here was given in the sentence dictated by the *Oidor* (audiencia magistrate) Francisco Tadeo Diez de Medina. The scribe Esteban de Loza gives a slightly different version, but the transcript of Diez de Medina's sentence would seem to be authoritative. (AGN IX 7-4-2, "Testimonios de confesiones del reo Julián Apaza y sentencia que se pronunció contra él," fols. 36–36v. Cf. AGI Charcas 595, "Diario que formo yo Esteban de Loza, escribano de Su Magestad . . . ," fols. 20–20v.)

26. For more on the provinces of Sicasica and Chulumani, see chapter 4; Lema (1988); Klein (1993).

27. Choque has written extensively on Pacajes from preconquest times until the twentieth century. For the colonial period, see Choque (1993).

28. On colonial Larecaja, see Saignes (1985b); and Thomson (1999a).

29. Málaga Medina 1974. Spalding 1984, 214–216. Gade 1991. Saignes 1991. Penry 1996. Abercrombie 1998.

30. Hunefeldt 1983. Cahill 1984. Cf. Taylor (1996) for Mexico.

31. The colonial tributary system and Andean responses to it are the subject of an extensive historiography. For Upper Peru, see Sánchez Albornoz (1978);

Saignes (1985c, 1987a); Larson (1988); and Klein (1993); cf. Wightman (1990) for Cuzco.

32. Platt 1982, 1988. There is also abundant historiography on the topic of the Potosí mita; for a set of references, see chapter 3.

33. Cf. Saignes (1991).

34. Rasnake (1988, 49–53) notes the great diversity of definitions of the ayllu in the literature and provides a working definition for Yura. The concept of "community" and the units of analysis used to understand Andean social organization have been interrogated in Segundo Moreno and Salomon (1991).

35. See list of archives consulted at end of text.

36. The model study of *longue durée* local history in the Andes is Spalding's *Huarochirí* (1984).

37. According to tributary records for 1797, Guarina's residents made up nine thousand of the sixty thousand inhabitants of the province of Omasuyos (AGN XIII 17-9-1, Libro 2, fol. 1084). An earlier parish report calculated roughly twelve thousand residents. See Archivo de la Catedral de La Paz (AC) Tomo 52, "Expediente sobre la demarcación de las doctrinas de Guarina, Laja, Pucarani" (1766) [1776], fols. 112–146; for the priest's testimony, see fol. 138v.

Chapter 2. The Inherited Structure of Authority

1. Diego Calaumana's second marriage seems to have been to a Spanish woman, for Matías charged that Francisco was a mestizo descendant of the Verástegui family. For this introductory sketch of the family lineage and Matías Calaumana's succesion, see AGN IX 30-3-2, "Dona María Justa Salazar, viuda de don Matías Calaumana cacique de Guarina, sobre esclarecer el derecho al cacicazgo," 1783, fols. 15–39v.

2. Archivo de la Curia Arzobispal de La Paz (AA) Libro 33, 1778 (X) No. 596, "Autos de Feliciana Hancara contra el Licenciado Miguel Irusta sobre maltratos," fol. 97.

3. Calaumana's phrase was "una voluntariedad fundada sólo en la equidad y gracia" (Archivo Nacional de Bolivia [ANB] Minas T. 128 No. 2/Minas Cat. No. 1754, fol. 37). For more on these land conflicts, see ANB EC 1774 No. 14, fols. 180–268v; ANB EC 1775 [1766] No. 174.

4. ANB Minas T. 128 No. 2/Minas Cat. No. 1754, fol. 4v. ANB EC 1776 No. 109. For the cacique's public dressing down of a local priest and his assertion that "no one could give orders but him" in the town, see AA Libro 30, 1770 (I) No. 502, "Autos de Martín Calahumana [*sic*] contra Lic. Juan de Mondaca sobre injurias."

5. This passage draws on AGN IX 30-2-1, "Recurso de don Francisco Calaumana, indio principal y noble del pueblo de Guarina, sobre que se le confirme . . . el empleo de alcalde mayor de naturales de dicha provincia," 1779; AGN IX

31-3-4, "Don Matías Calaumana a nombre de su hermano don José Calaumana sobre pertenecerle a éste el cacicazgo del pueblo de Laja . . . ," 1778; and a set of Guarina census registers in AGN Sala XIII.

6. While the full complexity of this issue cannot be addressed here, a note regarding racial and ethnic classification is in order at this point. "Indians"—most commonly termed *indios* or *naturales*—were assumed to be descended from the preconquest native population and to be free of the taint of mixture with another population. The category of "Spaniards" was broad. It included people of European birth *(peninsulares)* and creoles who were of pure European descent but born in the Americas. Yet, somewhat by default, it also included all others who were not Indian, mainly mestizos and blacks. The term "mestizo" was especially ambiguous. A strong component of its literal significance was racial, referring to "mixed" parentage from distinct preconquest populations. At the same time, the category of "mestizo" was loosely attributed to people according to a variety of different cultural markers and criteria. A common subcategory of the mestizo in the Andes was the "cholo." This term as well often carried a racial connotation, suggesting a high degree of Indian as compared to Spanish "blood." Yet it was equally applied to Indians who had acquired a superficial overlay of Spanish cultural attributes, such as European dress. Blacks *(negros),* most of whom were enslaved, and people of mixed African and Indian or European descent (known as *mulatos, zambos,* or *zambaigos*) made another intermediary group who fit awkwardly in the dualistic scheme of colonial discourse. Given the different overlapping criteria used to define collective identity in this period, I employ the language of both "race" and "ethnicity" for purposes of discussion.

7. See chapter 3 for a historiographic discussion of the forms of cacique ambivalence.

8. Lockhart 1992, 30–35.

9. Díaz Rementería (1977) offers a meticulous legal analysis of the Andean cacicazgo based on the abstract distinction between the statuses of cacique and governor. His work confirms the lack of colonial juridical clarity in this area and the predominance of hereditary over other Spanish criteria (whether election or appointment) for succession. The vagueness of the status of "governor" can be seen from the fact that Peruvian Viceroy Toledo's sixteenth-century ordinances establishing political jurisdiction within Indian towns make no mention of the post. See Sarabia Viejo (1989, 2:203–266).

10. ANB EC 1793 No. 11, fols. 1–3v. Henceforth I will indicate the province of a given town in parentheses.

11. ANB EC 1763 No. 129, fol. 1v. ANB EC 1808 No. 138, fol. 162.

12. ANB EC 1799 No. 121, fols. 150–150v.

13. ALP EC 1722 C. 54 E. 6, fol. 3v.

14. ALP EC 1783 C. 103 E. s.n. (sin número), fol. 13v. ANB EC 1783 No. 19, fol. 18v.

15. For a set of basic references on this issue, see Rowe (1954); Gisbert (1980); Flores Galindo (1987); Burga (1988).

16. Mesa and Gisbert 1982, 1:180. Burga 1988, 335. Rowe (1954, 21) also found that eighteenth-century Inka nobles in Cuzco practiced genealogical falsification.

17. ALP EC 1740 C. 67 E. 3, fol. 18. The Guarachis' cultural patrimony has been carefully examined by Gisbert (1980, 1992). On Guarachi family genealogy, kinship, and succession, see Archivo de la Biblioteca Central de la UMSA (ABUMSA) No. 191 (1805); Urioste (1978); and Choque (1993b).

18. A set of these paintings has been located and described by Gisbert (1992). On eighteenth-century portrait fever and the political uses of cacique paintings, see also Gisbert (1980, 97, 152).

19. The chronological distortions in the family's account of its lineage founders and Inka alliance are mentioned by Gisbert (1980, 93–94).

20. ABUMSA No. 191 (1805).

21. ALP EC 1740 C. 67 E. 3, fol. 23 and unnumbered folio at the end of the expediente. ABUMSA No. 191, fol. 13.

22. ABUMSA No. 191 (1805), fols. 33v–40. ABUMSA No. 186 (1801), fols. 1–3v.

23. ANB EC 1756 No. 72, fol. 39.

24. ANB EC 1802 No. 48, fols. 3v–4.

25. On traditional succession principles, see Platt (1988, 376–77). Cf. Choque (1993, 30).

26. Tutino 1983. Lavrin and Couturier 1979. For more on the dynamics of cacicazgo succession, see also Díaz Rementería(1977).

27. Cummins 1991. Cf. Gisbert (1980, 1992).

28. Buntinx and Wuffarden 1991. Their analysis of discursive ambivalence and the caciques' symbolic strategies in colonial painting complements the previous literary work, such as that of Adorno (1986), on the Indian chroniclers. See also Salomon (1982b). Their own argument is that Garcilaso provided a discursive blueprint for cacique strategies in the neo-Inka movement. See also Gisbert (1980, 1992).

29. Building on Flores Galindo's essay (1987) to answer a question posed by Stern (1987a, 75), we are in a position to bring together the literature on noble Indian culture, rural class formation, and Andean rebellion in order to account for the origins of neo-Inka "insurrectionary utopias" in the late-colonial period. See also chapters 5 and 6 here.

30. Buntinx and Wuffarden (1991) focus on cacique nobles in the regions of Cuzco, Huarochirí, and Lima. On the recurrent aspiration for "Andean utopia" in Peruvian history, see Flores Galindo (1987) and Burga (1988). They have used the term to indicate an ideal, at times unconscious and at times explicitly articulated in myth, literature, and political projects, of social transformation grounded in a distinctive sense of Andean identity and history, and often symbolically associated with ideas of the Inka and his return to sovereignty.

31. Rowe 1954.

32. On the de la Cueva engraving, its origins, variants, and interpretation, see Gisbert (1980, 117–146) and Buntinx and Wuffarden (1991).

33. ANB EC 1796 No. 97, fol. 11. The caciques' consciousness of hereditary transmission of indigenous nobility assumes historical continuity from the Inka to the Catholic kings who, in the final instance, sanctioned their elevated rank. For one illustration, see the case of Manuel Chiqui Inga Charaja of Juli (Chucuito). He traced his nobility *(hidalguía)* back to a gentile forefather "confirmed" by the Inka king Guayna Cápac and noted the reconfirmation of his lineage by Carlos II in the sixteenth century and Felipe V in 1701 (ALP EC 1722 C. 54 E. 6, fols. 3v–5).

34. Gisbert 1980, 95–97; and 1992, 78–83. Following the revisionism of Buntinx and Wuffarden, we might speculate that this motif, as part of more subtle political strategies and discourses, could actually reflect a qualification of cacique loyalism and an alliance with ecclesiastical forces that were semi–independent from the colonial state. See also Gisbert's comments on the allegory of Hercules and Apollo, another mural from the Carabuco church, with its similar message regarding secular and religious authority.

35. ALP EC 1783 C. 103 E. s.n., fols. 13v–15. On cacique family coats of arms, see Gisbert (1980, 157–162); and Arze and Medinaceli (1991).

36. ANB EC 1755 No. 66, fol. 131. ANB EC 1756 No. 130, fol. 12v.

37. This is obviously not to deny that, from the native Andean chroniclers in the early seventeenth century to Túpac Amaru, there were subversive currents that challenged the legitimacy of the conquest. However, it would be difficult to demonstrate any such challenge in the many official proclamations by caciques of military favors to the Crown. It is also worth noting how the issue, discussed above, of hereditary nobility sanctioned by the Spanish monarch could contain implicit legitimation of the conquest. For instance, the cacique of Juli (cited in n.33, this chapter) spoke out in defense of his nobility, ratified and recorded since the conquest (ALP EC 1722 C. 54 E. 6, fol. 4v).

38. ALP EC 1740 C. 67 E. 3, fols. 23–23v; reference to this painting is made on an unnumbered folio at end of the expediente. On the Uru rebellion, see Wachtel 1990, 382. For the services of Pedro Guarachi and his forefathers—"ever since the Spaniards arrived for the conquest and discovery of the natives of these kingdoms"—including Fernando Ajata Camaqui who dispatched a cargo of gold to Viceroy Toledo for Felipe II's wars against "the Turk," see ABUMSA No. 191 (1805), fols. 26–30, 40v.

39. ANB EC 1808 No. 138, fols. 150v, 151–151v, 153v, 154v, 157, 158, 164v.

40. ANB EC 1796 No. 97, fol. 9.

41. ANB EC 1771 No. 27, fol. 44. In Gisbert's (1980, 160) words, "The importance granted to noble distinction indicates just how close our caciques were to the excessive chivalric honor that characterized the Spaniards of the Golden Age."

42. Gutiérrez 1991, 148–150, 178–180, 190, 194, 206.

43. ANB EC 1771 No. 27, fols. 31v, 36v, 38, 41v. ALP EC 1786 C. 107 E. s.n., fol. 93v and unnumbered folio.

44. AGN IX 5-6-1, "Indios de Jesús de Machaca contra su cacique Pedro Ramírez de la Parra," 1795, fols. 1–11.

45. ANB EC 1783 No. 76, fol. 29. ANB Colección Ruck 1783 No. 113, fol. 42.

46. Arze and Medinaceli (1991) offer an interpretation of the subtle, intercultural symbolism in the escutcheon of the Ayaviri dynasty from Sacaca.

47. Rasnake (1988, 215–216) notes iconographic evidence of an Andean precursor to the colonial staff from Chavín and Tiahuanaco, and Patrice Lecoq (*Presencia,* 29 August 1992) located archaeological evidence from the southern altiplano.

48. In the 1795 Jesús de Machaca mobilization, rebels told an Indian authority (regidor) that he would be punished if he continued to brandish his staff (ALP EC 1795 C. 122 E. s.n., fol. 11). Rasnake (1988, 210–230) provides an important ritual and symbolic analysis of the staff of authority in Yura. He also discusses another community political symbol—the *rollo,* or pillar of justice standing in the plaza center—possessing a similar semantic ambivalence since colonial times.

49. This composite description is taken from the following expedientes: ANB EC 1793 No. 11, fols. 30, 123; ANB EC 1785 No. 4, fol. 5; ANB EC 1754 No. 62, fols. 27v–28; ANB EC 1745 No. 42, fols. 13–13v.

50. ANB EC 1808 No. 138, fol. 147.

51. One rather insignificant exception can be made here. The testimony from these events always duly notes that no one in attendance spoke out against the cacique's appointment. The opportunity to raise objections to the proceedings, which was common in feudal medieval ceremonies of possession, was apparently not meant specifically for community members, and in any case was not used by them.

52. For more of the historiography on caciques, mediation, and legitimacy, see chapter 3.

53. Cited in Campbell (1987, 133).

54. ANB EC 1758 No. 151, fols. 1–2. Consider also the case of the Indians of Yaco (Sicasica) who complained in 1769 about their cacique, "He never defends us as he should, and he doesn't even defend the boundaries of the community lands" (ANB EC 1772 No. 42, fol. 1).

55. ANB EC 1793 No. 11, fol. 162. ALP EC 1786 C. 107 E. s.n., fol. 60v.

56. Bertonio 1984, 1:342, and 2:275, 288, 314. Cf. Albó (1988, 404).

57. See Salomon's exhaustive review (1982a) of the Andean ethnography during the 1970s. Among the most in-depth and original treatments of traditional authorities, which hold the merit of combining historical and contemporary perspectives, are Rasnake (1988); Ticona and Albó (1997); and Abercrombie (1998). For an overview of authorities in Aymara communities today, see Carter and Albó (1988, 478–487); and Ticona et al. (1995, 79–95). For other Bolivian references, see Carter (1964, 35–42); Buechler and Buechler (1971, 68–89); Carter and Mamani (1982, 247–286); Ayllu Sartañani (1992, 55–107); and Fernández (2000).

For Ecuador historically, see Guerrero (1989); and Moscoso (1989). For Columbia, see Rappaport (1990, 1994). The Mexican literature is more extensive than the Andean in this field, paying particular attention to cabildo government in Indian towns and to the contemporary civil-religious cargo hierarchy. For examples of the historical work, see Gibson (1964); Farriss (1984); Chance and Taylor (1985); García Martínez (1987); Carmagnani (1988); Haskett (1991); and Lockhart (1992).

58. Toledo called for two alcaldes, four regidores, and one alguacil. See tít. I, ord. I of his decree "Ordenanzas generales para la vida común en los pueblos de indios," issued in Arequipa on 6 November 1575, which is published in Sarabia Viejo (1989, 2:217–266). The Laws of the Indies specified one alcalde for towns with more than forty families, and two alcaldes for towns of eighty or more families. See lib. VI, tít. III, ley xv of the Recopilación de leyes (1943). La Palata decreed that two alcaldes, two regidores, and one alguacil mayor should govern any town of two hundred or more tributaries (ANB EC 1760 No. 11, fol. 319v). A pair of references illustrate the local variability in the case of alcaldes. Ulloma (Pacajes) community members spoke of a norm of two alcaldes ordinarios and one alcalde mayor that was "prevalent in all the towns" (ANB EC 1752 No. 39, fol. 4). A list of the number of alcaldes in the towns of the Chulumani partido shows towns with three and four alcaldes (AGN IX 7-7-4, "Sobre el informe que hacen los comisionados para la revisita," 1802, fol. 17).

59. Explicit mention of the segunda's role as "lieutenant" comes from Challapata (Paria) (ANB EC 1790 No. 29, fol. 54). See also ANB EC 1785 No. 23, fol. 85. One segunda persona served thirty-three years in Tiahuanaco (Pacajes) (ANB EC 1779 No. 18, fol. 10v).

60. In Laja and Pucarani, hilacatas were responsible for the tribute in their own ayllus, while segundas collected the tribute of Indians working on Spaniards' estates within the jurisdiction (ALP EC 1790 C. 115 E. s.n., fol. 22v). In what was probably the most common arrangement, the segunda assisted the cacique in collecting tribute from the hilacatas for the moiety as a whole (ALP EC 1786 C. 107. E. s.n., fol. 2). In keeping with his primary tributary function, the segunda was sometimes labeled "contador" (accountant) or "receptor de tributos" (tribute receiver) (ANB EC 1778 No. 41, fol. 45v; ALP EC 1790 C. 115 E. s.n., fol. 1).

61. For comparative references on cabildo government, see Spalding (1984, 216–222, 234); Haskett (1991); and, for Spain, Behar (1986).

62. ANB EC 1779 No. 18, fols. 9v–10v. In the provincial capital of Azángaro, the alcalde ordinario de primer voto was enjoined to "administer justice in all civil and criminal cases. . . . In civil and ordinary matters, he will not hold trial but instead settle them briefly and summarily in favor of whomever he sees fit" (AGN IX 35-3-6, "Elecciones del pueblo de Azángaro del año 1780 por lo que respeta a los alcaldes indios," 1780, fol. 1). See also ALP 1783 C. 103 E. s.n., fols. 49–50v; and ANB Minas T. 148, EC 1731 No. 48, fol. 3v/Minas Cat. No. 1359a.

63. The diversity of local functions was sometimes expressed in titles such as "alcalde de cajas" (it seems a treasury guard—ANB EC 1777 No. 71, fol. 133),

"alcalde de balsas" (presumably in charge of Uru boatmen along the Desaguadero river—ANB EC 1757 No. 45, fol. 64), or "alcalde de mañazos" (perhaps a guild leader for meat purveyors—ALP EC 1787 C. 108 E. s.n., fol. 2).

64. There is substantial documentation of this, particularly for the neighboring provinces of Paria and Carangas, in the colonial expedientes for these decades located in the ANB. See, for example, ANB EC 1784 No. 17; ANB EC 1789 No. 38; ANB EC 1793 No. 136. Formal state approval of elected alcaldes was also carried out in La Paz at the same time (ALP EC 1789 C. 113 E. s.n. [34 fols.]).

65. ALP EC 1790 C. 115 E. s.n. (141 fols.), fols. 64–64v.

66. ALP EC 1795 C. 122 E. s.n., fols. 1, 4v.

67. ALP EC 1796 C. 123 E. s.n., fol. 2. ANB EC 1753 No. 70, fol. 1v. Cf. ANB EC 1796 No. 107, fols. 1–3.

68. ANB EC 1760 No. 11, fol. 326v.

69. The foregoing brief review of authority functions has privileged the principal political figures at the community level. The Potosí mita captain *(capitán enterador de la mita)* was another prestigious authority but one who did not exercise political power. The scribe *(escribano)* was uncommon in most towns, and church officers *(maestro de capilla, cantor, sacristan, fiscal),* and festival hosts *(alférez, prioste, estandarte)* were outside the civil system. The *contador* (accountant) cited in some towns was a tribute collector, at times identified with the segunda persona and with the moiety level of segmentation. One supracommunity honorary title held by Indian nobles and virtually obsolete by midcentury was the alcalde (mayor) provincial (ANB EC 1770 No. 125, fol. 17. AGN IX 30-2-1, "Recurso de don Francisco Calahumana . . . sobre que se le confirme por este superior gobierno el empleo de alcalde mayor de naturales de dicha provincia," 1779). Recall also José Fernández Guarachi's honorary title of alcalde mayor de los cuatro suyus, referred to above.

70. ANB EC 1802 No. 13, fols. 2–8v.

71. ALP EC 1790 C. 115 E. s.n., fol. 28. The subdelegate of Omasuyos confirmed that cacique designation of segundas was customary practice (ANB EC 1807 No. 12, fol. 14v). See also ANB EC 1790 No. 29, fol. 54. The occasional instance of colonial officials naming segundas was probably due to a breakdown of the cacicazgo locally; see, e.g., ALP EC 1797 C. 124 E. s.n.

72. Rasnake 1988, 100–101. Abercrombie notes that this arrangement resembled the balance of power between town councils and lords in feudal Castile. See his argument (Abercrombie 1998, 237–258) for the radical transformation of indigenous society under Toledo as ayllus were "reintegrated" within the new colonial towns. Toledo's prescriptions for elections form tít. I of the ordinances cited above.

73. The term appears only rarely in the documentation and is used mostly in the sense of "assembly" rather than to indicate a permanent cabildo institution. One subdelegate, for example, stated that he "formed a cabildo" (ALP EC 1783 C. 103 E. s.n., fol. 50). The following account of town authority elections is drawn

from a variety of sources, including a set of ANB documents from outside La Paz, especially for the partidos of Paria and Carangas in the 1780s and 1790s. This material fits with our more limited information about La Paz and helps to fill out the picture for the altiplano.

74. ALP EC 1783 C. 103 E. s.n. ANB EC 1786 No. 219.

75. ANB EC 1796 No. 245, fol. 6. For another document that refers to "majority" vote *(pluralidad),* see ANB EC 1796 No. 107, fol. 3. The Pacajes subdelegate in 1783 gave specific procedural orders: "Voters, . . . according to their rank, shall place their votes, written out in advance on slips of paper, in a jug or vessel. The acting authority will remove them and those who receive the most votes will be the officials." There are various reasons to suspect that the subdelegate's prescriptions were not always followed in actual practice, among them his very insistence on "proper formality" (ALP EC 1783 C. 103 E. s.n., fol. 3). Also, verbal election was surely a much more common practice than written ballots (ANB EC 1786 No. 36).

76. ALP EC 1783 C. 103 E. s.n., fols. 3v–4.

77. The colonial law on this point is given by Haskett (1991, 30) for New Spain.

78. Gibson (1953, 222), referring to the sixteenth-century Indian cabildo of Mexico City, argued that "the systematic rotation of alcaldes by their barrios derived directly from procedures in the mother country." In Peru, Toledo called for the distribution of posts between different moieties and ayllus to prevent an imbalance of power. See tít. I, ord. VIII of his ordinances in Sarabia Viejo (1989, 2: 217–266). It is unclear whether he had preexisting Spanish or Andean norms in mind. In the Peruvian case, we can only assume there was a coincidental convergence between some medieval Spanish municipal practices, the interests of the colonial state, and the mita principles of Andean ayllus.

79. ANB EC 1752 No. 39, fol. 4v. For other evidence of the alcalde post as service turn, see ANB EC 1774 No. 18, fol. 46v; ANB EC 1796 No. 245, fol. 2v; and ANB EC 1786 No. 36.

80. For the Guaqui case, see ANB EC 1771 No. 27, fols. 25v, 26v. For other hints suggesting alcalde representation for ayllus and moieties, see ANB EC 1802 No. 13, fols. 20, 22v; ANB EC 1779 No. 127, fol. 1v; ANB EC 1786 No. 219; ANB EC 1796 No. 107, fols. 1v, 3.

81. Platt (1987b) demonstrates similar ayllu organization for eighteenth-century cofradías and their twentieth-century festival equivalent in rural Potosí. Cf. Abercrombie's colonial and contemporary analysis (1998) of the civil-religious cargo system. Further ethnographic evidence comes from Rasnake (1988, 65–69); and Ticona and Albó (1997, 65–87).

82. ANB EC 1753 No. 70. See tít. I, ord. V from Toledo's ordinances cited in Sarabia Viejo (1989, 2:217–266).

83. Haskett 1991. Reporting on the elections in Tarabuco (Yamparaes), the subdelegate wrote: "The election was decided by majority vote of the governors,

alcaldes, and regidores of the respective ayllus and moieties of the town" (ANB EC 1796 No. 107, fol. 3).

84. ANB EC 1760 No. 11, fol. 150. ANB EC 1774 No. 18, fol. 46v.

85. On the ideology of service today, particularly the notions of cargos as burden and obligation toward the community, as well as the deference expected on the part of authorities, see Carter and Albó (1988, 478–482); Albó (1991c); Ticona et al. (1995, 79–85); and Ticona and Albó (1997, 65–87). See also Rasnake (1988, 72–89) on the service turns *(kamachi)* and deference of authorities in Yura.

86. ALP Padrones Coloniales (PC) Omasuyos 1757, fol. 132. A full explanation for noble decline awaits further research, but would presumably take into account restrictions on state recognition of nobles, demographic movements, and the effects of rural economic cycles. For comparative cases of noble fortunes over the colonial period, see Spalding (1984, 230–238); Gibson (1960); Farriss (1984, 227–255); García Martínez (1987, 182–190); Haskett (1991, 132–137, 196–202); Lockhart (1992, 110–117); and Garrett (2001).

87. ANB EC 1770 No. 125. For other cases of noble poverty, see ANB EC 1746 No. 66; ANB EC 1752 No. 76; ALP 1786 C. 106 E. s.n., fol. 10.

88. For noble artisans, see ANB EC 1758 No. 114; and the notable case of Blas Túpac Amaru Inka, who eventually found work in La Plata practicing the "noble craft" of painting (ANB EC 1771 No. 40, fol. 42v). In the 1750s, the Sanctuary of Copacabana's organist and harpist were nobles (ANB EC 1756 No. 119; ALP PC Omasuyos 1757), as was the maestro de capilla in Carabuco in 1754 (ANB EC 1759 No. 138).

89. In 1756, seventy-year-old Diego Fernández Guachalla was alcalde mayor in Pucarani while Hilario Chalco Yupanqui served as alcalde ordinario de primer voto in Copacabana (ANB EC 1773 No. 83, fol. 19v). Through the mid-eighteenth century, the aged noble Marcos Quispe of Tiahuanaco served thirty-three years as segunda persona and twice as alcalde ordinario (ANB EC 1779 No. 18, fols. 10v–14v).

90. In 1806, after years of litigation, Jacinto was also attempting to gain permanent status as the segunda of the same ayllus that his ancestors had represented. His very attempt to oblige caciques to recognize him and to have the state enforce this status suggests the tenuousness of his enterprise. See ANB EC 1807 No. 128.

91. While Inka nobles in Copacabana paid no tribute, those in Juli (Chucuito) were obliged to do so (ALP PC Omasuyos 1757, fol. 132; ANB EC 1746 No. 66). For other evidence on noble service exemptions and tribute payment, see ANB EC 1753 No. 40; ANB Minas T. 127 No. 8/Minas Cat. No. 1579; ANB EC 1758 No. 114; ANB EC 1762 No. 18.

92. ANB EC 1753 No. 40. ANB Minas T. 127 No. 9/Minas Cat. No. 1539, fol. 1. For a sample of other cacique-noble battles and noble discourse regarding status, see ANB EC 1746 No. 66; ANB Minas T. 127 No. 4/Minas Cat. No. 1508; ANB EC 1754 No. 106; ANB Minas T. 127 No. 8/Minas Cat. No. 1579; ANB EC 1759 No. 138; ANB EC 1762 No. 18; ANB EC 1771 No. 27, fols. 12–14, 69.

93. ANB EC 1807 No. 11, fol. 75.

94. ANB 1756 No. 130, fols. 18v, 27, 31, 37, 59v.

95. ALP EC 1803 C. 136 E. 34. This expediente is by far the most explicit account of the issues that concern us here; unfortunately it is badly deteriorated and a few important passages are now illegible.

96. Gibson 1964, 155. Spalding 1984, 220, 222. In colonial legislation, the term could be taken to mean simply "Indians of distinction" (Solórzano 1972, 335).

97. Community members challenged the cacique of Curaguara (Pacajes) for his punishment of alcaldes, regidores, and hilacatas, "with no regard for their honorable positions and the distinction with which they are adorned during the time of their offices" (ALP EC 1802 C. 134 E. 20, fol. 2).

98. For Viceroy La Palata's effort to clarify the question of exemptions for non-noble officers in the late seventeenth century, see ANB EC 1760 No. 11, fols. 319–320.

99. AGN Sala XIII 17-7-4, Padrones, La Paz, 1792–1794, Libro 3, fols. 347–348v. For further suggestions of the association between originarios, principales, and nobility, see ANB EC 1796 No. 97, fol. 11; ANB EC 1802 No. 32, fol. 1v; AGN IX 7-7-4, "Sobre el informe que hacen los comisionados para la revisita" (Chulumani), 1802, fol. 1. Contemporary ethnography confirms that today only landholding community members share the burden and status of the cargos. For the colonial period, see Wightman (1990).

100. It is worth recalling that principales were present during the ceremonies for authority designation. See, for example, ANB EC 1802 No. 13, fols. 2v–3; ANB EC 1786 No. 219.

101. For a political and gender analysis of community elders in late-colonial Mexico, see Stern 1995, 199–204.

102. On Mexico, see Chance and Taylor (1985); and Farriss (1984). Fuenazalida's classic article (1970) positing a unified hierarchy in contemporary Peru argues for the colonial matrix of the system, but he does not speculate on its integration and development over time. See also Abercrombie (1998, especially 291–304, 504) for the Andes. He too refrains from speculating on the origins of a presumably merged system, but hypothesizes that a consolidated fiesta-cargo system flourished in the Aymara highlands in the late eighteenth century. Cf. Saignes (1991, 122–124); and Platt (1987b).

103. ALP EC 1794 C. 121 E. s.n., fol. 1. For other evidence concerning the ladder of tandas, see the following references in the text as well as ALP EC 1754 C. 76 E. 11; ANB EC 1779 No. 18, fols. 1, 10v, 11v; ALP EC 1794 C. 121 E. s.n., fol. 7; ANB EC 1809 No. 14, fol. 8v.

104. Rasnake 1988, 67, 69. For other contemporary ethnography on the Aymara cargo hierarchy, see note 85 above.

105. ALP EC 1793 C. 119 E. s.n., fol. 128v.

106. Chance and Taylor (1985) consider prestigious individual sponsorship the key to civil-religious cargo integration historically in Mexico. They find other

forms of festival sponsorship predominant until the breakdown of the cofradías in the nineteenth century, and hence limited religious cargo integration in the colonial period.

107. ALP EC 1779 C. 99 E. 37.

108. ANB EC 1772 No. 215, fols. 33–34v.

109. Two specific factors introduced by Toledo would have contributed to the process. One of his ordinances for Indian towns (tít. I, ord. VII) called for only one of the two alcaldes to be a noble (principal) and the other to be a commoner *(particular)*, evidently in order to prevent noble domination within towns. Also, Toledo sought to winnow the upper ranks of indigenous society and ordered a reduction in the number of principales and authorities (mandones). See his "Instrucción general para los visitadores," issued in Lima in 1569–1570, which is published in Sarabia Viejo (1986, 1:20, 39).

110. Despite some contrary evidence (cf. Rasnake 1988, 69; Buechler and Buechler 1971, 73), Carter and Albó (1988, 481) maintain that civil-religious cargo integration is the norm on the altiplano today.

111. For Peru, see Celestino and Meyers (1981); Varón (1982); and Hunefeldt (1983).

112. ALP EC 1803 C. 136 E. 34.

Chapter 3. The Crisis of Andean Rule (I)

1. A carga was a measure of approximately six bushels (Larson 1988, 334).

2. This dispute comes from ANB Minas T. 128 No. 2/Minas Cat. No. 1754.

3. The one corregidor with whom Calaumana, along with other Omasuyos caciques, seems to have had tense relations was Antonio Calonje. See ANB EC 1757 No. 34; AGI Charcas 592, "Testimonio de los autos seguidos por don Agustín Siñani, cacique de Carabuco, contra don Antonio Calonje . . . ," fol. 27. For the landlord's comment, see ANB EC 1775 [1766] No. 174, fol. 16. The provincial situation in the late 1750s to early 1760s is further discussed below.

4. Sánchez Albornoz 1978, 100, 105.

5. Glave 1989, 284.

6. Saignes 1987b, 153. Glave 1989, 286. Spalding 1981, 18; and 1984, 210.

7. Saignes 1987b, 161.

8. In order to compensate for what he considers a generalized distortion in the historiography—the image of the cacique "tyrant" who lived from the plundering of his own community—Saignes (1989, 84) expresses his admiration of those seventeenth-century caciques of Charcas for their "formidable effort to effect the synthesis of two universes so scarcely compatible a priori."

9. The decline of the cacicazgo in the post-1780 period has recently received more historiographic attention. I have tried to use this work to clarify the problems for analysis and refine the explanation for the late-colonial crisis. In many cases, this literature attributes the cacicazgo breakdown to pressures stemming

from the colonial state such as postinsurrectionary repression or Bourbon reform legislation. One noteworthy contribution that contemplates a wide range of factors and processes from the mid-eighteenth century on is O'Phelan (1997). Along with the introductory discussion in this chapter, refer to chapter 7.

10. By "historical specificity" I do not mean empirical detail but rather temporality, in this case, the nature of the cacicazgo in its distinct moments and changes over time.

11. Stern 1982, 158–183. Spalding 1984, 221–223.

12. Glave 1989, 303–304. For the same period, Sánchez Albornoz (1978, 99–110) also refers to powerful tensions between caciques and communities as economic differentiation proceeded.

13. Rasnake 1988, 95–151. On the reduction of cacique power in Arica, Tarapacá, and Atacama in the late eighteenth century, see Hidalgo Lehuede (1986).

14. Hunefeldt 1982, 18–36. Referring to the internal authority of communities, Cahill (1986) speaks of a "destructuration" in the period from 1783 to 1824.

15. The social histories of Spalding on Huarochirí (1984) and Larson on Cochabamba (1988) offer the first approaches to this long view. Garrett (2001) gives a more in-depth view of Indian nobles and caciques in Cuzco for the colonial era, with an emphasis on the eighteenth century. Díaz Rementería (1977) studies the legislation regarding caciques over the colonial period. For a discussion of the specific changes in seventeenth-century kurakazgos, as the cacicazgo was known in Lower Peru, see Burga (1988, 310–368).

16. Another explanation suggested by scholars for the late-colonial period is that the crisis was provoked from above, by a reformist Bourbon state. See chapter 7 for a discussion of this specific position and some of the more recent literature on the post-1780 period.

17. Various authors emphasize this criterion for the late-colonial period. O'Phelan (1988, 155–159) asserts that "the hereditary tradition of the caciques was undermined" by the appointments made by corregidores from the mid-eighteenth century on. But see also her earlier work that addresses other factors, especially economic ones, for the cacicazgo crisis (O'Phelan 1978a, 159–185, 191–192; 1978b; 1983, 85–86; cf. O'Phelan 1997). Cahill (1986) points to the lineage factor for the period after 1783. On the rivalry between hereditary caciques from pre-Hispanic lineages and those *arrivistes* caciques who emerged in the early colonial period, see Saignes (1987b).

18. Stern (1982, 165–173) terms this phenomenon "Indian Hispanism."

19. Along with Stern (1982), for the early colonial era, and Spalding (1984), for the colonial period as a whole, Larson (1979, 1988) emphasizes the dynamics of class differentiation within indigenous society especially for the late period. For the late seventeenth century, Rivera (1978) suggests a creative and legitimate management by some caciques of private wealth, accumulated within the colonial economy, and its communal redistribution following Andean norms of reciprocity. Based on the

case of Chayanta, Cangiano (1987) takes issue with the image of the cacique as exploiter in the eighteenth century and argues that economic reciprocity within the community remained intact. Stavig (1988, 1999) argues rather for the erosion of moral economy ties between caciques and communities in eighteenth-century Cuzco. Serulnikov (1998) also links illegitimacy in northern Potosí to the failure to sustain community economic reproduction.

20. Wachtel (1990, 488–489). It seems plausible that conflict with caciques beginning in this period could have been related to the growing importance of the forced distribution of commodities *(reparto de mercancías)* following the 1678 institutional reform that fomented speculative bidding on the corregidor post. Cf. Lohmann Villena (1957, 125–134); Stern (1987a, 74). It is this same relation between the reparto regime and cacicazgos that we examine more deeply for the eighteenth century.

21. In this sense, our methodological approach could be expanded to *tracing* the cacicazgo in space as well as time, and *explaining* its geographical patterns as well as its historical processes.

22. It remains for future research to determine whether a comparable pattern existed in the Andes as a whole. For cacicazgos that suffered similarly gradual decline outside of the southern Andean highlands, references would include Larson (1998), Schramm (1990), and Presta (1995) on the eastern valleys of Charcas; and Hidalgo Lehuede (1986) on coastal Atacama, Arica, and Tacna. Cf. O'Phelan (1978a, 159–185, 191–192; 1997) on northern Peru; and Powers (1995) on the northern Andean district of Quito.

23. The reparto was a distribution of goods by the corregidor to Indians who were obliged to purchase them at inflated rates. It was a baldly exploitative institution that provoked substantial protest. (See chapter 4.)

24. The entire case comes from ANB EC 1793 No. 11. For this episode in the early part of the century, see fols. 1–30.

25. Elderly witnesses who supported Lucas de Meneses's cacicazgo claim testified only that María Vilamolle was the daughter of Bartolomé Cari. The discrepancies between Meneses, Sosa, and the witnesses over family forebears shows how genealogical lines could be braided and unbraided, or could fade into burnished legend—as in the case of lineage founder Apu Cari—when it was politically expedient.

26. Lucas claimed that Sosa had deliberately hidden the documents to prevent him from assuming office.

27. According to his detractors later, state officials had uncovered Alejo Hinojosa Cutimbo's tribute racketeering. They declared him traitor to the king and ignominiously discharged him.

28. On Berrazueta's military and other services, see fols. 124–164 of the expediente.

29. ANB EC 1793 No. 11, fol. 162.

30. See fols. 179–186v of the expediente.

31. One early instance took place in Italaque in 1755. The corregidor's Diego Torres sold the cacicazgo to Baltazar Calla for 150 pesos but subsequently withdrew it from his control (ANB EC 1756 No. 72, fol. 88v).

32. Recopilación de leyes, libro 6, título 7, leyes 1–4; Solórzano, libro 2, capítulo 27, números 14–27, 1972, 408–411. Díaz Rementería 1977.

33. See "Descripción y relación de la ciudad de La Paz" (1586), in Jiménez de la Espada (1965, 2: 347); and Platt (1988, 376–377).

34. Solórzano, libro 2, capítulo 27, números 20–22, 1972, 409–410. Díaz Rementería 1977, 119, 167. In Acora (Chucuito), interim caciques without legitimate hereditary claims controlled the post since the rightful heiresses, Isidora Catacora and then her daughter Petrona Pérez Catacora, were "orphaned and helpless," meaning husbandless. In the words of one elderly witness, "Petrona Pérez has been marginalized *(arrinconada)* all this time because of her poverty and because she is a woman, lacking someone to act on her behalf." She was finally granted possession after marrying Diego Felipe Hernani, a Spaniard with various local bureaucratic stints to his credit (ANB EC 1785 No. 4, fols. 3v, 16).

35. ANB EC 1754 No. 66, fol. 74. Consider also the case of the former cacique of Mocomoco (Larecaja) who attempted to transfer the cacicazgo as a dowry to a mestizo outsider about to wed his daughter. The maneuver was successfully blocked as illegal and potentially harmful to the community (ANB EC 1756 No. 5).

36. Not all cacique sons-in-law were resented. Vicente Salazar in Río Abajo, who was also a mestizo, was praised by Indians for observing local norms of reciprocity and guaranteeing community reproduction. In contrast to the situation under his replacement—"who governs as if over a foreign town, with the aim of bleeding us to death"—with don Vicente "the poor find relief because he either individually comes to their aid or distributes a share of the wealth enjoyed by others" (ANB EC 1798 No. 180, fol. 2).

37. This statement is primarily based on contemporary ethnography. On the "wife-taking" son-in-law, or yerno (*q'ata* or *masha* in Quechua), in the Peruvian kinship literature, see Bolton and Mayer (1977), especially the contributions of Lambert (20–22), Webster (36–41), Isbell (97–100), and Mayer; and Isbell (1978, 112–114, 174–175). For the Aymara equivalent *(tullqa)* in northern Potosí, see Harris (1994).

38. In the tributary sphere, we also know that communities in the seventeenth century referred to assimilated forasteros as subordinate sons-in-law (yernos) or nephews *(sobrinos)*. See Saignes (1987a, 141); Wightman (1990, 54, 88–89).

39. We might ask ourselves how the community adopted the ego position of the patriarch in viewing the encroaching successor as son-in-law. I suspect it reflects the perspective of principal elders with generational seniority who, as community representatives, established the discursive conjunction between community and patriarchal identity.

40. See Recopilación de leyes, libro 6, título 7, ley 6; Solórzano, libro 2, capítulo 26, número 43, 1972, 403.

41. Solórzano, libro 2, capítulo 27, número 49, 1972, 415. Díaz Rementería 1977, 132. In this sense, for example, the Crown reaffirmed the noble privileges of mestizos and Indians who were descendants of caciques in its *real cédula* of March 22, 1697; the decree guaranteed their rights to obtain ecclesiastical and secular posts and titles (ALP Gaveta 9, Cédulas Reales).

42. ANB EC 1803 No. 33, fol. 25. Mestizo and Spanish caciques accused of intrusion were numerous indeed; we will refer to many other cases in this chapter and chapter 7. For examples of attacks on "mulato" and "zambo" caciques, see ANB EC 1753 No. 99 and ANB EC 1772 No. 89.

43. ANB EC 1755 No. 56, fols. 2v, 5, 36.

44. For the full story of the struggle in Italaque, see ANB EC 1755 No. 56; ANB EC 1752 No. 12; and ANB EC 1756 No. 72. Another prominent cacicazgo that was subject to long-term conflict with community subjects was that of Urinsaya in Viacha. From the 1750s through 1780, the members of the Mercado family were challenged as intruders because of their abuses, mestizo blood, and because they had wrested the cacicazgo from the legitimate Sirpa line through marriage. See ANB EC 1756 No. 111; ALP EC 1767 C. 88 E. 18; ANB EC 1780 No. 108.

45. ANB EC 1754 No. 123, fols. 8–8v. According to charges, Tiburcio Fernández in Laja (Omasuyos) was brought up as a dependent in the cacique's household and later became his overseer in the brandy trade between Moquegua and Potosí. He finally took office fraudulently, posing as the cacique's kin. Indians insisted, "He made his fortune in silver coin and silverware, in livestock and foodstuffs, all from our sweat and labor" (ANB EC 1753 No. 99, fol. 8v).

46. ANB EC 1763 No. 129, fol. 1.

47. ANB EC 1768 No. 68, fol. 13v.

48. ANB EC 1766 No. 43, fol. 12v.

49. For an example of the procedure to obtain proprietary title, including testimony by twelve witnesses and documentary proof of family rights, see the case from Guaqui (Pacajes) in ANB EC 1771 No. 27, fols. 51–61.

50. Díaz Rementería 1977, 125–157, 173–187.

51. For one especially explicit example of an unauthorized corregidor appointment and possession ceremony, see the case from Caquiaviri (Pacajes) in ANB EC 1745 No. 42, fols. 41v–43, 47.

52. At the time of the suit in the 1730s, Canqui was said to be the *compadre* of Corregidor Mateo de Proleón, who failed to cooperate with the audiencia's investigation (ANB Minas T. 148, EC 1731 No. 48/Minas Cat. No. 1359a, fol. 108v).

53. The testimony both for and against the Canquis resulted in an unusually voluminous documentation. For the accusations, see ANB Minas T. 148, EC 1731 No. 48/Minas Cat. No. 1359a, especially fols. 2–6v; and ANB EC 1760 No. 11, especially fols. 148–150v, also fols. 5–8 (altered foliation). For earlier information about cacicazgo lineage in Calacoto, see ALP EC 1783 C. 103 E. s.n., "Conflicto sobre cacicazgo de Calacoto" (57 fols.).

54. For the itemized expenses of one irasiri, see ANB Minas T. 148, EC 1731 No. 48/Minas Cat. No. 1359a, fols. 115–115v.

55. The censo de comunidad was a quit-rent administered by the state in favor of the lending community.

56. ANB EC 1760 No. 11, fol. 158.

57. The cacique also speculated on local tithe and alcabala collection and would tax peasants arbitrarily.

58. For the Canquis' defense, see ANB EC 1760 No. 11, fols. 219–222, 266–274, 321–323.

59. On the female servants, see ANB EC 1760 No. 11, fols. 270v, 271v; for La Palata's retasa, see fols. 317–320.

60. ANB EC 1760 No. 11, fol. 274.

61. ANB EC 1760 No. 11, fol. 274.

62. The Canquis did not attempt to document this and we have scarce evidence of conflict relating to these issues: the isolated episode of Francisco Canqui's standoff before mass one Sunday; the assertion that Indians stayed away from town religious ceremonies in order to keep their mules from being requisitioned by the Canquis; and the church sacristan's testimony that the Indians were remiss in attending mass and that the cacique had ordered lashings as punishment (ANB EC 1760 No. 11, fol. 11, altered foliation).

63. To give but one example here, we know from later evidence that Calacoto caciques did indeed run the town store. While the store was formally owned by the church, as Canqui claimed, it was also rented to the cacique by the priest (ANB Minas T. 126 No. 20/Minas Cat. No. 1464, fol. 63v). The cacique in turn held the Indian designated for pulpería service responsible for the burden of the rent. Any losses against the rent due had to be made up by the Indian laborer, while any profits were pocketed by the cacique. In other towns we find the same arrangement, and that caciques intentionally selected wealthier peasants for pulpería service in order to guarantee themselves against losses. See ALP EC 1752 C. 75 E. 12; ANB EC 1771 No. 21, fols. 1v–2; ALP EC 1793 C. 119 E. s.n., fols. 128v, 156; ANB Minas Ruck No. 217/Minas Cat. No. 2165a, fols. 9, 127–127v, 132–132v, 142v–143.

64. On the marajaque practice in Pacajes, see Wachtel (1990, 461–465, 490–492); and Cañedo-Argüelles (1993, 86–88, 112–122). On the question of mita commutations in Potosí *(indios de plata* and *indios de faltriquera),* see Tandeter (1992, 91–100); Cole (1985); Bakewell (1984, 123–135, 161–164); Zavala (1978–80).

65. ANB EC 1760 No. 11, fol. 219v. Francisco Canqui said the money was paid to the mita captain obviously in order to avoid implicating his brother. Evidence from the mita literature, however, suggests that caciques were indeed the ones who handled (and mishandled) cash commutations at the community level. One example of a cacique who delivered over commutation payment for one Indian (known as a *yana)* to the mita captain comes from Guaqui (Pacajes) (ANB EC 1771 No. 21, fol. 21).

66. These references come from, respectively, ANB EC 1771 No. 21, fol. 2; ANB EC 1808 No. 203, fols. 4v–5; AGN IX 5-6-1, "Indios de Jesús de Machaca contra su cacique Pedro Ramírez de la Parra" (11 fols.), 4/III/1795, fol. 3v. See also the references to marajaques under subsequent Calacoto caciques Juan Machaca and the Cusicanquis, below.

67. This is obviously not to say that Potosí and the mita alone were responsible for the participation of Indians in colonial markets and for the developing exchange value of labor. Indians entered markets (including labor markets) shortly after the conquest and not only in response to the cycles of mining production. Other forms of extraeconomic coercion and new spaces for economic accumulation also drove or led them into market relations. For a general perspective and set of references on indigenous participation in markets, see Harris, Larson, and Tandeter (1987); and Larson and Harris (1995).

68. ANB EC 1760 No. 111, fol. 325v, emphasis is mine.

69. Two decades earlier, personal services for the cacique could be commuted in Caquiaviri (Pacajes) (Wachtel 1990, 490).

70. Wachtel (1990, 482–92) has treated the same conflict in Calacoto, seeing it as an example of the larger breakdown of cacique reciprocity in the eighteenth century. His comment on the historical evolution of mita services, with exploitation shifting increasingly to the local level, is particularly interesting. See also Larson on the collapse of cacique reciprocity in Cochabamba (1988, 152–170; 1991, 46–462, 473–475; 1995, 228–242), and for a general treatment of the moral economy concept and its historiographic application in the Andes (1991). Stavig (1988) emphasizes the deterioration of moral economy in cacique-community and community-state relations in Cuzco in the same period.

71. Again, Larson's discussion (1988, 152–170) deals with the controversies surrounding custom and cacique strategies for turning custom to private advantage. Cf. also Barragán and Thomson (1993, 337–338) on the political contestation over custom in colonial tithe collection; and Behar (1986, especially 274–285, 189–194) on the complex webs of custom in the European peasant setting. For general methodological references on this point, see Larson (1991, 462–466) on the Andes; and Hobsbawm and Ranger (1983).

72. ANB EC 1760 No. 111, fols. 289–291v.

73. ANB EC 1760 No. 111, fols. 415–416.

74. Other comparative references for La Paz can be found in the synthesis at the end of this section. Suffice it to mention here one example illustrating the problem we have identified of political nontransparency in a cacique-community conflict over labor services. In Viacha in 1756, the community rallied before the corregidor to denounce their cacique Manuel Mercado as a mestizo and for demanding improper personal services, threatening to revolt if he was not replaced by Pedro Adrián Sirpa. The corregidor informed them that only a higher authority could order a transfer in the possession of the cacicazgo, which actually belonged to Mercado's mother, and in order to calm them he inquired

into the alleged abuses. The Indians at first did not want to clarify their charges and then could only mention a few items, according to the official "of little importance," for which they would not receive money in compensation. The cacique stated that it was customary to give no payment for personal services, and the Indians acknowledged this was true. The encounter, which nearly turned into a riot, was finally settled when the troubled corregidor ordered that the mita for the cacique be scaled down and that the cacique not harm community members. While the accusations and settlement involving personal services were ostensibly the issue under negotiation, the original, underlying aim of the mobilization was to unseat Mercado. Soon thereafter the disturbance was renewed and the corregidor saw himself obliged to name community member Juan Vela as temporary tribute collector (ANB EC 1756 No. 111). The Mercados held onto the cacicazgo, however, and in 1780 Juan Vela once again led the community in a collective suit against the cacique family (ANB EC 1780 No. 108).

75. According to one witness, the cacique collected donations from the community along with the censo income, promising to distribute it among poor Indians and spend it on other town necessities, with the remainder being divided up among all other community members (ANB Minas T. 126 No. 20/Minas Cat. No. 1464, fol. 28v). For the charges against the cacique and scribe, see fols. 3–5.

76. ANB Minas T. 126 No. 20/Minas Cat. No. 1464, fols. 62–65v.

77. This was the case, for example, in Guaqui and Jesús de Machaca, though in the former the term *yana* was used (ANB EC 1771 No. 21, fols. 10, 21, 22, 43) and in the latter the term *colquechiri* (ANB EC 1792 No. 204, fol. 3v) as equivalents of the more common "colquejaque."

78. According to the caciques of Chucuito, community members "bear this charge willingly, because it falls alternately to each one of them and frees them from a voyage that is much worse than the price they pay in money. Since they know that their fate finds reciprocal relief, shared alternately by all, they embrace it without reservation" (AGN IX 6-2-3, "Caciques del partido de Chucuito se quejan de no poder aviar mitayos," [9 fols.], 1794, fol. 3v).

79. The colquejaque practice was in fact more complex and variable than we can show here, and evidently underwent slow modification, like marajaque practice, from the seventeenth to eighteenth centuries. It was likewise subject to the strategic contention within communities that we have been discussing throughout this section. On the abuses of colquejaques, see ANB EC 1758 No. 69, fols. 1–4v; ANB EC 1771 No. 21, fol. 1; AGN IX 6-2-3, "Caciques del partido de Chucuito se quejan de no poder aviar mitayos," (9 fols.), 1794, fols. 6–8v; ANB EC 1795 No. 154, fol. 4; ANB EC 1802 No. 32, fol. 5; also cf. ANB EC 1802 No. 48, fols. 3v–4. See also Sánchez Albornoz (1978, 102–103, 113–149).

80. Eighteenth-century observers regularly noted that colquejaque commutations left Potosí mita ranks filled with poor peasants.

81. In Zepita (Chucuito), the feasting (normally termed *hospicio* in the Spanish documents) was known by the Aymara expression *apumanqa,* which the

translator interpreted as "feast for the king" *(comida del Rey)* (ANB EC 1754 No. 123, fol. 7v).

82. Machaca's lawyer went on to challenge the accusations on various other grounds, namely that the cacique would have had no private interest in charging ineligible Indians tribute; the prosecution had invented "fantastic" charges (many of those allegedly enrolled improperly were healthy, of tributary age, of the other moiety, or unknown); and the witnesses for the prosecution were biased or unreliable (ANB Minas T. 126 No. 20/Minas Cat. No. 1464, fols. 210–215).

83. ANB Minas T. 126 No. 20/Minas Cat. No. 1464, fol. 65.

84. ANB Minas T. 126 No. 20/Minas Cat. No. 1464, fol. 13, 2nd foliation.

85. ANB Minas T. 126 No. 20/Minas Cat. No. 1464, fols. 12–20, 2nd foliation.

86. ANB Minas T. 126 No. 20/Minas Cat. No. 1464, fols. 36–39 (unnumbered), 2nd foliation.

87. See ANB EC 1760 No. 11, fols. 424–427v.

88. ANB EC 1759 No. 27, fols. 1–2. This Gregorio Machaca was probably the same character alluded to by the earlier cacique Juan Machaca as one who continually ignored his orders and opposed him (ANB Minas T. 126 No. 20/Minas Cat. No. 1464, fol. 28).

89. The Calacoto ruling from 1735 became a noted precedent in Pacajes. In 1762, the court cited it during the case against the cacique of Tiahuanacu (ANB EC 1762 No. 130).

90. Marca commented that throughout the province he was "fingered as having impeached priests and corregidores." We do not have positive proof of his involvement in litigation against priests, but we know that in 1748 Calacoto mitayos brought charges against their parish priest in Potosí for excessive exactions and violence. They described themselves as "destroyed, consumed, indebted, humiliated, beaten, and mistreated not only by miners, mayordomos, and other petty officials of the Rivera, but also by our priest." Their leader in the complaint, the mita captain whose name was given as Marcos Ramón, may well have been, after all, Francisco Marca's son, Marcos Ramos. See ANB Minas T. 148 (1748)/Minas Cat. No. 1454; for the quote, see fol. 3.

91. AGI Charcas 592, "Testimonio de los autos seguidos por los caciques e hilacatas del pueblo de Calacoto, provincia de Pacajes, contra el justicia mayor de ella, don Salvador de Asurza, sobre excesivos repartimientos," 1763 (76 fols.). AGI Charcas 592, "La Real Audiencia de Charcas informa con seis testimonios de autos los perjuicios que pueden seguirse de no tener aquel tribunal facultad para conocer a los recursos que hacen los indios contra sus corregidores sobre los repartimientos de efectos," 1/XII/1763 (4 fols.). AGI Charcas 592, "Respuesta del fiscal del consejo en vista de una carta de la Real Audiencia de Charcas respecto a repartos," 16/VIII/1764 (5 fols.). Moreno Cebrián 1977, 407–410.

92. AGI Charcas 592, "Testimonio de los autos seguidos por los caciques e hilacatas del pueblo de Calacoto, provincia de Pacajes, contra el justicia mayor de ella, don Salvador de Asurza, sobre excesivos repartimientos," 1763 (76 fols.), fols. 5, 72v.

93. In any event, Calacoto caciques made no protests against the corregidor when the investigator sent by Lima visited the community (AGI Charcas 592, 1763, fol. 12).

94. For this episode, see ANB EC 1757 No. 45 (in fact the expediente covers the years 1759–1763). Miguel Cusicanqui was accused of charging marajaques fifty-two pesos and not using the commutation for any known purpose. The marajaque was listed among the cacique's other personal servants (fol. 27).

95. For the grievances against Pedro Cusicanqui, see ANB EC 1757 No. 45, fols. 61–62v.

96. ANB EC 1757 No. 45, fols. 27v, 74.

97. An Uru family of balsa boatsmen also protested against the humiliating public punishments. Juan Ticona had been flogged while serving as alcalde of the balsa rafts for Calacoto (ANB EC 1757 No. 45, fols. 62–64).

98. They added, "Pedro Cusicanqui is of a temperament that is not natural, pacific, nor worthy of a governor. He is arrogant, wrathful, greedy, vengeful, and inclined toward destruction" (ANB EC 1757 No. 45, fols. 61, 62).

99. ANB EC 1757 No. 45, fol. 66v.

100. For Porlier's brief and the quotes given here, see ANB EC 1757 No. 45, fols. 73–76v. It was uncommon and even inappropriate for the Indian protector to distance himself from Indian plaintiffs so explicitly. Porlier's position and that of his predecessor Joseph López Lisperguer apparently derived from a political shift in the audiencia beginning in the late 1750s. The earlier protector Ignacio Negreiros was seen as too lenient toward communities and was forced out of office at a time when community opposition to corregidores and repartos was building. (See following chapter.)

101. On this episode, see ANB EC 1773 No. 12, fol. 47v; ANB EC 1777 No. 20, fols. 34–34v. Turmoil in the Calacoto cacicazgo also persisted into the early 1800s (ALP EC 1783 C. 103 E. s.n.; ANB EC 1800 No. 54; ANB EC 1804 No. 23). See chapter 7 for the postinsurrectionary period and process.

102. This and the following notes contain only samples of the abundant references to these issues from the 1740s to the 1800s. For tribute accusations, see ANB EC 1752 No. 12, fol. 3v; ANB EC 1754 No. 55; ANB EC 1755 No. 66, fol. 133v; ANB EC 1771 No. 74; ALP EC 1786 C. 107 E. s.n., fols. 13–14v, 16–16v, 18v–19, 20v, 45v/(3v–4)/(1–1v); ALP EC 1792 C. 117 E. s.n., fol. 13v; ALP EC 1793 C. 119 E. s.n., fols. 12v–14; ANB EC 1804 No. 33, fols. 7, 9, 16; ANB Minas Ruck No. 217/ Minas Cat. No. 2165a, fols. 13v, 18, 27–27v.

103. ANB EC 1752 No. 12, fols. 3–3v; ALP EC 1753 C. 76 E. 1, fol. 134; ANB EC 1769 No. 182, fols. 5–5v; ANB EC 1777 No. 96, fol. 10; ANB EC 1780 No. 108, fols. 2, 4–5; AGN IX 5-5-4, "Representación de indios de Irupana y Laza, partido de Chulumani, sobre extorciones del subdelegado y cacique," 7 fols., 19/VII/1784, fols. 4–5v; ALP EC 1786 C. 107 E. s.n., fols. 13v, 14v, 18v, 31v, 71–71v; ALP EC 1792 C. 117 E. s.n., 4 fols.; AGN IX 5-6-1, "Indios de Jesús de Machaca contra su cacique Pedro Ramírez de la Parra," 11 fols., 4/III/1795, fols. 2, 3v–4; ANB EC 1802

No. 32, fols. 1, 4, 6v–7; ANB Minas Ruck No. 217/Minas Cat. No. 2165a, fols. 11–11v, 18–18v, 27, 29, 31, 48, 49v, 91, 139v.

104. ANB EC 1755 No. 56, fols. 36v–38, 99v–101v, 107; ANB EC 1756 No. 111, fols. 3–5, 20–20v; ANB EC 1762 No. 130; ANB EC 1771 No. 27, fols. 1–3, 10, 13, 22; ANB EC 1780 No. 108, fols. 3–3v; ALP EC 1792 C. 117 E. s.n., fol. 13v; AGN IX 5-6-1, "Indios de Jesús de Machaca contra su cacique Pedro Ramírez de la Parra," 11 fols., 4/III/1795, fols. 2–6v; ALP EC 1797 C. 125 E. s.n.; ANB EC 1802 No. 32, fols. 1–2, 4–6; ANB Minas Ruck No. 217/Minas Cat. No. 2165a, fols. 7–11v, 15v, 28–28v, 31, 47v, 49, 129, 136–141.

105. ANB EC 1754 No. 123, fols. 8, 102v–103v; ANB EC 1755 No. 56, fols. 37, 100; ANB EC 1772 No. 89, fols. 41v–43v; ALP EC 1792 C. 117 E. s.n., fol. 13; ALP EC 1793 C. 119 E. s.n., fols. 11v–13, 17–18, 156–157; ANB EC 1802 No. 32, fols. 4v–6; ANB Minas Ruck No. 217/Minas Cat. No. 2165a, fols. 7, 9, 11v, 127–127v, 129v, 132–133v, 135, 142v–143; ANB EC 1809 No. 14, fols. 2v, 4, 19v, 35–36v, 39–39v.

106. ANB EC 1752 No. 12, fol. 2v; ANB EC 1762 No. 144, fols. 18–18v, 20, 22; ALP EC 1779 C. 99 E. 2, fols. 2–3; ALP EC 1786 C. 107 E. s.n., fols. 3, 64, 66, 67, 68v/(1, 5); ANB Minas T. 151 complemento (1789)/Minas Cat. No. 1945a, fols. 6–6v; ALP EC 1799 C. 129 E. s.n., fols. 6, 7v, 11, 15, 17; ANB EC 1804 No. 33, fols. 6–7, 13, 16v; ANB Minas Ruck No. 217/Minas Cat. No. 2165a, fols. 11v–12, 27v–28, 49v, 50v; ANB EC 1809 No. 14, fols. 3, 35v, 38v, 71, 107–107v.

107. ANB EC 1783 No. 76, fols. 17v, 23; ALP EC 1786 C. 107 E. s.n., fols. 3, 64–64v, 66, 71–71/(4v); ALP EC 1787 C. 109 E. s.n., sin foliación, deteriorated; ALP EC 1793 C. 119 E. s.n., fol. 46; ALP EC 1797 C. 125 E. s.n., fols. 1v–2, 12v, 14, 15, 27–28v, 52–52v; ALP EC 1802 C. 134 E. 20, fols. 1v–2; ANB EC 1802 No. 32, fols. 6–6v; ANB EC 1802 No. 48, fols. 3v–4, 6; ANB Minas Ruck No. 217/Minas Cat. No. 2165a, fols. 15v, 28–28v.

108. Abuses by caciques speculating on the collection of tithes were also cited in complaints. See ANB EC 1754 No. 55, fols. 3, 23v, 43v; ANB EC 1766 No. 43; ALP EC 1779 C. 99 E. 2, fols. 1v, 3v; ALP EC 1791 C. 116 E. s.n., fol. 2; ALP EC 1793 C. 119 E. s.n., fols. 10v–11; ALP EC 1799 C. 129 E. s.n., fol. 14v; ANB EC 1802 No. 32, fol. 6v; ANB EC 1802 No. 48, fols. 2, 4v–5.

109. ANB Minas T. 126 No. 20/Minas Cat. No. 1464, fol. 13, 2nd foliation.

Chapter 4. The Crisis of Andean Rule (II)

1. Golte 1980. Even O'Phelan (1988, 143), who objects to Golte's emphasis on the reparto as one-dimensional, refers to the reparto as "the underlying cause of the diversification of the revolts in the second half of the eighteenth century." Cf. Stern (1987a, 73–75).

2. For a general set of references on the reparto system, see Juan and Ulloa (1991 [1749]); Tord (1974); Tord and Lazo (1981); Moreno Cebrián (1977); Golte (1980); Larson and Wasserstrom (1983); Larson (1988).

3. Although circumstances varied according to the region, Serulnikov (1998) has also found that the interventions of corregidores at midcentury had major political consequences—generating conflicts over community government and conditions for rebellion—in northern Potosí.

4. See Thomson (1996a).

5. Golte 1980, 104–105. The sale price of this corregimiento was also the highest in the viceroyalty (Moreno Cebrián 1977, 97–98).

6. AGI Charcas 530, "Testimonio de los autos por el tumulto en el pueblo de Sicasica . . . ," 20/ VII/1778 (32 fols.), fol. 29. Following upon the 1771 crisis, Viceroy Amat declared it "the center where uprisings and trouble have always been plotted"; see AGI Charcas 592, "El Virrey Amat da cuenta con cinco documentos de la desgraciada muerte de don Josef del Castillo, corregidor de Pacajes . . . ," 12/I/1772 (8 fols.), fol. 8.

7. ANB EC 1756 No. 67.

8. ANB EC 1754 No. 53; ANB EC 1754 No. 54. Principales in Yanacachi protested against the corregidor's reparto in 1758; see AGI Charcas 592, "Testimonio de los autos seguidos por los caciques e hilacatas del pueblo de Calacoto, provincia de Pacajes, contra el justicia mayor de ella, don Salvador de Asurza, sobre excesivos repartimientos," 1763 (76 fols.), fols. 69–69v.

9. ALP EC 1753 C. 76 E. 31.

10. Moreno Cebrián (1977, 185–190) summarizes the legislation concerning tenientes and their problematic role in the reparto system. He describes the typical teniente as "a man well versed in the tricks of his office, a native or long-time resident in the provinces that he served, and hence familiar with the elasticity they afforded for business" (189).

11. ANB EC 1756 No. 108. ANB EC 1758 No. 151, with quotes from fols. 4v, 18v.

12. When the corregidor's term was later evaluated, in 1763, the colonial administration sanctioned him with a fine along with his "ministers, officials, and other magistrates." Among those mentioned were eight confirmed deputies (tenientes), alcaldes mayores, commissioners, one teniente de alcalde provincial, one alguacil mayor, and one scribe (ALP EC 1770 C. 91 E. 5).

13. The audiencia also fined and deposed the Indian protector in La Paz, named by Negreiros, who had defended the community members from Chulumani (ANB EC 1756 No. 71; for quote see fol. 3).

14. For an example of this political complexity in the town of Chulumani, see ANB EC 1766 No. 130. For the intricate battles over local power, cacicazgo maneuvering, and reparto resistance in the town of Sicasica, see AGI Charcas 592, "Autos seguidos por los indios del pueblo de Sicasica por various abusos," 1768 (52 fols.); and AGI Charcas 592, "Testimonio de los autos seguidos por los caciques e hilacatas del pueblo de Calacoto . . . ," 1763 (76 fols.), fol. 67.

15. AGI Charcas 592, "Autos seguidos por los indios del pueblo de Sicasica por varios abusos," 1768 (52 fols.), fols. 51–52.

16. For example, one landlord, Bernardino Argandoña, accused the deputies of Ocobaya and Chirca, Bernardo Illanes and Joaquín Sánchez, of repartos that burdened tenants *(arrenderos)* and peons (yanaconas) on landed estates. Other landlords blamed the corregidor for repartos, abuses against Indians, obstructing mine operations, and commercial speculation with goods and supplies needed by residents of the province. See AGI Charcas 593, "Autos sobre caso del corregidor Villahermosa," 7/II/1771 (106 fols.), fols. 1–3, 61. In the early 1760s, a previous case from the province served to clarify state policy regarding repartos on haciendas (Moreno Cebrián 1977, 182–183, 233).

17. ANB EC 1759 No. 74, fols. 16, 22v. ANB EC 1770 No. 22. AGI Charcas 593, "Autos sobre caso del corregidor Villahermosa," 7/II/1771 (106 fols.), fols. 1–8v, 54v–57.

18. ANB EC 1770 No. 86.

19. ANB EC 1777 No. 14, fol. 31v.

20. ANB EC 1777 No. 14, fols. 71–72v. AGI Charcas 593, "Autos sobre caso del corregidor Villahermosa," 7/II/1771 (106 fols.), fols. 40v–42v.

21. ANB EC 1759 [1769] No. 74.

22. Indians and townspeople in Sicasica presented repeated accusations against authorities in 1769 and 1770. See AGI Charcas 593, "Autos sobre caso del corregidor Villahermosa," 7/II/1771 (106 fols.), fols. 1–8v, 56v–63, 70–74v.

23. ANB EC 1769 No. 29, fol. 12v.

24. ALP 1770 C. 91 E. 5, fol. 11. ANB EC 1771 No. 74, fol. 21v.

25. ANB EC 1769 No. 94, fol. 12v.

26. ANB EC 1769 No. 94, fol. 12v; AGI Charcas 593, "Autos sobre caso del corregidor Villahermosa," 7/II/1771 (106 fols.), fols. 10v–14v.

27. There were also charges in Ayoayo and Yaco against Deputy Antonio Elisondo. In Araca, Deputy Pedro Nolasco Benítez came under investigation for having purchased his post from the corregidor for over eight thousand pesos and having administered justice without due confirmation by the audiencia. AGI Charcas 593, "Autos sobre caso del corregidor Villahermosa," 7/II/1771 (106 fols.), fols. 17–20. On Talavera, see fols. 20v–36v. See also ANB EC 1769 No. 94.

28. ANB EC 1769 No. 94, fols. 3–5.

29. For example, he sowed terror among the Indians saying that his reparto, which he called the "royal reparto," was from the king himself. AGI Charcas 593, "Autos sobre caso del corregidor Villahermosa," 7/II/1771 (106 fols.), fols. 28v, 30v.

30. ANB EC 1769 No. 94, fols. 12–13. AGI Charcas 593, "Autos sobre caso del corregidor Villahermosa," 7/II/1771 (106 fols.), fols. 23–23v.

31. AGI Charcas 593, "Autos sobre caso del corregidor Villahermosa," 7/II/1771 (106 fols.), fols. 14v–16v, 77v–79. Alejandro Chuquiguaman (first called Vicente, and sometimes cited in the documents as Chuquimamani) was exceptional among caciques in La Paz for his "rebelliousness" and the political influence that so troubled colonial functionaries. According to the first official reports, Chuquiguaman was not properly named as cacique by colonial authorities,

but rather personally assumed his title and sought to preserve his leadership among Indians through agitation. We might speculate, though the evidence does not allow us to say so with certainty, that Chuquiguaman emerged as a leader enjoying community support during the phase of intense local struggle over the Anansaya cacicazgo during the 1760s (fols. 78v–79). In his confession, Chuquiguaman stated that he had been named tribute collector by Deputy Talavera, with the mandate of Villahermosa; but the court questioned this point and held he had been chosen by the community. See AGI Charcas 530, "Testimonio de los autos por el tumulto en el pueblo de Sicasica . . . ," 20/VII/ 1778 (32 fols.), fols. 5–7, 21v. The political legitimacy of Chuquiguaman, from the community point of view, can be imagined from his confrontation with the town administrator of the royal sales outlet for tobacco. While this official insisted on the prohibition of unlicensed tobacco sales, Chuquiguaman defended the right of community members to sell the product, obtained from Indian traders from the Inquisivi valleys, in order to meet their tribute payments (fol. 22v). The nervousness of the authorities is evident from the fact that Chuquiguaman was released after his arrest, apparently in 1770 in the wake of the uprising. Deputy Mohedano, fearful of protest, acceded to the appeal of Indians who sought his release (fol. 6v). It is also worth noting that, during the same conjuncture, the other moiety of Urinsaya was upset with its cacique-tribute collector Alejandro Matías Nina Laura. One confrontation occurred between this cacique and Asencio Pinto, another leader along with Chuquiguaman of the 1769 uprising, who opposed Nina Laura's abuses (fols. 23, 24v). For the reference to "signs of uprising," consult AGI Charcas 593, "Expediente sobre lo ocurrido en la provincia de Sicasica . . . ," Plata y Lima, 1776 (18 fols.), fol. 9.

32. Another suit was brought against a tribute collector appointed by the corregidor in Caracato. Both Indians and townspeople raised a "universal clamor" against Miguel Ruíz because of his abuses of authority and against the corregidor's repartos. See ANB EC 1779 No. 73; ANB EC 1772 No. 89; AGI Charcas 593, "Autos sobre caso del corregidor Villahermosa," 7/II/1771 (106 fols.), fols. 49–53v.

33. AGI Charcas 593, "Autos sobre caso del corregidor Villahermosa," 7/II/1771 (106 fols.), fols. 74v–75v. ANB EC 1779 [1769] No. 127.

34. AGI Charcas 593, "Autos sobre caso del corregidor Villahermosa," 7/II/ 1771 (106 fols.), fols. 83–83v. AGI Charcas 530, "Testimonio de los autos por el tumulto en el pueblo de Sicasica . . . ," 20/VII/1778 (32 fols.), fols. 1–7.

35. Other motives cited for the mobilization were to liberate the hilacata jailed by Villahermosa for tributary debt and to prevent Chuquiguaman's mother from being sent to a textile workshop, as the corregidor had allegedly ordered. For the uprising, see AGI Charcas 530, "Testimonio de los autos por el tumulto en el pueblo de Sicasica . . . ," 20/VII/1778 (32 fols.); AGI Charcas 593, "Autos sobre caso del corregidor Villahermosa," 7/II/1771 (106 fols.).

36. AGI Charcas 593, "Autos sobre caso del corregidor Villahermosa," 7/II/1771 (106 fols.), fol. 89. AGI Charcas 593, "Auto sobre el caso de Villahermosa . . . ," traslado 13/XI/1770 (23 fols.), fol. 17. The corregidor himself, protesting Castro's activities, warned of the restive mood of the towns, while others blamed him for the disturbances.

37. AGI Charcas 593, "Autos sobre caso del corregidor Villahermosa," 7/II/1771 (106 fols.), fols. 29, 68, 76–86. AGI Charcas 530, "Testimonio de los autos por el tumulto en el pueblo de Sicasica . . . ," 20/VII/1778 (32 fols.), fol. 2.

38. AGI Charcas 593, "Autos sobre caso del corregidor Villahermosa," 7/II/1771 (106 fols.), fol. 69.

39. AGI Charcas 593, "Autos sobre caso del corregidor Villahermosa," 7/II/1771 (106 fols.), fols. 39v–40.

40. We lack other evidence of political links between the Chulumani uprising and that of Jesús de Machaca in 1771; however, it is interesting to note that Santos Mamani, a Chupe community member condemned as a leader in the Yungas movement, was originally from the highland town. See AGI Charcas 530, "Extracto, respuesta fiscales, confesiones de reos, y providencias sobre tumulto ocurrido en los Yungas de Sicasica," traslado 20/VII/1778 (69 fols.), fol. 14v. ANB EC 1773 No. 26.

41. AGI Charcas 530, "Extracto, respuesta fiscales, confesiones de reos, y providencias sobre tumulto ocurrido en los Yungas de Sicasica," traslado 20/VII/1778 (69 fols.), fol. 36v.

42. AGI Charcas 530, "Extracto, respuesta fiscales, confesiones de reos, y providencias sobre tumulto ocurrido en los Yungas de Sicasica," traslado 20/VII/1778 (69 fols.), fols. 15v–16, 22–23v, 36–37, 57.

43. AGI Charcas 530, "Extracto, respuesta fiscales, confesiones de reos, y providencias sobre tumulto ocurrido en los Yungas de Sicasica," traslado 20/VII/1778 (69 fols.), fol. 48.

44. AGI Charcas 530, "Testimonio de los autos sobre el alzamiento en Chulumani, encabezado por Juan Tapia mestizo," traslado 20/VII/1778 (15 fols.), fols. 1–2. AGI Charcas 530, "Extracto, respuesta fiscales, confesiones de reos, y providencias sobre tumulto ocurrido en los Yungas de Sicasica," traslado 20/VII/1778 (69 fols.), fols. 14–15.

45. On the Chulumani uprising, see the two documents cited in the previous note as well as ANB EC 1788 [1778] No. 29.

46. AGI Charcas 530, "Testimonio de los autos sobre el alzamiento en Chulumani, encabezado por Juan Tapia mestizo," traslado 20/VII/1778 (15 fols.), fol. 7. ANB EC 1788 [1778] No. 29, fol. 17v.

47. AGI Charcas 530, "Testimonio de los autos sobre el alzamiento en Chulumani, encabezado por Juan Tapia mestizo" traslado 20/VII/1778 (15 fols.), fol. 8. AGI Charcas 530, "Extracto, respuesta fiscales, confesiones de reos, y providencias sobre tumulto ocurrido en los Yungas de Sicasica," traslado 20/VII/1778 (69 fols.), fol. 16v. ANB EC 1788 [1778] No. 29, fol. 44v.

48. O'Phelan 1988, 134–135, 155–159.

49. ANB EC 1758 No. 151, fols. 1–2.

50. Cacique Bernardo Cachica signed one complaint by principales from Chupe in 1757, yet his vulnerability was manifest: "If the cacique says anything against the abuses, the deputy strikes him a violent blow in public" (ANB EC 1758 No. 1, fol. 8v). See also ANB EC 1756 No. 71; ANB EC 1769 No. 94, fols. 3–5, 9–10v.

51. Andrade reappears again in the documentation in 1774 as cacique of Palca testifying in an inquest that agitators could stir up the province anew. Archivo Histórico Nacional (AHN), Consejo de Indias 20,369, "Testimonio de diligencias relativas al pleito seguido entre el Regidor don Tadeo Medina y el señor Marqués de Feria . . . ," fol. 16; cf. ANB EC 1773 No. 26.

52. ANB EC 1769 No. 99. In 1762, Quinaquina's father had presented a complaint, in the name of his son and the community, against Deputy Antonio Montalvo for excessive repartos. AGI Charcas 592, "Testimonio de los autos seguidos por los caciques e hilacatas del pueblo de Calacoto . . . ," 1763 (76 fols.), fol. 76.

53. AGI Charcas 530, "Real Audiencia da cuenta con testimonio de lo que ha executado con motivo del tumulto y muerte que dieron los indios del pueblo de Sicasica . . . ," 10/X/1778.

54. For the tenacious opposition of the community to the authority of Clemente Escobar and the leadership exercised by González over the community in this conflictual period, see AGI Charcas 530, "Extracto, respuesta fiscales, confesiones de reos, y providencias sobre tumulto ocurrido en los Yungas de Sicasica," traslado 20/VII/1778 (69 fols.). For the sentence, see AGI Charcas 530, "Real Audiencia da cuenta con testimonio de los bullicios ocurridos en los pueblos de Yungas por haberse restituido a Clemente Escobar al cacicazgo de Chupe . . . ," 10/X/1778.

55. For other references that point to the nexus of relations between the reparto, the local structure of power, and the cacicazgo crisis, see Moreno Cebrián 1977, 183–185, 234–235, 238–242; O'Phelan 1988, 134–135, 155–159; Larson and Wasserstrom 1983; Larson 1988, 126–132; Cahill 1988.

56. A few years after the outbreak of insurgency in Sicasica, an adversary of the new corregidor Marqués de Feria asserted that caciques in the province, especially those of Yungas, were dependent members of the governor's faction. Those implicated included Dionicio Mamani of Chulumani, Clemente Escobar Cullo Inga of Chupe, and Casimiro Andrade of Palca. AHN, Consejo de Indias 20,369, "Testimonio de diligencias relativas al pleito seguido entre el Regidor don Tadeo Medina y el señor Marqués de Feria . . . ," fol. 17. Cf. ANB EC 1773 No. 26.

57. On the royalist stance of caciques in 1781, see chapter 6; and Choque 1991.

58. As we noted in chapter 2, at the start of the insurrection, when Túpac Amaru allegedly solicited his collaboration as a colonel to surprise the Yungas corregidor, Mamani turned the correspondence over immediately to the colonial authorities. He later aided the Spaniards in Yungas to escape to Cochabamba and fought for the royalist cause in numerous battles, alongside his sons and at the

head of his Indian troops, until he died in combat in Calacoto just outside La Paz. See AGN IX 5-6-1, "El cacique de Chulumani, don Martín Romero Mamani, solicita confirmación de empleo," 1796; ANB EC 1808 No. 138; and Choque (1991).

59. ANB EC 1745 No. 56. See also ANB EC 1740 No. 51; ANB EC 1745 No. 42.

60. ANB Minas T. 126 No. 20/Minas Cat. No. 1464.

61. Sensano replied that the priest and his mother had mounted the suit against him. According to him, in fact, it was the priest and his relatives who carried out illegal local repartos. If Indians went to Guacullani, they did so voluntarily to sell firewood and dung and to earn cash. If the cacique had carried out repartos, it was at the corregidor's orders: "He could not resist the precept and respect of his governor who demanded it under threat of arrest, just as he did with the other caciques of the province" (ANB EC 1754 No. 123, fols. 6–9v, 13–13v, 98–102v).

62. ANB EC 1755 No. 66, fols. 4, 133v–135. ANB EC 1755 No. 84, fols. 74–74v, 93v. Bartolomé Cachicatari's brother, Atanacio, who led the cacique's violent gangs in Yunguyo, was cacique himself in nearby Guaqui (Pacajes). After initially supporting a community suit against the priest, Atanacio was bought off for three hundred pesos and became the "enemy" of Indians in Guaqui. He was a known drunkard in the city of La Paz and the compadre of the corregidor. A community suit successfully deposed him in 1754 (ANB EC 1754 No. 49; ANB EC 1754 No. 66).

63. For the Chuani case, see ANB Minas T. 127 No. 6/Minas Cat. No. 1517; ANB EC 1753 No. 60; ANB EC 1754 No. 70; and, in relation to contemporary tithe conflict and the links between Larecaja and Paucarcolla, see Barragán and Thomson 1993, 331–333.

64. Chuani community leaders praised the Azángaro insurgents and vowed that "since those from Asillo were unsuccessful in their uprising, they would carry out an even greater one." (ANB Minas T. 127 No. 6/Minas Cat. No. 1517, fols. 12, 27v). In 1736, hundreds of armed Indians attacked the town of Asillo in order to remove an abusive parish priest and his entourage; later that year, when the corregidor returned to admonish them, he and his guard were put to flight. In the aftermath, Indians conspired to mobilize seventeen provinces throughout the southern Andes. Their leader, Andrés Ignacio Caxma Condori, and dozens of cadre were arrested in Omasuyos, the province situated above the Larecaja valleys (Colin 1966, 171–173; O'Phelan 1988, 85–86, 104, 131, 299).

65. Bertonio (1984 [1612], 1:405; 2:290) gives the Aymara term *quespiyri* as the equivalent of *redentor*. He glosses the term *quespi* as "resplendent object like glass or crystal."

66. ANB Minas T. 127 No. 6/Minas Cat. No. 1517, fols. 5v–6, 11v, 35v.

67. Exasperation overcame cacique Lorenzo Corina: "Because of the Pallis, this cacique has been blamed for the revolts. They shamelessly claimed he was their leader; even in their petitions, which he never saw, they pretended he was the

author of their mischief. This is quite believable, since no one would assume that Indians were not subject to their cacique, but they never have been. . . . They were also so bold as to tell him to his face that if he did not back them in their designs, they would burn his house down." He objected to others acting in the name of the community and insisted that he fulfilled his political responsibilities as cacique: "The community should find the relief it needs from the hand of the cacique, as in the past I have been able to negotiate for them, rather than from greedy Indians [who raise money for themselves saying it will be used to obtain decrees from the court]" (ANB Minas T. 127 No. 6/Minas Cat. No. 1517, fols. 11, 12, 51–51v).

68. For more on the Larecaja struggles, see ANB EC 1752 No. 12; ANB EC 1754 No. 132; ANB EC 1755 No. 56; ANB EC 1756 No. 72; for the final quote see ANB EC 1755 No. 58, fol. 5. The community of Chuma protested against repartos and other exactions by authorities in 1759; see AGI Charcas 592, "Testimonio de los autos seguidos por los caciques e hilacatas del pueblo de Calacoto . . . ," 1763 (76 fols.), fols. 69v–70.

69. ANB EC 1753 No. 70. ANB EC 1753 No. 99. ANB EC 1753 No. 148. ANB EC 1754 No. 125.

70. ANB EC 1756 No. 130, fol. 25v.

71. ANB EC 1760 No. 116, fol. 52v. AGI Charcas 592, "Carta del corregidor de Omasuyos, Francisco Antonio de Trelles, al virrey," 20/XI/1771 (2 fols.).

72. ANB EC 1756 No. 111, fol. 28v.

73. ANB CR No. 613.

74. ANB EC 1760 No. 116, fols. 55, 77–77v.

75. The community suit was presumably heard in December 1759, not 1760 as cited in the expediente; see AGI Charcas 592, "Testimonio de los autos seguidos por los caciques e hilacatas del pueblo de Calacoto . . . ," 1763 (76 fols.), fols. 70–71v, 72–72v. Though we do not have full details on the 1759 attack, there is reason to believe it was related to the reparto conflict; see AGI Charcas 592, "Carta del corregidor de Omasuyos, Francisco Antonio de Trelles, al virrey," 20/XI/1771 (2 fols.).

76. Grievances against Calonje had also been filed by Guarina cacique Matías Calaumana. For the disputes involving Calonje, see ANB EC 1761 No. 97 (for quotes, fols. 60, 69v–70); ANB EC 1762 No. 169; AGI Charcas 592, "Testimonio de los autos seguidos por don Ildefonso Fernández, cacique de Laja, sobre agravios que le ha inferido su corregidor don Antonio Calonje," 1763 (33 fols.); AGI Charcas 592, "Testimonio de los autos seguidos por don Augustín Siñani, cacique de Carabuco, contra don Antonio Calonje, corregidor que fue de dicha provincia," 1762 (28 fols.).

77. In locations where the corregidor's reparto system relied more on caciques than on other agents from outside the community, the chain of obligation extended down to local Indian collectors who were principales or particularly hilacatas. They generally derived no profit from this arrangement, unlike the cacique who drew a salary from the corregidor, but served out of obedience

to their governor. For one indictment of this reparto hierarchy, see AGI Charcas 592, "Testimonio de los autos seguidos por los caciques e hilacatas del pueblo de Calacoto . . . ," 1763 (76 fols.), fols. 59–60. The audiencia ruled in 1759 that caciques should not be forced to participate in the system and should be paid for all voluntary contracted services (fol. 70v). Immediately following the uprisings of 1771 it went on to ban cacique participation outright. But these regulations were not observed (AGI Charcas 592, "Autos de la Real Audiencia de Charcas and real cédula sobre repartos," [14 fols.]). The audiencia also reiterated that only private agents *(cajeros)* should operate in the reparto system, not deputies (tenientes) who were ostensibly the agents of colonial justice. This stipulation was also ineffective (fols. 9v–11).

78. The hacendado was none other than Antonio Pinedo, Corregidor of La Paz at the same time. See ANB EC 1775 [1766] No. 174, fol. 16.

79. In a similar and contemporaneous case from Charazani (Larecaja), the widow of cacique Juan Miguel Sirena appealed for the cancellation of her husband's debts to Corregidor Miguel Fernández Duarte. The corregidor had allegedly coerced Sirena into acting as a financial backer for Deputy Josef Manzaneda who owed Duarte money for reparto goods distributed in his jurisdiction. See AGI Charcas 592, "Testimonio de los seguidos por doña Michaela Llavilla, viuda de don Juan Miguel Sirena, cacique que fue de Charazani, contra el corregidor de Larecaja don Miguel Fernández Duarte," 1762 (81 fols.).

80. Other regional studies in the Andes are needed to determine whether the La Paz case is generally representative. Golte (1980, 160–161) suggests that La Paz and Charcas were distinct from other parts of the Peruvian viceroyalty due to a more active cacique participation in legal struggles and an alliance between caciques and communities that afforded a supralocal character to the protests. Our study of La Paz shows, however, the weakness of this alliance and that the political organization of the resistance did not depend in the end on caciques.

81. O'Phelan 1985, 163–166.

82. In a succinct explanation of the method and efficacy of colonial rule, Corregidor Lafitta justified the need for responding with a crackdown on the population: "The Indian has a propensity toward disturbance, novelty, and movement. But this only persists in a system while he does not see the threat of punishment, or, simply put, the arm raised over him. It is the threat that keeps these people in order. It is remarkable, since they are not subjects who act out of respect for religion nor honor and loyalty, that such large towns of Indians can be maintained by a corregidor with no more weapons or support than the name of the king whom he represents. But it is true that there is no other basis of respect and that only that name and the threat of punishment are what contain them." See AGN IX 5–5–2, "Corregidor de La Paz, Lafita, sobre levantamiento de Pacajes," 9/XI/1771 (2 fols.). On the Pacajes insurgency, see the documents in AGN IX 5–5–2; ALP EC 1771 C. 92 E. 24; Amat y Junient (1947, 296–304); AGI Charcas 592, "Carta del Contador Pedro Nolasco Crespo al Virrey Amat," 26/XI/1771 (2 fols.).

83. For Bartolina Sisa's account, see AGI Buenos Aires 319, "Cuaderno No. 4," fol. 59; for Katari's testimony see AGN IX 7–4–2, "Testimonio de las confesiones del reo Julián Apaza, alias Tupa Catari, y sentencia que se pronunció contra él," (38 fols.), fols. 4–4v. Lewin dates the planning of Túpac Amaru's project back to 1770. The regional and local factors contributing to the importance of this conjuncture in Cuzco merit comparative research.

84. The corregidor of Carangas, the province directly south of Pacajes, also reported an uprising the same year. However, it turned out to be a false alarm to disguise the fact that Indians were resisting his reparto in the courts and fleeing to the hills when he pretended to practice a revisita. See AGI Charcas 592, "Autos de la Real Audiencia de Charcas y real cédula sobre repartos," (14 fols.), fols. 6–6v; and ANB EC 1771 No. 66.

85. We cannot undertake here a full account of viceregal and metropolitan state responses to popular resistance and the building crisis in this period. References for the summary in this paragraph come especially from the set of expedientes in AGI Charcas 592; and Moreno Cebrián (1977).

86. ANB EC 1777 No. 71. For the quotes, see fols. 10, 371; on the corregidor's perception of a threat and the antecedent conflicts in Paucarcolla, see fols. 345v–347, 370.

87. For this and the following quote, see AGN IX 32–1–6, "Informe del Corregidor Vial al virrey sobre disturbios en la provincia," 19/I/1777, fol. 2. In fact, punishment was meted out to alleged leaders in both cases. In the case of Pacajes, dozens of Indians languished in La Paz jails during the 1770s.

88. See AGN IX 32–1–6, "Informe del Corregidor Vial al virrey sobre disturbios en la provincia," 19/I/1777, fol. 2; AGN IX 32–1–6, "Autos criminales seguidos contra don Augustín Catacora, cacique, su segunda Ignacio Cruz, y los indios de la parcialidad de Anansaya de Acora sobre el tumulto que acaeció el 16/IX/1775, y el que preparaban en el presente año de 1777; y de los demás delitos que constan de este proceso," 1777 (67 fols.); and the other expedientes included with them. The strong pressures exerted from above by corregidores and from below by communities to control cacicazgos are evident, for example, in Pomata. In 1773, Indians rose up in defense of cacique Josef Toribio Castilla, whom Corregidor Mateo de la Cuadra intended to replace. Five years later, when the same cacique intervened attempting to pacify the community as it attacked Corregidor Vial, peasants ignored his entreaties and declared that "he had sold them out and allied himself with the governor." See, amongst the other expedientes, "Autos criminales seguidos de oficio contra el común de indios de Pomata por el tumulto que hicieron el 11/I y el perdimiento de respeto a la real justicia," fol. 4v.

89. ANB EC 1780 No. 111.

90. On the Condocondo episode, see Cajías (1987, 315–317); O'Phelan (1988, 158–159); and Penry (1996: 24–146).

91. ANB EC 1777 No. 71, fol. 408v.

92. ANB EC 1777 No. 20, fols. 15–16v. When the investigatory commission arrived in Calacoto, the community of Viacha registered its own complaints against the reparto abuses of corregidores and their debt collectors (ANB EC 1773 No. 12, fols. 14–14v, 27–31v).

93. ANB EC 1773 No. 12, fol. 47v. ANB EC 1777 No. 20, fols. 34–34v. In 1779, Agustín Canqui (calling himself Cusicanqui) protested against the pressures exerted by corregidores upon caciques to distribute their goods. Yet this complaint, coming after years of compliance, surfaced because of a breakdown in relations and the designation of a new interim governor for Urinsaya, Juan Josef Cusicanqui. The community now attempted to defend Agustín Canqui, in order to rid themselves of the new cacique. Battles over the cacicazgos in Calacoto lasted into the early nineteenth century, with a key point of dispute being the succession rights of the heirs of Juan Eusebio Canqui who had been deposed in the 1730s. See ANB EC 1779 No. 47; ALP EC 1783 C. 103 E. s.n., "Conflicto sobre cacicazgo de Calacoto" (57 fols.).

94. AHN, Consejo de Indias 20,369, "Testimonio de diligencias relativas al pleito seguido entre el Regidor don Tadeo Medina y el señor Marqués de Feria . . . ," fols. 7v–16. Cf. ANB EC 1773 No. 26.

95. There was probably a significant strain of resentment by creoles against the peninsular Spaniards who occupied privileged positions, particularly that of corregidor, in the regional political and economic regime. However Valle de Siles (1990, 549–569) maintains that prior to 1781 such tensions were slight in La Paz compared to Oruro (Cajías 1987), Chuquisaca, and Potosí. For peninsular domination of the corregidor post in Peru, see Moreno Cebrián (1977, 136–166). See also Barragán (1996) on elite factions and identity in La Paz.

96. Francisco Tadeo Diez de Medina, the author of a bombastic, self-promoting diary of the siege of La Paz, would earn for himself a notorious place in the annals of history as the judge who dictated Túpaj Katari's death sentence. (See Valle de Siles 1980, 1994; and chapter 6.) For more of his antecedents, see ANB EC 1776 No. 72, fols. 19v–20v. Diez de Medina was also personally hostile toward Marqués de Feria due to legal disputes involving his family and Yungas property (fol. 15; ANB EC 1773 No. 26).

97. ANB EC 1776 No. 72. ANB EC 1778 No. 7, fols. 4v–5v. Valle de Siles 1990, 484–487. For more on this case, see the expedientes in AGN XIII 28–3–1, 2.

98. ANB EC 1776 No. 72, fols. 1–9. ANB EC 1778 No. 7.

99. ANB EC 1776 No. 240. ANB EC 1776 146.

100. AGN IX 36–9–6, "La Real Audiencia remite testimonio de los autos obrados en La Paz, con motivo del alboroto de los indios," 1778 (76 fols.). ANB EC 1781 No. 57, fols. 168–182. AGI Charcas 595, "Testimonio N. 1 LA de la sublevación que se temía en Cochabamba por el establecimiento de la aduana," (167 fols.). AGI Charcas 595, "Testimonio del expediente formado sobre la exacción de alcabalas a los indios de la ciudad de La Paz," (51 fols.). For a general treatment of the impacts of Bourbon reform and their importance for the

insurrection of 1780–1781, see O'Phelan (1988), especially chapter 4. For more on the episodes in La Paz, see Valle de Siles (1990, 475–489). Valle de Siles may be right that Marqués de Feria sought to curry favor with Indians in compensation for the burden of his own reparto. However, in her account, she underestimates Indian resentment against the new collection system and places too much faith in the version of treasury officials whom she considers "enlightened" agents of Bourbon reform. Resentment ran high not only because of the chafing controls (which contributed to a steep increase in alcabala income, especially within the rubric of Andean products, or *efectos de la tierra*), but due to their irreconcilability (especially in the *guía/tornaguía* system) with Indian strategies of commercial circulation. Also, political rifts within the regional elite had a large role to play in the controversy surrounding Marqués de Feria.

101. For the 1780 disturbances, see AGN IX 32-2-5, "Intento de sublevación en la ciudad de La Paz," 1780 (140 fols.); AGN IX 30-2-2, "Testimonio de la información secreta hecha por el señor fiscal don Fernando Márquez de la Plata sobre las inquietudes acaecidas en la ciudad de La Paz," 1780 (24 fols.); AGN IX 5-5-3, "Sobre negación de la renuncia de don Bernardo Gallo de la Aduana de La Paz," 24/III/1780 (3 fols.). See also AGI Charcas 594; and Lima 1039. For a fuller secondary account, consult Valle de Siles (1990, 489–506). The original language and punctuation of the later quote is: "Viva la Ley de Dios y la puresa de Maria, y Muera El Rey de España, y se acabe el Peru; pues el es causa de tanta eniquidad; Si el Monarca no sabe de las insolensias de sus ministros de los Robos Publicos, y como tienen ostilisados a los pobres Viba el Rey y Mueran todos estos ladrones publicos, ya que no quieren poner enmienda en lo que se les pide." For interpretation of the passage, see Valle de Siles (1990, 491–492, 503–504); and Lewin (1967, 151–153).

102. On the size and diversity of the plebeian elements, see the testimony of witnesses in AGN IX 32-2-5, "Intento de sublevación en la ciudad de La Paz," 1780 (140 fols.); and Valle de Siles 1990, 501–506. For the quote from the Indians congregated at the outskirts of the city, see the same expediente, fol. 96. Another manifestation of creole radicalism in La Paz is the letter to Father Mazo, fols. 114–115; see Lewin 1967, 151–153, 722–724.

103. For Areche's response, see AGN IX 32-2-5, "Intento de sublevación en la ciudad de La Paz," 1780 (140 fols.), fols. 129–134v. Márquez de la Plata's reports are contained in AGN IX 5-5-3; see also AGI Charcas 447B.

104. Stern 1987a, 73–75. While New Spain did not experience a political crisis comparable to that of Peru, both Carmagnani and Chance (1989, 146–150) have proposed that the reparto system in parts of Oaxaca similarly effected changes in Indian political and social relations. Larson and Wasserstrom (1983) offer a comparison between the impacts of the reparto on peasantries in the Andes and central Chiapas. Cf. Basques (2000).

105. This pact could be strategically (and disingenuously) invoked while harboring more radically autonomous objectives, but it was more often appealed to as

a legitimate alternative to abusive conditions under regional authorities. Serulnikov (1996) has developed an original interpretation of Tomás Katari's movement in Chayanta between 1777 and 1780 that illuminates a number of aspects of the common community struggles that did not seek a rupture with the colonial state. While the Chayanta movement took on a distinctive character, the analysis offers important insights for other regions especially regarding the combination of legal maneuvering and collective direct action and regarding Indian appropriation of colonial discourses and institutions.

Chapter 5. Emancipation Projects and Dynamics of Native Insurgency (I)

1. As is true of many revolutionary moments, the age of Andean insurrection has been remembered and represented as a time of glory or a time of terror ever since it came to pass. It is curious that we have so little in the way of historiographic essays and critical reviews of these representations in the arts and public discourse.

2. ANB EC 1797 No. 56, fol. 11v. "The revolution was thus a return to the past" (Flores Galindo 1987, 142, 361–368).

3. "The Indians were now like ferocious beasts, hunting the miserable refugees in caves, on the hills, and on farms. . . . The untamed savage spirit in the natives was unleashed" (L. E. Fisher 1966, 247, 257).

4. "Even at a distance one is still impressed—though not as much as the Spanish themselves must have been—by the sudden transformation of these tribute-paying, submissive Indians into columns of thousands of silent, armed combatants, guided by their own banners and trumpets, standing on a hill to then charge without mercy on the despised city of the whites" (Cornblit 1995, 143–144).

5. For general reviews of this historiography, see Stern (1987a, 36–42); Campbell (1979); Flores Galindo (1989).

6. Lewin 1967, expanded 3rd edition. C. D. Valcárcel 1946, 1947, 1975, 1977. Loayza 1945, 1947. Cornejo Bouroncle 1949. Durand Flórez 1973. The second tome of the massive *Colección documental de la independencia del Perú* (1971–1975), edited by C. D. Valcárcel, is devoted to Túpac Amaru's insurgency. In contrast to most of the work from this generation, which cast eighteenth-century Indian rebellion as the precursor of Peruvian independence, Rowe's work (1954; reprinted in Flores Galindo 1976) was pioneering in identifying a protonational Indian project. Cf. Campbell (1979, 14–21); Stern (1987a, 36–38); and Walker (1999, 16–54).

7. Within the field of Andean studies, whose pioneers would include John Rowe, John Murra, and Tom Zuidema, a loose school or paradigmatic intellectual project has employed ethnohistorical and symbolic structuralist approaches to Andean culture to ascertain its distinctiveness, an effort which at times has led to an essentialized notion of "Andeanness" *(lo andino)*. Flores Galindo 1976. Golte 1980. Hidalgo Lehuede 1983. Szeminski 1993 (1st ed. 1983). O'Phelan 1988 (originally published in English in 1985). Flores Galindo 1987. Stern 1987.

8. Hidalgo Lehuede 1983. Szeminski 1983, 1987. Abercrombie 1991b.

9. Serulnikov (1996) shows how this is played out in the documentation and historiography about Tomás Katari, and we will see a related problem with regard to Túpaj Katari.

10. Cf. Guha (1983), who draws from Gramsci, on the "negative" consciousness of anticolonial peasant insurgents in India.

11. ANB Minas T. 127 No. 6/Minas Cat. No. 1517, fols. 5v–6, 11v, 35v.

12. ALP EC 1795 C. 122 E. 25, fol. 8v. One might speculate that the principle of rotating authority within the community contributed to the peasant political notion that it was the turn of new authorities or Indians to rule. However, I believe that the sense of illegitimate authority or unjust government was the primary criterion in any anticolonial mobilization or political project.

13. The unusual Chuani case bears comparison with that of Andagua (Arequipa) where, in the same period, opposition to the state was sustained by Indians who participated in a local mummy cult (Salomon 1987).

14. See chapter 4 for more on the events in Sicasica in 1769 and Chulumani in 1771.

15. ANB EC 1788 [1778] No. 29, fol. 11v. Naturally we must exercise discretion when reading the evidence assembled against alleged Indian rebels. Exaggerated accusations were a common tactic to discredit leaders and malign them as traitors to the Crown. Nevertheless, I believe a full scrutiny of the evidence justifies our interpretation here.

16. ANB EC 1788 [1778] No. 29, fol. 12.

17. ANB EC 1788 [1778] No. 29, fols. 11–16; see also the testimony of Indians from Chupe in AGN Charcas 530, "Extracto sobre tumulto ocurrido en los Yungas de Sicasica," 20/VII/1778 (69 fols.), especially fols. 47v–48, 49v–50v.

18. ANB EC 1788 [1778] No. 29, fols. 43, 45.

19. For the details of the siege reported in original testimony, see ANB EC 1788 [1778] No. 29, fols. 6v–22, 39v–45v; AGN Charcas 530, "Extracto sobre tumulto ocurrido en los Yungas de Sicasica," 20/VII/1778 (69 fols.), fols. 25–51v.

20. ANB EC 1788 [1778] No. 29, fol. 19v.

21. AGN Charcas 530, "Extracto sobre tumulto ocurrido en los Yungas de Sicasica," 20/VII/1778 (69 fols.), fol. 14. ANB EC 1788 [1778] No. 29, fols. 6v–22. By one account, Tapia coerced reticent community members into the mobilization by threatening to seize their property, an action that would have resembled the procedures, authority, and fearsomeness of Spanish corregidores (ANB EC 1788 [1778] No. 29, fol. 21).

22. ANB EC 1788 [1778] No. 29, fols. 83v–84.

23. See chapter 4 for more description of the uprising in Jesús de Machaca and Caquiaviri in 1771. This account is based on the documents in IX 5–5–2, especially the expediente of 22 fols. with the heading "Al señor Diez de Medina en La Paz. Venta de estancia en Sicasica," 1774; and ALP EC 1771 C. 92 E. 24.

24. The phrase should be understood to mean that if the soldiers were marching against the community (in Machaca), then the peasants in Caquiaviri would stand against the the soldiers. AGN IX 5–5–2, "Al señor Diez de Medina en La Paz . . . ," 1774 (22 fols.), fol. 18v.

25. AGN IX 5–5–2, "Al señor Diez de Medina en La Paz . . . ," 1774 (22 fols.), fols. 19, 20v. ALP EC 1771 C. 92 E. 24, fol. 1v.

26. *"Muerto el corregidor ya no había Juez para ellos sino que el REY era el común por quien mandaban ellos"* (upper-case emphasis preserved from original document; AGN IX 5–5–2, "Al señor Diez de Medina en La Paz . . . ," 1774 [22 ff], fol. 20v). I thank Mark Thurner for help with interpretation of this phrase.

27. The testimony of witnesses is less than perfectly clear and consistent, particularly on the precise sequence of events.

28. By another account, the mulatto was moved to such pity by the scene in the town that he told the Indians that he would kill them if he had a knife because they were seizing innocent people (AGN IX 5–5–2, "Al señor Diez de Medina en La Paz . . . ," 1774 [22 ff], fol. 20v).

29. ALP EC 1771 C. 92 E. 24, fol. 2. Another account attributed the lapse to the disappearance of the jail attendant (AGN IX 5–5–2, "Al señor Diez de Medina en La Paz . . . ," 1774 [22 fols.], fol. 21).

30. AGN IX 5–5–2, "Al señor Diez de Medina en La Paz . . . ," 1774 (22 fols.), fol. 20v.

31. Romero was described by Spanish witnesses as a "mozo," a "mozo mestizo," and as one of a number of "mozos españoles." See ALP EC 1771 C. 92 E. 24, fol. 1v; AGN IX 5–5–2, "Al señor Diez de Medina en La Paz . . . ," 1774 (22 fols.), fol. 21.

32. AGN IX 5–5–2, "Al señor Diez de Medina en La Paz . . . ," 1774 (22 fols.), fols. 19, 21. Another report had it that the Indians killed a mozo named Josef Hinojosa because he had seized mules for the soldiers as they set out for Jesús de Machaca; this was probably a confusion with the case of Josef Romero (fol. 18).

33. This threat was made during the siege of Chulumani (AGI Charcas 530, "Extracto sobre tumulto ocurrido en los Yungas de Sicasica," 20/VII/1778 [69 fols.], fol. 14), as it was during the purported Indian conspiracy in Coroico in 1800 (AGN IX 5–6–3, "Autos sobre rumores de levantamiento de indios en Coroico," 1800 [21 fols.], fols. 15v–16v).

34. The quote from the previous sentence comes from ALP EC 1771 C. 92 E. 24, fols. 2–2v. The claim and perspective indicated here echo that of the Indians in Jesús de Machaca who appropriated all the belongings of the dead corregidor, including his very bed, or destroyed them. They burned his papers and collected his money, saying that "it was theirs to drink with" (AGN IX 5–5–2, "Al señor Diez de Medina en La Paz . . . ," 1774 [22 fols.], fol. 17v).

35. ALP EC 1771 C. 92 E. 24, fol. 2v.

36. AGN IX 5–5–2, "Al señor Diez de Medina en La Paz . . . ," 1774 (22 fols.), fols. 18–18v.

37. Three years later, this same agenda resurfaced in the town of Condocondo (Paria province) when peasants rose up in the name of "King Community" *(el rey común)* and killed the Llanquepacha brothers of one local cacicazgo lineage. See the suggestive analysis of Penry (1996). A comparable case of collective Indian identification with royal sovereignty and repudiation of other colonial authorities occurred with a contingent of mitayos on their way to Potosí in 1801. See Tandeter (1992, 39–43).

38. The quote is from ALP EC 1771 C. 92 E. 24, fol. 2. Rivera's title, that of *secretario,* is also of uncertain origin.

39. The accounts presented in this and the preceding paragraph are from AGN IX 5–5–2, "Al señor Diez de Medina en La Paz . . . ," 1774 (22 fols.), fols. 19–21v. A key sentence reads, "*Mandaron que todos los vecinos jurasen el domicilio y sujeción a ellos, vistiendo mantas, camisetas y monteras, y sus mujeres de axsu a semejanza de ellos, y que así saldrían libres con vida*" (AGN IX 5–5–2, "Al señor Diez de Medina en La Paz . . . ," 1774 [22 fols.], fols. 21–21v).

40. It is certainly the first documented case in eighteenth-century La Paz; I am not aware of other historically previous instances of cross-dressing and Indian rebellion elsewhere in the Andes.

41. See Mallon (1995).

42. Compared to the altiplano setting, where usually only Indian forasteros were absorbed into the community, it was more common in the Yungas valleys for mestizos to hold community lands or to enter the community through marriage. In Yungas, community identification probably followed less clear-cut cultural boundaries, and community responsibilities may have even been more flexibly assigned (e.g., mestizo landholders paid a form of rent that was applied toward community tribute payments, while they may not have been subject to other forms of community labor service).

43. AGN IX 5–5–2, "Al señor Diez de Medina en La Paz . . . ," 1774 (22 fols.), fol. 21v.

44. Immediately after announcing that "all were vassals of the king" and proposing mancomunidad, peasants became disturbed and threatened to kill everyone because Garicano violated orders and attempted to leave the jail (ALP EC 1771 C. 92 E. 24, fol. 2).

45. AGN IX 5–5–2, "Al señor Diez de Medina en La Paz . . . ," 1774 (22 fols.), fol. 21v.

46. See Hidalgo Lehuede 1983; Szeminski 1983; Flores Galindo 1987, 107–143; also cf. Platt 1993.

47. Vélez de Córdoba was a creole who proclaimed his own Inka lineage and the legitimacy of Inka monarchy. The Oruro conspiracy, primarily organized by creoles and mestizos, purportedly involved coordination with a group of caciques on the Pacific coast and others in Cochabamba; there is no evidence that La Paz caciques participated in the project (O'Phelan 1988, 104–111). Juan Santos Atahualpa, also claiming the right to govern Peru as Inka heir, waged an

impressive guerrilla war against Spanish troops from 1742 until 1761 (Stern 1987a, 34–93).

48. Cited in Hidalgo Lehuede (1983, 120). It was also said that a Spanish gazette had predicted a time of disaster for the "year of the three sevens."

49. Consider another of the tavern opinions: "One of the signs of the prophecy's fulfillment was the disturbance and sedition by the mestizo Indians against the corregidores, killing some of them and expelling others from their provinces." (Hidalgo Lehuede 1983, 121) On the unrest in the final phase prior to the insurrection, see O'Phelan (1988, 188–221, 304–306).

50. It is likely that the reading of Garcilaso contributed to this notion, which was explicitly asserted by Vélez de Córdoba in his Oruro declaration of 1739 (Rowe 1976, 25–32; Lewin 1967, 118–120, 382–383). However, given the process of politicization in the eighteenth century, it was not a view familiar only to literate Indian nobles. In La Paz, for example, the idea was communicated to peasants by insurgent leaders during the 1781 siege, as we note in this paragraph; also, as we saw above in the case of Ambaná, rural Indians held the related historical view that the Spanish conquest had brought an end to their "liberty."

51. Cited in Hidalgo Lehuede (1983, 122). On the Huarochirí uprising, see Spalding (1984, 270–293); Sala i Vila (1996a); and O'Phelan (1988, 111–116).

52. Cited in Lewin (1967, 420–421); Durand Flórez 1973, 173–176. The historical shadow cast by the sixteenth-century conquest must have been ever present for Túpac Amaru. He referred to Visitador Areche, who arrived in Peru in the 1770s to introduce a battery of onerous Bourbon reforms, as a "second Pizarro." He also spoke forcefully of the tears shed by Indians over the previous three hundred years (Comisión Nacional del Sesquicentenario de la Independencia del Perú [CDIP] 2: 2:346, 379).

53. CDIP 2:2:810.

54. AGI Buenos Aires 319, "Cuaderno No. 4," fol. 39.

55. Cited in Lewin (1967, 352).

56. For example, he named local tribute collectors, directed the payment of tribute to the royal treasury in Potosí, and, moving about the province as well as receiving Indians who came to him in Macha, he served as magistrate in the resolution of disputes (even involving Spaniards). On the Chayanta movement, see Lewin (1967); Hidalgo Lehuede (1983); S. Arze (1991); Andrade (1994); Penry (1996); Serulnikov (1996).

57. Hidalgo Lehuede 1983, 123–124, 128, 133 n.20. Lewin 1967, 375–376, 739, 774. Perhaps adding to the millenarian mood, Katari's movement was preceded by a miracle in Surumi, part of Macha territory, which became an important regional sanctuary (Platt 1993, 176).

58. Katari sent communications to Indians in Sicasica announcing that he had obtained a reduction in tribute payments, and Gregoria Apaza testified that in early 1781 Indians in Sicasica were expecting the arrival of a shadowy figure identified as Tomás Katari who would eliminate corregidores, tax collectors, and

Europeans (CDIP 2:2:555; AGI Buenos Aires 319, "Cuaderno No. 5," fols. 3v–4). It is also worth noting that Túpac Amaru did not acquire political ascendancy throughout the southern Andes until after Tomás Katari was killed in early January of 1781. That same month, Indians in the province of Carangas were said to recognize Túpac Amaru "as their king and lord after the death of Tomás Katari" (CDIP 2:2:474).

59. Serulnikov 1996.

60. When the full-scale mobilization of communities became essential, Katari eventually did assert falsely that the viceroy had authorized a tribute reduction, which regional authorities refused to carry out. He did so under dire circumstances and evidently in spite of himself. See the confessions of his brothers Dámaso and Nicolás Katari (CDIP 2:2:555–556, 606).

61. The sheer demographic superiority of the Indian population was another factor contributing to the confidence of insurgents throughout the southern Andes. Consider the threat made by Indians in Chayanta to their corregidor— "The entire kingdom will be roused since their numbers are greater than those of the Spaniards, all of which may be avoided by not disturbing them" (Cited in Serulnikov 1996, 236). Of course few leaders anticipated that significant numbers of Indians would also be mobilized as royalist troops.

62. CDIP 2:2:255.

63. Túpac Amaru himself spoke confidently of the prophecies then in circulation: "He would say that the time of the prophecy of Santa Rosa de Lima had come. Control of the kingdom would return to its former possessors, and this was why he was going to exterminate and get rid of all Europeans existing in it." In response to Bishop Moscoso's excommunication edict, Amaru complained: "Who got the cleric involved in all this? Does he not realize that the time of the prophecy has arrived? Let him tend to his church; he has enough to worry about with that." *Colección Documental del Bicentenario de la Revolución Emancipadora de Túpac Amaru* (CDTA) 2:380. Another account by a priest reported: "He affects piety, and even attempts to persuade others that heaven favors him" (Cited in Lewin 1967, 391).

64. AGN XIII, 28–3–2, "Autos sobre el juicio de las cuentas de Ramón de Anchoríz por todo el tiempo que fue corregidor (Sicasica)," 1780–1783, fols. 171v–172. Valle de Siles 1994, 59.

65. Campbell (1987, 121) states, "These dualistic authority symbols, King and Inkarrí, are at the heart of the confusion surrounding the meaning of the Great Rebellion of 1780." The following discussion relies especially on Lewin (1967, 394–426); Durand Flórez (1973, 107–147); and Szeminski (1983, 1st ed.; 1993, 2nd ed.). It accords with the analysis in Walker (1999, 16–54).

66. Lewin (1967, 415) observed that Amaru employed the fiction of being commissioned by the king primarily in his dealings with other Indians at the beginning of the campaign; since this would have been less credible to creoles, he presented himself to them as the natural political representative of the population

and as morally compelled to defend it against oppression, without asserting independent sovereignty.

67. See Túpac Amaru's letter cited in Lewin (1967, 456–457).

68. See L. E. Fisher (1966, 22, 99, 135–136, 241); Valcárcel (1946, 117–125, 162–165); and the first edition of Valcárcel's *La rebelión de Túpac Amaru* (1947, 177–188). In the later editions of this work (the second edition appeared in 1965), Valcárcel proposed that Amaru's initial and "ingenuous" loyalism gave way to separatism with the unfolding of events; see Valcárcel (1975, 167–172, 234–237) as well as Valcárcel (1977, 111–115). A similar view is sustained, for example, by Moreno Cebrián (1988, 114–124).

69. The first edition of Lewin's magisterial study was published in 1943 as *Túpac Amaru, el rebelde: Su época, sus luchas y su influencia en el continente* (Buenos Aires: Editorial Claridad).

70. The edict is cited and analyzed in Lewin (1967, 419–422). Durand Flórez 1973, 141–147, 173–176; and Szeminski (1983, 220–224).

71. Szeminski 1983, 201–286. Lewin 1967, 397–412.

72. In fact, Amaru's call for tithe payments to priests involved a significant reform of colonial tithe farming. Under the existing system, the Church rented tithe-collection rights to private speculators, usually local landlords, who realized profits by marketing the tithed crops and animals for a value above the original bidding price. On tithing and the social conflict it generated, see Barragán and Thomson (1993).

73. The phrase comes from the edict for the province of Chichas; cited in Lewin (1967, 398).

74. CDIP 2:2:549.

75. Cajías 1987, 186–187.

76. The following account of the insurrection in Oruro is based on Cajías (1987); Lewin (1967, 538–566); and Cornblit (1995). See also Robins (1997).

77. Cited in Cajías (1987, 738–739, 744).

78. One European was spared because of his marriage to a creole woman (ibid., 513–516).

79. For example, upon entering the city, Indians would first visit Jacinto Rodríguez; they rendered homage to him, embraced him and kissed his hand, and vowed to defend his life. Likewise in the countryside, Indians respected the safe-conduct passes he issued, and obeyed the calls of other prominent creoles for Indians to march to the city (Cornblit 1995, 152; Cajías 1987, 538–543). The incident involving Manuel Herrera is cited in Cajías (1987, 532).

80. Cajías 1987, 528–532.

81. Spanish women were also forced to dress as Indians during the 1781 uprising in Calama (Atacama) (Hidalgo Lehuede 1986, 289–290).

82. Cornblit 1995, 155.

83. Cajías 1987, 572–577.

84. Cited in ibid. (748).
85. Cited in ibid. (375–377).
86. Cited in ibid. (737–738); Cornblit (1995, 179–180).
87. Cited in Cajías (1987, 738–739); Cornblit (1995, 166).

Chapter 6. Emancipation Projects and Dynamics of Native Insurgency (II)

1. Stern (1987a, 29–33, 34–93) highlights the methodological issue of spatial analysis in the literature on eighteenth-century rebellion, assessing its contributions and limitations.

2. O'Phelan (1982, 461–488; 1988, 223–287) and Valle de Siles (1990, 507–548) have tabulated the data contained in the interrogations of prisoners in order to draw a set of conclusions about the movement, its regional (and conjunctural) characteristics, and the contrasts between Cuzco and La Paz.

3. Lewin did, however, mistakenly conceive of the insurrection as radiating out from Cuzco, with Tomás Katari and Túpaj Katari having been in previous contact with the Cuzco leadership. See Lewin (1967). O'Phelan's work has been published in two books (1988, 1995) and a spate of articles. (For a partial set of O'Phelan's references, see bibliography. For a larger register of her production, see the bibliographies in her two books.) Though neither of these historians have dealt at length with La Paz, they have clearly signaled the importance of the region within the greater insurrectionary territory.

4. On La Paz, see Valle de Siles (1990). On Oruro, see Cajías (1987); Cornblit (1995); Robins (1997). On Arica, Tarapacá, and Atacama, see Hidalgo Lehuede (1986). For Chayanta, more of the new research has appeared in shorter texts. See S. Arze, Cajías, and Medinaceli (n.d.); S. Arze (1991); Andrade (1994); Penry (1996); Serulnikov (1996, 1998). See also Ramos Zambrano (1982) on Puno.

5. This is the common view as O'Phelan (1982, 461–462) notes; see also O'Phelan (1988, 223–287; 1995).

6. This assessment is supported by the excellent documentary base available for historical examination of the La Paz theater. Of the surviving diaries concerning the sieges and pacification campaigns—an unusually wealthy and intimate source of information about Indian activities during the war—the majority correspond to the city and provinces of La Paz. See the prologue by Gunnar Mendoza in Valle de Siles (1994); and Valle de Siles (1980). There is also a voluminous documentation in the Archives of La Paz, Sucre, Buenos Aires, and Spain. A valuable portion of the La Paz material—including diaries, Spanish and Indian correspondence, and the testimony of Katari and his partner Bartolina Sisa after their capture—are available in published form.

7. Flores Galindo 1987, 143. For his overall interpretation of the movement, see pp. 133–143.

8. O'Phelan 1988, 260–263; and 1995, 195. Valle de Siles 1990, 530.

9. O'Phelan 1988, 265–267; for her broader treatment, see pp. 223–272. Campbell 1987, 127, 132. Zavaleta 1986, 84–91, 117.

10. AGN IX 7–4–2, fol. 36v. Diez de Medina's febrile imagination and overheated prose may have been fired by his correspondent, Doctor Juan Josef de Segovia, who wrote of Katari as "a base Indian by birth, barbarous in his customs, and even ferocious looking. . . . Truly, only one so ignorant and vile could have such a monstrous body. And once reason has been obscured, it embraces the shadows as things of splendor" (ANB MSS Moreno 1781 No. 96, fol. 226). The reference to Katari's physical deformities is here used to enhance the image of horror.

11. There has been much unnecessary confusion over Katari's place of birth or residence. For an extended biographical treatment of Túpaj Katari, see Valle de Siles (1990, 1–30).

12. Ballivián y Roxas [1872] 1977, 148. This error has been freely repeated in the historiography. It seems that the original rumor confused Julián Apaza with his sister's husband, Alejandro Pañuni, who was indeed the sexton of Ayoayo. Gregoria Apaza testified that the whereabouts of her husband were unknown, and that she presumed he had died in the war (AGI Buenos Aires 319, "Cuaderno No. 5," fols. 2v, 13–13v). In fact, after a journey to Cochabamba, Pañuni joined the camp of Carlos Silvestre Choqueticlla in the Inquisivi valley area where he was not captured until mid-1782. He refrained from acknowledging that he was Túpaj Katari's brother-in-law, yet he was executed all the same (AGN IX 21–2–8, "Copia de testimonio de la sumaria formada a Isabel Guallpa, viuda de Carlos Choqueticlla," 26/VII/1782, fol. 4).

13. Valle de Siles 1994, 301–302. Valle de Siles 1990, 565–566. AGN IX 7–4–2, fol. iv.

14. Ballivián y Roxas [1872] 1977, 144. Borda's report is shot through with the most denigrating and uncomprehending terms of colonial discourse, yet it remains an extraordinarily valuable document for historians of the Indian siege of La Paz. The text may also be consulted in AGI Charcas 595, and in published form in CDIP 2:2:801–818.

15. AGI Charcas 595, "Diario que formo yo Esteban de Loza, escribano de Su Magestad . . . ," fol. 19. The mestizo Bolaños of Sicasica also attested to Katari's low station and character (Valle de Siles 1994, 301–302).

16. Zavaleta 1986, 87, 91.

17. For Borda's report, see Ballivián y Roxas [1872] 1977, 140–156. For Spanish Commander Segurola's notes on Katari as impostor, see p. 24; for Diez de Medina's version, see Valle de Siles 1994, 61–62.

18. Campbell 1987, 129, 131.

19. Ballivián y Roxas [1872] 1977, 131. Germán Arciénagas, cited in Valle de Siles 1980, 17.

20. Valle de Siles 1990, 10–11, 40. Valle de Siles 1994, 121 n.1.

21. Montenegro ([1943] 1993), for example, ignored him altogether. Finot (1954, 130) did see the insurrection as a harbinger of independence, though he contradicts himself by also referring to it as a race war. Cf. also Imaña Castro (1971).

22. An early work in this vein is Paredes ([1897] 1973); see also Aranzaes (1915, 36–43). For the work of other La Paz historians, see Imaña Castro (1971, 1973); Costa de la Torre (1974); Crespo Rodas (1974, 1982, 1987). For a fictional representation, see Díaz Machicao (1964, 1969).

23. Valle de Siles 1980. Fellman Velarde 1968, 234. Valencia Vega 1984, 511–512.

24. The paceñista literature, then, avoids the more overt colonial stereotypes and prejudices we have identified in other work. Yet the sense of horror at what happened two centuries ago and an ulterior identification with the urban camp remain unspoken. On this point, Silvia Rivera's verdict—"And so the nightmare of the Indian siege continues to trouble the sleep of the Bolivian Creole class"— cannot be dismissed (Rivera 1984, 170).

25. Her work on the diaries of the siege was published in Valle de Siles (1980, 1994). Older articles on the insurrection were republished in her principal monograph, Valle de Siles (1990).

26. Valle de Siles 1990, 1–30, 40. There is another current in Bolivian historiography that directly identifies with the Indian forces in 1781 or seeks to recover the experience and struggles of the Aymara people historically. See Grondín (1975); Albó (1984, 1987); Albó and Barnadas (1984, 1990); Cárdenas (1988); Choque (1991); Rivera (1993, 41–45). Not coincidentally, this current has surfaced since the 1970s along with the peasant trade-union movement in Bolivia and the rise of a contemporary "katarista" political and ideological project that critiques present-day internal colonialism and cultural oppression. So far, this work has been forced to rely on published primary sources and has not produced extensive or in-depth monographs. Nevertheless, it has made certain advances in the analysis of socioeconomic and political dynamics of the insurgency. The figure of Túpaj Katari himself has yet to receive careful treatment. For instance, this literature has not addressed the problems posed by his confession before the Spaniards, the colonial and neocolonial stereotypes about his conduct, or the complex cultural and religious dimension to the man. Nonetheless, due to its cultural sensitivity and the energy of political engagement, this current has the potential of providing original insight into the insurrection and recasting the field of late-colonial social history. For other interpretive work that has dealt with Indian political perceptions in the siege of La Paz, see Hidalgo Lehuede (1983); Szeminski (1983, 1993); Thurner (1991); and O'Phelan (1995).

27. AGI Buenos Aires 319, "Cuaderno No. 4," fol. 59.

28. On Katari's early activities, see the confessions of Katari and Bartolina Sisa. The quote is from AGI Buenos Aires 319, "Cuaderno No. 4," fols. 59v–60. On Amaru's circulation, see O'Phelan (1995, 93).

29. CDIP 2:2:555. Valle de Siles 1994, 59.

30. AGN XIII, 28-3-2, "Autos sobre el juicio de las cuentas de Ramón de Anchoríz por todo el tiempo que fue corregidor (Sicasica)," 1780–1783, fols. 171v–172. Valle de Siles 1994, 59.

31. Lewin 1967, 340–341. CDIP 2:2:509.

32. AGI Buenos Aires 319, "Cuaderno No. 5," fols. 3v–4. The reference to "up there" *(lugares de arriba)* was not mystical or mythological, as Szeminski (1993, 242–244) assumed. It was common colonial usage to speak of the "upper provinces," meaning inland and to the south. Here it refers to Buenos Aires, whence travelers were also said to "come down."

33. In one version, he had "spoken and feasted with the king" (S. Arze, Cajías, Medinaceli n.d., 8, 71). In another, he had kissed the king's feet and been shown great love by him; on learning of the abuses in the realm, the king had ordered that repartos be abolished and tribute reduced by two-thirds (CDIP 2:2:237).

34. AGI Buenos Aires 319, "Cuaderno No. 5," fols. 3v–4.

35. CDIP 2:2:509.

36. Diez de Medina gives these accounts in Valle de Siles 1994, 61–62. Hidalgo Lehuede (1983, 128) must be credited as the first author to perceive the importance of Apaza's identification with Tomás Katari.

37. AGN IX 7-4-2, fol. 1v. The emphasis is mine.

38. Apaza first appeared in Ayoayo wearing a veil. Only after he reached La Paz, to mount the siege, did he expose himself to his followers. His own sister, Gregoria Apaza, suggested that the revelation had surprised her (AGI Buenos Aires 319, "Cuaderno No. 5," fol. 4).

39. ANB EC 1782 No. 42, fol. 7. Ballivián y Roxas [1872] 1977, 149–150. Lewin 1967, 876–877.

40. Túpaj Katari also manifested Inka identity through dress, and by travelling in a litter in the traditional manner of an Andean lords (Valle de Siles 1994, 117; 1990, 629; see also O'Phelan 1995, 161–166).

41. Ballivián y Roxas [1872] 1977, 141, 149–152.

42. ANB EC 1781 No. 248, fol. 1. In his decrees, Túpac Amaru declared himself "descendant of the native king" of Peru and Indian of the "royal blood and principal trunk" of the Inka lineage (Lewin 1967, 398, 415–416).

43. Valle de Siles 1994, 61. Ballivián y Roxas [1872] 1977, 24. It should be noted that Szeminski's collection of linguistic evidence does not corroborate Diez de Medina's translation of "túpac." In sum, he glosses the term as "a lord who introduced order" (Szeminski 1993, 218–223). Besides the oidor's own boasting of his polyglot faculties, the fact that, after the surrender or capture of the insurgent leaders, Diez de Medina addressed the Indians assembled at Peñas in both Aymara and Quechua does give him linguistic credibility (Valle de Siles 1994, 120; AGN IX 21-2-8, "Sobre la pacificación de los pueblos sometidos por la expedición de Reseguín," 1782 [54 fols.], fol. 41v).

44. One Felipe Tupacatari assumed the role of loyal interim cacique in Sica-sica in the aftermath of the insurrection (AGN IX 7-7-4, "Don Ramón Anchoríz da la noticia pedida en orden circular . . . ," 7/IX/1783 [11 fols.], fol. 1; ANB EC 1782 No. 30, fol. 1). See also ALP EC 1790 C. 114 E. s.n. (169 fols.), fol. 7v; ANB EC 1775 No. 171, fols. 15a, 16a; as well as ALP EC 1774 C. 95 E. 2, fol. 2.

45. Ballivián y Roxas [1872] 1977, 148.

46. ALP EC 1781 C. 101 E. 2, fol. 10. AGN IX 7-4-2, fols. 5-5v. Ballivián y Roxas [1872] 1977, 167, 172.

47. This account is from Fray Borda in Ballivián y Roxas ([1872] 1977, 153-154). Cf. Valle de Siles (1994, 203). We have now seen two stories about Túpaj Katari intercepting correspondence—in the first case the letter of Tomás Katari and in the second case the letter of Túpac Amaru—and using seized documents for his own political purposes. Given their resemblance, the two stories could be alternate renditions of a single event, but they probably had separate origins. They refer to different moments in the uprising, and Katari's own testimony approximately matches one but not the other story. The Spanish commander Segurola also re-ferred in passing to Katari intercepting correspondence between the Cuzco and Chayanta leaders. But his version sheds no light on the two accounts, and in all likelihood it was based on one or both of them (Ballivián y Roxas [1872] 1977, 24). Cf. also Valle de Siles (1990, 37, 39).

48. For Túpac Amaru's fictional correspondence, see Ballivián y Roxas ([1872] 1977, 158-161). For the new uprising in Pacajes under the Inka Esteban Atahualpa, see ANB EC 1782 No. 32; and ANB EC 1782 No. 42.

49. Within such a politically charged atmosphere, fabricated documentary claims by Indians were in some ways a response to the actual denial or suppression of real documents by regional colonial authorities. When the letter attributed to the communities of four provinces in La Paz declared that Túpac Amaru's legiti-mate decrees had been suppressed, it would have been a credible assertion to many (Ballivián y Roxas [1872] 1977, 135).

50. Valle de Siles 1994, 61. Ballivián y Roxas [1872] 1977, 146-150.

51. ALP EC 1781 C. 101 E. 2, fols. 39v-40, 43-43v. AGN IX 7-4-2, fols. 5v-8v.

52. Valle de Siles 1990, 37. ALP EC 1781 C. 101 E. 2, fol. 49v. Valle de Siles 1994, 260.

53. Ballivián y Roxas [1872] 1977, 147, 148.

54. AGN IX 7-4-2, fols. 2v, 6v. Katari's own declaration about executing Calle diverged from other evidence. In one of his letters, Katari said he was sending the head of Marcelo Calle to Segurola because Calle had been in communication with the Spanish commander. Segurola denied this and said he had independent knowledge that Calle had died in battle a few days earlier (Ballivián y Roxas [1872] 1977, 59; Valle de Siles 1994, 227).

55. AGN IX 7-4-2, fol. 7-8v.

56. AGN IX 7-4-2, fols. 7v-8.

57. One morning when Katari appeared in his fine garb on the hill just above

the central plaza, Spanish soldiers insulted him, calling him a "thief made of nothing but wax." He reacted furiously, charging down the hill with his sword unsheathed, "in the belief that the authority he imagined for himself had been violated." It took fifteen Indians to subdue him and carry him back to their camp (Valle de Siles 1994, 205).

58. Ballivián y Roxas [1872] 1977, 148, 133. Valle de Siles 1994, 190–191.

59. The bishop of La Paz wrote that Katari was an Indian "of low sphere and full of vices . . . a rebellious and insubordinate spirit" . . . who carried out in the towns of Sicasica province . . . the worst atrocities ever known to history." He continued, "I leave to Your Excellency's comprehension the exertions, cares, and anguish that we all suffered, the continual assaults by the rebel and his followers with no regard for the hour of the day or night . . . such that there was never an instant when we were not in the greatest apprehension, since not even the most innocent child was exempt from his atrocities" (Valle de Siles 1990, 189–190; Cf. AGI Charcas 595, "El obispo de La Paz, don Gregorio Francisco Campos, da cuenta a VM del asedio de 109 días . . . ," 30/VII/1781, [4 fols.]).

60. Harris 1994, 59. The analysis in this section is indebted to Harris's insights about the connections between violence and gender in northern Potosí. For more on the role of violence in Andean culture, see Platt (1988); and Urbano (1991).

61. Bertonio [1612] 1984 2:38. Van den Berg 1985, 93. Tschopik 1951, 203–204. See also Mamani (1989, 54–56). For more on the significance of the amaru, usually identified as a snake or a bull that rages at the time of torrential flooding of rivers, see Szeminski (1993, 219–220).

62. ALP EC 1782 C. 102 E. 1. It is also interesting to note that the word *palli,* the surname of the anticolonial community leaders in Ambaná in the 1740s, also signified a large and venomous rattlesnake (Bertonio [1612] 1984 1:94; 2:246). One of the Palli's principal collaborators, Diego Cutili, also went by the alias of "Katari" (ANB Minas T. 127 No. 6/Minas Cat. No. 1517).

63. Ballivián y Roxas [1872] 1977, 132–133. Valle de Siles 1994, 118, 127. Tschopik 1951, 243.

64. Guaman Poma [1615, 64–78] 1980, 1:50–61. The quote is from Guaman Poma, [1615, 65] 1980, 1:52.

65. Valle de Siles 1994, 120–121. Ballivián y Roxas [1872] 1977, 35–36.

66. Saignes 1987b, 153. For more on the cultural and religious role of drinking in the Andes, see Saignes (1993).

67. AGI Charcas 595, "Diario que formo yo Esteban de Loza, escribano de Su Magestad . . . ," fols. 17v–18.

68. Ballivián y Roxas [1872] 1977, 146. See Harris (1994) on the condor as Andean sexual and kin metaphor for the wife-taking son-in-law.

69. ALP EC 1781 C. 101 E. 2, fols. 39v–40, 42v–44, 49v.

70. Lewin 1967, 428–429, 447–461.

71. O'Phelan 1995, 148–156.

72. Ballivián y Roxas [1872] 1977, 135, 150. AGN IX 7-4-2, fols. 17v–18.

73. This account is based on a variety of sources: Ballivián y Roxas [1872] 1977, 144, 151; Valle de Siles 1994, 120–129; AGN IX 7–4–2, fols. 8v–10; Valle de Siles 1990, 19–22, 178–179, 577–579; 1980, 90; and Crespo Rodas 1987, 52–53. Pedro Obaya testified that the peasant interpretation was true and that the priest had confirmed it to him personally, though this may have been a fabrication to convince his interrogators that he was secretly on the side of the Spaniards (Crespo Rodas 1987, 53).

74. Ballivián y Roxas [1872] 1977, 151.

75. Ibid., 135.

76. Ibid., 150. Valle de Siles 1994, 177. According to Esteban de Loza, Katari consulted the box to determine whether a prisoner would be executed or pardoned (AGI Charcas 595, "Diario que formo yo Esteban de Loza, escribano de Su Magestad . . . ," fol. 19).

77. Ballivián y Roxas [1872] 1977, 150.

78. Charcas 595, "Diario que formo yo Esteban de Loza, escribano de Su Magestad . . . ," fols. 19–19v. CDIP 2:3:81. Under interrogation, Katari later denied these reports (AGN IX 7–4–2, fol. 28v). For the evidence regarding Túpac Amaru, see Szeminski (1993, 205, 248).

79. ABUMSA No. 129, fol. s.n. O'Phelan (1995, 176–180) suggests that Indians in the Aymara camp may have been enacting a ritual drama, resembling a Passion play, during Easter week. While there certainly was a heightened ritual atmosphere during the week, there is little evidence of a sustained religious performance. When Katari gave food to the poor, it was a gesture of Christian charity rather than an enactment of the Last Supper. In any case, the killing of the clergyman, as we have seen, was not meant as a sacrificial rite in imitation of Christ's martyrdom.

80. Wachtel 1990, 63–64. Harris 1995, 320. On illas, cf. Van den Berg (1985, 62); Tschopik (1951, 238–240). Abercrombie (1998, 493) poses an alternative hypothesis that the box was a retablo used to hold a Christian saint.

81. Ballivián y Roxas [1872] 1977, 150. Valle de Siles 1994, 177.

82. Their importance was great in solar-oriented Inka ritual before the conquest. Wachtel also notes among the Uru Chipaya, as part of the chthonic cult of the ancestors, that champi found in tombs are said to be able to revive, reflecting "like mirrors" the light of the full moon (Wachtel 1990, 63). For more on the symbolic aspects of mirrors, metals, and money, see Harris (1995, especially pp. 317–318).

83. Bertonio [1612] 1984, 1:405; 2:290. Cf. De Lucca (1983, 245).

84. Bertonio [1612] 1984, 1:405. Harris 1995, 317–318.

85. Katari also sought to prove his power over other dangerous, potentially malignant *(saxra)* forces of nature. He unsheathed his sword and fearlessly attacked the whirlwinds on the altiplano, showing that they would die down while he contracted no sickness from them. For Spaniards unfamiliar with Andean beliefs about malignant winds *(saxra wayra),* such behavior seemed lunacy (AGI

Charcas 595, "Diario que formo yo Esteban de Loza, escribano de Su Magestad . . . ," fol. 19).

86. Harris 1995, 316–318. Tschopik 1951, 262–265.

87. Valle de Siles 1994, 177.

88. When Julián Apaza first appeared publicly in Ayoayo, with peasants expecting to encounter Tomás Katari who had died but was rumored to have resuscitated, he wore a veil that he did not remove. Xavier Albó suggested that this episode may also have been related to the practices of the ch'amakani: "[The ch'amakani] has the power to speak with beings beyond the grave, like the dead themselves, but also with the *achachilas* (lit. ancestors, but now become divine and identified with the mountain peaks that are guardians of the area) and others. He can also bring back the *ajayu,* the spirit or 'shadow' of living beings, which can be lost to fright or illness. The ceremony in which he summons the dead or the achachilas usually takes place in a dark setting, with him squatting in the center, totally covered by a poncho and acting as a ventriloquist. He uses a normal or deep voice when he is talking; and a falsetto to indicate the dead person or achachila or other being summoned. In any case, though the ch'amakani can bring back the spirit or ajayu of sick or crazy people, these ceremonies do not lead to a 'resurrection'" (cited in Hidalgo Lehuede 1983, 134). On the ch'amakani, see also Van den Berg (1985, 49). Cf. Tschopik (1951) on the Aymara ritual specialist known as the *paqo* in Chucuito.

89. AGN IX 7–4–2, fols. 8–8v.

90. AGI Charcas 595, "Diario que formo yo Esteban de Loza, escribano de Su Magestad . . . ," fol. 19v.

91. AGI Charcas 595, "Diario que formo yo Esteban de Loza, escribano de Su Magestad . . . ," fol. 19.

92. Ballivián y Roxas [1872] 1977, 148, 150.

93. Ibid., 154.

94. Ibid., 132, 133, 135–136.

95. Ibid., 145, 149.

96. Ibid., 167.

97. Ibid., 133, 172. These expressions were also used by the Quechua leaders in La Paz and were part of the general vision of Amaru. Consider this exposition by Diego Cristóbal: "It was ordered that the *chapetones* and foreigners be distanced from these dominions, being usurers in them, and kept to their destinations, where they should subsist in the service of the Majesty that ruled them, and whence they came as apostates and escapees" (CDIP 2:3:127).

98. The following passage illustrates this thinking. It is given in the original Spanish in order to demonstrate the full flavor of the letters reputed to be "incoherent": "Y así Cristianos V.V. quieren a malas mañana lo verán con el favor de Dios, ya les tengo por donde pegar avance, y así no hay más remedio que tenga; si V.V. se porfían más no hay ni para tres horas con el favor de Dios para mis soldados, le dice acaban sin duda, y así no hay más remedio tengan los que tuvieren las

armas, no será caso para mí con el favor de Dios; y sepan han de volver por tierra y polvo, y a ver cual nos ayudará de Dios y cual seremos hombres de carajos, y así este es de lo alto" (Ballivián y Roxas [1872] 1977, 132). For a sample of his published correspondence, see the documents published with Segurola's diary therein; and Valle de Siles (1990, 36–40).

99. Valle de Siles 1990, 37. Ballivián y Roxas [1872] 1977, 132.

100. AGN IX 21–2–8 "Sobre la pacificación de los pueblos sometidos por la expedición de Reseguín," 1782. AGN IX 7–4–2, fol. 16.

101. This interpretation of Katari's death, with accompanying quotations, is based on AGI Charcas 595, "Diario que formo yo Esteban de Loza, escribano de Su Magestad . . . ," fols. 20v–21.

102. The linguistic evidence for the storm analogies comes from Bertonio. He noted not only the Aymara association of cloudbursts with warriors' collective outcry, but that of lightening and thunder with rifle or artillery fire ([1612] 1984, 2: 126–127, 173). See also Platt (1988, especially 398–403). For examples of Indian din and commotion, see Valle de Siles (1994, 117–119).

103. Ballivián y Roxas [1872] 1977, 149, 135–136.

104. S. Arze, Cajías, and Medinaceli n.d., 9. The slogan was also heard in Oruro (Cornblit 1995, 183, 186).

105. Ballivián y Roxas [1872] 1977, 134, 148–152. AGN IX 7–4–2, fols. 21v–22. Crespo Rodas 1987.

106. It was reported that Chuquimamani had worked in the ecclesiastical tribunal and the notary's office in La Paz (Ballivián y Roxas [1872] 1977, 145, 149; Valle de Siles 1994, 108, 119, 212).

107. AGN IX 7–4–2, fol. 21. In colonial state administration, the oidor was a magistrate on the political and judicial tribunal of the audiencia, which was subject to the authority of the viceroy (the title assumed by Túpaj Katari).

108. For this episode see Ballivián y Roxas [1872] 1977, 140–143.

109. Borda interpreted the undoing of the knot as similar to the opening of a sealed letter, in this case Katari's decree. Aymara linguistic evidence, both historical and contemporary, suggests that the tearing or cutting of thread is abstractly associated with separation and delimitation, and, in an explicit politico-legal sense, with judgment, sentencing, and the settlement of disputes (De Lucca 1983, 419–420. Bertonio [1612] 1984, 2:345–346).

110. Ballivián y Roxas [1872] 1977, 145.

111. Two elements of Christian religious practice that Indians apparently did continue to spurn were confession and the invocation of Jesus when they expired (Ballivián y Roxas [1872] 1977, 150; CDIP 2:3:147–148). The other evidence of overtly nativist policy in La Paz was the report that European livestock and seed were to be destroyed (ANB EC 1782 No. 97, fol. 1v).

112. Valle de Siles 1994, 117, 271. Ballivián y Roxas [1872] 1977, 131–132. AGN IX 7–4–2, fol. 4.

113. Katari reportedly announced to his troops that Túpac Amaru had nearly

conquered Cuzco and that as soon as he reached La Paz, Katari would accompany him all the way to Buenos Aires (Crespo 1987, 60, 65).

114. AGN IX 21–2–8, "Copia de testimonio de la sumaria formada a Isabel Guallpa, viuda de Carlos Choqueticlla," 26/VII/1782, fol. 4v. ALP EC 1781 C. 101 E. 2, fol. 14.

115. Valle de Siles 1990, 31–43.

116. While "racial" discourse, narrowly defined, did not possess the salience for eighteenth-century elites that it would come to acquire a century later, there were important colonial origins for the scientific or scientistic discourse on race that would develop in the nineteenth century.

117. For the prophecy, see CDTA 2:229. Katari's remark echoed the haughty Andrés Túpac Amaru who used the same term, referring to creoles and Europeans, in a letter to the city (Ballivián y Roxas [1872] 1977, 170–171). For other examples of evidence that Indians targeted "whites," see ALP EC 1781 C. 101 E. 2, fols. 39v–40, 76, 80.

118. Ballivián y Roxas [1872] 1977, 141; 135–136.

119. Hardman 1988, 197–199. For other references in the same volume, see Albó (1988, 438, 443, 601).

120. Ballivián y Roxas [1872] 1977, 152. Valle de Siles 1994, 138. For the quote from Oruro, see Cajías (1987, 738–739); Cornblit (1995, 166). For Chayanta, see S. Arze, Cajías, Medinaceli (n.d., 82–83).

121. O'Phelan (1995, 105–137) has also analyzed the radicalization of the insurrection in terms of the violence applied to political "traitors." It should be noted that the idea of the "traitor" was initially framed, by Túpac Amaru, not only in relation to himself but to the king of Spain. In general perception and practice, the traitor came to be seen most immediately as a rebel against the Inka ruler.

122. Ballivián y Roxas [1872] 1977, 139, 149–150.

123. Hence Katari testified that caciques along with corregidores and customs-house officials were the three primary targets of the insurgents besieging the city (AGN IX 7–4–2, fol. 4v). The Quechua colonel Andrés Laura also included caciques along with corregidores, deputies, and customshouse officials as forming an insufferable band of thieves (Ballivián y Roxas [1872] 1977, 168).

124. ANB EC 1801 No. 25; for quotes see fols. 60–60v, 69v. We have already cited the similar case of Dionicio Mamani, cacique of Chulumani, who spurned an order from Túpac Amaru to seize the corregidor of Sicasica. After notifying the corregidor of the letter, he fled to Cochabamba and later returned to die in battle outside the city of La Paz (ANB EC 1808 No. 138).

125. ANB EC 1782 No. 97, fols. 21–21v.

126. Szeminski 1993, 235–236. Diego Cristóbal Túpac Amaru publicly maintained José Gabriel's moral-religious arguments after the latter's death, while Andrés Túpac Amaru, during informal moments in La Paz, voiced the more radical line equating all "traitors" with "devils" who must die (CDIP 2:3:127; ANB EC 1782 No. 62, fols. 64v–65).

127. Ballivián y Roxas [1872] 1977, 152.

128. Valle de Siles 1994, 160–161. As we noted in the previous chapter, radical community forces in Oruro aimed to decapitate the icon that they saw as the spiritual patroness of that city. They held that the Virgen del Rosario de Santo Domingo was a witch whose evil powers stymied their efforts (Cajías 1987, 737–738; Cornblit 1995, 179–180).

129. Valle de Siles 1994, 121. The emphasis is mine.

130. ANB EC 1781 No. 244, fol. 2.

131. On the complex, cross-cutting lines of solidarity and antagonism in La Paz, see also Albó (1984).

132. AGN IX 5–5–2, "Corregidor de La Paz, Lafitta, sobre levantamiento de Pacajes," 9/XI/1771 (2 fols.).

133. AGN IX 7–4–2, fols. 4–4v, 28. Separate evidence supports Katari's version that the Indians decided to attack the city because Spanish military forces had organized against them; see Valle de Siles (1990, 563–564). On the Viacha massacre, see Valle de Siles (1994, 81–84).

134. ANB EC 1782 No. 97, fol. 13. Valle de Siles 1994, 249, 161, 126.

135. Gregoria Apaza testified that at the start of the insurrection the leaders only sought to eliminate corregidores, Europeans, and others employed as collectors of taxes, but later, for reasons she did not clarify, they resolved to destroy all whites and level the cities of Sorata and La Paz (AGI Buenos Aires 319, "Cuaderno No. 5," fol. 8v).

136. For Túpac Amaru's letters to Cuzco, see Lewin (1967, 398–399, 456–457). For the letters of Andrés, see the documents in Ballivián y Roxas ([1872] 1977, especially 158–161).

137. See Katari's letters among the documents in Ballivián y Roxas ([1872] 1977), including the fabricated letter from José Gabriel Túpac Amaru (131–132). In the latter, the Inka states that those "who are not obedient to my command will be destroyed from the root, for the bad fruit should be entirely wiped out." Indians in Oruro also understood that Túpac Amaru had ordered the "annihilation" of the city (Cornblit 1995, 183).

138. ANB EC 1801 No. 25, fol. 61. ALP EC 1781 C. 101 E. 2, fol. 67.

139. Costa de la Torre 1974.

140. Platt 1988, 397–403.

141. See Szeminski (1993, 236–240); and also Hidalgo Lehuede (1983, 125, 133), including Albó's comment. For other ethnographic evidence of the radical destruction (including the act of cannibalism) of evil sorcerers, see Bandelier (1910, 127).

142. Platt 1988; for his interpretive comments on the Andean insurrection, see 428–430.

143. This spatial hypothesis coincides with the microlevel findings of Morner and Trelles (1987) for Cuzco. They establish a correlation between insurgent areas and higher-altitude zones with fewer haciendas and non-Indians.

144. ANB EC 1782 No. 42. For more on the cacicazgo in Santiago de Machaca and Berenguela, see ANB EC 1799 No. 83.

145. AGN IX 7–4–2, fols. 7–7v. ANB EC 1808 No. 109, fols. 40v, 54, 58v; I thank Ana María Lema for calling my attention to this document.

146. ANB EC 1801 No. 25. ANB EC 1808 No. 138. ANB EC 1807 No. 11.

147. ANB EC 1801 No. 25, fols. 44–44v. AGI Charcas 429, "Testimonio del expediente obrado sobre méritos y servicios de don Juan de Dios Thomás Balboa, cacique de Laja," 1786, fols. 55, 56v. The generalization given here about the role of caciques throughout the region during the insurrection is drawn from abundant documentation in Bolivian, Argentine, and Spanish archives.

148. AGI Buenos Aires 319, "Cuaderno No. 4," (88 fols.), fol. 53. ALP EC 1781 C. 101 E. 2, fols. 40, 49–49v, 80.

149. AGN IX 7–4–2, fols. 5–5v, 12.

150. AGN IX 7–4–2, fol. 9v. AGI Buenos Aires 319, "Cuaderno No. 4," fols. 47–47v.

151. Ballivián y Roxas [1872] 1977, 145–146, 154. For historiographic reference points, see O'Phelan (1985, 260–263); Hidalgo Lehuede (1986, 287); and Campbell (1987, 131).

152. Valle de Siles 1990, 538–540. AGN IX 7–4–2, fol. 2v.

153. ALP EC 1781 C. 101 E. 2, fols. 49–49v. AGI Buenos Aires 319, "Cuaderno No. 1," fols. 24–26v; and "Cuaderno No. 3," fol. 74.

154. AGN IX 7–4–2, fols. 3, 25.

155. O'Phelan 1995, 115–116.

156. On the Sorata episode, see ANB EC 1782 No. 82; ANB EC 1782 No. 62; ANB EC 1781 No. 244; and Valle de Siles (1990, 79–129).

157. Cornblit 1995, 154–155. AGI Charcas 597, "Representación de fray Eugenio Gutierrez sobre las causas de la sublevación," 1783, primer informe, fol. 8; segundo informe, fols. 8–8v.

158. AGI Buenos Aires 319, "Cuaderno No. 4," fols. 60v, 77.

Chapter 7. The Aftermath of Insurgency and Renegotiation of Power

1. A report on tithe collection in Guarina in 1782 described wholesale loss of life in the mountain hamlets where insurgents had sought refuge and general poverty in the town's jurisdiction. An important site for insurgent forces, Guarina was a prime target of military repression and endured the subsequent burden of sustaining royalist troops (AA Juzgado Episcopal 1782 [XII] No. 133).

2. A week later he managed to scrape up another 1,246 pesos. The cacique claimed he had collected them from his subjects, but treasury officials were not entirely convinced this was so (AGN IX 6–2–3, "Méritos y servicios del Capitán de Cavallería Don Francisco Antonio Guerrero y Oliden, Justicia Mayor de Omasuyos," 1783, fol. 9; AGN IX 30–3–2, "Doña María Justa Salazar viuda de don

Matías Calaumana, cacique de Guarina, sobre esclarecer el derecho al cacicazgo," 1783, fol. 10).

3. AGN IX 30–3–2, "Doña María Justa Salazar viuda de don Matías Calaumana, cacique de Guarina, sobre esclarecer el derecho al cacicazgo," 1783, fol. 12.

4. AGN IX 30–3–2, "Doña María Justa Salazar viuda de don Matías Calaumana, cacique de Guarina, sobre esclarecer el derecho al cacicazgo," 1783, fols. 1–12. ANB EC 1782 No. 43.

5. Her lawyer argued, "A certain affection or spirit of partiality among the Indians arises for whomever governs. Consequently there is a growing lack of subordination and disaffection toward the legitimate successor, because everyone, and especially the Indian due to his idiotic nature, follows the rising sun, as the common saying goes, that is, the current ruler. This is even more so if he governs in full view and with the knowledge and tolerance of the woman they know is the legitimate proprietress." AGN IX 30–3–2, "Doña María Justa Salazar viuda de don Matías Calaumana, cacique de Guarina, sobre esclarecer el derecho al cacicazgo," 1783, fols. 1–8, 43–46v; the quote is from fol. 43v.

6. ALP Padrones Coloniales, Omasuyos, 1790, "Testimonio del expediente formado sobre los sobrantes de tributos del pueblo de Guarina." Silverio Torres would take over a second time and was succeeded after the turn of the century by Manuel Bustillos. Bustillos had family ties in Guarina, and also married the heiress to the Carabuco cacicazgo, with whom he joined in the lengthy legal battle against Juan Bautista Goyzueta. On the complex regional links between these and related creole, mestizo, and cacique families, see for example ANB EC 1807 No. 11. Matías Calaumana's daughter married José Santa Cruz y Villavicencio, a creole military man who had fought in 1781 and became governor of Moxos and never seems to have sought local political authority in Guarina. Their son, Andrés de Santa Cruz y Calaumana, would later come to fame as the Mariscal de Zepita— independence hero, president of Bolivia, and protector of the Peruvian-Bolivian Confederation.

7. The reference was to "*el particular y económico gobierno que llevan allá entre sí los tributarios con los hilacatas y segundas*" (ALP Padrones Coloniales, Omasuyos, 1790, "Testimonio del expediente formado sobre los sobrantes de tributos del pueblo de Guarina," fol. 17v).

8. ALP EC 1787 C. 109 E. s.n., esp. fols. 6–7, 13, 51–51v, 58v, 60–60v. ALP EC 1805 C. 139 E. 27, fol. 2. For references to other such land struggles in Guarina in this period, see AC, Cuaderno de documentos referentes a la Hacienda de Cullucachi, No. 7, Instrumentos de la hacienda y posesión adjudicada a don Pedro Aliaga y su esposa doña Isabel Dorado (1801); and ALP EP 1893 [1898] C. 119 E. s.n., fols. 17v–18. I am grateful to Seemin Qayum for the last reference.

9. For stimulating work that has begun to address this, see Abercrombie (1998); O'Phelan (1997); Penry (1996); Rasnake (1988); Saignes (1991); and Sala i Vila (1996b).

10. Valle de Siles 1990, 349–412.

11. ANB EC 1781 No. 241. ANB EC 1782 No. 32. ANB EC 1782 No. 42. ANB EC 1782 No. 149d (número borrado/s.n.). For other reports of ongoing agitation in the lake district, with purported ties to the Tupamarus to the north and other allies as far south as Chuquisaca (La Plata), see ALP EC 1782 C. 102 E. 2.

12. Lewin 1967, 526, 794.

13. His campaign was nonetheless effective in instilling fear among the local population. Said one witness: "Due to the urgency of the summons to appear, everyone thought it meant another [uprising] like the last time. Hence their confusion because they didn't want to find themselves involved in similar travails. . . . The superior authorities would think they were to blame, and would wipe them out in war." This was evidently the psychological effect desired by authorities. In the words of the subdelegate of Oruro: "It would be appropriate to punish them in order that the memory of this incident intimidate them and let them come to see, as they do now only in a vacillating way, that the king is powerful" (ALP EC 1786 C. 107 E. s.n.).

14. CDIP 2:3:213. According to colonial law, Indians were not under the jurisdiction of the Inquisition. Indians and their representatives in court regularly appealed to the Laws of the Indies, which contained a series of provisions establishing the legal and civil rights of Indians.

15. AGN IX 5–5–5, "El modo de conservar el reino del Perú (borrador)." It is quite possible that Juan Bautista Zavala, or someone close to him, was also the anonymous peninsular Spanish author of this tract. In its tone and contents, it resembles Zavala's letters written during and after the insurrection.

16. Santamaría 1977, 268–269.

17. Barragán 1990, 85–122.

18. Barragán and Thomson 1993.

19. During one political conflict in Calamarca (Pacajes) in 1790, the interim cacique and the local priest threatened to bring troops from La Paz to kill community members. It was the priest, during his Sunday sermon, who threatened to let flow "rivers of blood" as in 1781. Thus, even a decade later, the repression of the war remained deeply etched in local memory, and the specter of future military violence was invoked to instill community quiescence (ALP EC 1790 C. 115 E. s.n. (18 fols.); for the quote, see fol. 3v).

20. ALP EC 1786 C. 107, fol. 2v. ANB EC 1783 No. 180, fol. 4v.

21. ANB EC 1802 No. 32. ANB EC 1802 No. 48; the quote is from fol. 2. Other examples of this could be given for many towns in each of the provinces of La Paz from the 1780s through the 1800s. To cite only one, the cacique of Caquiaviri (Pacajes), Manuel Francia, was also alguacil mayor of the partido, alcalde pedáneo, alcabala collector, while having other unmentioned "other occupations." He was also named on an interim basis to fill the vacant cacicazgo in nearby Santiago de Berenguela. See ALP EC 1789 C. 113 E. s.n. (1 fol.); ALP EC 1799 C. 129 E. s.n.; ANB EC 1799 No. 83, fol. 12; and ANB EC 1804 No. 23, fol. 18v.

22. The alcalde pedáneo was occasionally also referred to as *alcalde de aldea* or alcade mayor, but should not be confused with the Indian alcalde mayor. The candidacy of the alcalde pedáneo was proposed by the subdelegate, for whom he acted as commissioner, and his title was granted by the intendant. His formal functions were to administer justice in all cases that required prompt remedy; to prevent public sins; to assist the collection of tribute; and to resolve verbally debt squabbles involving less than fifty pesos. In cases of theft, death, or injury, he was to receive summary testimony, arrest the delinquents, confiscate their property, and inform the subdelegate so that he could rule on the case. The alcalde pedáneo did not possess the authority to draft judicial documents. See ANB EC 1801 No. 36, fol. 23; ANB EC 1800 No. 54, fol. 116; and AGN IX 35–3–6, "Autos seguidos por los vecinos del pueblo de Irupana sobre que se les nombren dos alcaldes ordinarios," 1807, fol. 6.

23. ANB EC 1803 No. 109, fols. 17–17v. Cf. ALP EC 1796 C. 123 E. 31, fol. 31.

24. For general appraisals along these lines, see Lynch 1958; Fisher 1970; Fisher 1982; Fisher et al. 1990; Pietschmann 1996.

25. In particular, O'Phelan (1988, 1996) has emphasized the impacts of the reforms, especially in their economic dimension, as a cause of rebellion. Serulnikov (1998, 1999) has analyzed the local consequences of the reforms—in their economic, political, and cultural dimensions—as a leading cause of Indian protest in Potosí.

26. For urban studies of the impacts of the reforms, see O'Phelan (1978); McFarlane (1990); and Cahill (1990). For sustained examination of the impacts in the Andean countryside, see Larson (1998); Sala I Vila (1996b); Serulnikov (1998, 1999).

27. The 1782 regulations of the Ordinance for Buenos Aires were extended to the rest of the realm, and the intendancy system was installed in the Viceroyalty of Peru in 1784. In 1786, an updated Ordinance for New Spain superseded the original one everywhere outside of Río de la Plata (Lynch 1958).

28. The tensions between the viceroy and the superintendant quickly led, in 1788, to the suppression of the new post, with the viceroy absorbing the superintendant's functions (Lynch 1958, 83–84).

29. This northern tip of the viceroyalty was subject to ongoing changes and overlapping jurisdictional claims. The Puno intendancy's political integrity was fragmented in 1787 when Lampa, Azángaro, and Carabaya were attached to the new Audiencia of Cuzco, ruled by Peru's viceroy, while Puno and Chucuito remained subject to the Audiencia of Charcas and the viceroy in Buenos Aires. In 1796, this problem was resolved when the entire intendancy of Puno shifted to the Viceroyalty of Peru. In its ecclesiastical administration, no such unity was achieved. Puno and Chucuito remained within the bishopric of La Paz, while Lampa, Azángaro, and Carabaya belonged to the bishopric of Cuzco.

30. Lynch 1958. Fisher 1970. Pietschmann (1996) offers a comparable view for New Spain.

31. Lynch (1958) notes the problems in La Paz and the Viceroyalty of La Plata as a whole. To cite a representative case from La Paz, community members in Irupana and Laza protested against the subdelegate Pedro Flores Larrea for his reparto practices, local monopoly over coca trade, land accumulation, and manipulation of community authorities. A dependent and reparto agent of previous corregidores, he allegedly acquired his post through the influence of the outgoing corregidor Albizuri who needed someone to collect his outstanding reparto debts. Flores Larrea continued his predecessor's abuses and managed to go from rags to riches (AGN IX 5-5-4, "Representación de indios de Irupana y Laza, partido de Chulumani, sobre extorsiones del subdelegado y cacique," 1784 [7 fols.]). Colonial authorities were aware that subdelegates continued to distribute goods illegally and debated how to deal with this issue. However, due particularly to the power of vested commercial interests, the reparto problem was never resolved (Moreno Cebrián 1977; Stein 1981). For other local complaints about the pervasiveness of illegal repartos and the ongoing abuses of subdelegates in La Paz, see ALP EC 1792 C. 117 E. s.n. (22 fols.), fols. 12–12v; ANB EC 1792 No. 204; ALP EC 1795 C. 122, E. s.n. (6 fols.); AGN IX 5-6-1, "Indios de Jesús de Machaca contra su cacique Pedro Ramírez de la Parra," 4/III/1795 (11 fols.); AGN IX 5-6-3, "Obispo don Remigio de la Santa y Ortega, de La Paz, sobre varios asuntos," 1800, fol. 2; ALP EC 1802 C. 134 E. 20; and ANB EC 1803 No. 78, fol. 16v. On treasury corruption, see ALP Gaveta No. 6. Neoreparto practices and subdelegate abuses have also been extensively documented in the Viceroyalty of Peru. See, for example, Fisher (1970); Moreno Cebrián (1977); Cahill (1988).

32. Larson 1988, 276–284.

33. ALP EC 1781 C. 101 E. 14.

34. ALP EC 1784 C. 104 E. s.n. (4 fols.).

35. AGN IX 7-7-4, "Sobre el informe que hacen los comisionados para la revisita (del Partido de Chulumani)," 1802. AGN XIII 17-7-4, Libro 3, 1792, fols. 344, 347–353v. ANB Minas Ruck No. 217/Minas Cat. No. 2165a, fols. 1–5, 25v, 27, 147–159. On community property, treasuries, and mortgage funds, see Escobedo Mansilla (1997); and Quiroz (1993, 59–67; 1994, 206–209).

36. ANB EC 1777 [1771] No. 68. ANB EC 1779 [1787?] No. 219. AGI Charcas 531. Real Academia de la Historia (RAH), Mata Linares 20:282–282v. Similar radical cultural measures—preventing certain forms of dress and dance, for example, or the use of Quechua—were proposed in Cuzco during and after the civil war. It is possible that where repressive measures were directed against specific elements of Inka political culture, they were more effective (Walker 1999, 53–54).

37. Vollmer 1967. Santamaría 1977, 254. TePaske and Klein 1982 (note especially 2:x). Klein 1973, 1993, 1998. See also Larson (1988, 284 ff.); Fisher (1970, 111–114, 123); and Sala i Vila (1996, 33–42).

38. ANB EC 1782 No. 58, fol. 11 (emphasis is mine). For more on initial reconstruction efforts in Azángaro, Lampa, and Carabaya, see also ANB EC 1782 No. 59.

39. See the discussion of cacicazgo historiography in chapter 3.

40. While the periodization and causality may differ from region to region, my understanding of La Paz complements other work for Upper and Lower Peru that points to the midcentury origin of cacicazgo decline. Stern (1987a, 75), Larson (1979; 1988), Rasnake (1988), Penry (1996), and Serulnikov (1998) all suggest or conclude that cacique powers were seriously challenged over decades prior to 1780. Ultimately, my own findings coincide with the periodization of O'Phelan (1997) in her treatment of the gradual collapse of the cacicazgo in the late-colonial period.

Important new work is emerging on the post-1780 period in the Andean countryside. For a sampling, consult, along with the earlier work of Cahill (1984, 1986, 1988), Hunefeldt (1982), and Jacobsen (1993), the recent contributions of Peralta (1991), Sala i Vila (1996b), Soux (1999), Thurner (1996), and Walker (1999). The cacicazgo studies of Díaz Rementería (1977) and Garrett (2001) also emphasize the institution's post-1780 decline.

41. In the age of Toledan reform, Juan Polo de Ondegardo and Juan de Matienzo had favored replacing hereditary lords with elected municipal officials as community governors (Sala i Vila 1996, 68–69).

42. O'Phelan (1985, 229) calculates that a total of twenty-five caciques sided with Túpac Amaru. Of these, twelve were from his province of Canas y Canchis or Tinta.

43. Díaz Rementería 1977, 189–196. Sala i Vila 1996b, 65–74.

44. For the following discussion, see AGI Buenos Aires 319, "Cuaderno No. 5," fols. 409v–418; and AGI Buenos Aires 321. For Pacheco's document see AGI Buenos Aires 321, No. 16, "Testimonio del expediente obrado por el superior gobierno del Río de la Plata para informar a su magestad con justificación del estado de su distrito . . . ," (37 fols.). Valle de Siles (1990, 583–620) provides a helpful synthesis of this material.

45. AGI Buenos Aires 321, No. 16, "Testimonio del expediente obrado por el superior gobierno del Río de la Plata para informar a su magestad con justificación del estado de su distrito . . . ," fols. 12–12v.

46. AGI Buenos Aires 321, No. 16, "Testimonio del expediente obrado por el superior gobierno del Río de la Plata para informar a su magestad con justificación del estado de su distrito . . . ," fols. 19, 20, 26. Pacheco also described the task as one of "trying to finish making them into true Spaniards" (fol. 25).

47. Pacheco seems to have been particularly influenced by the cultural recommendations of Diez de Medina. See Abercrombie (1998) on the attempts to colonize indigenous memory, especially for the early-colonial era.

48. For the range of opinions, see AGI Buenos Aires 321. Another example of the radical anticacique stance, similar to that of Areche, comes from the Oruro friar Eugenio Gutiérrez. He considered caciques one of the prime causes of the insurrection because they symbolically evoked a native sovereignty at odds with that of the Spanish Catholic monarchs. They also, he maintained, stirred up Indian subjects with tales of their gentile past and ancient emperors (AGI Charcas 597,

"Representación de fray Alonso [Eugenio] Gutiérrez sobre las causas de la sublevación," 10/VIII/1783).

49. For the quotes in this and the previous paragraphs, see AGI Buenos Aires 321, No. 16, "Testimonio del expediente obrado por el superior gobierno del Río de la Plata para informar a su magestad con justificación del estado de su distrito . . . ," fols. 28v, 30, 31.

50. *Encomenderos* were the Spanish conquistadors who held the large estates known as *encomiendas* in the sixteenth century.

51. AGI Buenos Aires 321, No. 16, "Testimonio del expediente obrado por el superior gobierno del Río de la Plata para informar a su magestad con justificación del estado de su distrito . . . ," fols. 28–28v.

52. As he dispatched the files of Pacheco and his informants to Spain in early 1783, Viceroy Vértiz noted that the survey of opinions was incomplete and insufficient to draw up a definitive policy. Nonetheless, he preferred to submit the reports as an indication of the state of debate rather than suffer additional delays. I have not found a definitive statement of policy from a later date.

53. AGI Charcas 595, "Al virrey de Buenos Aires para que haciendo entender a la audiencia de La Plata que no admita de los indios informaciones algunas de las que solían presentar para calificar su descendencia de los primitivos reyes gentiles, recoja la obra o historia del Inka Garcilaso con los demás papeles que se expresan. Reservada," 21/IV/1782. AGI Lima 1049, "Carta reservada (de la real resolución) a los virreyes del Perú y Buenos Aires sobre provisión de cacicazgos," 28/IV/1783.

54. ALP Gaveta No. 9; reproduced in Arze Aguirre (1987, 227–230). For further discussion of legislation, see Díaz Rementería (1977) and Sala I Villa (1996b).

55. ANB EC 1785 No. 23. ANB EC 1782 No. 100.

56. ANB EC 1782 No. 100, fols. 127–127v. ALP EC 1791 C. 116 E. s.n. (1 fol.). ANB EC 1795 No. 154, fol. 8. ANB EC 1796 No. 97, fols. 9–10. Nuria Sala i Vila (1996b) has carefully examined the problems surrounding the collection of tribute in this period and the ways in which they contributed to the cacicazgo crisis. The dynamics she describes for Lower Peru are closely matched by those in La Paz. On this point, however, there is one important clarification to make. Sala contends that the intendancy legislation formally separated caciques from tribute collection, thereby constituting one of the two prime causes of the cacicazgo crisis. In the viceroyalty of Río de La Plata, the Ordinance of Intendants continued to allow caciques to carry out their traditional role as tribute collectors, and there is evidence of legitimate, titled caciques doing so. I see the loss of tributary functions by many caciques as a contingent result of local political maneuvers by regional officials and local town notables rather than an explicit policy legislated by the state.

57. In Callapa, community members complained: "If they could remove and replace caciques every day or every week, they would do so because it brings them a fine profit" (ALP EC 1791 C. 116). In Ayoayo, the community asserted: "We are not satisfied with the rule of the interim caciques due to the continual mutation of them and their different characters and the little love they have for us. . . . As town

residents, many of them extort us for their own profit" (ANB EC 1801 No. 25, fol. 53). See also ANB EC 1796 No. 97, fol. 9; and ANB EC 1804 No. 33, fol. 15.

58. The audiencia's orders were emitted on December 20, 1795 and February 27, 1796. See next note for the archival source.

59. RAH, Colección Mata Linares, Tomo 7:416–441; Tomo 78:80–83. The superintendant's report (of July 26, 1796) is included in the latter tome.

60. AGI Charcas 446, "La audiencia de Charcas informa a su magestad con documentos los excesos del gobernador intendente de La Paz y la inobservancia de la real cédula de 9/V/1790," 25/IX/1798. For the quotes, see fols. 1–2, 9v.

61. ALP EC 1797 C. 125 E. s.n., fols. 15v–16. ANB EC 1800 No. 140. On the Instrucción Metódica del Ramo de Contribución de Indios of 1815 and the debate surrounding it, see ANB EC 1821 No. 5, fols. 12–14v, 33–36v. See also Sala I Vila (1996b, 247–251).

62. AGN IX 5–6–1, "Indios de Jesús de Machaca contra su cacique Pedro Ramírez de la Parra," (11 fols.). ALP EC 1795 C. 122 Expedientes 4, 8, 25. For a general indictment (whose authorship is unknown) of caciques in the districts of Pacajes, Sicasica, and Yungas, see ANB EC 1792 No. 204.

63. ANB Minas T. 151 Complemento (1789)/Cat. No. 1945a. ALP EC 1790 C. 115 Expedientes s.n. (2 expedientes of 1 fol. each). ANB EC 1791 No. 166. ANB EC 1802 No. 32. ANB EC 1802 No. 48. ANB EC 1803 No. 137. ANB EC 1818 No. 51.

64. ANB EC 1771 No. 27; for the quote, see fol. 41v. Another witness echoed the same notion: "The Indians are a people who have always got it backwards *[gente al revés]*. The bad seems good to them, and the good bad. Thus, they understand the cacique's zeal in a contrary fashion" (fol. 35v).

65. See the treatment of the Pacajes insurgency in chapters 4 and 5. Limachi's acquittal by the audiencia is cited in AGI Charcas 592, "Autos de la Real Audiencia de Charcas y real cédula sobre repartos," (14 fols.), fols. 7–7v.

66. ANB EC 1792 No. 204, fol. 4v. ALP EC 1799 C. 129 E. s.n. (2 fols.).

67. Extensive evidence for this, especially in the preinsurrectionary period, is given in the community conflicts examined in chapters 3 and 4. The same activities of lower-level political representatives are reflected in the postinsurrectionary documentation.

68. ANB EC 1753 No. 99, fol. 20. ANB EC 1756 No. 5, fol. 5. For other examples from the mid- to late eighteenth century, see ANB EC 1754 No. 62, fol. 26v; ANB EC 1770 No. 160, fol. 14; ANB EC 1771 No. 74, fols. 21v; ALP EC 1789 C. 113 E. s.n., fol. 15; ALP EC 1790 C. 115 E. s.n. (18 fols.), fols. 2v–3; and ALP EC 1797 C. 125 E. s.n. (128 fols.), fol. 16. At the turn of the century in Berenguela, two segundas came forward offering to take over community tributary functions in order to prevent the interim appointment of outsiders as caciques and tribute collectors (ANB EC 1799 No. 83, fol. 6v).

69. ANB EC 1780 No. 58, fol. 1. ALP EC 1802 C. 134 E. 20, fol. 4. ANB EC 1804 No. 33, fols. 15, 18v. For other references to lower-level authorities supplanting (or proposing to supplant) caciques in community government and

administration, see ANB EC 1760 No. 11, fols. 289–291v (case is from 1734); and ALP Padrones Coloniales Omasuyos 1790, fol. 17v.

70. ALP EC 1795 C. 122 E. 3, fols. 11–12v. See also ALP EC 1808 C. 144 E. 53, fol. 4; and ALP EC 1794 C. 121 E. s.n., fol. 7.

71. ANB EC 1809 No. 14, f 77.

72. ALP EC 1793 C. 119 E. s.n. (2 fols.).

73. For the Laza case, see ANB EC 1796 No. 97, fols. 9–14v (the quote is from fol. 9); and ANB EC 1821 No. 2. Indians in Italaque had also called for new authorities to take the place of the abusive cacique in office: "We request with shouts and loud voices that your lordship have named for us another cacique whom we have elected and who has a proprietary claim" (ALP EC 1792 C. 117 E. s.n. [22 fols.], fol. 1v). There are many other examples of communities proposing their own candidates for the posts of cacique and tribute collector. For example, see ANB EC 1756 No. 111; ANB EC 1782 No. 100; and ANB EC 1794 No. 8, fol. 19.

74. ALP EC 1795 C. 122 E. 29; for the quote, see fols. 1v–2. For other evidence of the belief that community members ought to have caciques of their own choice, see ANB EC 1802 No. 48, fol. 6; and ANB EC 1809 No. 14, fol. 99.

75. ALP EC 1795 C. 122 E. 28, fol. 1.

76. ANB EC 1801 No. 25, fol. 53.

77. Protector Juan Baptista Rebollo's analysis of the political problem and his paternalist rhetoric are worth noting: "The painful, bitter, and oppressive life that these miserable Indians lead is occasioned by the great neglect of the subdelegates, who leave their partidos abandoned, without leadership, and delivered into the hands of the tribute collectors. These tribute collectors do as they please with the poor Indians, and each considers himself a duke or marquis. From one day to the next they become powerful, because they drink the Indians' blood down to the very last drop" (ANB EC 1809 No. 14, fols. 76–78).

78. My overall conception of this period in La Paz fits with Walker's work on Cuzco (1999). Nuria Sala's vision of Lower Peru (1996) at this time is also one of disintegration, complex conflict, and precarious political projects, although she tends to see a more effective penetration of Indian towns and subordination of community authorities, especially by non-Indians manipulating the tributary apparatus. Cf. Thurner (1996); Larson (1999).

Chapter 8. Conclusions

1. On this conflict, see ALP EC 1795 C. 122 E. 25 (the quote is from fol. 8v); and ALP EC 1795 C. 122 E. 8.

2. This account, and the following treatment of intracommunity hierarchy, draws on the eighteenth-century documentation as well as contemporary ethnography that coincides with and illuminates the colonial evidence. See, in general, the work of Xavier Albó. For a synthetic view of local and community government

among the Aymara today, see Ticona, Albó, and Rojas (1995, 79–120). For an in-depth case study, see Ticona and Albó (1997).

3. Cf. Mallon's processual analysis (1995) of internal power relations and collective political identity, which focuses on indigenous communities in the Puebla highlands of nineteenth-century Mexico.

4. Ethnic hierarchy—involving the inferiority of Uru people relative to Aymaras—also existed within some communities and was strongly ascriptive. We can speculate that the democratizing tendency of the eighteenth-century political transformation did not significantly alter Uru subordination. On the Uru, see Wachtel (1990).

5. Here again see Ticona, Albó, and Rojas (1995, 79–120); Ticona and Albó (1997); and Rasnake (1988).

6. Albó 1972, 1985. Carter and Albó 1988. Rivera 1990. Rojas 1994. My own thinking has been inspired by Wood's analysis (1988) of classical Athens as a democratic smallholding regime. For more on Greek antiquity and its significance for rethinking popular and modern forms of democracy, see Euben, Wallach, and Ober (1994); and Ober and Hendrick (1996).

7. Saavedra [1903] 1995, 144. In the 1990s, a century later, the "reconstitution" of the system of ayllu authorities again emerged as a primary objective of many highland communities facing critical cultural and political challenges. See M. E. Choque and C. Mamani (2001).

8. Choque and Ticona 1996, 175.

9. Rasnake 1988, 155.

10. The term "apoderado" means legal representative. For more on Llanqui and the struggle of the Jesús de Machaca community, see Choque (1986); Choque and Ticona (1996); Ticona and Albó (1997). For other references to the indigenous movements of the early twentieth century as well as the political role of collective historical memory, see Taller de Historia Oral Andina 1984, 1986); Rivera (1986, 1991); Mamani (1991); Choque et al. (1992); Condori and Ticona (1992); and Fernández (1996).

11. Rasnake 1988, 263–267. Wachtel (1992) has offered a comparative reflection, based on the findings of Abercrombie (1986), Rasnake (1988), and Wachtel (1990), on the "crystallization" of contemporary ethnic or collective organization and identity in the latter eighteenth century. (Cf. also Saignes 1991.) This remains an open question, for there has so far been limited evidence brought to bear on key issues under debate. It is, nonetheless, an important question insofar as it challenges us to think of indigenous social formations integrally, considering the relations between territorial, religious, and political spheres of social organization and their respective temporal development. My findings coincide with Rasnake's in the view that the latter part of the eighteenth century was the time of important change in the structure of political authority. The evidence for La Paz does not show internal changes in the "cargo system." Nevertheless, rotating authorities did acquire greater political importance, so we can infer at least that a

loosely structured and ayllu-based civil cargo system, which had emerged with the gradual decline of Indian nobility, acquired greater salience with the conjunctural collapse of cacique power. (Cf. Abercrombie 1998.) Other aspects of territorial and religious organization at the reducción level were evidently in place much earlier, and larger-scale preconquest ethnic identity was presumably lost in La Paz before it was further south in Charcas. Judging from La Paz, it appears overstated to think of an overall "crystallization" of collective identity in the late eighteenth century; however, closer regional comparison may clarify differences between La Paz and southern Charcas.

Bibliography

Abercrombie, Thomas. 1986. The Politics of Sacrifice: An Aymara Cosmology in Action. Doctoral thesis, University of Chicago.

————. 1991a. "Articulación doble y etnogénesis." In Segundo Moreno Yañez and Frank Salomon, eds. *Reproducción y transformación de las sociedades andinas, siglos XVI–XX.* Quito: ABYA-YALA and MLAL.

————. 1991b. "To Be Indian, to Be Bolivian: 'Ethnic' and 'National' Discourses of Identity." In Greg Urban and Joel Sherzer, eds. *Nation States and Indians in Latin America.* Austin: University of Texas Press.

————. 1998. *Pathways of Memory and Power: Ethnography and History among an Andean People.* Madison: University of Wisconsin Press.

ACI (Comisión Nacional del Bicentenario de la Rebelión Emancipadora de Túpac Amaru). 1982. *Actas del coloquio internacional: "Túpac Amaru y su tiempo."* Lima: P. L. Villanueva.

Adorno, Rolena. 1986. *Guaman Poma: Writing and Resistance in Colonial Peru.* Austin: University of Texas Press.

Adorno, Rolena, ed. 1982. *From Oral to Written Expression: Native Andean Chronicles of the Early Colonial Period.* Foreign and Comparative Studies, Latin American Monograph Series, no. 4. Syracuse, New York: Maxwell School of Citizenship and Public Affairs, Syracuse University.

Albó, Xavier. 1972. "Dinámica en la estructura intercomunitaria de Jesús de Machaca." *América Indígena* 32:773–81.

————. 1979a . *Achacachi: Medio siglo de lucha campesina.* La Paz: CIPCA.

————. 1979b. *Khitipxtansa: Quiénes somos? Identidad localista étnica y clasista en los aymaras de hoy.* 2d ed. La Paz: CIPCA and Instituto Indigenista Interamericano.

————. 1984. "Etnicidad y clase en la gran rebelión Aymara/Quechua: Kataris, Amarus y bases, 1780–1781." In Fernando Calderón and Jorge Dandler, eds. *Bolivia: La fuerza histórica del campesinado.* Cochabamba: UNRISD and CERES.

————. 1985. *Desafíos de la solidaridad aymara.* La Paz: CIPCA.

————. 1987. "From MNRistas to Kataristas to Katari." In Steve Stern, ed.

Resistance, Rebellion, and Consciousness in the Andean Peasant World, Eighteenth to Twentieth Centuries. Madison: University of Wisconsin Press.

———. 1991a. "El retorno del indio." *Revista Andina* 11:299–345.

———. 1991b. "El sinuoso camino de la historia y de la conciencia hacia la identidad nacional aymara." In Segundo Moreno Yañez and Frank Salomon, eds. *Reproducción y transformación de las sociedades andinas, siglos XVI–XX*. Quito: ABYA-YALA and MLAL.

———. 1991c. "El thaki o 'camino' en Jesús de Machaca." In Raquel Thiercelin, ed. *Cultures et sociétés Andes et Meso-Amérique: Mélanges en hommage a Pierre Duviols*. 2 vols. Aix-en-Provence: Université de Provence.

———. 1993. *¿Y de kataristas a MNRistas? La sorprendiente y audaz alianza entre aymaras y neoliberales en Bolivia*. La Paz: CEDOIN and UNITAS.

———, ed. 1988. *Raíces de América: El mundo aymara*. Madrid: Alianza Editorial.

Albó, Xavier, Thomas Greaves, and Godofredo Sandoval. 1981–1987. *Chukiyawu: La cara aymara de La Paz*. 4 vols. La Paz: CIPCA.

Albó, Xavier, and Josef Barnadas. 1984. *La cara campesina de nuestra historia*. La Paz: UNITAS.

———. 1990. *La cara india y campesina de nuestra historia*. La Paz: UNITAS.

Allen, Catherine. 1988. *The Hold Life Has: Coca and Cultural Identity in an Andean Community*. Washington: Smithsonian Institution Press.

Amat y Junient, Manuel de. *Memoria de gobierno*. 1947. Vicente Rodríguez Casado and Florentino Pérez Embid, eds. Sevilla: Escuela de Estudios Hispano-Americanos.

Anderson, Perry. 1978. *Lineages of the Absolutist State*. London: Verso.

Andrade, Claudio. 1994. *La rebelión de Tomás Katari*. Sucre: IPTK.

Aranzaes, Nicolás. 1915. *Diccionario histórico biográfico de La Paz*. La Paz: Editorial Gráfica La Prensa.

Arze Aguirre, René. 1978. "El cacicazgo en las postrimerías coloniales." *Avances* 1: 47–50.

———. 1987. *La participación popular en la Independencia de Bolivia*. La Paz: Fundación Cultural Quipus.

Arze, Silvia. 1991. "Organización y crisis: La rebelión en los ayllus de Chayanta en 1781." *Estado y Sociedad* 7:89–111.

Arze, Silvia, and Rossana Barragán. 1988. *La Paz–Chuquiago. El escenario de la vida de la ciudad. Fascículo 1. La fundación y el centro urbano hasta 1781*. La Paz: Ediciones Casa de la Cultura.

Arze, Silvia, and Ximena Medinaceli. 1991. *Imágenes y presagios: El escudo de los Ayaviri, mallkus de Charcas*. La Paz: HISBOL.

Arze, Silvia, Magdalena Cajías, and Ximena Medinaceli. N.d. Mujeres en rebelión: La presencia feminina en las rebeliones de Charcas en el siglo XVIII. Unpublished manuscript.

Ayllu Sartañani. 1992. *Pachamamax tipusiwa: Qhurqhi (La pachamama se enoja)*. La Paz: Aruwiyiri.

Bakewell, Peter. 1984. *Miners of the Red Mountain: Indian Labor in Potosí, 1545–1650*. Albuquerque: University of New Mexico Press.

Ballivián y Roxas, Manuel Vicente de. [1872] 1977. *Archivo boliviano. Colección de documentos relativos a la historia de Bolivia durante la época colonial*. La Paz: Casa de la Cultura Franz Tamayo.

Bandelier, Adolfo. 1910. *The Islands of Titicaca and Koati*. New York: The Hispanic Society of America.

Barnadas, Josef. 1973. *Charcas: Orígenes históricos de una sociedad colonial, 1535–1565*. La Paz: CIPCA.

Barragán, Rossana. 1990. *Espacio urbano y dinámica étnica: La Paz en el siglo XIX*. La Paz: HISBOL.

———. 1996. "Españoles patricios y españoles europeos: Conflictos intra-elites e identidades en la ciudad de La Paz en vísperas de la independencia, 1770–1809." In Charles Walker, ed. *Entre la retórica y la insurgencia: Las ideas y los movimientos sociales en los Andes, Siglo XVIII*. Cuzco: Centro Bartolomé de las Casas.

Barragán, Rossana, and Ramiro Molina Rivero. 1987. "De los señoríos a las comunidades: Caso Quillacas." Paper presented at the Reunión Anual de Etnología, MUSEF, La Paz.

Barragán, Rossana, and Sinclair Thomson. 1993. "Los lobos hambrientos y el tributo a Dios: Conflictos sociales en torno a los diezmos en Charcas colonial." *Revista Andina* 11:305–348.

Basques, Jeremy. 2000. *Indians, Merchants, and Markets: A Reinterpretation of the Repartimiento and Spanish-Indian Economic Relations in Colonial Oaxaca, 1750–1821*. Stanford: Stanford University Press.

Behar, Ruth. 1986. *The Presence of the Past in a Spanish Village, Santa María del Monte*. Princeton: Princeton University Press.

Benjamin, Walter. 1976. *Illuminations*. New York: Schocken Books.

Bertonio, Ludovico. [1612] 1984 . *Vocabulario de la lengua aimara*. La Paz: CERES and MUSEF.

Bolton, Ralph. 1973. "Aggression and Hypoglycemia among the Qolla: A Study in Psychobiological Anthropology." *Ethnology* 12:227–57.

———. 1976. "Aggression in Fantasy: A Further Test of the Hypoglycemia Aggression Hypothesis." *Aggressive Behavior* 2:251–274.

Bolton, Ralph, and Enrique Mayer, eds. 1977. *Andean Kinship and Marriage*. American Anthropological Association Special Publication no. 7. Washington, D.C.: AAA.

———. 1987. "Comunidades indígenas y estado nación en el Perú." In Heraclio Bonillat al. *Comunidades campesinas: Cambios y permanencias*. Chiclayo y Lima: Centro de Estudios Sociales Solidaridad y CONCYTEC.

Bonilla, Heraclio, ed. 1992. *Los conquistados: 1492 y la población indígena de las Américas*. Quito: Tercer Mundo Editores, FLACSO, Ediciones Libri Mundi.

Bonilla, Heraclio et al. 1987. *Comunidades campesinas: Cambios y permanencias.* Chiclayo y Lima: Centro de Estudios Sociales Solidaridad y CONCYTEC.

Bouysse-Cassagne, Thérèse. 1986. "*Urco* and *Uma:* Aymara Concepts of Space." In John Murra, Nathan Wachtel, and Jacques Revel, eds. *Anthropological History of Andean Polities.* Cambridge: Cambridge University Press.

———. 1987. *La identidad aymara: Aproximación histórica (siglo XV–XVI).* La Paz: HISBOL and IFEA.

Bouysse-Cassagne, Thérèse, Olivia Harris, Tristan Platt, and Verónica Cereceda. 1987. *Tres reflexiones sobre el pensamiento andino.* La Paz: HISBOL.

Buechler, Hans, and Judith–Marie Buechler. 1971. *The Bolivian Aymara.* New York: Holt, Rinehart, and Winston.

Buntinx, Gustavo, and Luis Eduardo Wuffarden. 1991. "Incas y reyes españoles en la pintura colonial peruana: La estela de Garcilaso." *Márgenes* 8:151–210.

Burga, Manuel. 1988. *El nacimiento de una utopía: Muerte y resurección de los incas.* Lima: Instituto de Apoyo Agrario.

———. 1992. "El corpus christi y la nobleza inca colonial. Memoria e identidad." In Heraclio Bonilla, ed. *Los conquistados: 1492 y la población indígena de las Américas.* Quito: Tercer Mundo Editores, FLACSO, Ediciones Libri Mundi.

Cahill, David. 1984. "*Curas* and Social Conflict in the *Doctrinas* of Cuzco, 1780–1814." *Journal of Latin American Studies* 16 (2):241–276.

———. 1986. "Caciques y tributos en la sierra del sur del Perú después de la rebelión de los Túpac Amaru." Paper presented at VII Simposio de Historia Económica, Lima.

———. 1988. "Repartos ilícitos y familias principales en el sur andino: 1780–1824." *Revista de Indias* 48 (182–183):449–473.

———. 1990. "Taxonomy of a Colonial 'Riot': The Arequipa Disturbances of 1780." In Fisher et al., eds. *Reform and Insurrection in Bourbon New Granada and Peru,* Baton Rouge: Louisiana State University Press.

Cajías, Fernando. 1987. La sublevación tupacamarista de 1781 en Oruro y las provincias aledañas: Sublevación de indios y revuelta criolla. Doctoral thesis, Universidad de Sevilla.

Calderón, Fernando, and Jorge Dandler. 1984. *Bolivia: La fuerza histórica del campesinado.* Cochabamba: UNRISD and CERES.

Calla Ortega, Ricardo. 1993. "Hallu hayllisa huti: Identificación étnica y procesos políticos en Bolivia (1973–1991)." In Alberto Adrianzén et al., *Democracia, etnicidad y violencia política en los países andinos.* Lima: Instituto de Estudios Peruanos and Instituto Francés de Estudios Andinos.

Campbell, Leon. 1979. "Recent Research on Andean Peasant Revolts, 1750–1820." *Latin American Research Review* 14:3–49.

———. 1987. "Ideology and Factionalism During the Great Rebellion, 1780–1782." In Steve Stern, ed. *Resistance, Rebellion, and Consciousness in the Andean Peasant World, Eighteenth to Twentieth Centuries.* Madison: University of Wisconsin Press.

Cañedo-Argüelles Fabrega, Teresa. 1993. *Potosi: La versión aymara de un mito euro-peo. La minería y sus efectos en las sociedades andinas del siglo XVII (la provincia de Pacajes).* Madrid: Editorial Catriel.

Cangiano, María Cecilia. 1987. "Curas, caciques y comunidades en el Alto Perú: Chayanta a fines del siglo XVIII." Unpublished manuscript, Jujuy.

Canny, Nicholas,and Anthony Pagden, eds. 1987. *Colonial Identity in the Atlantic World, 1500–1800.* Princeton: Princeton University Press.

Cárdenas, Víctor Hugo. 1988. "La lucha de un pueblo." In Xavier Albó, ed. *Raíces de América: El mundo aymara.* Madrid: Alianza Editorial.

Carmagnani, Marcello. 1988. *El regreso de los dioses: El proceso de la reconstitución de la identidad étnica en Oaxaca, siglos XVII y XVIII.* Mexico City: Fondo de Cultura Económica.

Carter, William. 1964. *Aymara communities and the Bolivian Agrarian Reform.* Gainesville, Florida: University of Florida Press.

Carter, William, and Mauricio Mamani. 1982. *Irpa Chico: Individuo y comunidad en la cultura aymara.* La Paz: Editorial Juventud.

Carter, William, and Xavier Albó. 1988. "La comunidad aymara: Un mini-estado en conflicto." In Xavier Albó, ed. *Raíces de América: El mundo aymara.* Madrid: Alianza Editorial.

CDIP (Comisión Nacional del Sesquicentenario de la Independencia del Perú). 1971–1975. *Colección documental de la independencia del Perú.* 27 vols. Lima: Talleres Gráficos Cecil.

CDRTA (Comisión Nacional del Bicentenario de la Rebelión Emancipadora de Túpac Amaru). 1980–82. *Colección documental del bicentenario de la revolución emancipadora de Túpac Amaru.* 5 vols. Lima: Talleres Gráficos P. L. Villanueva.

CDRTA (Comisión Nacional del Bicentenario de la Rebelión Emancipadora de Túpac Amaru). 1981. *La revolución de los Túpac Amaru: Antología.* Lima: P. L. Villanueva.

Celestino, Olinda, and Albert Meyers. 1981. *Las cofradías en el Perú: Región central.* Frankfurt/Main: K. D. Vervuert.

Céspedes del Castillo, Guillermo. 1946. *Lima y Buenos Aires: Repercusiones económicas y políticas de la creación del virreinato de La Plata.* Sevilla: Escuela de Estudios Hispanos (CSIC).

Chance, John. 1989. *Conquest of the Sierra: Spaniards and Indians in Colonial Oaxaca.* Norman: University of Oklahoma Press.

Chance, John, and William Taylor. 1985. "Cofradías and Cargos: An Historical Perspective on the Mesoamerican Civil-Religious Hierarchy." *American Ethnologist* 12 (1):1–26.

Choque, María Eugenia. 1992. La estructura de poder en la comunidad originaria de Salasaca. M.A. thesis, FLACSO-Quito.

———. 1995. "Dominación colonial y subordinación de la mujer indígena." *Presencia Literaria,* 30 July 1995.

Choque, María Eugenia, and Carlos Mamani. 2001. "Reconstitución del ayllu y derechos de los pueblos indígenas: El movimiento indio en los Andes de Bolivia." *Journal of Latin American Anthropology* 6 (1):202–224.

Choque, Roberto. 1979. Situación social y económica de los revolucionarios del 16 de Julio de 1809. Thesis in History, Universidad Mayor de San Andrés.

———. 1986. *La masacre de Jesús de Machaca*. La Paz: Chitakolla.

———. 1988. Historia de Machaca (Diagnóstico, Cantón San Andrés de Machaca). Unpublished manuscript.

———. 1991. "Los caciques frente a la rebelión de Túpak Katari en La Paz." *Historia y Cultura* 19:83–93.

———. 1992. "Los aymaras y la cuestión colonial." In Heraclio Bonilla, ed. *Los conquistados: 1492 y la población indígena de las Américas*. Quito: Tercer Mundo Editores, FLACSO, Ediciones Libri Mundi.

———. 1993a. *Sociedad y economía colonial en el sur andino*. La Paz: HISBOL.

———. 1993b. El parentesco entre los caciques de Pakaxe. Unpublished manuscript.

Choque, Roberto et al. 1992. *Educación indígena: ¿Ciudadanía o colonización?* La Paz: Aruwiyiri.

Choque, Roberto, and Esteban Ticona. 1996. *Sublevación y masacre de 1921 (Jesús de Machaqa: La marka rebelde 2)*. La Paz: CEDOIN and CIPCA.

Clendinnen, Inga. 1987. *Ambivalent Conquests: Maya and Spaniard in Yucatán, 1517–1570*. Cambridge: Cambridge University Press.

Coatsworth, John. 1988. "Patterns of Rural Rebellion in Latin America." In Friedrich Katz, ed. *Riot, Rebellion, and Revolution: Rural Social Conflict in Mexico*. Princeton: Princeton University Press.

Cole, Jeffrey. 1985. *The Potosí Mita, 1573–1700: Compulsory Indian Labor in the Andes*. Stanford: Stanford University Press.

Colin, Michèle. 1966. *Le Cuzco à la fin du XVIIe et au début du XVIIIe siècle*. Paris: Institut des Hautes Études de l'Amérique Latine.

Condarco Morales, Ramiro. 1966. *Zárate, el "temible" willka. Historia de la rebelión indígena de 1899*. La Paz: Talleres Gráficos Bolivianos.

———. 1985. *Atlas histórico de Bolivia*. La Paz: Ed. y Imp. San José.

Condori, Leandro y Esteban Ticona. 1992. *El escribano de los caciques apoderados*. La Paz: HISBOL and Taller de Historia Oral Andina.

Cornblit, Oscar. 1970. "Society and Mass Rebellion in Eighteenth-Century Peru and Bolivia." In Raymond Carr, ed. *Latin American Affairs*. Oxford: Oxford University Press.

———. 1995. *Power and Violence in the Colonial City: Oruro from the Mining Renaissance to the Rebellion of Túpac Amaru (1740–1782)*. New York: Cambridge University Press.

Cornejo Bouroncle, Jorge. 1949. *Túpac Amaru. La revolución precursora de emancipación continental*. Cuzco: Universidad Nacional del Cuzco.

Costa de la Torre, Arturo. 1974. *Episodios históricos de la rebelión indígena de 1781.* La Paz: Camarlinghi.

Crespo Rodas, Alberto. 1974. "Los coroneles de Túpac Catari." *Presencia Literaria,* 21 April 1974.

———. 1982. "Las armas de los rebeldes." In ACI *"Tupac Amaru y su tiempo."* Comisión Nacional del Bicentenario de la Rebelión Emancipadora de Túpac Amaru. Lima: P. L. Villaneva.

———. 1987. "Pedro Obaya, el rey chiquito." *Historia y Cultura* 11:41–72.

Crespo, Rodas, Alberto, René Arze Aguirre, Florencia Romero, and Mary Money. 1975. *La vida cotidiana en La Paz durante la guerra de Independencia, 1800–1825.* La Paz: Universidad Mayor de San Andrés.

Crespo Rodas, Alberto et al. 1989. *La ciudad de La Paz. Su historia—su cultura.* La Paz: Alcaldía Municipal.

Cummins, Tom. 1991. "We Are the Other: Peruvian Portraits of Colonial Kurakakuna." In Kenneth Andrien and Rolena Adorno, eds. *Transatlantic Encounters: Europeans and Andeans in the Sixteenth Century.* Berkeley: University of California Press.

De Angelis, Pedro. [1836] 1971. *Colección de obras y documentos relativos a la historia antigua y moderna de las provincia del Río de La Plata.* Tome 7. Buenos Aires: Plus Ultra.

De Lucca, Mario. 1983. *Diccionario aymara-castellano, castellano-aymara.* La Paz: CALA.

Desan, Suzanne. 1989. "Crowds, Community, and Ritual in the Work of E. P. Thompson and Natalie Davis." In Lynn Hunt, ed. *The New Cultural History.* Berkeley: University of California Press.

Díaz Machicao, Porfirio. 1964. *Tupac Catari, la sierpe.* La Paz: Amigos del Libro.

———. 1969. *Historía del rey chiquito.* 2d ed. La Paz: Difusión.

Díaz Rementería, Carlos. 1977. *El cacique en el virreinato del Perú. Estudio histórico-jurídico.* Sevilla: Seminario de Antropología Americana.

Dollfus, Olivier. 1991. *Territorios andinos: Reto y memoria.* Lima: IFEA and IEP.

Durand Flórez, Luis. 1973. *Independencia e integración en el plan político de Túpac Amaru.* Lima: P. L. Villanueva.

Eguiguren, Luis Antonio, ed. 1952. *Guerra separatista: Rebeliones de indios en Sur América. La sublevación de Túpac Amaru. Crónica de Melchor de Paz.* 2 vols. Lima: N.p.

Escobedo Mansilla, Ronald. 1997. *Las comunidades indígenas y la economía colonial peruana.* Bilbao: Servicio Editorial de la Universidad del País Vasco.

Espinoza Soriano, Waldemar. 1960. "El alcalde mayor indígena en el virreinato del Perú." *Anuario de Estudios Americanos* 17:183–300.

———. 1981. "1780: Movimientos antifiscales en la sierra norte de la Audiencia de Lima y repercusiones tupamaristas en la misma zona." *Allpanchis* 15: 169–201.

Eubin, J. Peter, John Wallach, and Josiah Ober, eds. 1994. *Athenian Political Thought and the Reconstruction of American Democracy.* Ithaca: Cornell University Press.

Ferrer, Ada. 1999. *Insurgent Cuba: Race, Nation, and Revolution, 1868–1898.* Chapel Hill: University of North Carolina Press.

Farriss, Nancy. 1984. *Maya Society under Colonial Rule: The Collective Enterprise of Survival.* Princeton: Princeton University Press.

Fellman Velarde, José. 1968–1970. *Historia de Bolivia.* 3 vols. Cochabamba: Editorial Los Amigos del Libro.

Fernández, Marcelo. 1996. El poder de la palabra: Documento y memoria oral en la resistencia de Waquimarka contra la expansión latifundista (1874–1930). Thesis in sociology, Universidad Mayor de San Andrés.

———. 2000. *La ley del ayllu: Práctica de "jach'a" justicia y "jisk'a" justicia (Justicia Mayor y Justicia Menor) en comunidades aymaras.* La Paz: PIEB.

Finot, Enrique. 1954. *Nueva historia de Bolivia. Ensayo de interpretación sociológica.* 2d ed. La Paz: Gisbert.

Fisher, John. 1970. *Government and Society in Colonial Peru: The Intendant System, 1784–1814.* London: Athlone.

———. 1982. "Soldiers, Society, and Politics in Spanish America, 1750–1821." *Latin American Research Review* 17 (1):217–222.

Fisher, John, Allan Kuethe, and Anthony McFarlane, eds. 1990. *Reform and Insurrection in Bourbon New Granada and Peru.* Baton Rouge: Louisiana State University Press.

Fisher, Lillian Estelle. 1966. *The Last Inca Revolt, 1780–1783.* Norman: University of Oklahoma Press.

Flores Galindo, Alberto. 1987. *Buscando un inca: Identidad y utopia en los Andes.* Lima: Instituto de Apoyo Agrario.

———. 1989. "Las revoluciones tupamaristas: Temas en debate." *Revista Andina* 13:279–287.

Flores Galindo, Alberto, ed. 1976. *Túpac Amaru II—1780. Sociedad colonial y sublevaciones populares.* Lima: Retablo de Papel.

Forbes, David. 1870. *On the Aymara Indians of Bolivia and Peru.* London: Taylor and Francis.

Fuenzalida, Fernando. 1970. "La estructura de la comunidad de indígenas tradicional: Una hipótesis de trabajo." In Robert Keith et al. *La hacienda, la comunidad y el campesino en el Perú.* Lima: IEP.

Gade, Daniel. 1991. "Reflexiones sobre el asentamiento andino de la época toledana hasta el presente." In Segundo Moreno Yañez and Frank Salomon, eds. *Reproducción y transformación de las sociedades andinas, siglos XVI–XX.* Quito: ABYA-YALA and MLAL.

García Martínez, Bernardo. 1987. *Los pueblos de la sierra: El poder y el espacio entre los indios del norte de Puebla hasta 1700.* Mexico City: El Colegio de México.

Garrett, David. 2001. The Shadows of Empire: The Indian Nobility of Bourbon Cusco. Doctoral thesis, Columbia University.

Gibson, Charles. 1953. "Rotation of Alcaldes in the Indian Cabildo of Mexico City." *Hispanic American Historical Review* 33 (2): 212–223.

———. 1960. "The Aztec Aristocracy in Colonial Mexico." *Comparative Studies in Society in History* 2: 169–196.

———. 1964. *The Aztecs Under Spanish Rule: A History of the Indians of the Valley of Mexico, 1519–1810.* Stanford: Stanford University Press.

Gisbert, Teresa. 1980. *Iconografía y mitos indígenas en el arte.* La Paz: Gisbert.

———. 1992. "Los curacas de Collao y la conformación de la cultura mestiza andina." In Tomoeda Hiroyasu and Luis Millones, eds. *500 años de mestizaje en los Andes.* Osaka: National Museum of Ethnohistory.

Glave, Luis Miguel. 1989. *Trajinantes: Caminos indígenas en la sociedad colonial, siglos XVI/XVII.* Lima: Instituto de Apoyo Agrario.

Glave, Luis Miguel, and María Isabel Remy. 1983. *Estructura agraria y vida rural en una región andina: Ollantaytambo entre los siglos XVI y XIX.* Cuzco: Centro Bartolomé de Las Casas.

Golte, Jürgen. 1980. *Repartos y rebeliones: Túpac Amaru y las contradicciones de la economía colonial.* Lima: Instituto de Estudios Peruanos.

Grondín, Marcelo. 1975. *Túpaj Katari y la rebelión campesina de 1781–83.* Oruro: INDICEP.

Guaman Poma de Ayala, Felipe. [1615] 1980. *El primer nueva corónica y buen gobierno.* Critical edition by John Murra and Rolena Adorno; translation and textual analysis of Quechua by Jorge Urioste. 3 vols. Mexico City: Siglo XXI.

Guerrero, Andrés. 1989. "Curagas y tenientes políticos: La ley de la costumbre y la ley del estado (Otavalo 1830–1875)." *Revista Andina* 7:321–66.

Guha, Ranajit. [1983] 1988. "The Prose of Counter-Insurgency." In R. Guha and Gayatri Spivak, *Selected Subaltern Studies.* New York: Oxford University Press.

———. [1983] 1999. *Elementary Aspects of Peasant Insurgency in Colonial India.* Durham, N.C.: Duke University Press.

Gutiérrez, Ramón. 1991. *When Jesus Came the Corn Mothers Went Away: Marriage, Sexuality, and Power in New Mexico, 1500–1846.* Stanford: Stanford University Press.

Hardman, Martha. 1988. "Jaqi aru: La lengua humana." In Xavier Albó, ed. *Raíces de América: El mundo aymara.* Madrid: Alianza Editorial.

Harris, Olivia. 1994. "Condor and Bull: The Ambiguities of Masculinity in Northern Potosí." In Penelope Harvey and Peter Gow, eds. *Sex and Violence: Issues in Representation and Experience.* London: Routledge.

Harris, Olivia, Brooke Larson, and Enrique Tandeter, eds. 1987. *La participación indígena en los mercados surandinos: Estrategias y reproducción social, siglos XVI–XX.* La Paz: CERES.

————. 1995. "The Sources and Meanings of Money: Beyond the Market Paradigm in an Ayllu of Northern Potosí." In Larson, Brooke and Olivia Harris, eds. *Ethnicity, Markets, and Migration in the Andes: At the Crossroads of History and Anthropology*. Durham: Duke University Press.

Haskett, Robert. 1991. *Indigenous Rulers: An Ethnohistory of Town Government in Colonial Cuernavaca*. Albuquerque: University of New Mexico Press.

Hidalgo Lehuede, Jorge. 1983. "Amarus y Cataris: Aspectos mesiánicos de la rebelión indígena de 1781 en Cusco, Chayanta, La Paz y Arica." *Chungará* 10: 117–138.

————. 1986. Indian Society in Arica, Tarapacá, and Atacama, 1770–1793, and Its Response to the Rebellion of Tupac Amaru. Doctoral thesis, University of London.

Hobsbawm, Eric, and Terence Ranger, eds. 1983. *The Invention of Tradition*. Cambridge: Cambridge University Press.

Huanca, Tomás. 1984. La desestructuración de los espacios socioeconómicos en el altiplano lacustre: Agresión colonial o resistencia comunitaria. Thesis in sociology, Universidad Mayor de San Andrés, La Paz.

Hunefeldt, Christine. 1982. *Lucha por la tierra y protesta indígena: Las comunidades de Perú entre colonia y república, 1800–1830*. Bonn: Bonner amerikanistische Studien.

————. 1983. "Comunidad, curas y comunarios hacia fines del período colonial." *HISLA* 2:3–31.

Hurtado, Javier. 1986. *El katarismo*. La Paz: HISBOL.

Imaña Castro, Teodosio. 1971. "Katari y la acción pre-emancipadora." *Presencia Literaria,* 14 March 1971.

————. 1973. "De lo pasional en la vida de los caudillos indígenas de 1780." *Historia y Cultura* 1:125–142.

Isbell, Billie Jean. 1977. "'Those Who Love Me': An Analysis of Andean Kinship and Reciprocity within a Ritual Context." In Ralph Bolton and Enrique Mayer, eds. *Andean Kinship and Marriage*. American Anthropological Association Special Publication No. 7. Washington, D.C.: AAA.

————. 1978. *To Defend Ourselves: Ecology and Ritual in an Andean Village*. Austin: University of Texas at Austin.

Jacobsen, Nils. 1993. *Mirages of Transition: The Peruvian Altiplano, 1780–1930*. Berkeley: University of California Press.

James, C. R. L. [1938] 1963. *The Black Jacobins: Toussaint L'Ouverture and the Santo Domingo Rebellion*. New York: Vintage Books/Random House.

Jiménez de la Espada, Marcos. 1965. *Relaciones geográficas de Indias: Perú*. 3 vols. Madrid: Ed. Atlas.

Juan, Jorge and Antonio de Ulloa. 1991. *Noticias secretas de América*. Madrid: Historia 16.

Katz, Friedrich. 1988. "Rural Uprising in Preconquest and Colonial Mexico." In Friedrich Katz, ed. *Riot, Rebellion, and Revolution: Rural Social Conflict in Mexico*. Princeton: Princeton University Press.

Katz, Friedrich, ed. 1988. *Riot, Rebellion, and Revolution: Rural Social Conlict in Mexico*. Princeton: Princeton University Press.

Klein, Herbert. 1973. "Structure and Profitability of Royal Finance in the Viceroyalty of the Rio de la Plata in 1790." *Hispanic American Historical Review* 53:440–469.

———. 1982. *Bolivia: The Evolution of a Multi-Ethnic Society*. New York: Oxford University Press.

———. 1993. *Haciendas and Ayllus: Rural Society in the Bolivian Andes in the Eighteenth and Nineteenth Centuries*. Stanford: Stanford University Press.

———. 1998. *The American Finances of the Spanish Empire: Royal Income and Expenditures in Colonial Mexico, Peru, and Bolivia, 1680–1809*. Albuquerque: University of New Mexico Press.

La Barre, Weston. [1948] 1969. *The Aymara Indians of the Lake Titicaca Plateau, Bolivia*. New York: American Anthropological Association.

Lambert, Bernd. 1977. "Bilaterality in the Andes." In Ralph Bolton and Enrique Mayer, eds. *Andean Kinship and Marriage*. American Anthropological Association Special Publication No. 7. Washington, D.C.: AAA.

Larson, Brooke. 1979. "Caciques, Class Structure and the Colonial State in Bolivia." *Nova Americana* 2:197–235.

———. 1980. "Rural Rhythms of Class Conflict in Eighteenth-Century Cochabamba." *Hispanic American Historical Review* 60:407–430.

———. 1988. *Colonialism and Agrarian Transformation in Bolivia: Cochabamba, 1550–1900*. Princeton: Princeton University Press.

———. 1991. "Explotación y economía moral en los andes del sur andino: Hacia una reconsideración crítica." In Segundo Moreno Yañez and Frank Salomon, eds. *Reproducción y transformación de las sociedades andinas, siglos XVI–XX*. Quito: ABYA-YALA and MLAL.

———. 1998. *Cochabamba, 1550–1900: Colonialism and Agrarian Transformation in Bolivia*. Exp. 2d ed. Durham: Duke University Press.

———. 1999. "Andean Highland Peasants and the Trials of Nation-Making during the Nineteenth Century." In Frank Salomon and Stuart Schwartz, eds. *The Cambridge History of Native American Peoples: South America*. Cambridge: Cambridge University Press.

Larson, Brooke, and Olivia Harris, with Enrique Tandeter, eds. 1995. *Ethnicity, Markets, and Migration in the Andes: At the Crossroads of History and Anthropology*. Durham: Duke University Press.

Larson, Brooke, and Robert Wasserstrom. 1983. "Coerced Consumption in Colonial Bolivia and Guatemala." *Radical History Review* 27:49–78.

Lavrin, Asunción, and Edith Couturier. 1979. "Dowries and Wills: A View of Women's Socioeconomic Role in Colonial Guadalajara and Puebla, 1640–1790." *Hispanic American Historical Review* 59 (2):280–304.

Lema, Ana María. 1988. Production et circulation de la coca en Bolivie (Alto Perú), 1740–1840. Doctoral thesis, Ecole des Hautes Etudes en Sciences Sociales, Paris.

Lewin, Boleslao. 1943. *Túpac Amaru, el rebelde: Su época, sus luchas y su influencia en el continente.* Buenos Aires: Editorial Claridad.

Lewin, Boleslao. 1967. *La rebelión de Túpac Amaru y los orígenes de la independencia de hispanoamérica.* Exp. 3d ed. Buenos Aires: Hachette.

Loayza, Francisco. 1945. *Mártires y heroinas, documentos inéditos del año de 1780 a 1782.* Lima: Pequeños Grandes Libros de Historia Americana.

Loayza, Francisco. 1946. *Genealogía de Túpac Amaru por José Gabriel Túpac Amaru (Documentos inéditos del año 1777). Causas de la Sublevación.* Lima: Pequeños Grandes Libros de Historia Americana.

Loayza, Francisco. 1947. *Preliminares del incendio: Documentos del año de 1776 a 1780, en su mayoría inéditos, anteriores y sobre la rebelión.* Lima: Pequeños Grandes Libros de Historia Americana.

Lockhart, James. 1992. *The Nahuas after the Conquest: A Social and Cultural History of the Indians of Central Mexico, Sixteenth through Eighteenth Centuries.* Stanford: Stanford University Press.

Lohmann Villena, Guillermo. 1957. *El corregidor de indios en el Perú bajo los Austrias.* Madrid: Ediciones Cultura Hispánica.

Loy, Jane. 1957. "Forgotten Comuneros: The 1781 Revolt in the Llanos of Casanare." *Hispanic American Historical Review* 61:235–57.

Lynch, John. 1958. *Spanish Colonial Administration, 1782–1810: The Intendant System in the Viceroyalty of the Río de la Plata.* London: Athlone.

———. 1986. *The Spanish American Revolutions, 1808–1826.* New York: Norton.

Málaga Medina, Alejandro. 1974. "Las reducciones en el Perú (1532–1600)." *Historia y Cultura* 8:141–72.

Mallon, Florencia. 1983. *The Defense of Community in Peru's Central Highlands: Peasant Struggle and Capitalist Transition, 1860–1940.* Princeton: Princeton University Press.

———. 1995. *Peasant and Nation: The Making of Postcolonial Mexico and Peru.* Berkeley: University of California Press.

Mamani, Carlos. 1989. "History and Prehistory in Bolivia: What about the Indians?" In R. Layton, ed. *Conflict in the Archaeology of Living Traditions.* London: Unwin Hyman.

Mamani, Carlos. 1991. *Taraqu. Masacre, guerra y renovación en la biografía de Eduardo L. Nina Qhispi. 1886–1935.* La Paz: Aruwyiri.

Manrique, Nelson. 1993. *Vinieron los Sarracenos. El universo mental de la Conquista de América.* Lima: DESCO.

Maúrtua, Víctor, ed. 1906–7. *Juicio de límites entre el Perú y Bolivia.* 12 vols. Barcelona: Henrich.

Mayer, Enrique. 1977. "Beyond the Nuclear Family." In Ralph Bolton and Enrique Mayer, eds. *Andean Kinship and Marriage.* American Anthropological Association Special Publication No. 7. Washington, D.C.: AAA.

McFarlane, Anthony. 1984. "Civil Disorders and Popular Protests in Late Colonial Granada." *Hispanic American Historial Review* 64:17–54.

————. 1990. "The Rebellion of the *Barrios:* Urban Insurrection in Bourbon Quito." In Fisher et al., eds. *Reform and Insurrection in Bourbon New Granada and Peru,* Baton Rouge: Louisiana State University Press.

————. 1992. "Challenges from the Periphery: Rebellion in Colonial Spanish America." In Werner Thomas, ed. *Rebelión y resistencia en el mundo hispánico del s. XVII.* Leuven: Leuven University Press.

————. 1995. "Rebellions in Late Colonial Spanish America: A Comparative Perspective." *Bulletin of Latin American Research* 14 (3):313–338.

Mesa, José de and Teresa Gisbert. 1982. *Historia de la pintura cuzqueña.* 2 vols. Lima: Fundación Augusto N. Wiese.

Montenegro, Carlos. [1943] 1993. *Nacionalismo y coloniaje.* La Paz: Juventud.

Moreno Cebrián, Alfredo. 1977. *El corregidor de indios y la economía peruana en el siglo XVIII (los repartos forzosos de mercancías).* Madrid: Instituto Gonzalo Fernández de Oviedo.

————. 1988. *Túpac Amaru: El cacique que rebeló los Andes.* Madrid: Anaya.

Moreno Yañez, Segundo, and Frank Salomon, eds. 1991. *Reproducción y transformación de las sociedades andinas, siglos XVI–XX.* Quito: ABYA-YALA and MLAL.

Morner, Magnus, and Efraín Trelles. 1987. "A Test of Causal Interpretations of the Túpac Amaru Rebellion." In Steve Stern, ed. *Resistance, Rebellion, and Consciousness in the Andean Peasant World, Eighteenth to Twentieth Centuries.* Madison: University of Wisconsin Press.

Moscoso, Martha. 1989. "Comunidad, autoridad indígena y poder republicano." *Revista Andina* 7:481–500.

Murra, John. 1968. "An Aymara Kingdom in 1576." *Ethnohistory* 15:115–151.

Murra, John. 1975. *Formaciones políticas y económicas en el mundo andino.* Lima: Instituto de Estudios Peruanos

————. 1978. "Aymara Lords and their European Agents at Potosí." *Nova Americana* 1:231–43.

Murra, John, Nathan Wachtel, and Jacques Revel, eds. 1986. *Anthropological History of Andean Polities.* Cambridge: Cambridge University Press.

Ober, Josiah, and Charles Hedrick, eds. 1996. *Demokratia: A Conversation on Democracies, Ancient and Modern.* Princeton: Princeton University Press.

O'Phelan, Scarlett. 1978a. "El carácter de las revueltas campesinas del siglo XVIII en el norte del Virreinato del Perú." Cuadernos del Taller de Estudios Rurales No. 19, Departamento de CC.SS. Universidad Católica, Lima.

————. 1978b. "El sur andino a fines del siglo XVIII: Cacique o corregidor." *Allpanchis* 11:17–32.

————. 1979. "La rebelión de Túpac Amaru: Organización interna, dirigencia y alianzas." *Histórica* 3 (2):89–121.

————. 1982 "El movimiento Tupacamarista: Fases, coyuntura económica y perfil de la composición social de su dirigencia." In ACI *"Túpac Amaru y su tiempo."* Lima: P. L. Villaneva.

————. 1983. "Tierras comunales y revuelta social: Perú y Bolivia en el siglo XVIII." *Allpanchis* 22:75–91.

————. 1985. *Rebellions and Revolts in Eighteenth Century Peru and Upper Peru.* Lateinamerikanische Forschungen 14. Köln: Böhlau Verlag.

————. 1988. *Un siglo de rebeliones anticoloniales. Perú y Bolivia, 1700–1783.* Cuzco: Centro Bartolomé de Las Casas.

————. 1995. *La gran rebelión en los Andes: De Túpac Amaru a Túpac Katari.* Cuzco: Centro Bartolomé de las Casas.

————. 1996. "Algunas reflexiones sobre las reformas borbónicas y las rebeliones del siglo XVIII." In C. Walker, ed. *Entre la retórica y la insurgencia: Las ideas y los movimientos sociales en los Andes, siglo XVIII,* Cuzco: Centro Bartolomé de las Casas.

————. 1997. *Kurakas sin sucesiones: Del cacique al alcalde de indios (Perú y Bolivia 1750–1835).* Cuzco: Centro Bartolomé de las Casas.

Ossio, Juan. 1973. *Ideología mesiánica del mundo andino.* Lima: Prado Pastor.

Pacheco, Diego. 1992. *El indianismo y los indios contemporáneos en Bolivia.* La Paz: HISBOL and MUSEF.

Paredes, M. Rigoberto. 1906. *Provincia Inquisivi. Estudios geográficos, estadísticos y sociales.* La Paz: Gamarra.

————. [1897] 1973. *Tupac Catari: Apuntes biográficos.* La Paz: Ediciones ISLA.

Penry, Elizabeth. 1996. "Transformations in Indigenous Authority and Identity in Resettlement Towns of Colonial Charcas (Alto Perú)." Doctoral thesis, University of Miami.

Peralta, Víctor. 1991. *En pos del tributo. Burocracia estatal, elite regional y comunidades indígenas en el Cusco rural (1826–1854).* Cuzco: Centro Bartolomé de las Casas.

Phelan, John Leddy. 1978. The People and the King: The Comunero Revolution in Columbia, 1781. Madison: University of Wisconsin Press.

Pietschmann, Horst. 1996. *Las reformas borbónicas y el sistema de intendencias en Nueva España. Un estudio político administrativo.* México: Fondo de Cultura Económica.

Platt, Tristan. 1982. *Estado boliviano y ayllu andino: Tierra y tributo en el Norte de Potosí.* Lima: Instituto de Estudios Peruanos.

————. 1986. "Mirrors and Maize: The Concept of *Yanantin* among the Macha of Bolivia." In John Murra, Nathan Wachtel, and Jacques Revel, eds. *Anthropological History of Andean Polities.* Cambridge: Cambridge University Press.

————. 1987a. "The Andean Experience of Bolivian Liberalism, 1825–1900: Roots of Rebellion in 19th-Century Chayanta (Potosí)." In Steve Stern, ed. *Resistance, Rebellion, and Consciousness in the Andean Peasant World, Eighteenth to Twentieth Centuries.* Madison: University of Wisconsin Press.

————. 1987b. "The Andean Soldiers of Christ: Confraternity Organization, the Mass of the Sun, and Regenerative Warfare in Rural Potosí (Eighteenth to Twentieth Centuries)." *Journal de la Société des Américanistes.* 73: 139–191.

————. 1988. "Pensamiento político aymara." In Xavier Albó, ed. *Raíces de América: El mundo aymara*. Madrid: Alianza Editorial.

————. 1993. "Simón Bolívar, the Sun of Justice and the Amerindian Virgin: Andean Conceptions of the Patria in Nineteenth-Century Potosí." *Journal of Latin American Studies* 25:159–185.

Powers, Karen. 1995. *Andean Journeys: Migration, Ethnogenesis, and the State in Colonial Quito*. Albuquerque: University of New Mexico Press.

Presta, Ana María, ed. 1995. *Espacio, etnías, frontera. Atenuaciones políticas en el sur del Tawantinsuyu. Siglos XV–XVIII*. Sucre: ASUR.

Presencia. 29 August 1992. "Restos arqueológicos en el Salar de Uyuni."

Quiroz, Alfonso. 1993. *Deudas olvidadas: Instrumentos de crédito en la economía colonial peruana, 1750,–1820*. Lima: Universidad Católica.

————. 1994. "Reassessing the Role of Credit in Late Colonial Peru: *Censos, Escrituras*, and *Imposiciones*." *Hispanic American Historical Review* 74 (2):193–230.

Ramos Zambrano, Augusto. 1982. *Puno en la rebelión de Tupac Amaru*. Puno: Universidad Nacional Técnica del Altiplano.

Rappaport, Joanne. 1990. *The Politics of Memory: Native Historical Interpretation in the Colombian Andes*. Cambridge: Cambridge University Press.

————. 1994. *Cumbe Reborn: An Andean Ethnography of History*. Chicago: University of Chicago.

Rasnake, Roger. 1988. *Domination and Cultural Resistance: Authority and Power among an Andean People*. Durham: Duke University Press.

Recopilación de leyes de los reynos de las Indias, mandados imprimir y publicar por la Ma. Católica del Rey D. Carlos II. [1681] 1943. Madrid: Gráficas Ultra.

Rivera, Silvia. 1978. "El mallku y la sociedad colonial en el siglo XVII." *Avances* 1: 7–27.

————. 1984. *"Oprimidos pero no vencidos": Luchas del campesinado aymara y qhechwa, 1900–1980*. La Paz: UNRISD, HISBOL, CSUTCB.

————. 1987. *Oppressed but Not Defeated: Peasant Struggles among the Aymara and Qhechwa in Bolivia, 1900–1980*. Geneva: United Nations.

————. 1990. "Liberal Democracy and *Ayllu* Democracy in Bolivia: The Case of Northern Potosí." *Journal of Development Studies* 26 (4): 96–121.

————. 1991. "'Pedimos la revisión de límites': Un episodio de incomunicación de castas en el movimiento de caciques-apoderados de los Andes bolivianos, 1919–1921." In Segundo Moreno Yañez and Frank Salomon, eds. *Reproducción y transformación de las sociedades andinas, siglos XVI–XX*. Quito: ABYA-YALA and MLAL.

————. 1993. "El raíz: Colonizadores y colonizados." In Xavier Albó and Raúl Barrios, eds. *Violencias encubiertas en Bolivia 1*. La Paz: CIPCA and Aruwiyiri.

Robins, Nicholas. 1997. *El mesianismo y la rebelión indígena: La rebelión de Oruro en 1781*. La Paz: HISBOL.

Rojas, Gonzalo. 1994. *Democracia en Boliva, hoy y mañana: Enraizando la democracia con las experiencias de los pueblos indígenas*. La Paz: CIPCA.

Roseberry, William. 1989. *Anthropologies and Histories: Essays in Culture, History, and Political Economy.* New Brunswick: Rutgers University Press.

———. 1993. "Beyond the Agrarian Question in Latin America." In Frederick Cooper et al. *Confronting Historical Paradigms: Peasants, Labor, and the Capitalist World System in Africa and Latin America.* Madison: University of Wisconsin Press.

Rowe, John. 1954. "El movimiento nacional inca del siglo XVIII." *Revista Universitaria* 43:17–47.

———. 1976. "El movimiento nacional inca del siglo XVIII." In Alberto Flores Galindo, ed. *Túpac Amaru II—1780. Sociedad colonial y sublevaciones populares.* Lima: Retablo de Papel.

Saavedra, Bautista. 1903. *La criminalidad aymara en el proceso de Mohoza.* La Paz: Imprenta Artística Velarde, Aldazosa y Cia.

———. 1906. *Defensa de los derechos de Bolivia en el litigio de fronteras con la república del Perú.* 2 vols. Buenos Aires: Talleres de la Casa Jacobo Peuser.

———. [1903] 1995. *El ayllu. Estudios sociológicos.* La Paz: Editorial Juventud.

Saignes, Thierry. 1985a. "'Algún día todo se andará': Los movimientos étnicos en Charcas (siglo XVII)." *Revista Andina* 3 (2):425–450.

———. 1985b. *Los Andes orientales: Historia de un olvido.* Cochabamba: CERES.

———. 1985c. "Caciques, Tribute, and Migration in the Southern Andes." Institute of Latin American Studies Occasional Papers No. 15, University of London.

———. 1986. *En busca del poblamiento étnico de los Andes bolivianos (Siglos XV y XVI).* La Paz: MUSEF.

———. 1987a. "Ayllus, mercado y coacción colonial: El reto de las migraciones internas en Charcas (siglo XVIII)." In Harris, Olivia, Brooke Larson, and Enrique Tandeter, eds. *La participación indígena en los mercados surandinos: Estrategias y reproducción social, siglos XVI–XX.* La Paz: CERES.

———. 1987b. "De la borrachera al retrato: Los caciques andinos entre dos legitimidades (Charcas)." *Revista Andina* 5 (1):139–170.

———. 1989. "Les caciques coloniaux, médiateurs ambivalents (Charcas, XVIIe siecle)." In *Les médiations culturelles.* Cahiers de l'UFR d'Etudes Ibériques et Latino-Américaines 7. Paris: Publications de la Sorbonne Nouvelle.

———. 1991. "Lobos y ovejas: Formación y desarrollo de los pueblos y comunidades en el sur andino (Siglos XVI–XX)." In Segundo Moreno Yañez and Frank Salomon, eds. *Reproducción y transformación de las sociedades andinas, siglos XVI–XX.* Quito: ABYA-YALA and MLAL.

Saignes, Thierry, ed. 1993. *Borrachera y memoria: La experiencia de lo sagrado en los Andes.* La Paz: IFEA and HISBOL.

Sala i Vila, Nuria. 1991a. "Mistis e indígenas: La lucha por el control de las comunidades indígenas en Lampa, Puno, a fines de la colonia." *Boletín Americanista* 41:35–66.

———. 1991b. "La revuelta de Julí en 1806: Crisis de subsistencia y economía campesina." *Revista de Indias* 51 (192):343–374.

————. 1996a. "La rebelión de Huarochirí en 1783." In Charles Walker, ed. *Entre la retórica y la insurgencia: Las ideas y los movimientos sociales en los Andes, Siglo XVIII*. Cuzco: Centro Bartolomé de las Casas.

————. 1996b. *Y se armó el tole tole: Tributo indígena y movimientos sociales en el virreinato del Perú. 1784–1814*. Huamanga: IER José María Arguedas.

Salomon, Frank. 1975. "Don Pedro de Zambiza, un varayuj del siglo XVI." *Cuadernos de historia y arqueología* 42:285–315.

————. 1982a. "Andean Ethnology in the 1970s: A Retrospective." *Latin American Research Review* 17 (2):75–128.

————. 1982b. "Chronicles of the Impossible: Notes on Three Peruvian Indigenous Historians." In Rolena Adorno, ed. *From Oral to Written Expression: Native Andean Chronicles of the Early Colonial Period*. Foreign and Comparative Studies, Latin American Monograph Series, no. 4. Syracuse, New York: Syracuse University.

————. 1986. *Native Lords of Quito in the Age of the Incas: The Political Economy of North-Andean Chiefdoms*. New York: Cambridge.

————. 1987. "Ancestor Cults and Resistance to the State in Arequipa, ca. 1748–1754." In Steve Stern, ed. *Resistance, Rebellion, and Consciousness in the Andean Peasant World, Eighteenth to Twentieth Centuries*. Madison: University of Wisconsin Press.

Sánchez Albornoz, Nicolás. 1978. *Indios y tributos en el Alto Perú*. Lima: Instituto de Estudios Peruanos.

Santamaría, Daniel. 1977. "La propiedad de la tierra y la condición social del indio en el Alto Perú, 1780–1810." *Desarrollo económico* 66:253–271.

————. 1989. *Hacendados y campesinos en el Alto Perú colonial*. Buenos Aires: Fundación Simón Rodríguez.

Santos, Roberto. 1989. "Información y probanza de don Fernando Kollatupaj, Onofre Maskapongo y Juan Pizarro Limachi, Inkas de Copacabana: Siglo XVII." *Historia y Cultura* 16:3–19.

Sarabia Viejo, María Justina. 1986–1989. *Francisco de Toledo. Disposiciones gubernativas para el virreinato del Perú, 1569–1580*. 2 vols. Seville: Escuela de Estudios Hispano-Americanos.

Schramm, Raimund. "Mosaicos etnohistóricos del valle de Cliza (valle alto cochabambino), siglo XVI." *Historia y Cultura* 18:3–41, 1990.

Scott, James. 1976. *The Moral Economy of the Peasant: Rebellion and Subsistence in Southeast Asia*. New Haven: Yale University Press.

————. 1985. *Weapons of the Weak. Everyday Forms of Peasant Resistance*. New Haven: Yale University Press.

————. 1987. "Resistance without Protest and without Organization: Peasant Opposition to the Islamic *Zakat* and the Christian Tithe." *Comparative Studies in Society and History* 29:417–452.

————. 1990. *Domination and the Arts of Resistance: Hidden Transcripts*. New Haven: Yale University Press.

Sempat Assadourian, Carlos. 1982. *El sistema de la economía colonial: Mercado interno, regiones y espacio económico*. Lima: Instituto de Estudios Peruanos.

Serulnikov, Sergio. 1996. "'Su verdad y su justicia': Tomás Catari y la insurrección aymara de Chayanta, 1777–1780." In Charles Walker, ed. *Entre la retórica y la insurgencia: Las ideas y los movimientos sociales en los Andes, Siglo XVIII*. Cuzco: Centro Bartolomé de las Casas.

————. 1998. Peasant Politics and Colonial Domination: Social Conflicts and Insurgency in Northern Potosí, 1730–1781. Doctoral thesis, State University of New York at Stony Brook.

————. 1999. "From the Everyday Forms of Colonial Politics to the Politics of Anticolonialism (Northern Potosí, ca. 1770–1777). *Colonial Latin American Review* 8 (2) 245–274.

Solórzano Pereyra, Juan de. [1647] 1972. *Política indiana*. Madrid: Compañía Ibero-Americana de Publicaciones.

Soux, María Luisa. 1999. Autoridad, poder y redes sociales entre colonia y república. Laja, 1800–1850. Thesis, Universidad Internacional de Andalucía (Sede iberoamericana de La Rábida).

Spalding, Karen. 1970. "Social Climbers: Changing Patterns of Mobility among the Indians of Colonial Peru." *Hispanic American Historial Review* 50:645–664.

————. 1973. "*Kurakas* and Commerce: A Chapter in the Evolution of Andean Society." *Hispanic American Historial Review* 53:581–599.

————. 1974. *De indio a campesino: Cambios en la estructura social del Perú colonial*. Lima: Instituto de Estudios Peruanos.

————. 1981. "Resistencia y adaptación: El gobierno colonial y las élites nativas. *Allpanchis* 17–18:5–21.

————. 1984. *Huarochirí: An Andean Society Under Inca and Spanish Rule*. Stanford: Stanford University Press.

Stavig, Ward. 1988. "Ethnic Conflict, Moral Economy, and Population in Rural Cusco on the Eve of the Thupa Amaro II Rebellion." *Hispanic American Historical Review* 68 (4):737–770.

————. 1999. *The World of Túpac Amaru: Conflict, Community, and Identity in Colonial Peru*. Lincoln: University of Nebraska Press.

Stein, Stanley. 1981. "Bureaucracy and Business in the Spanish Empire, 1759–1804: Failure of a Bourbon Reform in Mexico and Peru." *Hispanic American Historical Review* 61 (1):2–21.

Stern, Steve. 1982. *Peru's Indian Peoples and the Challenge of Spanish Conquest: Huamanga to 1640*. Madison: University of Wisconsin Press.

————. 1983. "The Struggle for Solidarity: Class, Culture, and Community in Highland Indian America." *Radical History Review* 27:21–45.

————. 1987a. "The Age of Andean Insurrection, 1742–1782: A Reappraisal." In Steve Stern, ed. *Resistance, Rebellion, and Consciousness in the Andean Peasant World, Eighteenth to Twentieth Centuries*. Madison: University of Wisconsin Press.

————. 1987b. "New Approaches to the Study of Peasant Rebellion and Consciousness: Implications of the Andean Experience." In Steve Stern, ed. *Resistance, Rebellion, and Consciousness in the Andean Peasant World, Eighteenth to Twentieth Centuries*. Madison: University of Wisconsin Press.

————. 1992. "Paradigmas de la Conquista. Historia, historiografía y política." In Heraclio Bonilla, ed. *Los conquistados: 1492 y la población indígena de las Américas*. Quito: Tercer Mundo Editores, FLACSO, Ediciones Libri Mundi.

————. 1995. *The Secret History of Gender: Women, Men, and Power in Late Colonial Mexico*. Chapel Hill: University of North Carolina Press.

Stern, Steve, ed. 1987. *Resistance, Rebellion, and Consciousness in the Andean Peasant World, Eighteenth to Twentieth Centuries*. Madison: University of Wisconsin Press.

Szeminski, Jan. 1987. "Why Kill the Spaniard? New Perspectives on Andean Insurrectionary Ideology in the 18th Century." In Steve Stern, ed. *Resistance, Rebellion, and Consciousness in the Andean Peasant World, Eighteenth to Twentieth Centuries*. Madison: University of Wisconsin Press.

————. 1993. *La utopía tupamarista*. 2d ed. Lima: Universidad Católica.

Taller de Historia Oral Andina. 1984. *El indio Santos Marka T'ula, cacique principal de los ayllus de Callapa y apoderado general de las comunidades de la República*. La Paz: Tallerde Historia Oral Andina.

————. 1986. *Mujer y resistencia comunaria: Historia y memoria*. La Paz: HISBOL.

Tandeter, Enrique. 1980. "La rente comme rapport de production et comme rapport de distribution. La cas de l'industrie minière de Potosí, 1750–1810." Doctoral thesis, Ecole des Hautes Etudes en Sciences Sociales, Paris.

————. 1992. *Coacción y mercado: La minería de la plata en Peru colonial, 1692–1826*. Buenos Aires: Editorial Sudamericana.

————. 1995. "Población y economía en los Andes (siglo XVIII)." *Revista Andina* 13:7–42.

Tandeter, Enrique, and Nathan Wachtel. 1984. *Precios y producción agraria: Potosí y Charcas en el siglo XVIII*. Buenos Aires: CEDES.

Tapia, Luciano. 1995. *Ukhamawa Jakawisaxa (Así es nuestra vida): Autobiografía de un Aymara*. La Paz: HISBOL.

Taylor, William. 1979. *Drinking, Homicide and Rebellion in Colonial Mexican Villages*. Stanford: Stanford University Press.

————. 1996. *Magistrates of the Sacred: Priests and Parishioners in Eighteenth-Century Mexico*. Stanford: Stanford University Press.

TePaske, John, and Herbert Klein. 1982. *The Royal Treasuries of the Spanish Empire in America*. 2 vols. Durham: Duke University Press.

Thompson, E. P. 1963. *The Making of the English Working Class*. New York: Vintage.

Thomson, Sinclair. 1996a. "Quiebre del cacicazgo y despliegue de los poderes en Sicasica, 1740–1771." In Xavier Albó et al., eds., *La integración surandina: Cinco siglos después*. Cuzco: Centro Bartolomé de las Casas.

———. 1996b. Colonial Crisis, Community, and Andean Self-Rule: Aymara Politics in the Age of Insurgency (Eighteenth-Century La Paz). Doctoral thesis, University of Wisconsin–Madison.

———. 1998. "¿Transmisión o intromisión? Propiedad, poder y legitimidad cacical en el mundo aymara de la colonia tardía." *Historias* 2:169–186.

———. 1999a. "En las terrazas del pasado: Geografía histórica de un valle andino." In Ricardo Rivas, Caterina Carenza, Cécile Claudel, Sinclair Thomson, John Earls, *Promoción económica y tecnológica en el municipio de Mocomoco: Recuperación de andenes prehispánicos*. La Paz: Ricerca e Cooperazione.

———. 1999b. "'We Alone Will Rule . . .': Recovering the Range of Anticolonial Projects among Andean Peasants (La Paz, 1740s to 1781)." *Colonial Latin American Review* 8 (2):275–299.

Thurner, Mark. 1991. "Guerra andina y política campesina en el sitio de La Paz, 1781: Aproximaciones etnohistóricas a la práctica insurreccional a través de las fuentes editadas." In Henrique Urbano and Mirko Lauer, eds. *Poder y violencia en los Andes*. Cuzco: Centro Bartolomé de Las Casas.

———. 1996. *From Two Republics to One Divided: Contradictions of Postcolonial Nationmaking in Andean Peru*. Durham: Duke University Press.

Ticona, Esteban. 2000. *Organización y liderazgo aymara, 1979–1996*. La Paz: AGRUCO and Universidad de la Corillera.

Ticona, Esteban y Xavier Albó. 1997. *La lucha por el poder comunal*. La Paz: CIPCA/CEDOIN.

Ticona, Esteban, Xavier Albó, and Gonzalo Rojas. 1995. *Votos y wiphalas: Campesinos y pueblos originarios en democracia*. La Paz: CIPCA.

Tord Nicolini, Javier. 1974. "El corregidor de indios del Perú: Comercio y tributos." *Historia y Cultura* (Lima) 8:173–214.

Tord Nicolini, Javier, and Carlos Lazo. 1981. *Hacienda, comercio, fiscalidad y luchas sociales (Perú colonial)*. Lima: BPHES.

Tschopik, Harry. 1951. "The Aymara of Chucuito, Peru. Magic I." *Anthropological Papers of the American Museum of Natural History* 44:133–308.

Tutino, John. 1983. "Power, Class, and Family: Men and Women in the Mexican Elite, 1750–1810." *The Americas* 39 (3):359–381.

———. 1986. *From Insurrection to Revolution in Mexico: Social Bases of Agrarian Violence, 1750–1940*. Princeton: Princeton University Press.

Untoja, Fernando. 1992. *Re-torno al ayllu*. La Paz: CADA.

Urbano, Henrique, and Mirko Lauer, eds. 1991. *Poder y violencia en los Andes*. Cuzco: Centro Bartolomé de Las Casas.

Urioste, Martha. 1978. "Los caciques Guarache." In Martha Urioste et al., *Estudios bolivianos en homenaje a Gunnar Mendoza*. La Paz: mimeo.

Urton, Gary. 1991. "Las unidades de análisis en el estudio de la reproducción y transformación de las sociedades andinas." In Segundo Moreno Yañez and Frank Salomon, eds. *Reproducción y transformación de las sociedades andinas, siglos XVI–XX*. Quito: ABYA-YALA and MLAL.

Valcárcel, Carlos. 1946. *Rebeliones indígenas.* Lima: Editorial P. T. C. M.

———. 1947. *La rebelión de Túpac Amaru.* Mexico City: Fondo de Cultura Económica.

———. 1977. *Túpac Amaru, precursor de la independencia.* Lima: OEA and Universidad Mayor de San Marcos.

———. 1981. "Fidelismo y separatismo de Túpac Amaru." In CDRTA. *La revolución de los Túpac Amaru: Antología.* Lima: P. L. Villanueva.

Valencia Vega, Alipio. 1984. *Historia política de Bolivia.* Vols. 1–2. La Paz: Editorial Juventud.

Valle de Siles, María Eugenia del. 1980. *Testimonios del cerco de La Paz: El campo contra la ciudad.* La Paz: Ultima Hora.

———. 1989. "Cronología de la rebelión de Túpac Catari en las provincias paceñas." *Historia y Cultura* 16:51–64.

———. 1990. *Historia de la rebelión de Túpac Catari, 1781–1782.* La Paz: Don Bosco.

Valle de Siles, María Eugenia del, ed. 1994. *El cerco de La Paz. Diario del Franciso Tadeo Diez de Medina.* Exp. 2d ed. La Paz: Don Bosco.

Van den Berg, Hans. 1985. *Diccionario religioso aymara.* Puno and Iquitos: IDEA and CETA.

Varón, Rafael. 1982. "Cofradías de indios y poder local en el Perú colonial: Huaráz, siglo XVII." *Allpanchis* 20:127–166.

Vollmer, Günter. 1967. *Bevölkerungspolitik und Bevölkerungsstruktur im Vizekönigreich Peru zu Ende der Kolonialzeit (1741–1821).* Bad Homburg: Gehlen.

Wachtel, Nathan. 1977. *The Vision of the Vanquished. The Spanish Conquest of Peru through Indian Eyes, 1530–1570.* New York: Barnes and Noble.

———. 1990. *Le retour des ancêtres. Les Indiens Urus de Bolivie XXe–XVIe siècle. Essai d'histoire regressive.* Paris: Gallimard.

———. 1992. "Note sur le problème des identités colectives dans les Andes méridionales." *L'Homme* 32:122–124.

Walker, Charles. 1989. "El estudio del campesinado en las ciencias sociales peruanas: Avances, limitaciones y nuevas perspectivas." *Allpanchis* 33:161–205.

———. 1991. "La violencia y el sistema legal: Los indios y el estado en el Cusco después de la rebelión de Túpac Amaru." In Henrique Urbano and Mirko Lauer, eds. *Poder y violencia en los Andes.* Cuzco: Centro Bartolomé de Las Casas.

———. 1999. *Smoldering Ashes: Cuzco and the Creation of Republican Peru, 1780–1840.* Durham: Duke University Press.

Walker, Charles, ed. 1996. *Entre la retórica y la insurgencia: Las ideas y los movimientos sociales en los Andes, Siglo XVIII.* Cuzco: Centro Bartolomé de las Casas.

Webster, Steven. 1977. "Kinship and Affinity in a Native Quechua Community." In Ralph Bolton and Enrique Mayer, eds. *Andean Kinship and Marriage.* American Anthropological Association Special Publication No. 7. Washington, D.C.: AAA.

Wightman, Ann. 1990. *Indigenous Migration and Social Change: The Forasteros of Cuzco, 1570–1720*. DurhamJuly 9, 2002: Duke University Press.

Wolf, Eric. 1966. *Peasants*. Englewood Cliffs, N.J.: Prentice-Hall.

Wood, Ellen Meiksins. 1988. *Peasant-Citizen and Slave: The Foundations of Athenian Democracy*. London: Verso.

Zavala, Silvio. 1978–1980. *El servicio personal de los indios en el Perú*. 3 vols. Mexico City: El Colegio de México.

Zavaleta, René. 1986. *Lo nacional-popular en Bolivia*. Mexico City: Siglo XXI.

Index

Abuse of power: and anticolonial options for peasants prior to 1781, 144, 146–48; and breakdown of colonial authority, 270; in early twentieth century, 278; and final downfall of *cacicazgo,* 252, 254–55, 258, 259, 260, 261, 346–47n.57; and institutional and intracommunity strife, 64–65, 70, 78, 79, 80, 83–94, 95; and insurrections of 1780–1781, 141, 165, 166, 168, 169, 170; and intendancy, 241, 242, 243; in late colonial period, 278–79; and reconstitution of community power, 275; and Spanish reconquest and reform, 344n.31; and structure of authority, 30, 34, 38, 40, 53, 54, 299n.97; and takeover of *ayllus,* 348n.73. *See also* Repartimiento system
Accountability, 80, 82, 105, 160, 236, 255, 266
Achacachi (Omasuyos), 21, 61, 125–26, 132, 197–98
Acora (Chucuito), 55, 303n.34, 319n.88
Age of insurgency, 15–16, 35, 269, 287n.9
Age of Revolution, 6–7, 15
Agregados, 23, 275
Albizuri, José de, 344n.31
Albó, Xavier, 277, 289n.19, 336n.88
Alcabala (taxes), 134–36, 170, 238
Alcalde pedáneo, 238, 239, 243, 259, 342–43nn.21–22
Alcaldes, Indian: accountability of, 160; and anticolonial options for peasants prior to 1781, 152, 155, 160; and final downfall of *cacicazgo,* 249, 252–53, 255, 257, 258; functions of, 46–47;

and institutional and intracommunity strife, 84, 85, 86, 93, 96, 309n.97; and insurrections of 1780–1781, 164, 169, 170, 215; and race/ethnicity, 215; and reconstitution of community power, 276; and repartimiento and breakdown of mediation, 109, 114, 118, 119, 311n.12; and structure of authority, 44, 45, 46–47, 48, 49, 50, 51, 52, 53, 54, 58, 60, 61, 295n.58; 295–96nn.62–63, 296n.69, 297n.78, 297–98n.83, 300n.109; and takeover of *ayllus,* 262, 263
Aldonza, María, 73
Alférez de voto (festival standard-bearer), 59, 60, 61
Alguaciles: and anticolonial options for peasants prior to 1781, 152; and institutional and intracommunity strife, 84, 93, 96; and repartimiento and breakdown of mediation, 108, 109, 311n.12; and Spanish reconquest and reform, 342n.21; and structure of authority, 44, 46, 47, 50, 53, 54, 61, 295n.58; and takeover of *ayllus,* 263
Ali, Felipe, 160
Alvarez, Felipe, 102, 113, 217, 224
Alvarez, Melchor, 265–66
Amat y Junient, Manuel de, 130, 242, 311n.6
Ambaná (Larecaja), 123, 145–46, 154, 162, 164, 178, 271, 326n.50
Ananea (Larecaja), 229
Anchoríz, Ramón, 167, 188
Ancoraimes (Omasuyos), 32, 226

of, 8, 10, 271; and self rule, 8, 10, 12,
140–43, 163–77, 223, 231, 271, 322–
23nn.1–9, 325–29nn.46–87; "silencing" and "trivialization" of, 7; and social reordering, 205–6, 231; and socioeconomic structure, 222–23; stages of,
181; and structure of authority, 39, 41,
43; symbolic significance of, 8; and
takeover of *ayllus,* 267; and utopianism, 7, 227; and violence, 181, 182, 183,
210, 212, 214, 219–23, 228, 229, 271,
279. *See also* Annihilation of enemy;
Cacicazgo/caciques—and insurrection/
insurgencies of 1780–1781; Inka restoration; Pacification; Radicalism; Traitors; *specific insurrection or leader*
Intendancy system: and aftermath of insurgency, 235–36, 240–47; and final downfall of *cacicazgo,* 248, 253, 257, 258, 264,
346n.56; and Spanish reconquest and
reform, 343n.22, 343n.27, 343n.29;
and structure of authority, 46–47, 51;
and takeover of *ayllus,* 264; and viceroys, 343n.28. *See also* Ordinance of
Intendants
Intermarriage, 30, 253, 255
Iruitu (Pacajes), 39
Irupana (Sicasica/Chulumani), 40, 43–44,
117, 265, 344n.31
Italaque (Larecaja), 79, 124, 303n.31,
348n.73

Jaúregui, Agustín, 250
Jesús de Machaca (Pacajes): and aftermath
of insurrections, 272; and anticolonial
options for peasants prior to 1781,
150–51, 152, 153, 154, 157, 161, 323n.23,
324nn.24, 32, 34; in early twentieth
century, 277–79, 280; and final downfall of *cacicazgo,* 260, 261; and institutional and intracommunity strife, 85,
90; and regional insurrections in 1781,
165, 326n.56; and repartimiento and
breakdown of mediation, 122, 128,
129, 314n.40; structure of authority in,
32–33, 37, 40, 55, 56, 58–59, 61, 62, 63,
294n.48; uprising in 1771 in, 314n.40;

uprising of 1795 in, 145, 260, 272,
294n.48
Jujuy, 167
Juli (Chucuito), 32, 293nn.33, 37, 298n.91
Junta de Corregidores, 99, 111
Juntas, 49, 50. *See also* Assembly
Justice/judicial system, 46, 47, 144, 230,
234, 239, 247, 295n.62

Katari: meaning and spelling of word, 190,
285n.3
Katari, Dámaso, 171, 327n.60
Katari, Nicolás, 327n.60
Katari, Tomás: aims of, 178; and anticolonial options for peasants prior
to 1781, 178; Buenos Aires trip of,
188–89, 332n.33; and Chayanta insurrection of 1781, 4, 11, 142, 143, 149,
164–66, 178, 322n.104, 326n.58; cult
surrounding, 204; and Cuzco as
source of insurrections of 1780–1781,
329n.3; death/assassination of, 149,
165, 166, 189, 211, 327n.58, 336n.88; images of, 165–66; importance of, in La
Paz, 191; and La Paz insurgency of 1781,
228, 230; lineage of, 189; loyalty to
king of, 178; and millenarianism,
326n.57; political program of, 142, 143,
167, 184; as redeemer/savior, 165, 178,
189, 326–27n.58; release from prison
of, 166; and religion, 201–2, 204; "resurrection" of, 201, 336n.88; and self
rule, 271; and Spanish Crown, 178,
188–89, 332n.33; spelling of, 285n.3;
state decree for, 188–89, 332n.33; and
tribute, 188, 332n.33; and Túpac Amaru, 166, 168, 169, 189, 191–92; and
Túpaj Katari, 188, 189, 201, 231, 272,
332n.36, 333n.47
Katarismo, 331n.26
"King was the community," 155–56, 159,
179, 230, 271, 325n.37

La Palata, Duque de: and institutional and
intracommunity strife, 85–86, 88, 93,
97, 98; and structure of authority, 44,
46, 295n.58, 299n.98

Living in Latin America

Robert Levine
General Editor